MW00997407

VOICE OF JUSTICE

The First Amendment rights of lawyers are ethereal. Most lawyers fail to realize that courts may deny them access to the First Amendment's protective shield in many regulatory and disciplinary contexts. Overall, attorneys cannot and should not assume that they can obtain First Amendment protection – especially when acting *as an attorney* in their role as an "officer of the court." Yet, it is precisely in the lawyering context – where attorneys engage in speech, association, and petitioning for the very purpose of securing client rights, invoking law, enabling the judicial power, and obtaining justice – that the need for First Amendment protection is the most acute. If regulators silence that voice, they silence justice. From overarching theory to specific real-world contexts, this illuminating book provides a critical resource for lawyers, judges, and scholars to understand the relationship between the First Amendment rights of lawyers and the integrity of the justice system.

MARGARET TARKINGTON is a professor of law at the Indiana University Robert H. McKinney School of Law. Her scholarship bridges specialties in constitutional law, lawyer regulation, and procedure – harnessing the First Amendment as a means to protect the integrity of government processes. In addition to teaching and writing on these topics, she has served as an expert consultant on disciplinary proceedings brought against attorneys for their speech, association, and petitioning. She serves as the 2018 Chair of the AALS Professional Responsibility Section. She previously practiced law in New York, Indiana, and Utah and is the mother of six children.

Voice of Justice

RECLAIMING THE FIRST AMENDMENT RIGHTS OF LAWYERS

MARGARET TARKINGTON

Indiana University Robert H. McKinney School of Law

CAMBRIDGE
UNIVERSITY PRESS

CAMBRIDGE
UNIVERSITY PRESS

University Printing House, Cambridge CB2 8BS, United Kingdom

One Liberty Plaza, 20th Floor, New York, NY 10006, USA

477 Williamstown Road, Port Melbourne, VIC 3207, Australia

314–321, 3rd Floor, Plot 3, Splendor Forum, Jasola District Centre, New Delhi – 110025, India

79 Anson Road, #06–04/06, Singapore 079906

Cambridge University Press is part of the University of Cambridge.

It furthers the University's mission by disseminating knowledge in the pursuit of education, learning, and research at the highest international levels of excellence.

www.cambridge.org
Information on this title: www.cambridge.org/9781107146839
DOI: 10.1017/9781316544549

First published 2018

Printed in the United States of America by Sheridan Books, Inc.

A catalogue record for this publication is available from the British Library.

ISBN 978-1-107-14683-9 Hardback
ISBN 978-1-316-60098-6 Paperback

For my children,
Joseph, Eli, Maisy, Cyrus, Gabriel, and Hal,
and with gratitude to
Alexander Meiklejohn,
whose work shaped my view of the relationship
between government processes and the First Amendment, and
Monroe H. Freedman,
who greatly encouraged me as a new scholar
and helped me understand lawyers' ethics.

Contents

Acknowledgments

A special thanks to participants of the 2017 Legal Ethics Schmooze, UCLA School of Law, who gave helpful comments and encouragement of this project, including Benjamin Barton, Scott L. Cummings, Bruce A. Green, Renee Newman Knake, Carol A. Needham, Russell G. Pearce, Deborah L. Rhode, Rebecca Roiphe, Ann Southworth, Norm Spaulding, W. Bradley Wendel, and Ellen Yaroshefsky.

Heartfelt appreciation also is given to my father, Jim Robertson, for providing insightful comments and edits to the manuscript.

I would like to thank the following for permission to include the identified materials:

> The American Bar Association for quotations from the MODEL RULES OF PROFESSIONAL CONDUCT and the STANDARDS FOR CRIMINAL JUSTICE: THE PROSECUTION AND DEFENSE FUNCTIONS.
>
> Paul K. Ogden, for quotations from his blog post, *Pennsylvania Supreme Court Silenced Attorney Whistleblowers Who Could Have Reported "Kids for Cash" Judicial Scandal*, DISBARRING THE CRITICS, Jan. 9, 2014, http://disbarringthecritics.blogspot.com/2014/01/pennsylvania-supreme-court-disciplinary.html.

Additionally, some material contained in this book was previously published in the following articles, of which I am the sole author, and is included herein with permission:

> *Lost in the Compromise: Free Speech, Criminal Justice, and Attorney Pretrial Publicity*, 66 FLA. L. REV. 1873 (2014).
>
> *Freedom of Attorney-Client Association*, UTAH L. REV. 1071 (2012).

A First Amendment Theory for Protecting Attorney Speech, 45 U.C. DAVIS
   L. REV. 27 (2012).
A Free Speech Right to Impugn Judicial Integrity in Court Proceedings,
   51 B.C. L. REV. 363 (2010).
*The Truth Be Damned: The First Amendment, Attorney Speech, and Judicial
   Reputation*, 97 GEO. L. J. 1567 (2009).

Introduction

The First Amendment rights of lawyers in the United States are ethereal. Although attorneys are largely responsible for the realization of the power of the First Amendment of the United States Constitution in protecting the rights of others, attorneys have failed to appropriately realize and invoke the power of the First Amendment to protect their own speech, association, assembly, and petitioning. But this failure affects far more than merely securing the individual lawyer's exercise of constitutional rights – for the First Amendment rights of lawyers, when properly defined, protect the integrity of the justice system itself.

Most lawyers don't realize that they lack First Amendment rights. They are aware of the Supreme Court's protection of lawyer advertising and proceed on the assumption that they possess the full panoply of First Amendment rights. Yet the caselaw does not bear that out in many regulatory and disciplinary contexts. Particularly, when attorneys are acting *as an attorney* in their role as an "officer of the court," attorneys cannot and should not assume that they can obtain First Amendment protection from regulation or professional discipline.

Yet it is precisely in that context – where attorneys engage in speech and association for the very purpose of securing client rights and obtaining justice – that First Amendment protection must instead be understood as indispensable. The lawyer's role in the justice system, the client's rights, and even justice itself can be undermined where attorneys lack First Amendment rights to speak and associate as lawyers.

Nevertheless, a dominant premise in modern state court cases – and one that members of the US Supreme Court endorse from time to time – is that attorneys voluntarily relinquished their First Amendment rights when they became members of a State's bar and swore to abide by regulations imposed upon them. Other scholars and courts – including, again, the US Supreme Court – purport to allow attorneys full First Amendment rights when acting as independent citizens, but deny them First Amendment protection when acting as an attorney or in a representative capacity.

The US Supreme Court has only amplified lower court confusion regarding attorney First Amendment rights. The Court's protection and recognition of attorney speech and association rights is near schizophrenic – widely vacillating between recognizing First Amendment rights for attorneys and refusing them any such rights. Moreover, the Court often fails to even acknowledge its own authority to the contrary. On the whole, conflicting cases are not distinguished; they are ignored. Scholarship as to the scope of attorney First Amendment rights, where it exists, similarly runs the gamut from the view that attorneys have full First Amendment rights to a complete denial of any such rights for attorneys. If there is a dominant consensus, legal scholarship would deny First Amendment rights to lawyers when acting in their role as attorneys. The result is that State Supreme Courts can selectively choose a line of cases to either protect or refuse attorneys' appeals to First Amendment protection. And where State regulations are under attack, refusal is a natural choice.

What is more, the practice of law is performed nearly entirely through speech, meaning the written and spoken word. This fact itself creates several challenges to recognizing and protecting attorneys' First Amendment rights. First, nearly all regulations on attorneys can be perceived as restrictions on attorney speech. Further, many restrictions on attorney speech are in fact essential to the just and proper functioning of the judicial system. Thus, courts and scholars have supposed that recognition of First Amendment rights for lawyers would either frustrate the United States justice system or would undermine the First Amendment itself – or both.

But the problems with recognizing lawyers' First Amendment rights are illusory and come from a misconception of the appropriate and powerful role that the First Amendment should play in protecting the rights of attorneys, their clients, and, perhaps most importantly, the integrity of the justice system. United States lawyers no longer practice in a local self-regulation bubble. Rather, attorneys are subject to regulation from state and federal legislatures, agencies, and even intergovernmental entities on a global scale. Such governing bodies can be subject to majoritarian pressures and may lack specialized knowledge regarding the proper functioning of the justice system. Because lawyers can only obtain justice for their clients through speech, regulators can undermine justice itself by limiting and punishing attorney speech made to that end. Thus, contrary to prevailing views, the core of First Amendment protection for attorneys should encompass speech made as attorneys – specifically, attorney speech invoking and avoiding government power in the protection of client life, liberty, and property.

Regulation of attorney speech, association, and petitioning surrounding litigation can also interfere with the proper functioning of the judicial power itself – as that branch of government is limited to adjudicating cases and controversies. Attorneys play a critical role in our system of justice by enabling the effective exercise of the judicial power. Regulation that undermines the ability of the attorney to bring and argue colorable cases equally undermines the power of the judiciary.

First Amendment protection, thus, must be shaped to safeguard the role of the attorney in the justice system. Such shaping has a two-fold beneficial effect: It recognizes and protects the First Amendment rights of attorneys and their clients, and it creates a constitutional protection for the essential role of the attorney in our system of justice from regulation that would undermine that role. The results are truly First Amendment rights *for* lawyers – defined both to fit their role and to protect that role.

Attorneys are the voice of justice. That is so not because all lawyers are altruistic warriors for the public good – they certainly are not. The legal profession includes its fair share of those who are jaded, crass, stingy, or self-centered, to identify only a few faults. Nevertheless, lawyers are still the voice of justice precisely because justice can only be achieved through their voice – by invoking and avoiding government power in protecting client life, liberty, and property and by enabling the judiciary to exercise its power to interpret the law and protect constitutional and other legal rights. If regulators can silence that voice, they can silence justice.

PART I

Understanding the Puzzle

1

Do Lawyers Have First Amendment Rights?

"They say that Justice is blind, but it took Municipal Judge Willard Dullard to prove that it is also DEAF and DUMB!" So began a leaflet written and distributed by Gene W. Glenn, an attorney in Ottumwa, Iowa. Glenn apparently believed, as most attorneys probably do, that he had a First Amendment right to free speech to publish his bitter brochure. But ultimately he found himself completely bereft of the First Amendment, and instead received a one-year suspension from the practice of law.[1]

In numerous contexts, lawyers have, like Glenn, discovered to their dismay that they lack access to the protective shield of the First Amendment as to their speech, association, and petitioning. Nevertheless, at other times courts assert their commitment to lawyers' First Amendment rights. The caselaw and commentary on the subject is nothing short of a morass. Yet distilling the primary theoretical bases both for rejecting and for recognizing attorney First Amendment rights is the first step to unraveling this puzzle and to framing a workable methodology that will protect both attorney First Amendment rights and the administration of justice.

THE CONSTITUTIONAL CONDITIONS THEORY

A century ago, Benjamin Cardozo stated what has become the traditional theoretical conception of attorneys' First Amendment rights – or, rather, the lack of such rights. "[T]he practice of law is a privilege burdened with conditions."[2] That is, attorneys voluntarily relinquish their First Amendment rights as a condition of the "privilege" of a license to practice law as a member of a State's bar. A more recent source for the theory – relied on by State Supreme Courts to this day – is the concurrence of Justice Stewart in *In re Sawyer*.[3] Justice Stewart said:

---

[1] *In re Glenn*, 130 N.W.2d 672, 675 (Iowa 1964).
[2] *In re Rouss*, 221 N.Y. 81, 84 (N.Y. 1917).
[3] 360 U.S. 622, 646–47 (1959) (Stewart, J., concurring).

> If ... there runs through the principal opinion an intimation that *a lawyer can invoke the constitutional right of free speech to immunize himself from even-handed discipline for proven unethical conduct,* it is an intimation in which I *do not join.* A lawyer belongs to a profession with inherited standards of propriety and honor, which experience has shown necessary in a calling dedicated to the accomplishment of justice. He who would follow that calling must conform to those standards. *Obedience to ethical precepts may require abstention from what in other circumstances might be constitutionally protected speech.*[4]

The problem with this formulation is apparent from the opening line – it has no limits. Justice Stewart asserts that whenever there is "even-handed discipline for proven unethical conduct" – apparently any violation of a rule of professional conduct – a lawyer cannot "invoke the constitutional right of free speech" as a defense.[5] Stewart assumes that *all* "inherited standards of propriety and honor" or "ethical precepts" are "necessary in a calling dedicated to the accomplishment of justice" and thus must be complied with, even though they "may require abstention" from First Amendment rights. For Stewart, attorneys *cannot* "invoke the constitutional right of free speech" in the face of professional regulation, but instead "must conform" and "[o]be[y]."

This constitutional conditions theory is often undergirded by reliance on the oath to which an attorney is required to swear when admitted to a State's bar. In *Gentile* v. *State Bar of Nevada,*[6] Justice Rehnquist, speaking for four members of the Court, adopted the constitutional conditions theory, relying on the attorney's oath taken at admission. He stated:

> When petitioner was admitted to practice law before the Nevada courts, the oath which he took recited that "I will support, abide by and follow the Rules of Professional Conduct as are now *or may hereafter* be adopted by the Supreme Court ..." *The First Amendment does not excuse him from that obligation, nor should it forbid the discipline imposed upon him* by the Supreme Court of Nevada.[7]

According to this variant on the constitutional conditions theory, attorneys are apparently irrevocably bound by their oath to abide by whatever rules of professional conduct or other attorney regulations are created by the State Supreme Court or bar – regardless of how patently unconstitutional or violative of First Amendment rights such a rule may be. And this divestiture of constitutional rights is achieved very simply – by requiring anyone who wishes to practice law to swear at their admission to obey the rules that the judiciary will impose upon them.

---

[4] *Id.* (emphasis added).
[5] *See also Gardner,* 793 N.E.2d at 429 (paraphrasing and concluding from Stewart's concurrence that "attorneys may not invoke the federal constitutional right of free speech to immunize themselves from even-handed discipline for proven unethical conduct").
[6] 501 U.S. 1030, 1081 (1991) (Rehnquist, J.).
[7] *Id.* (emphasis added).

Courts continue to require attorneys to promise compliance with rules enacted by the judiciary (even ones of dubious constitutionality) as a condition of obtaining or maintaining a law license. The Utah State Bar (of which I am an inactive member) adopted "Standards of Professionalism and Civility" in 2003, which, among other things, require attorneys to "treat all other counsel, parties, judges, witnesses, and other participants in all proceedings *in a courteous and dignified manner*" and "*avoid hostile, demeaning, or humiliating words in written and oral communications with adversaries.*"[8] Even a First Amendment novice would recognize that the rule directly prohibits speech and thus enforcement may have constitutional ramifications.[9] Yet in June 2017, as part of the online annual registration with the Utah State Bar, attorneys were only able to complete and submit the registration if the attorney checked a box that said "Affirm that you are familiar with and *pledge to abide by* the Utah Standards of Professionalism and Civility." Attorneys could not complete the registration without checking the box (I know because I tried), which means that every attorney who wanted to renew their license for 2017–18 had to "pledge to abide by" the Professionalism and Civility standards. Under Rehnquist's view, that pledge exposes the attorney to discipline for violation of the standards while stripping the attorney of any First Amendment defense thereto.

An important, yet distinct, corollary to the constitutional conditions theory is that attorneys also have no speech rights for speech that they are enabled to engage in by virtue of their license to practice law. Thus, because attorneys could not have spoken as representatives of a client in court proceedings or filed anything on behalf of litigants prior to becoming attorneys, they have no preexisting free speech right that could be violated by punishing or restricting that speech as an attorney.[10]

The constitutional conditions theory has retained an astonishing staying power in the area of lawyer First Amendment rights in general – despite being rejected as unconstitutional in other contexts[11] and despite the comprehensive transformation

---

[8] Utah Standards of Professionalism and Civility ¶¶ 1 and 3 (emphasis added); *see also id.* ¶ 3 ("Neither written submissions nor oral presentations should disparage the integrity, intelligence, morals, ethics, or personal behavior of an adversary unless such matters are directly relevant under controlling substantive law.").

[9] Chapter 14 discusses the constitutionality of civility codes.

[10] Bradley Wendel illustrated the corollary in the following hypothetical:

> Suppose a lawyer is disciplined for making racist remarks in a closing argument at trial. It is to no avail to claim that the disciplinary agency is requiring the lawyer to surrender a constitutional right in exchange for the privilege of trying cases before the courts of the state because the lawyer *had no preexisting right to address a jury in a courtroom.* W. Bradley Wendel, *Free Speech for Lawyers*, 28 Hastings Const. L. Q. 305, 373–74 (2001) (emphasis added).

[11] The normal understanding of this idea is the exact reverse of what it is in the attorney context: It is the "unconstitutional conditions" doctrine, because it is unconstitutional to make relinquishment of a constitutional right a condition of obtaining a government-supplied benefit. *See* Kathleen Sullivan, *Unconstitutional Conditions*, 102 Harv. L. Rev. 1413, 1415 (1989) (explaining that the unconstitutional conditions doctrine "holds that government may not

of First Amendment doctrine over the last century since Cardozo made his statement in 1917. Indeed, when Cardozo made his statement, the First Amendment had
not even been incorporated by the Fourteenth Amendment as being applicable to
states, and thus it was not even applicable to state bars and judiciaries, which would
happen in 1925. Yet on March 6, 2018, the American Bar Association (ABA) issued
Formal Opinion 480 regarding client confidentiality and seemingly embraced the
constitutional conditions theory – explaining that a lawyer only has a "privilege of
practicing law" and that a lawyer's free speech rights are "not without bounds." The
ABA concluded: "Lawyers' professional conduct may be constitutionally constrained
by various professional regulatory standards as embodied in the Model Rules, or
similar state analogs."[12] The ABA cited modern cases espousing the constitutional
conditions theory, most of which arose out of the specific context of attorney speech
that impugns judicial integrity – a context where the constitutional conditions
theory has maintained particular resilience.[13] As the Missouri Supreme Court
summarized: "[A]n attorney's voluntary entrance to the bar acts as a voluntary waiver
of the right to criticize the judiciary."[14] Importantly, the resilience of the theory in
that specific context is not happenstance – it is an intrinsic piece of the misconception of the attorney's power and role in the United States justice system, as will be
addressed in Chapter 4.

THE FIRST AMENDMENT IS INAPPLICABLE

While scholarly commentary has not entirely embraced the constitutional conditions theory, it fails to account for or persuasively counter it and generally offers an
equally emasculated – and frankly misconceived – account of attorney First Amendment rights. Frederick Schauer argues that because attorney speech – especially
when made as an attorney – is subject to a near "omnipresence of speech regulation," "the First Amendment has, ... properly never been thought to apply" to
"a vast array of lawyer and legal system activity." Thus speech made as a lawyer is
(and should remain) "unencumbered by either the doctrine or the discourse of the
First Amendment."[15]

One of the major problems with the constitutional conditions approach and
Schauer's argument that the First Amendment is inapplicable is that the Supreme
Court has repeatedly held attorney regulations unconstitutional as violative of

---

grant a benefit on the condition that the beneficiary surrender a constitutional right, even if the
government may withhold that benefit altogether").

[12] AM. BAR ASS'N, STANDING COMM. ON ETHICS AND PROF'L RESPONSIBILITY, Formal Op. 480, at
4–5 (2018).

[13] *See id.* at 4 n. 18.

[14] *In re Westfall*, 808 S.W.2d 829, 834 (Mo. 1991).

[15] Frederick Schauer, *The Speech of Law and The Law of Speech*, 49 ARK. L. REV. 687, 694–95
(1997).

lawyers' First Amendment Rights.[16] Thus it appears that despite the Supreme Court's occasional pronouncements flirting with the constitutional conditions theory, it has ultimately rejected it and recognized that lawyers have not voluntarily surrendered their First Amendment rights as a condition of practicing law, nor have lawyers waived their First Amendment rights by swearing an oath to obey all regulations imposed by a state bar. The problem with both the constitutional conditions and inapplicability approaches is that they are inaccurate. Lawyers have enforceable First Amendment rights – which means the real question becomes determining what the scope of those rights should be.

THE CATEGORICAL APPROACH

One major approach to determining the scope of attorney First Amendment rights – adopted by commentators through various permutations – is what I will call the "categorical approach." Under the categorical approach, if the attorney is acting as a private citizen, the attorney has access to normal First Amendment rights, but where the attorney is acting in their capacity as an attorney or "officer of the court," the attorney is divested of those First Amendment rights.

For example, several commentators have analogized attorney speech protection to other areas of limited First Amendment protection, including comparison to speech protection for public employees, to speech made in a nonpublic forum, and to government-funded speech.[17] Under each of these analogies, the ultimate result is that there is little or no protection for attorney speech when made in the capacity of an attorney. The premise of the government-funded speech theory, for example, is that the government has funded the court systems and made attorneys officers of the court, and thus can restrict attorney speech made in that capacity. Further, in the analogy to public employee speech, the attorney as "officer of the court" is treated in like manner to an employee of the court whose speech rights vis-à-vis the judiciary are extremely circumscribed. Finally, in the nonpublic forum analogy, the entire legal system is viewed as a nonpublic forum where the government, which created the forum, can restrict the speech of participant attorneys. Although some of the analogies are more problematic than others, none of them are satisfactory, and all of

---

[16] *See, e.g., Republican Party of Minnesota* v. *White*, 536 U.S. 765 (2002); *Legal Services Corp.* v. *Velazquez*, 531 U.S. 533, 541 (2001); *Zauderer* v. *Office of Disciplinary Counsel of the Supreme Court of Ohio*, 471 U.S. 626 (1985); *NAACP* v. *Button*, 371 U.S. 415 (1963); *Bates* v. *State Bar of Arizona*, 433 U.S. 421 (1977); *In re Primus*, 436 U.S. 412 (1978); *In re R.M.J.*, 455 U.S. 191 (1982).

[17] *See* Kathleen Sullivan, *The Intersection of Free Speech and the Legal Profession: Constraints on Lawyers' First Amendment Rights*, 67 FORDHAM L. REV. 569, 585–87 (1998–99) (analogizing attorney speech to public employees, government-funded speech and speech in a nonpublic forum); Wendel, *supra* Note 10, at 375–81 (same); Terri R. Day, *Speak No Evil: Legal Ethics v. The First Amendment*, 32 J. LEGAL PROF. 161, 187–90 (2008) (analogizing attorney speech to public employee speech).

them fail to protect speech of attorneys made in the role of attorney, counselor, or representative of others.[18]

Additionally, all of the analogies are limited to examining restrictions on attorney speech made in or related to a court proceeding. The analogies fail to even acknowledge other areas of potential restriction on attorney speech, including speech made in an advisory role to clients, or in transactions and other practice contexts where attorneys are invoking the protection of the law on behalf of the client.

Claudia Haupt recently advanced a theory that partakes of both the constitutional conditions theory and the categorical approach. Haupt argues that lawyers, as members of a "professional knowledge community," should have the same free speech rights as any other citizen when acting as a private person (the categorical approach).[19] As to speech within one's profession, she argues that the First Amendment forbids *state interference* with the professional knowledge community's ability to communicate their professional insights.[20] However, Haupt argues that "the First Amendment is *not* a roadblock to regulation of *professionals' speech by the profession*."[21] At heart, Haupt's concept as to regulation of speech undertaken as a lawyer is merely constitutional conditions arguments dressed in the new linguistic clothing of "professional knowledge communities." Her idea is that, as a member of a professional knowledge community, one agrees to (and thus waives rights against) regulations imposed *by that community* in an exercise of self-regulation. Basically, "membership in the bar is a privilege burdened with conditions"[22] as prescribed by the bar.

In line with the categorical approach, Kathleen Sullivan has argued that the Supreme Court's inconsistent caselaw in the area of First Amendment rights of lawyers can be understood as providing normal First Amendment protection when attorneys are speaking "as participants in ordinary public or commercial discourse on a par with other speakers in those realms," but that their free speech rights are limited (or even lost) when attorneys are speaking in their role of attorney as "officers of the court" or "delegates of state power."[23]

Indeed, the Supreme Court's own statements in *Gentile* and *Holder* v. *Humanitarian Law Project*[24] can be read to accept the categorical approach. The *Gentile* Court stated that "[i]t is unquestionable that in the courtroom itself, during a

---

[18] *See* Margaret Tarkington, *A Free Speech Right to Impugn Judicial Integrity in Court Proceedings*, 51 B.C. L. Rev. 392–413 (2010) at 393–401 (fully analyzing each of these analogies).

[19] *See* Claudia E. Haupt, *Professional Speech*, 125 Yale L. J. 1238, 1255 (2016) (when professionals are speaking as "ordinary citizens," they "enjoy ordinary First Amendment protection").

[20] *See id.* at 1297 and 1303.

[21] Claudia E. Haupt, *Antidiscrimination in the Legal Profession and the First Amendment: A Partial Defense of Model Rule 8.4(g)*, 19 J. Const. L. 1, 21 (2017).

[22] *In re Rouss*, 221 N.Y. 81, 84 (N.Y. 1917).

[23] *See* Sullivan, *supra* Note 17, at 569 and 584.

[24] 561 U.S. 1 (2010).

judicial proceeding, whatever right to 'free speech' an attorney has is extremely circumscribed" and, moreover, even outside the courtroom, "lawyers in pending cases [are] subject to ethical restrictions on speech to which an ordinary citizen would not be."[25] State and federal courts have relied on these statements from *Gentile* for the generalized proposition that attorneys acting in a representative capacity or in connection with a legal proceeding have few, if any, First Amendment rights.[26]

In *Humanitarian Law Project*, the Supreme Court again appeared to embrace the categorical approach when it held that attorneys lacked First Amendment protection for lawful, nonviolent legal advice and assistance to or on behalf of organizations designated by the Secretary of State as Foreign Terrorist Organizations. The determining factor for the Court in holding that the plaintiff attorneys lacked a First Amendment right to engage in such speech was that "[t]he statute does not prohibit *independent* advocacy or expression of any kind."[27] According to the Court, "plaintiffs may say anything they wish on any topic," and thus there allegedly was no suppression of "ideas or opinions in the form of 'pure political speech'."[28] Rather, the plaintiff attorneys were *only* prohibited from speech performed "under the direction of, or in coordination with" their proposed clientele.[29] *Holder* exemplifies this categorical approach where attorneys enjoy free speech rights in their private citizen capacity (and thus the plaintiffs could engage in "independent advocacy or expression" on "any topic"), but lack free speech rights for speech made in their role as attorney (and thus plaintiffs can be prohibited from engaging in all speech undertaken "under the direction of, or in coordination with" their proposed clientele).

The primary problem with the categorical approach is that it provides no First Amendment protection for speech and association that is essential for lawyers to fulfill their role in the system of justice – their rights to associate with and advocate on behalf of clients in the protection of life, liberty, and property. Indeed, the categorical approach is repudiated by two critically important Supreme Court cases where the Court recognized that attorneys have First Amendment rights specifically when acting as lawyers representing clients. In both *Legal Services Corp.* v. *Velazquez*[30] and *NAACP* v. *Button*,[31] the Court held that attorneys had First Amendment rights in associating with clients, instigating litigation, and making relevant claims and arguments in court proceedings. The *Velazquez* Court noted

[25] *Gentile v. State Bar of Nev.*, 501 U.S. 1030, 1071 (1991).
[26] *See, e.g., In re Anonymous Member of South Carolina Bar*, 709 S.E.2d 633, 635 (S.C. 2011); *In re Cobb*, 838 N.E.2d 1197, 1211 (Mass. 2005); *Office of Disciplinary Counsel v. Gardner*, 793 N.E.2d 425, 433 (Ohio 2003); *In re Shearin*, 765 A.2d 930, 938 (Del. 2000).
[27] *Humanitarian Law Project*, 561 U.S. at 26 (emphasis added).
[28] *Id.* at 25–26.
[29] *Id.* at 26.
[30] 531 U.S. 533 (2001).
[31] 371 U.S. 415 (1963).

that attorneys' First Amendment rights are essential, not only to the vindication of their clients' rights, but also to the proper functioning of the judiciary itself. These cases will be discussed throughout this book and correctly undermine the categorical approach – as well as the constitutional conditions theory and its corollary – not merely as a matter of precedent but, more importantly, in demonstrating the critical need to protect attorneys' First Amendment rights.

REGULAR FIRST AMENDMENT PROTECTION

Other commentators – and again, the Supreme Court itself – have asserted that attorneys enjoy the regular protection of the First Amendment. Erwin Chemerinsky has repeatedly asserted and analyzed attorney First Amendment rights under the normal doctrines of the First Amendment. For example, in the context of restrictions on attorney pretrial publicity, Chemerinsky argues that strict scrutiny is required for what is clearly a content-based restriction on political speech.[32] Similarly, Renee Newman Knake relies on regular First Amendment cases and doctrines in analyzing restrictions on attorney speech. For example, she argues that the Supreme Court's decision in *Sorrell* v. *IMS Health, Inc.*,[33] regarding the First Amendment's protection for the creation and dissemination of information, should likely apply to lawyer regulation, potentially undermining the constitutionality of certain restrictions on confidentiality, multidisciplinary practice, unauthorized practice of law, and advertising.[34]

In a similar vein, the Supreme Court has itself applied strict scrutiny in cases dealing with attorney speech. In *Republican Party of Minnesota* v. *White*,[35] the Court struck down Minnesota's announce clause, a rule of professional conduct that prohibited attorney candidates for judicial positions from expressing their views on certain political issues, as violating the Speech Clause. The *White* Court subjected the state's restrictions to strict scrutiny because the announce clause restricted "speech that is at the core of our First Amendment freedoms – speech about the qualifications of candidates for public office."[36] Moreover, in *In re Primus*,[37] the Supreme Court held that an ACLU attorney's solicitation of a potential client who had been sterilized as a condition of receiving medical benefits was protected speech and involved "core First Amendment rights" since the ACLU was engaged in a "form of political expression" in its solicitation.[38]

---

[32] Erwin Chemerinsky, *Silence Is Not Golden: Protecting Lawyer Speech under the First Amendment*, 47 EMORY L. J. 859, 863–67 (1998).

[33] 564 U.S. 552 (2011).

[34] *See* Renee Newman Knake, *Legal Information, the Consumer Law Market, and the First Amendment*, 82 FORDHAM L. REV. 2843, 2844–45 (2014).

[35] 536 U.S. 765 (2002).

[36] *Id.* at 774–75.

[37] 436 U.S. 412 (1978).

[38] *Id.* at 432, 442.

Similarly, the Supreme Court has analyzed restrictions on attorney advertising by applying the *Central Hudson* commercial speech test. The Court has not modified the test based on the fact that a regulation restricts attorney speech.[39] Although the state interests and the regulations themselves may involve interests specific to attorneys, the analysis used to test the constitutionality of the restriction, along with the level of scrutiny employed, are the same as is used for regulation of any other service provider or regulated industry.

Unfortunately, the regular First Amendment doctrines and caselaw fail to properly identify attorney speech that should be protected or that can be restricted by regulators. For example, in determining whether rules restricting lawyers from disclosing client confidences violate the First Amendment, a court's examination of whether the restriction is content-based or content-neutral and whether the speech involves issues of public concern do not seem to be the appropriate metrics. In the pretrial publicity scenario, Chemerinsky is right as a matter of First Amendment law that pretrial publicity limitations are content-based restrictions on political speech that impose a prior restraint – which requires application of strict scrutiny and results in free speech for nearly all attorney pretrial publicity.[40] Nevertheless, scholars and regulators have not embraced Chemerinsky's arguments precisely because of the damage prosecutors have imposed on individuals through pretrial publicity – with the Duke lacrosse case providing an excellent example.[41] Neither courts nor regulators desire to expand the ability of prosecutors to use the damaging information they obtain through coercive state power in ways that impair the lives and liberties of criminal defendants and subvert the presumption of innocence. Yet the traditional doctrines of the First Amendment fail to provide a methodology or a principled distinction on which courts or regulators can lean to protect both criminal justice interests and comply with the First Amendment.

The problem with using traditional doctrines is also illustrated by the Supreme Court's 2010 decision, *Milavetz, Gallop & Milavetz v. United States.*[42] In *Milavetz*, attorneys challenged the constitutionality of congressional restrictions applicable to attorneys when advising clients in contemplation of bankruptcy. The restrictions directly circumscribed the advice an attorney would be allowed to give to a client. The Court in *Milavetz* employed typical First Amendment methodologies, examining whether the statute was overbroad or vague. During the *Milavetz* oral

---

[39] *See, e.g., Fla. Bar v. Went For It, Inc.*, 515 U.S. 618, 623–24 (1995); *Shapero v. Ky. Bar Ass'n*, 486 U.S. 466, 472 (1988); *Zauderer v. Office of Disciplinary Counsel of the Sup. Ct. of Ohio*, 471 U.S. 626, 637–44 (1985); *In re R.M.J.*, 455 U.S. 191, 203–06 (1982); *Bates v. State Bar of Ariz.*, 433 U.S. 350, 365 (1977).

[40] Chemerinsky, *supra* Note 32, at 862–67.

[41] *See* Robert P. Mosteller, *The Duke Lacrosse Case, Innocence, and False Identifications: A Fundamental Failure to "Do Justice,"* 76 FORDHAM L. REV. 1337, 1349–52 (2007).

[42] 559 U.S. 229 (2010).

argument, Chief Justice Roberts indicated a concern that the regulation achieved its substantive objective (getting debtors to avoid incurring more debt) "indirectly [] by interfering with the attorney-client relationship."[43] Indeed, the regulation did *not* prohibit debtors from incurring debt; rather, *it prohibited attorneys from advising clients* to incur debt when contemplating bankruptcy. Yet normal First Amendment doctrines did not account for the problematic interference with the attorney–client relationship. Indeed, counsel for the plaintiffs agreed that if the statute was unconstitutional as applied to attorneys, it would be unconstitutional as applied to everyone – again highlighting the lack of a methodology for reaching the distinctive problems of the statute as applied to attorney speech and to the interference with the attorney–client relationship.[44] The Supreme Court ultimately avoided interfering with the attorney–client relationship by interpreting the statute narrowly.[45] Importantly, the protection of the attorney–client relationship came from the Court's attorney-friendly interpretation of the statute and not from the First Amendment.

IGNORING THE FIRST AMENDMENT

A number of scholars simply ignore the First Amendment as a limitation on attorney regulation. For example, in the pretrial publicity context, Gerald Uelmen addresses solely "the ethical dimensions of trial publicity" because "the fact that we have a right to do something does not mean it is the right thing to do."[46] Similarly, Judith Maute "urges all persons involved with either prosecution or defense of criminal matters steadfastly to refrain from all, or practically all, extrajudicial communications" but notes that whether such restraints "can withstand First Amendment challenge is beyond the scope of this essay."[47] Finally, Kevin Cole and Fred Zacharias discuss "the propriety of lawyer statements to the press" apart from the constitutionality of restrictions thereon.[48] The fact that scholars propose ethical restrictions on lawyers but

---

[43] *Milavetz, Gallop & Milavetz v. United States*, Nos. 08–119, 08–1225, Oral Arg. Trans. at 47 (Dec. 1, 2009).

[44] Counsel for appellants agreed with Justice Scalia that if the statute was vague or overbroad for attorneys it would be equally problematic for anyone else to whom the statute applied. *See id.* at 20 ("don't bring in the fact that, well, and moreover, if it's applied to attorneys, it's unconstitutional ... [b]ecause if it's applied to anybody it's unconstitutional, according to your [vagueness] argument.").

[45] The Court interpreted the statute to prohibit only advice to a debtor "to incur more debt *because* the debtor is filing for bankruptcy, rather than for a valid purpose." *Milavetz*, 559 U.S. at 243 (emphasis added).

[46] Gerald F. Uelmen, *Leaks, Gags and Shields: Taking Responsibility*, 37 Santa Clara L. Rev. 943 (1997).

[47] Judith L. Maute, *"In Pursuit of Justice" in High Profile Criminal Matters*, 70 Fordham L. Rev. 1745, 1746 (2002).

[48] Kevin Cole and Fred C. Zacharias, *The Agony of Victory and the Ethics of Lawyer Speech*, 69 S. Cal. L. Rev. 1627, 1628–30 (1996).

avoid addressing whether those restrictions would violate the First Amendment is indicative of the quagmire surrounding attorney First Amendment rights.

THE PUZZLE

What is it about attorney speech and association that makes application of the First Amendment so difficult? As indicated by the foregoing overview of the leading approaches, not only are there divergent and inconsistent views as to attorneys' First Amendment rights but the Supreme Court has seemingly embraced each one in differing opinions. Further, the Court generally does not even acknowledge the conflicting authority, but proceeds as if it doesn't exist. For example, in *Humanitarian Law Project*, the Court embraced a categorical approach denying lawyers First Amendment rights when acting as lawyers, but the Court neither mentioned nor attempted to distinguish its prior caselaw found in *Button* and *Velazquez*, both of which squarely hold that attorneys have enforceable First Amendment rights when acting in the capacity of lawyers representing clients.

Faced with this divergence of views and no attempt by the Supreme Court to explain or even acknowledge the inconsistency, state courts are left to selectively choose a line of authority to either accept or refuse attorneys' appeals to First Amendment protection. And states, in fact, do exactly that. State courts wishing to employ the constitutional conditions theory cite Stewart's concurrence from *Sawyer* and Rehnquist's concurrence from *Gentile*, and those wishing to adopt a categorical approach can rely on *Gentile* or *Humanitarian Law Project*.[49] Where the attorney is asserting that the state's own actions or regulations are unconstitutional, state courts naturally tend to adopt one of the approaches that denies attorney access to the First Amendment.

Why are there such divergent and inconsistent views? And why hasn't the Supreme Court just adopted one approach and then stuck with it? In order to understand the cause of the confusion – and to see how to appropriately get out of the morass we are in – we must understand the special complications, both practical and theoretical, surrounding the recognition of First Amendment rights for lawyers. These complications illuminate why application of the First Amendment hasn't been straightforward in many attorney speech contexts, and include (1) the fact that the practice of law is accomplished precisely through speech, association, and petitioning; (2) the traditional self-regulation of lawyers; and (3) the source of attorney power and the designation of attorneys as officers of the court. In the next three chapters, each of these special problems will be examined and accounted for as a necessary precondition to creating any workable approach to the First Amendment rights of lawyers.

---

[49] *See, e.g., supra* Note 26 and accompanying text.

2

"Speech Is All We Have"[1]

The Supreme Court's 1954 *Brown* v. *Board of Education*[2] decision did not go down easily with the Southern States. Many tactics of resistance were used to avoid complying with desegregation, which necessitated the filing of lawsuits – sometimes for each and every school board – to try to secure desegregation and compliance with the Court's ruling.[3] In 1956, Virginia's legislature enacted five bills "as part . . . of the general plan of massive resistance to the integration of schools of the state under the Supreme Court's decrees."[4] One of the bills enacted took direct aim at attorney speech, association, and petitioning. The legislature's method of foreclosing the implementation of *Brown* was to amend Virginia's rules regulating lawyers to redefine prohibited "solicitation" in such a way as to prohibit the NAACP's solicitation of plaintiffs and instigation of desegregation lawsuits. The Virginia Supreme Court held that the NAACP's activities – of holding meetings with parents of school children, advising them of their legal rights, offering to represent them in desegregation lawsuits, and then instigating litigation on their behalf – were *prohibited* by the redefined professional conduct rule and constitutionally so. Virginia was not the only state to enact such attorney regulations. Following *Brown*, similar statutes were enacted in Arkansas, Florida, Georgia, Mississippi, South Carolina, and Tennessee – all in an attempt to shut down the NAACP's desegregation campaign.[5]

---

[1] Frederick Schauer, *The Speech of Law and the Law of Speech*, 49 ARK. L. REV. 687 (1997). Some material contained in this chapter, as well as Chapters 7, 9, and 10, was previously published in *A First Amendment Theory for Protecting Attorney Speech*, 45 U.C. DAVIS L. REV. 27 (2012).

[2] 347 U.S. 483 (1954).

[3] *See NAACP* v. *Button*, 371 U.S. 415, 435–36, n. 16 (1963) (listing over sixty lawsuits filed in Virginia alone in separate counties against specific school boards).

[4] *Id.* at 445–46 (Goldberg, J., concurring) (quoting federal district court's finding).

[5] *See id.*

In a powerful opinion, the Supreme Court in *NAACP v. Button*[6] reversed the Virginia Supreme Court, holding that Virginia's statute, as interpreted to prohibit the NAACP's attorney's activities, violated the First Amendment rights of "speech, petition, [and] assembly" – First Amendment rights of *both* the attorneys and their clients "to petition for the redress of grievances," as well as the *regulated attorneys'* rights to engage in "political expression and association."[7] The Court eloquently explained: "[A]bstract discussion is not the only species of communication which the Constitution protects"; rather, the First Amendment also protects "litigation . . . [as] a means for achieving the lawful objectives of equality of treatment by all government."[8] The Court explained that, for the NAACP lawyers:

> [L]itigation is not a technique of resolving private differences; it is a *means for achieving the lawful objectives of equality of treatment by all government*, federal, state and local, for the members of the Negro community in this country. *It is thus a form of political expression.* Groups which find themselves unable to achieve their objectives through the ballot frequently turn to the courts . . . And under the conditions of modern government, *litigation may well be the sole practicable avenue open to a minority to petition for redress of grievances.*[9]

The *Button* Court thus expressly recognized speech and association rights belonging to the regulated attorney. These rights of expression and association for the attorney were essential to preserve the rights to petition the government through litigation held by both the attorneys and the people whom the NAACP would be representing. Virginia technically had only foreclosed *attorney speech* – but that restriction on attorney speech had the effect of (and was intended to have the effect of) denying African Americans the ability to assert their constitutional rights by means of desegregation litigation. The *Button* Court emphasized that the racial setting of the lawsuit was "irrelevant to the ground of our decision" and that the First Amendment protections recognized by the Court would apply equally in other circumstances.[10]

As illustrated by the bundle of First Amendment rights the *Button* Court held to be violated by Virginia's statute, nearly everything a lawyer does in representing a client falls under the First Amendment's umbrella. The First Amendment guarantees rights to speech, association, and petition – and those three rights succinctly encapsulate the primary activities of lawyers: associating with clients, petitioning the government, and speaking, both orally and via written documents. Indeed, the practice of law is performed almost entirely through speech. As Frederick Schauer famously observes:

---

[6] 371 U.S. 415 (1963).
[7] *Id.* at 430–31 (majority opinion).
[8] *Id.* at 429–30.
[9] *Id.* at 428–29 (emphasis added).
[10] *Id.* at 444–45.

As lawyers, speech is our stock in trade. Speech is all we have. Our tools are books and not saws or scalpels. Our product is argument, persuasion, negotiation, and documentation, so speaking (by which I include writing) is not only central to what the legal system is all about, and not only the product of law as we know it, but basically the only thing that lawyers and the legal system have.[11]

This fact severely complicates the appropriate recognition of attorney First Amendment rights. If lawyers are recognized as having full access to the protections of the First Amendment and if nearly all activities of law practice fall within the First Amendment's ambit, does that mean that all regulations on attorneys are subject to constitutional attack?

Further, as Schauer notes, lawyer speech is highly regulated in many legal contexts – constituting a near "omnipresence" of speech regulation.[12] Restrictions on courtroom speech, for example, are abundant – restricting the identity of speakers, the timing of speech, and the content of speech to relevant, admissible evidence as determined by a government official (the judge).[13] Yet these restrictions seem essential to the proper functioning of the justice system and to the integrity of the trial process. If such restrictions could be stricken as an unconstitutional abridgement of speech, then it would seem that the proper functioning of the justice system would be thwarted.

On the other hand, because these restrictions on speech are essential to the workings of our justice system, Schauer believes there is perhaps a more likely problem that if the First Amendment is applied to such regulations then the First Amendment itself will be watered down to allow for these essential restrictions. Thus application of the First Amendment to attorney speech could undermine the proper functioning of the First Amendment itself for other contexts. As Schauer posits, if there is full recognition of First Amendment rights for attorney speech, one of two negative results appears to follow: Either regulations essential to the system of justice will be stricken as unconstitutional or the First Amendment itself will have to be watered down to ensure that essential regulations survive constitutional attack. Thus Schauer contends that, in large part, the speech of law should properly remain "unencumbered by either the doctrine or the discourse of the First Amendment."[14]

Schauer's concerns are not illusory. Indeed, the Supreme Court's 2015 decision in *Williams-Yulee* v. *Florida Bar*[15] appears to validate those concerns. In *Williams-Yulee*, the Court said that it was applying strict scrutiny – requiring that the regulation be "narrowly tailored to serve a compelling government interest" – to determine the constitutionality of a prohibition on personal campaign solicitations

---

[11]   Schauer, *supra* Note 1, at 688.
[12]   *Id.* at 697.
[13]   *Id.* at 689–90.
[14]   *Id.* at 691.
[15]   135 S. Ct. 1656 (2015).

for money by judicial candidates.[16] But the strict scrutiny applied by the Court didn't seem very strict. The Court expressly noted that Florida's asserted governmental interest of "public confidence in judicial integrity" was neither easily defined nor proved.[17] Moreover, the Court asserted that the "intangible" nature of the governmental interest created an "impossibility of perfect tailoring."[18] Nevertheless – with an unproven governmental interest and admittedly imperfect tailoring – the Court held that the regulation survived strict constitutional scrutiny.

Arguably, the Court applied a watered-down version of the often fatal strict scrutiny. Thus *Williams-Yulee* may be an example of what Schauer was describing. The Court applied traditional First Amendment doctrines, which pointed to application of strict scrutiny. Yet the Court felt it was important to allow states to prohibit judicial candidates from making personal solicitations for campaign donations. The result is that strict scrutiny was itself diluted to allow for the regulation. How much, if any, effect this dilution will have to other cases outside the judicial speech realm is hard to say, but it is an illustration that Schauer was rightly concerned.

Despite correctly diagnosing one of the central difficulties inherent in recognizing lawyers' First Amendment rights, Schauer's solution – that the First Amendment should be inapplicable to much of the world of lawyer speech and activity – is misguided. It is true that many of the doctrines of the First Amendment (like the content-based distinction) fail to accurately identify which prohibitions on lawyer speech should be stricken as unconstitutional and which should withstand constitutional attack. But ignoring the First Amendment's protections is a drastic and detrimental remedy. Lawyers are engaged in speech and association that are essential to our justice system – and that speech and association is in dire need of protection from inappropriate government regulation and punishment.

LAWYER SPEECH AND GOVERNMENT POWER

Failing to protect certain categories of lawyer speech and association is a very significant problem – for lawyers, for clients, and for the system of justice. And that is because lawyer speech, association, and petitioning are directly tied to access to government power. Thus, while Schauer is right that law is a "speech-constituted activity,"[19] he actually overstates his case when he says that "speech is *all*" that lawyers have.[20] Although speech is the tool lawyers use – their "saws or scalpels" as Schauer says – speech is not the end product of the law or the service that clients seek. Lawyers have something far greater than "argument, persuasion, negotiation,

[16] *Id.* at 1672.
[17] *Id.* at 1667.
[18] *Id.* at 1671.
[19] Schauer, *supra* Note 1, at 688.
[20] *Id.*

and documentation" – they have access to government power.[21] A journalist and a professor are stuck with speech – with argument, persuasion, and documentation. But clients come to lawyers because lawyers can invoke the law on their behalf and thus gain access to or protection from government power.

For example, when a client hires a lawyer to write a will, the client is not looking for eloquence or persuasion. Rather, the client is hiring a lawyer because the lawyer knows what to say to effectively invoke the law. The lawyer knows what is required to make the will legally enforceable so that the client's property will be devised according to the client's wishes. Similarly, when a client meets with a lawyer to write a contract or to set up a business, the purpose for selecting a lawyer is not eloquence or persuasion. Instead, a lawyer is selected because the lawyer knows what words to use to create a legally recognized agreement or business association that will maximize wealth and limit liability. If the lawyer is competent, then the contact or business association is recognized by law and its terms can and will be enforced through government power. If a corporation is created competently for individuals, the individuals will not be held personally liable for their corporate dealings – they are effectively shielded from government imposition of liability. And that is precisely why a lawyer was consulted – to obtain that legally enforceable shield, not for persuasion or eloquence. Endless similar examples exist. Clients go to lawyers to merge businesses, obtain temporary restraining orders or preliminary injunctions, adopt children, obtain a certain immigration status, enter a plea, enforce or modify a judgment, evict a tenant, enforce a lease, declare bankruptcy, collect a debt – and the list goes on and on.

In each of these scenarios clients retain lawyers to obtain access to government power. They want something, but, more importantly, they want that something to be legally enforceable at the end of the day. If it is legally enforceable, then the full weight of government power can be invoked to obtain it or protect that interest – wages can be garnished, titles to property can be changed, and people can be restrained, enjoined, held in contempt, and imprisoned.

Even in the litigation context where argument and persuasion seem to play a somewhat larger role than in the transactional speech context, it is still not eloquence or public relations that the client seeks. The attorney's knowledge of the law enables the lawyer to assess what legal claims or defenses exist and what arguments in favor of such claims and defenses are likely to be legally viable. Regardless of whether the argument would be persuasive in a newspaper article, what counts in litigation is the lawyer's ability to understand the current law and the client's possible claims and defenses, and then to recognize how to fit the client's case within the existing precedent to obtain the client's desired ends.

Even legal advice from lawyers to clients is not primarily about speech in the abstract. Clients want to know how to act or what to do in order to invoke or avoid

<hr>

[21] *Id.*

the full weight of government power being brought against them through litigation, prosecution, and other forms of legal enforcement. The purpose in asking a lawyer is precisely to obtain access to or avoidance of government power.

Although it is through speech that lawyers obtain their client's legal ends, clients do not come to lawyers for speech. Clients come to lawyers to invoke government power in their favor or to avoid the execution of government power against them. As will be shown, because such speech is tied to government power and to individual access to government power, it is essential that attorney speech and association enjoy First Amendment protection attuned to its function – for the very purpose that regulators cannot undermine access to government.

PROTECTION OF CLIENT LIFE, LIBERTY, AND PROPERTY

Lawyer speech and association also need protection because they are directly tied to the protection of individual life, liberty, and property. In the United States, life, liberty, and property are specifically protected against state and federal deprivation by the Fifth and Fourteenth Amendments. Additionally, they are listed among the inalienable rights of citizens in the Declaration of Independence – the protection of which was a specified basis for creating the United States government.

Clients come to lawyers not merely to invoke government power but to invoke that power in the protection of their life, liberty, and property. As Geoffrey Hazard posited, "The lawyer's work consists of resistance to government intervention in the lives, liberty, or property of private parties."[22] Monroe Freedman and Abbe Smith similarly argue that the rights comprising the adversary system (and that should shape the professional responsibilities of the lawyer) are "included in the broad and fundamental concept that no person may be deprived of life, liberty, or property without due process of law."[23] Hazard, Freedman, and Smith were discussing the professional responsibilities of lawyers – not First Amendment rights – but their discussions illustrate the fact that lawyers, through their speech, association, and petitioning, play an important role in the United States justice system as defenders of due process.

ACCESS TO JUSTICE

Lawyer speech, association, and petitioning are essential to securing access to justice for individuals and organizations. As used herein, the idea of "access to justice" is far

---

[22] Geoffrey C. Hazard, *The Future of Legal Ethics*, 100 YALE L. J. 1239, 1246 (1991). *See also id.* at 1266 ("[T]he legal profession's traditional ideal viewed the lawyer as the protector of life, liberty, and property through due process.").

[23] *See* MONROE H. FREEDMAN AND ABBE SMITH, UNDERSTANDING LEGAL ETHICS 15–16 (4th edn. 2010).

broader than the constitutionally recognized, although ill-defined, right to court access[24] or the constitutionally recognized right to counsel for indigent defendants.[25] Additionally, it is significantly broader than "access to justice" in the oft-used sense of providing legal services to those of low or moderate income.[26]

Instead, "access to justice" as used herein indicates access to law and legal processes *by anyone*. It encompasses the work of a lawyer (whether paid or not, whether transactional or litigation, whether civil, administrative, or criminal) that serves to invoke or avoid the power of the government in securing individual or collective life, liberty, or property. The idea of access to justice includes at least (1) the ability to invoke the protection of the law; (2) the ability to obtain legal advice about the lawfulness or unlawfulness of proposed or past conduct; (3) the ability to access court and government processes and to raise relevant and colorable arguments therein; and (4) the ability to secure people's constitutional rights.[27]

Lawyers are absolutely essential to effective access to justice as just defined. Even where litigants do not have a constitutional right to have the state provide legal counsel for them, they still have a constitutional right to hire a lawyer and have the lawyer speak on their behalf and act as their advocate and advisor.[28] As Freedman and Smith have summarized, "the Supreme Court has reiterated that the right to counsel is 'the most precious' of our rights, because it affects one's ability to assert any other right."[29] The Supreme Court, in recognizing the constitutional right for indigent criminal defendants to be supplied with counsel, explained: "The right to be heard would be, in many cases, of little avail if it did not comprehend the right to be heard by counsel."[30] The Court also recognized that "assistance of counsel" is "deemed necessary to insure fundamental human rights of life and liberty" without which justice cannot be done.[31] Attorneys *are* the gateway to effective access to the third branch of government. Litigants have constitutional rights to due process and court access, but those rights would be of little value if attorneys could be restricted from associating with or speaking on behalf of clients or from securing clients' underlying rights. Moreover, in many jurisdictions, corporate entities are not allowed to proceed pro se, but must be represented by an attorney. Thus, attorneys provide sole access for corporate entities to the judiciary. Lawyer speech, association,

---

[24] *See, e.g., Christopher v. Harbury*, 536 U.S. 403, 415 n. 12 (2002) ("Decisions of this Court have grounded the right of access to courts in the Article IV of the Privileges and Immunities Clause, the First Amendment Petition Clause, the Fifth Amendment Due Process Clause, and the Fourteenth Amendment Equal Protection and Due Process Clauses . . . " [citations omitted]).

[25] *See Gideon v. Wainwright*, 372 U.S. 335 (1963).

[26] *See, e.g.,* DEBORAH RHODE, ACCESS TO JUSTICE (2004).

[27] Margaret Tarkington, *A First Amendment Theory for Protecting Attorney Speech*, 45 UC DAVIS L. REV. 27, Part III (2011).

[28] *Powell v. Alabama*, 287 U.S. 45, 68–69 (1932); *see also Potashnick v. Port City Const. Co.*, 609 F.2d 1101 (5th Cir. 1980) (discussing the "constitutional right to retain hired counsel").

[29] FREEDMAN AND SMITH, *supra* Note 23, at 16.

[30] *Powell*, 287 U.S. at 68–69.

[31] *Gideon v. Wainwright*, 372 U.S. 335, 343 (1963).

and petitioning play a critical role in providing access to justice to individuals and entities through invoking and avoiding government power on behalf of clients and thus preserving their individual or collective life, liberty, and/or property.

ENABLING THE JUDICIAL POWER

The judicial power is not self-executing. The judiciary's role is to interpret the law – to "say what the law is" – including determining the constitutionality of laws, and providing remedies and punishment for law violation and legal injury. These principles were set out in the early years of the American Republic in *Marbury* v. *Madison*,[32] where the Supreme Court asserted that "[t]he very essence of civil liberty certainly consists in the right of every individual to claim the protection of the laws, whenever he receives an injury."[33] The Court explained that such protection is generally afforded through judicial remedies, and thus "where there is a legal right, there is also a legal remedy by suit or action at law."[34]

Yet, the judiciary only has power to fulfill its role to interpret the law and provide remedies to the extent that cases and controversies are brought before it, properly invoking its jurisdiction. And who is it that brings those cases into the judicial power on behalf of individual people, corporate entities, organizations, and even governments? Lawyers. Lawyers file cases, invoking a court's jurisdiction and enabling the judiciary to exercise its governmental powers as the third branch of government. In this sense, lawyers are "officers of the court" because lawyers are integral to the invocation and exercise of the judicial power in our system of government. Courts cannot hear matters, cannot determine the constitutionality, legality, or proper interpretation of laws or the acts of government officials, cannot remedy individual harms or resolve disputes, and cannot convict or sentence criminals without cases being brought before them. The judiciary is absolutely powerless – it cannot protect or enforce rights; it cannot check the use of government power (including its own) – without attorneys who bring cases before it.

In theory, individuals – but not business entities – could still bring cases pro se, but it is a fact that attorneys are essential to the *meaningful* invocation of court processes to vindicate legal rights. Thus, a major defect of both the constitutional conditions theory and the categorical approach is that silencing attorneys when acting in the role of attorney limits the judiciary's *own* power. To the precise extent that lawyers are and can be silenced in what they are allowed to present to courts, the courts lose power to address those problems.

---

[32] 5 U.S. 137, 177 (1803).
[33] *See id.* at 163.
[34] *Id.* (internal quotations omitted).

SPEECH *IS* ALL WE HAVE

I argue above that Schauer inaccurately asserts that "speech is all we have" because attorney speech is tied to government power and is not speech in the abstract.[35] Yet, the invocation and avoidance of government power to preserve client life, liberty, and property by an attorney can only happen *through speech*. The NAACP lawyers in *Button* could only inform African American parents of their legal rights *through speech*; they could only instigate litigation and petition the courts for redress from Virginia's patent disregard of the rights of African Americans *through speech*. The bottom line is that justice can only be obtained *through speech*.

And *Button* is not the only case illustrating this point. In *Velazquez* and *Humanitarian Law Project* the federal legislature attempted to undermine access to law by a disfavored group (welfare recipients and alleged terrorists, respectively) through restricting *attorney* speech, association, or petitioning.[36]

Thus, in a sense, Schauer is absolutely correct that "speech is all we have" because speech is the only *means* that attorneys have to fulfill their role in the justice system – to provide access to justice by invoking and avoiding government power in the protection of client life, liberty, and property. Speech is the only tool of attorneys, their sole "saw ... [or] scalpel ... "[37] to accomplish their work. To turn Schauer's point on its head – it is precisely because "speech is all we have" that the role of the attorney in the administration of justice can be frustrated and even defeated through restricting attorney speech that is essential to that role.

---

[35] *See* Schauer, *supra* Note 1, at 688.

[36] *See Legal Services Corp.* v. *Velazquez*, 531 U.S. 533 (2001); *Holder* v. *Humanitarian Law Project*, 561 U.S. 1 (2010).

[37] *See* Schauer, *supra* Note 1, at 688.

3

Self-Regulation

Myth and Reality

As *Button* illustrates, attorney speech and association is vital for access to government power – particularly, access to the judicial power – and requires protection from regulations that could undermine the attorney's role in the justice system to protect due process. Yet, as noted in Chapter 1, the traditional constitutional conditions view is that lawyers lack or have waived their First Amendment rights – an idea that survives obdurately in cases decided in the twenty-first century.[1]

Nevertheless, the theory underlying the traditional view is that the conditions to which the attorney agrees are themselves necessary to the lawyer's function. As Justice Stewart explained in *In re Sawyer*, "A lawyer belongs to a profession with inherited standards of propriety and honor, *which experience has shown necessary in a calling dedicated to the accomplishment of justice*." It is these standards – purportedly "necessary ... to the accomplishment of justice" – that Stewart states a lawyer cannot avoid by "invok[ing] the constitutional right of free speech."[2]

Thus, the arguable redeeming feature of the traditional view is found in the professional independence of the legal profession – the fact that attorneys are a self-regulated profession. With self-regulation, even though attorneys purportedly waive their First Amendment rights, the regulators (the state judiciary and the organized bar) fully understand the legal system and theoretically will only impose appropriate restrictions. Indeed, a primary justification for allowing attorneys and other traditional professions to self-regulate is that attorneys "alone have the specialized knowledge to understand the unique nature of their profession's problems and hence, [will alone know how] to apply effective cures."[3]

---

[1]   *See, e.g., In re Anonymous Member of South Carolina Bar*, 709 S.E.2d 633, 635 (S.C. 2011); *In re Cobb*, 838 N.E.2d 1197, 1211 (Mass. 2005); *Office of Disciplinary Counsel v. Gardner*, 793 N.E.2d 425, 429 (Ohio 2003).

[2]   In re Sawyer, 360 U.S. 622, 646–47 (Stewart, J., concurring).

[3]   William T. Gallagher, *Ideologies of Professionalism and the Politics of Self-Regulation in the California State Bar*, 22 PEPP. L. REV. 485, 490 (1995).

Claudia Haupt advocates this basic premise. She argues for First Amendment protection from *state interference* with a profession's ability to communicate that profession's insights but asserts that "the First Amendment is *not* a roadblock to regulation of professionals' speech *by the profession.*"[4] At least in theory, self-regulation should preserve the special role that attorneys play in the administration of justice – it should increase the likelihood that regulations on attorney speech, association, or related rights will be tailored to the attorney's function in our system of government. Judicial and bar association regulators should generally protect speech and association that are essential to the attorney's role and should prohibit speech and association only as required to safeguard that role.

There are two critical flaws with this theory: First, attorney "self-regulation" is a misnomer, and second, even if attorneys were entirely self-regulated, the theory assumes we can trust the judiciary and/or state bars to protect lawyers' essential First Amendment rights such that lawyers can safely waive those rights as to such regulation.

THE MISNOMER OF SELF-REGULATION

It is a central (yet inaccurate) tenet of United States lawyers that they belong to a self-regulated profession. The Preamble to the Model Rules of Professional Conduct laud lawyer self-regulation as largely "obviat[ing]" the need for "government regulation," explaining that

> Self-regulation helps maintain the legal profession's independence from government domination. An independent legal profession is an important force in preserving government under law, for abuse of legal authority is more readily challenged by a profession whose members *are not dependent on government for the right to practice.*[5]

Nevertheless, it is something of a misnomer to say that lawyers are or ever really were "self-regulated." As Fred Zacharias put it, Self-regulation is a "myth" – a myth that is increasingly disassociated with realty. He explains, "Whatever its actual meaning, the term 'self-regulation' produces an image of lawyers unilaterally controlling the behavior of their peers. That image is patently false."[6] As reviewed in this chapter, until well into the twentieth century, there was little regulation of American lawyers at all – other than disbarments for committing significant crimes. So even if this era

---

[4] *See* Claudia E. Haupt, *Antidiscrimination in the Legal Profession and the First Amendment: A Partial Defense of Model Rule 8.4(g)*, 19 J. Const. L. 1, 21 (2017); Claudia E. Haupt, *Professional Speech*, 125 *Yale L. J.* 1238, 1297, 1303 (2016).

[5] Model Rules of Prof'l Conduct pmbl. ¶ 11 (Am. Bar Ass'n) (emphasis added).

[6] *See, e.g.*, Fred Zacharias, *The Myth of Self-Regulation*, 93 Minn. L. Rev. 1147, 1188 (2009); *see also*, Carol Rice Andrews, *Standards of Conduct for Lawyers: An 800-Year Evolution*, 57 S.M.U. L. Rev. 1385 (2004).

included periods with some flavor of "self-regulation," it was heavy on "self" and light to nonexistent on "regulation." In the last half century, the tables have turned. Lawyers are heavily regulated – but it is not by themselves but by state and federal judiciaries, legislatures, administrative agencies, and even global entities.

A Picture of Lawyer Regulation in the United States

Numerous scholars have chronicled the history of lawyer regulation in the United States. As recognized today, the ultimate authority as to lawyer discipline in each state is generally the State Supreme Court. The authority of courts to regulate lawyer conduct through in-court sanctions and disbarment has a long history. Before there were written codes of professional conduct in the United States, attorneys could only appear before a court if the court admitted the lawyer to practice before it. The court in turn had the concomitant power to disbar attorneys whom it had previously admitted. As Charles Wolfram chronicles, from colonial times to the mid-twentieth century, courts exercised this power primarily by issuing an order to show cause, which required a lawyer to respond and show why he should not be disbarred. The order to show cause could be based on a complaint filed with the court by aggrieved individuals (including ultimately, local bar associations).[7]

In fact, in *In re Rouss*, Cardozo was specifically addressing the ability of the judiciary to admit and disbar attorneys when he stated that "[m]embership in the bar is a privilege burdened with conditions." Cardozo maintains that the power to disbar is not a punishment but merely the exercise of judicial "discretion" in determining that a particular person is no longer worthy of being on the court's roll of attorneys.[8]

Thus lawyers have been regulated to some extent by the courts throughout the history of the United States through the process of admission to that court and disbarment – although certainly not to the same extent and in the same manner that they are today. Reviewing such disbarment proceedings throughout the history of the United States, Wolfram states that "well into the twentieth century, most court decisions on professional discipline of lawyers sort into two short stacks."[9] One stack is disbarment following a significant criminal conviction and the other stack is disbarment following egregious conduct that is likely worthy of a significant criminal conviction.[10] There are some important historical outliers where disbarment was based on speech critical of the judiciary or for political reasons, as in the 1831 disbarment of Luke Lawless for criticizing federal judge James Peck,[11] and the 1735 disbarments of William Smith and James Alexander in representing printer

---

[7] Charles W. Wolfram, *Toward a History of the Legalization of American Legal Ethics – I. Origins*, 8 U. CHI. L. SCH. ROUNDTABLE 469, 474–76 (2001).

[8] *In re Rouss*, 221 N.Y. 81, 84–85 (1917).

[9] Wolfram, *supra* Note 7, at 480.

[10] *See id.* at 480–82.

[11] The disbarment of Lawless is discussed *infra*, Chapter 11.

Peter Zenger[12] – disbarments that caused a political backlash. But overall, court discipline of attorneys was rare, and even when an attorney was disbarred, it was only disbarment as to that court – the attorney could still be admitted in another jurisdiction and practice there. As Wolfram recounts, the mobility to other courts proved problematic because scoundrel attorneys could commit atrocities and then move to another state and repeat such conduct.[13]

In colonial America, there was also nonjudicial regulation of lawyers by the colonial legislative and executive branches. As William Gallagher summarized, colonial regulation of lawyers varied among the colonies, yet was "often quite extensive and generally entailed some combination of control of the legal profession by the executive, the legislature, and the courts."[14] He concludes: "Thus, it was the state rather than the profession that typically regulated lawyers."[15]

While the judiciary has long since had the power to disbar lawyers whom it had admitted to appear before them, the idea that the judiciary had the ultimate or perhaps even the sole power to regulate lawyers did not surface until the late nineteenth and early twentieth centuries. The doctrine of the courts' "inherent power" to regulate lawyers – to the exclusion of other branches of government – rose approximately concurrently with the formal education of lawyers at professional law schools and the rise of powerful bar associations.[16] Relying on the denomination of admitted lawyers as "officers of the court," the judiciary indicated that it had the ultimate power to regulate its own officers.[17] Gallagher notes that although "courts have sometimes claimed inherent regulatory power of lawyers as an ancient preroga-tive of the judiciary, [yet] this power is a thoroughly modern development."[18] English lawyers have also long since been denominated "officers of the court" (before the founding of the United States); nevertheless, the English legal profession has been (and is) subject to regulation by Parliament.[19]

In the United States, two versions of the inherent powers doctrine arose largely in the early twentieth century: A weaker version asserted that the judiciary had the ultimate authority to regulate lawyers, while a stronger version asserted that the

---

[12] Wolfram, *supra* Note 7, at 480.

[13] *Id.* at 478–79.

[14] *See* Gallagher, *supra* Note 3, at 508–10.

[15] *Id.* at 509.

[16] *See* Thomas M. Alpert, *The Inherent Power of the Courts to Regulate the Practice of Law: An Historical Analysis*, 32 Buff. L. Rev. 525 (1983); Zacharias, *supra* Note 5, at 1158–59.

[17] *See* Alpert, *supra* Note 16, at 539

[18] Gallagher, *supra* Note 3, at 528.

[19] For example, Blackstone wrote that attorneys are "officers of the respective courts in which they are admitted" and thus "subject to the censure and animadversion of the judges," but also noted that "many subsequent statutes have laid them under farther regulation." *See* W. Blackstone, Commentaries on the Laws of England, *26 (quoted in Alpert, *supra* Note 15, at 531); *see also* Andrews, *supra* Note 5, at 1395 (reviewing parliamentary regulation of attorneys in England starting in 1275); Legal Services Act of 2007, c. 29 (Eng.).

judiciary had the sole authority to regulate lawyers.[20] Relying on this doctrine, state judiciaries struck down legislative regulation of lawyers as unconstitutional for interfering with the state judiciary's exclusive regulatory power over the legal profession.[21]

The idea of the court's inherent power as the ultimate authority over lawyer regulation became further entrenched with the unified or integrated bar movement. Local voluntary bar associations had arisen in the late nineteenth and early twentieth centuries. Some local bar associations imposed discipline on their members – and bar associations also petitioned courts to issue orders to show cause for disbarment of particular attorneys.[22] The American Bar Association – the first national bar association – was founded in 1878 and promulgated its first code of ethics in 1908, the Canons of Professional Ethics, which were intended to influence bar associations and the judiciary, but which were not intended or adopted as positive law.[23]

The unified bar movement sought to "create an autonomous, self-regulating, prosperous, and influential legal profession" by *requiring* all lawyers within a jurisdiction to join a state bar association that was generally under the control of the state judiciary.[24] The dues from mandatory membership would fund and improve state regulation and discipline of lawyers.[25] While voluntary bar associations continued, the mandatory bar association was no longer a social or economic association of like-minded professionals engaged in peer-review but instead an agency of the state headed by the state judiciary.

The rise of both the voluntary bar associations in the late nineteenth century and the unified bar associations in the mid-twentieth century had mixed motivations – some apparently laudable and some clearly not. For example, voluntary bar associations in New York City and Chicago in the late nineteenth century arose in part to curb judicial and political corruption.[26] These were the days of Tammany Hall, and the New York City bar association sought disbarment of corrupt lawyers and impeachment of corrupt judges.[27]

Yet the rise of both voluntary and integrated bar associations had reprehensible motivations as well. Nativism appears to have been a major motivation in both movements. Socially elite lawyers did not approve of sharing a profession with immigrants and others perceived to be ethnically or socially undesirable.[28] Further, both movements secured and broadened the legal professional monopoly for the

---

[20] Gallagher, *supra* Note 3, at 527–28.
[21] *See id.* at 528–29; Alpert, *supra* Note 16, at 536–48.
[22] Gallagher, *supra* Note 3, at 516.
[23] Zacharias, *supra* Note 6, at 1160–61.
[24] Gallagher, *supra* Note 3, at 518–19; Alpert, *supra* Note 15, at 544.
[25] Gallagher, *supra* Note 3, at 519–20.
[26] *See id.* at 515–16.
[27] *See id.*
[28] *See* Alpert, *supra* Note 16, at 538; Gallagher, *supra* Note 3, at 514 n. 164.

established lawyer class – foreclosing competition from lower classes, immigrants, nonlawyers, and businesses.[29] Despite the rhetoric of improving the quality and standing of the profession as the reason for establishing bar associations, there was significant self-dealing to this alleged self-regulation.

The modern result of these movements is that most states have adopted a unified bar of some sort, requiring dues from all lawyers, which pays for a state regulatory machine with the resources to discipline lawyers. State Supreme Courts generally have ultimate authority over regulation and discipline of lawyers. The ABA, comprised of lawyers, promulgates model rules, which are then reviewed and either adopted, modified, or rejected by the states.

In a sense, then, this primary regulation of lawyers is a "self-regulation" of sorts. The judiciary (nearly all of whom were previously lawyers) has the ultimate authority to adopt the general rules of professional conduct and to oversee the discipline of lawyers within the state – and the rules adopted primarily come from the ABA's Model Rules of Professional Conduct, also promulgated by lawyers.

But in another sense it is *not* self-regulation. Fred Zacharias contends that regulation by the judiciary is regulation external to the profession.[30] The traditional ideal of lawyer independence and even the ABA's assertion of self-regulation in the Model Rules envision a profession free from "government domination."[31] Judicial regulation is only self-regulation and professional independence if one considers the judiciary *not* to be part of the government. Moreover, because state judiciaries have delegated primary disciplinary authority to a state agency, most state discipline of lawyers is actually accomplished by a state regulatory agency with judicial review of that agency's determinations. That looks an awful lot like government domination of lawyer regulation.

Indeed, the Supreme Court has repeatedly recognized that state judicial regulation of lawyers is governmental (and not just self) regulation of lawyers, subject to constitutional requirements. The Court has stricken as unconstitutional regulations enacted by the state bar and judiciary, including advertising regulations, restrictions on campaign speech, restrictions on pretrial publicity, and refusals to admit certain applicants to the bar – to name a few examples.[32] The current system is not self-regulation – it is mandated government regulation of lawyers.

---

[29] *See* Gallagher, *supra* Note 3, at 519–20; Alpert, *supra* Note 16, at 536.
[30] Zacharias, *supra* Note 6, at 1154.
[31] MODEL RULES OF PROF'L CONDUCT pmbl. ¶ 11.
[32] *See, e.g., Republican Party of Minnesota v. White,* 536 U.S. 765 (2002); *Gentile v. State Bar of Nev.,* 501 U.S. 1030, 1071 (1991); *Zauderer v. Office of Disciplinary Counsel of the Supreme Court of Ohio,* 471 U.S. 626 (1985); *Bates v. State Bar of Arizona,* 433 U.S. 421 (1977); *In re Primus,* 436 U.S. 412 (1978).

Co-Regulation by Other Government Entities

Perhaps more importantly, lawyers today are not exclusively regulated by the judiciary or the state bar. Despite the inherent powers doctrine and judicial attempts to squelch lawyer regulation by other governmental entities, the fact remains that lawyers are regulated by state and federal legislatures, as well as administrative agencies (such as the SEC, PTO, or the IRS). As Laurel Terry has explained:

> Although the ABA recently reaffirmed the traditional view that lawyers should be regulated by the state judicial branch, commentators have noted that lawyers already are subject to multiple sources of regulation. The combination of globalization and the service providers paradigm means that lawyers are likely to face regulation from more and more entities ... U.S. lawyers face regulation from many new sources, including global entities.[33]

Further, in 2010, the Supreme Court undercut the strong version of the inherent powers doctrine by expressly rejecting that judicial regulation excludes regulation by other government entities. In *Milavetz, Gallop & Milavetz v. United States*,[34] attorneys challenged the constitutionality of congressional restrictions on attorneys when advising clients in contemplation of bankruptcy. The ABA argued in an amicus brief that "the licensing and regulation of attorneys has been reserved to, and performed by, the State judicial systems."[35] The Supreme Court flatly rejected "self-regulation" as a defense that shielded attorneys from congressional regulation. It noted that "Congress and the bankruptcy courts *have long overseen aspects of attorney conduct* in this area of substantial federal concern," and summarily concluded that an argument that Congress had "impermissibly trenche[d] on an area of traditional state regulation ... *lacks merit*."[36]

The fact that regulations on lawyers do not come solely from the judiciary or lawyers – those who know and understand the legal profession – undercuts the constitutional conditions theory. Do lawyers consent to regulation from any potential regulators? Have they waived their First Amendment rights as to any and all state or federal legislation? Regulation by state and federal agencies? International treaties and global entities? How far does it go?

Moreover, legislators are answerable to their constituents – and can be subject to majoritarian and special interest capture. Democratic majorities have not consistently appreciated the need to protect legal rights of and processes for disfavored minorities (including, for example, criminal defendants) and could easily undermine access to

---

[33] Laurel S. Terry, *The Future Regulation of the Legal Profession: The Impact of Treating the Legal Profession as "Service Providers*," 2008 J. PROF. LAW. SYMP. ISSUES 189, 205–06 (2008).
[34] 559 U.S. 229 (2010).
[35] Brief for Amicus Curiae American Bar Association Supporting Petitioners, *Milavetz, Gallop & Milavetz v. United States*, 559 U.S. 229 (2010) (No. 08–1119), 2009 WL 2875367, at *8.
[36] *Milavetz*, 559 U.S. at 237 (emphasis added).

law by disfavored groups if their elected representatives regulate lawyers to foreclose lawyer speech and association on behalf of such groups. While this possibility sounds ludicrously unlikely, history demonstrates otherwise.

For example, the Virginia legislation at issue in *Button* foreclosed the activities of NAACP lawyers for the very purpose of forestalling desegregation.[37] Similarly, federal legislation in *Velazquez* prohibited lawyers for the Legal Services Corporation from bringing constitutional challenges to welfare laws on behalf of welfare recipients.[38] And federal legislation in *Humanitarian Law Project* forbad lawyers from providing legal assistance or legal advice regarding lawful nonviolent conduct to groups that the Secretary of State has designated as Foreign Terrorist Organizations (FTOs).[39] Each of these examples is a situation where a legislature sought to undermine access to the law as to a particular unpopular group by regulating attorney speech, association, or petitioning.

It actually is not inherently problematic to allow legislative or other external regulation of attorneys. Historically, such regulation existed in colonial America and it has reemerged in recent decades. But it is absolutely problematic and a threat to our justice system to have external regulation if attorneys lack the ability to withstand regulation that violates their First Amendment rights and, more particularly, interferes with their role in the justice system of protecting client life, liberty, and property.

IS SELF-REGULATION THE ANSWER?

What if lawyers were exclusively regulated by the judiciary and/or state bars so that only those who understand the legal system and appreciate the need for lawyers were regulating them? Would that solve the problem? Is the inherent powers doctrine that forbids regulation by government entities other than the judiciary the solution to securing attorneys' essential functions in the justice system? If regulation were solely in judicial and state bar hands, could we trust them to protect lawyers' First Amendment rights such that lawyers could safely waive those rights as to such regulation?

The problem is that neither the judiciary nor the state bars have a clean record in the process of alleged "self-regulation." As noted earlier, both the voluntary state bar association movements and the unified bar movements had nefarious and self-serving motives – keeping out allegedly undesirable populations of lawyers and forestalling competition. The Supreme Court has repeatedly stricken various

---

[37] *See* NAACP v. *Button*, 371 U.S. 415, 445–46 (1963) (Goldberg, J., concurring).
[38] *See Legal Services Corp.* v. *Velazquez*, 531 U.S. 533 (2001).
[39] *See* Holder v. *Humanitarian Law Project*, 561 U.S. 1 (2010).

regulations *enacted by state bars and judiciaries* as unconstitutional infringements on attorneys' First Amendment rights.[40]

Another example can be found in the bar admission cases regarding the applicant's membership or affiliation with the communist party. Although success before the US Supreme Court was mixed, the fact remains that bar associations actively worked to forbid those with connections to alleged communists from being admitted to state bars.[41] Although all lawyers would hope that state bar associations and state judiciaries would be above popular hysteria and distrust concerning disfavored groups and causes, they have not lived up to that ideal.

State judiciaries also have failed to protect attorney speech that absolutely should be protected – and they cannot just be "trusted" to do so. As will be discussed in Chapters 4 and 11, the courts have failed miserably in protecting attorney speech that is critical of the judiciary – even though such speech is at the core of First Amendment freedoms and should enjoy near impregnable protection. Even when attorneys are raising a relevant argument of judicial bias in a court proceeding, the judiciary has failed to protect such speech.[42] This failure has undermined one of the attorney's core functions – to check the abuse of governmental power, including the misuse and abuse of judicial power.

Judiciaries (and state bars) are not immune to self-serving purposes. They are not immune to popular and political pressures. Notably, state judiciaries do not generally enjoy the salary and tenure protections afforded to the federal judiciary. Thus, state judges are answerable to an electorate, as are legislators. Some states hold partisan or nonpartisan elections as to their State Supreme Court – and among states that appoint their supreme court, retention elections are common.[43] Even retention elections can exert popular pressure on State Supreme Court justices. In 2010, three of the justices of the Iowa Supreme Court lost their seats in a retention election because they had voted to protect the rights of homosexuals to marriage under the Iowa state constitution.[44] Similarly, Penny White lost her seat as a justice on the Tennessee Supreme Court for overturning a death sentence.[45]

Even if lawyers were truly self-regulated, that should not erase the First Amendment. Our entire system of government is one of self-government, and yet everyone

---

[40] *See supra* Note 32 and accompanying text.

[41] *See, e.g., Schware v. Board of Bar Examiners of New Mexico*, 353 U.S. 232 (1957); *Konigsberg v. State Bar of California*, 366 U.S. 36 (1961).

[42] *See generally* Margaret Tarkington, *A Free Speech Right to Impugn Judicial Integrity in Court Proceedings*, 51 B.C. L. REV. 392–413 (2010).

[43] *See* NAT'L CENTER FOR STATE COURTS, *Methods of Judicial Selection*, www.judicialselection .us/judicial_selection/methods/selection_of_judges.cfm?state (last visited Jan. 1, 2018).

[44] *See* A.G. Sulzberger, *Ouster of Iowa Judges Sends Signal to Bench*, N.Y. TIMES, Nov. 3, 2010, *available at* www.nytimes.com/2010/11/04/us/politics/04judges.html.

[45] Maya Srikrishnan, *Conservatives Nationwide Target Tennessee Supreme Court Justices*, L.A. TIMES, Aug. 6, 2014, *available at* www.latimes.com/nation/nationnow/la-na-tennessee-supreme-court-20140805-story.html.

understands the need for a First Amendment even with self-regulation – particularly to protect minority viewpoints from majoritarian tyranny. What happens when a majority of a "self-regulating" profession wishes to abridge the speech or other rights of a disliked minority of that profession? Certainly, tyranny of the majority can happen among professionals.

If the Virginia legislature had not enacted the statute in *Button* foreclosing the activities of the NAACP lawyers, might the Virginia judiciary have promulgated it instead as a rule of professional conduct? Considering the fact that the Supreme Court of Virginia not only upheld the law as constitutionally permissible regulation of lawyers but interpreted the law as forbidding *all* of the NAACP lawyer activities in obtaining clients and instigating desegregation litigation on their behalf, it is not too far-fetched a supposition that if the legislature had not acted, the Virginia Supreme Court would have willingly adopted such a rule, especially if proposed through its rule-making procedures.

Attorney speech, association, and petitioning are not solely core constitutional rights of attorneys but are also essential to the protection of the attorney's role in the justice system and in protecting client life, liberty, and property. Such rights cannot be left to the good graces of the regulators – whether those regulators are the bar itself, the judiciary, legislatures, agencies, or others.

4

Attorneys as Officers of the Court and Delegates of State Power

Under both the constitutional conditions theory and categorical approach (where attorneys lack First Amendment rights when acting as attorney), attorneys are understood as delegates of state power, whose powers and rights derive top-down from the sovereign (the judiciary) who has given them a license to practice law. Thus the attorney's legal power and rights can be freely defined, limited, and revoked by that sovereign. Although not expressly recognized by courts or commentators, the reality is that under this construct, attorneys become subjects of that sovereign, and they, like the subjects of monarchical regimes before them, swear fealty to that sovereign, owe the sovereign reverence, and subject themselves to the sovereign's absolute power. It is a construct that is entirely antithetical to the United States system of government and, ironically, ultimately holds within it the undermining of the sovereign – here the integrity of the judicial power and thus the overall justice system.

A proper understanding of the US lawyer's power, role, and rights as an "officer of the court" must instead be firmly grounded in political theory forming the basis for the United States Constitution and system of government, which results in an entirely different construct of the attorney's powers, role, and rights. Most importantly, the proper conception results in the proper and just protection of not only the lawyer's rights but also the rights of the lawyers' clients and ultimately the integrity of judicial power and the overall system of justice.

THE LAWYER AND THE JUDICIAL SOVEREIGN

Although not stated in these terms, the constitutional conditions theory and categorical approaches holding that lawyers lack First Amendment rights when acting as officers of the court partake of a Hobbesian notion of top-down power flowing from the judicial sovereign. There are several critical aspects of this misconception that permeate the caselaw and theory regarding attorneys' First Amendment rights.

Delegation of Sovereign Power

Lawyers are delegates of state power and, as such, are often referred to as "officers of the court." This basic idea is both noncontroversial and accurate. State judiciaries in fact grant licenses to attorneys, who use that grant of state power in the practice of law. Overarchingly, lawyer speech, association, and petitioning are unique precisely because they are directly tied to access to government power. It is only through attorneys that individuals (citizen or noncitizen) or entities can gain effective access to the judiciary – the branch of government constitutionally designed to provide remedies for individualized harms. Even outside of court proceedings, attorneys provide effective access to the force of law itself (by creating legally binding agreements and structures), as well as advising people regarding their legal rights so that people can structure their conduct to protect their life, liberty, and property.

Attorneys thus have access to governmental power that nonlawyers do not have. For example, lawyers are able to represent others in court proceedings and bring and defend claims on their behalf, depose and subpoena people, examine witnesses, and compel the production of private information through discovery. In the criminal context, prosecutors are able to charge people with crimes and obtain the most damaging information possible about people through the police powers of the state. These and other similar powers are delegated to attorneys as part of their license to practice law.

The misstep in the theory is not the premise that lawyers are delegates of state power – they clearly are, and can be properly termed "officers of the court" in that they obtain their license from the judiciary upon admission to the bar. Instead, the misstep is the unwarranted assumption that because the judiciary has given the attorney a license to access government power on behalf of clients, then any use of such powers, including through attorney speech or association, *can be freely controlled, defined, and revoked by the judiciary* – the government entity that granted such powers (and perhaps even by Congress or other governmental entities that regulate attorneys).

This view of delegation of powers is similar to that held by sixteenth- and seventeenth-century political theorists who defended absolute monarchy. For example, Jean Bodin explained as to delegation of the sovereign's power:

> However much [the sovereign] gives there always remains a reserve of right in his own person, *whereby he may command or intervene by way of prevention, confirmation, evocation, or any way he thinks fit, in all matters delegated* to a subject, whether in virtue of an office or a commission. Any authority exercised in virtue of an office or a commission *can be revoked or made tenable* for as long as the sovereign wills.[1]

---

[1] Jean Bodin, Six Books of the Republic, *as translated in* Michael Curtis, 1 The Great Political Theories 304–05 (Harper Perennial Modern Classics edn., 2008) (1961) (emphasis added).

Similarly, Thomas Hobbes in *Leviathan* explained that public ministers, as dele-gates of the sovereign's power, "have no other right, but what depends on the Soveraign's Will."[2]

As noted, according to both scholarly commentary and numerous court opinions (whether under the constitutional conditions theory or the categorical approach), attorneys are viewed as being divested of First Amendment rights when acting as a lawyer. Under both theories, then, as delegates of state power, the attorneys' use of that power in the practice of law can be freely limited, controlled, or revoked by the sovereign – just as Bodin and Hobbes had theorized regarding delegates of the power of an absolute monarch.

Covenant and Oath of Allegiance

Recall also that in *Gentile* v. *State Bar of Nevada*, Justice Rehnquist, speaking for four members of the Court, adopted the constitutional conditions theory but relied on the attorney's oath taken at admission: "The First Amendment does not excuse" attorneys from their oath to abide by attorney regulation.[3] According to this version of the constitutional conditions theory, attorneys are irrevocably bound by their oath to abide by whatever rules of professional conduct are created by the State Supreme Court or bar – regardless of how patently unconstitutional or violative of First Amendment rights such a rule may be.

This idea is reminiscent of the Hobbesian "covenant" made (whether actually, allegedly, or impliedly) by subjects to an absolute sovereign to obey all that the sovereign may choose to require of the people. Hobbes argues that this covenant is made either in the first instance to escape the state of nature (where every man is warring against every man) or it is made when a conqueror grants the conquered their lives in exchange for such a covenant of obedience. Having made such a covenant, the subjects are bound and cannot disobey or even claim that the sovereign's actions are unjust.[4] Indeed, for Hobbes, the only injustice – the "defin-ition of Injustice" – is "no other than" the breaking of one's covenant to the sovereign.[5] Further, having made a covenant to a sovereign, "they that are subjects to a Monarch, cannot without his leave cast off Monarchy," but instead are "bound" to everything that the sovereign "shall do, and judge fit to be done."[6] The covenant not only binds the subject to what the monarch is currently doing but also to what

[2] THOMAS HOBBES, LEVIATHAN chap. 23, 167 (Richard Tuck, ed., Cambridge University Press, 1996).
[3] *Gentile* v. *State Bar of Nevada*, 501 U.S. 1030, 1081 (1991) (Rehnquist, J.).
[4] *See, e.g.*, HOBBES, *supra* Note 2, chap. 21, 148 ("Nothing the Soveraign ... can doe to a Subject, on what pretence soever, can properly be called Injustice, or Injury ... ").
[5] *See id.* at chap. 15, 100 ("But when a Covenant is made, then to break it is *Unjust*: And the definition of INJUSTICE, is no other than *the not Performance of Covenant.*").
[6] *Id.* at chap. 18, 122.

the king will do in the future. Similarly, the oath that Rehnquist relied on bound the attorney not only to the rules that the state had enacted at the time the attorney took the oath but also to any rules that "may hereafter be adopted."[7]

Artificial Promotion of the Sovereign's Integrity

Accompanying any assertion of absolute sovereignty is the need to preserve the public belief in and commitment to the legitimacy of the sovereign's power and right to reign. To stave off rebellion and sedition, the public must maintain confidence in the right and the integrity of the absolute sovereign. Not surprisingly, a number of the political theorists favoring absolute monarchy and top-down power advocated methods whereby the legitimacy and integrity of the sovereign would be promoted to the public. Indeed, doctrines such as the divine right of kings were developed to promote the legitimacy of absolute sovereignty. Robert Filmer's work *Patriarcha* argued that monarchy was God's divine method of governance, which dated back to the creation of Adam, and, thus, "the greatest liberty in the world . . . is for a people to live under a monarch."[8] And King James I argued that "Monarchy is the true pattern of Divinity."[9]

Similarly, the United States judiciary fixated itself on the term "officer of the court" to legitimize its ultimate – and under the strong "inherent powers" doctrine, exclusive – power to regulate lawyers. As Thomas Alpert explains, the judiciary "justified" its assertion of exclusive power "by using the traditional characterization of lawyers as officers of the court and then claiming that interference with these officers in turn interfered with the functioning of the judicial branch."[10]

In addition to promotion of the legitimacy of absolute sovereignty through the propagation of such theories, seventeenth-century political theorists supporting absolute power employed two closely related methods for artificially promoting the public perception of the integrity of the sovereign: (1) prohibiting criticism of the sovereign[11] and (2) requiring reverence toward the sovereign.

---

[7] *Gentile*, 501 U.S. at 1081 (Rehnquist, J.).

[8] ROBERT FILMER, PATRIARCHA (1653) *in* ROBERT FILMER, PATRIARCHA AND OTHER WRITINGS 6 (Johann P. Sommerville, ed., Cambridge University Press 1991).

[9] JAMES I, THE TRUE LAW OF FREE MONARCHIES, *in* MICHAEL CURTIS, 1 THE GREAT POLITICAL THEORIES 313 (Harper Perennial Modern Classics edn., 2008) (1961) (spelling modernized).

[10] *See* Thomas M. Alpert, *The Inherent Power of the Courts to Regulate the Practice of Law: An Historical Analysis*, 32 BUFF. L. REV. 525, 538–39 (1983).

[11] Notably, Spinoza doesn't entirely disallow criticism. He argues for absolute monarchy but would allow citizens to complain to proper authorities "that a law is repugnant to sound reason and should therefore be repealed." However, even there, the citizen is prohibited from "accus[ing] the authorities of injustice, and stirs up the people against them, or if he seditiously strives to abrogate the law without their consent, he is a mere agitator and rebel." BARUCH SPINOZA, TRACTATUS THEOLOGICO-POLITICUS, *as translated in* MICHAEL CURTIS, 1 THE GREAT POLITICAL THEORIES 355–56 (Harper Perennial Modern Classics edn., 2008) (1961).

For example, Hobbes argues:

> [The People] ought to be informed, *how great a fault it is to speak evill* of the Soveraign ... or to argue and dispute his Power, or *any way to use his Name irreverently*; whereby he may be brought into Contempt with his People, and their Obedience (in which *the safety of the Common-wealth consisteth*) slackeneth.[12]

Notably, this quote from Hobbes reveals the theoretical justification for prohibiting criticism and requiring reverence – namely, that without such, the people may cease to obey the sovereign, and this would undermine "the safety of the commonwealth."

Hobbes further invokes the ancient Roman crime *crimen laesae majestatis*, in which it was high treason to commit a crime against the sovereign's person or dignity. Hobbes includes in his definition of that crime "all endeavors by word or deed to diminish the Authority of the [Sovereign], either in the present time, or in succession."[13] Similarly, James I, in a speech in the Star Chamber in 1616, explained: "That which concerns the mystery of *the King's power is not lawful to be disputed*; for that is to wade into the weakness of Princes and to take away the mystical *reverence* that belongs unto them that sit in the Throne of God."[14] Notably, James specifically asked the Star Chamber to take "special care to blunt the sharp edge and vain popular humor of some Lawyers at the Barre that ... meddle with the King's Prerogative." James admonished that "the absolute Prerogative of the Crown ... is no subject for the tongue of a lawyer, nor is [it] lawful to be disputed."[15]

In a similar vein, United States attorneys are generally prohibited from and severely punished for impugning judicial integrity. As will be discussed in Chapter 11, in scores of cases from across the United States both state and federal courts have disciplined attorneys for making disparaging remarks about the judiciary, and have almost universally rejected the constitutional standard established by the Supreme Court in *New York Times* v. *Sullivan*[16] and *Garrison* v. *Louisiana*[17] for punishing speech regarding government officials. The punishment imposed for impugning judicial reputation is often severe, with suspension from the practice of law being typical. Attorneys have been punished regardless of whether they were engaged in a representative capacity when making the statements and regardless of the forum in which the statements were made.

Like the Hobbesian notions underlying absolute sovereignty, attorneys are not free to criticize the judiciary, who is seen as the sovereign over attorneys that granted attorneys their powers. It is not happenstance that the constitutional conditions

---

[12] *See* HOBBES, *supra* Note 2, chap. 30, 234 (emphasis added).

[13] *See id.* at chap 27, 212.

[14] JAMES I, *Speech in Star Chamber, 1616, in* MICHAEL CURTIS, 1 THE GREAT POLITICAL THEORIES 318–19 (Harper Perennial Modern Classics edn., 2008) (1961) (emphasis added; spelling modernized).

[15] *Id.* at 319.

[16] 376 U.S. 254 (1964).

[17] 379 U.S. 64 (1964).

theory has maintained a resilient presence in the caselaw dealing with punishing attorneys for impugning judicial integrity. The attorney is seen as having no constitutional rights when the attorney is attacking the judiciary – the perceived source of the attorney's power. Just as the absolute sovereign can freely limit, define, and revoke power delegated to a public minister, the attorney (as delegate of the judiciary) has no right to use the power given other than as defined by the judiciary – and certainly cannot use that power to undermine the integrity of the judiciary itself.

Additionally, as with Hobbes's rationale of protecting the "safety of the commonwealth" by preventing any slacking in obedience, the primary reason that courts reject the constitutional standard from *New York Times* v. *Sullivan* and impose serious sanctions for attorney speech impugning judicial integrity is the belief that such measures are justified by "the state's compelling interest in preserving public confidence in the judiciary."[18]

The overarching rationale is based in fear: The judiciary is afraid that if lawyers – who are constantly exposed to and thus intimately familiar with the workings of the judiciary, including any judicial incompetence, abuse, mistakes, weaknesses, or even corruption – are free to expose the weaknesses of the judiciary or of specific judges to the public, then the public will lose their confidence in the integrity of the judiciary, will cease to recognize the validity of court orders and processes, and then will flout judicial decrees and, more generally, the rule of law. This parade of horribles flowing from attorney criticism of the judiciary is why the Supreme Court of Indiana, in oft-quoted language, claimed that attorneys who disparage the judiciary commit "a wrong ... against society as a whole, the preservation of a fair, impartial judicial system, and the system of justice as it has evolved for generations."[19] It is this fear – the fear that the judiciary will lose its power if lawyers are

---

[18] *Fla. Bar* v. *Ray*, 797 So. 2d 556, 559 (Fla. 2001); *see also In re Wilkins*, 777 N.E.2d 714, 718 (Ind. 2002) (citing the "state's interest in preserving the public's confidence in the judicial system and the overall administration of justice"); *Idaho State Bar* v. *Topp*, 129 Idaho 414, 416 (1996) (citing "the state's legitimate interests in preserving the integrity of its judicial system"); *Office of Disciplinary Counsel* v. *Gardner*, 99 Ohio St.3d 416, 423 (2003) (citing the "state's compelling interest in preserving public confidence in the judiciary" and "in the fairness and impartiality of our system of justice"); *In re Westfall*, 808 S.W.2d 829 (Mo. 1991) (relying on "the state's substantial interest in maintaining public confidence in the administration of justice"); *In re Holtzman*, 78 N.Y.2d 184, 185 (1991) (relying on the need "to adequately protect the public interest and maintain the integrity of the judicial system"); *In re Evans*, 801 F.2d 703, 707 (4th Cir. 1986) (positing that "the public interest and administration of the law demand that the courts should have the confidence and respect of the people" and thus "[u]njust criticism, insulting language and offensive conduct toward the judges, personally, by attorneys, who are officers of the court, which tend to bring the courts and the law into disrepute and to destroy public confidence in their integrity, cannot be permitted"; *In re Meeker*, 76 N.M. 354, 363 (1966) (characterizing attorney's comments about judiciary as an "attempt ... to destroy the trust of the people of New Mexico, and elsewhere, in their courts and in their judges").

[19] *In re Terry*, 271 Ind. 499, 502 (1979); *Cobb*, 445 Mass. at 471 (2005) (same, quoting *Terry*); *Holtzman*, 78 N.Y.2d at 192 (same, quoting *Terry*); *Graham*, 453 N.W.2d at 322 (same, quoting *Terry*).

permitted to speak freely – that is used to justify the suppression of lawyer speech regarding the judiciary. From the judiciary's point of view, it is nothing less crucial than the continued functioning of the judicial system itself that is threatened by seemingly careless lawyer speech.

New York attorney Frederick Oberlander has referred to this as the Tinkerbell solution to judicial integrity.[20] In the play version of *Peter Pan*, Tinkerbell is dying, and her revival depends upon, and is secured by, the audience clapping to show their belief in fairies.[21] Similarly, lawyers are required to demonstrate their faith in the judiciary, to refrain from disparagement or criticism, and to show reverence and respect – to keep clapping – in an attempt to keep the judiciary alive in the eyes of the public. The concern is that if lawyers fail to show their faith in and reverence for the judiciary, the public will cease to believe – and if the public ceases to believe and everyone stops clapping, the judiciary will lose its power; in essence, it will die. Like the promotion of the divine right of kings to the public to artificially inflate public confidence in and support of absolute sovereign power, attorneys are required to promote the public perception of judicial integrity.

Moreover, when attorneys refuse to clap, the judiciary supposes that it has in its own hands (and feels it must use in self-preservation) the power to avert its feared downfall – namely, the judiciary has power over lawyers and the ability to punish them and even disbar them. By punishing severely the lawyers who dare impugn judicial integrity (including with mandatory suspension or even disbarment – taking away their very livelihood), the judiciary sends a clear message to all other lawyers to keep clapping.

OFFICERS OF THE COURT AS DEFENDERS OF THE UNITED STATES SYSTEM OF JUSTICE

Contrary to the fears of American judicial bodies, rejecting these constructs will kill neither Tinkerbell nor the judiciary – nor does it leave us without a framework for understanding the power, role, and rights of lawyers. Indeed, a correct conception of the lawyer's source of political power, grounded in the democratic theories that underlie the US Constitution, brings into relief the proper understanding of attorneys' powers delegated from the judiciary, the shaping of the attorneys' rights, and the preservation of judicial integrity and the justice system. Yes, Tinkerbell continues to live under the correct conception – even if attorneys stop clapping – but that is because we actually diagnose problems and provide life-saving medical treatment rather than clapping in the vain hope that somehow if we "believe" enough she will not really be sick.

---

[20] Telephone conversation with Frederick Oberlander, Attorney, The Law Office of Frederick M. Oberlander (May 2017).
[21] J. M. BARRIE, PETER PAN, Act IV.

Delegates of State Power – A Construct Comporting with Popular Sovereignty

As noted in the previous sections, attorneys are in fact delegates of state power. But it isn't Hobbes's or Bodin's notion of delegation of absolute power, top-down, which power is then freely defined, limited, controlled, and revoked by the sovereign. In order to understand what state power attorneys actually have been delegated, we must understand what power the American judiciary has to delegate.

As John Locke explained regarding the delegation of political power, "no Body can transfer to another more power than he has in himself."[22] Thus the judiciary can only delegate to the attorney the political power that state and federal judiciaries in the United States actually possess. And here is where the democratic political theory that laid the groundwork for and is incorporated into US constitutional structures matters – because the *limited* (not absolute) state power that the judiciary has and which it "delegates" by admission to the bar to attorneys derives from the entire body politic, of which the attorney remains a part. Political power in the United States that is delegated to attorneys contains permanently embedded within it the guarantee that the power can and will be checked by the people – because the ultimate sovereign in American political theory is the people. The Supreme Court reiterated this fact in *New York Times v. Sullivan*,[23] quoting James Madison, "the Constitution created a form of government under which 'The people, not the government possess the absolute sovereignty.'"[24]

As Alexander Meiklejohn explained, through the constitutional compact, the people delegated limited powers to "*subordinate agencies*, such as the legislature, the executive, [and] the judiciary," but not all of their sovereign powers.[25] Meiklejohn maintains that we "must have a freedom *unabridged by our agents*. Though they govern us, *we, in a deeper sense, govern them*. Over our governing they have no power. *Over their governing we have sovereign power*."[26]

Even viewing attorneys as delegates of state power, attorneys retain their sovereign rights as citizens over their subordinate governmental agents, including the judiciary. Perhaps more importantly, in light of the lawyer's role in the system of justice to represent clients and provide them with access to law, the lawyer also must be able to assert the client's rights as a citizen with the ultimate sovereignty to check government power, including judicial power.

---

[22] JOHN LOCKE, SECOND TREATISE OF GOVERNMENT ¶ 135 in JOHN LOCKE, TWO TREATISES OF GOVERNMENT 357 (Peter Laslett ed., Cambridge University Press, 2005).

[23] 376 U.S. 254 (1964).

[24] *Id.* at 274..

[25] Alexander Meiklejohn, *The First Amendment Is an Absolute*, 1961 SUP. CT. REV. 245, 254 (emphasis added).

[26] *Id.* at 257 (emphasis added).

As Locke explained, the people "perpetually retain ... a supreme power" over their governmental agents who are to act as fiduciaries of the people.[27] Political power is, according to Locke, the power given by "every Man ... into the hands of the Society, and therein to the Governors, whom the Society hath set over it self, with this express or tacit Trust, That it shall be imployed for their good" and "can have no other *end or measure*, when in the hands of the Magistrate, but to preserve the Members of that Society in their Lives, Liberties, and Possessions; and so cannot be an Absolute, Arbitrary Power over their Lives and Fortunes."[28] If government actors break that trust, the people can remove that actor – be that through election or other democratic correctives.

So who gets to decide if there has been a breach of trust by a government actor? Locke responds directly: *"The People shall be Judge."*[29] And why are the people the judge? Because the government officials work for the sovereign people. Government actors are the agents and fiduciaries put into positions of trust by the people and are responsible to them.

But how can people make such judgments if they are kept from knowing anything about their governmental servants? Attorneys are the very class of people with the requisite legal knowledge and training to understand what the judiciary should (and should not) be doing and with the exposure to the judiciary to observe and evaluate judicial conduct. Yet attorneys are effectively silenced by threats of severe discipline for impugning judicial integrity.

Further, the fear of public reaction to information or public displeasure with governmental officials cannot constitutionally support suppression of speech – absent incitement to imminent lawless action.[30] Under the First Amendment, the theoretical fear (and entirely hypothesized and unsupported by any evidence) that allowing criticism of judges by lawyers might undermine the public's *perception* of judicial integrity, which might in turn lead to disenchantment with judicial power or the rule of law, cannot support suppression of speech. The public absolutely has a right to know about the actual integrity of the judiciary (not the inflated, one-sided, censored view).

In *Bridges* v. *California*,[31] the Supreme Court analyzed the validity of a California court's contempt citation against a newspaper and a nonattorney individual for publications about a pending case. One of the justifications proffered by California was the possibility that the publications might create disrespect for the judiciary. The Court gave that interest precisely zero weight and eloquently explained:

[27] LOCKE, *supra* Note 22, ¶ 149.
[28] *Id.* at ¶ 171.
[29] *Id.* at ¶ 240.
[30] *Brandenburg* v. *Ohio*, 395 U.S. 444 (1969).
[31] 314 U.S. 252 (1941).

The assumption that respect for the judiciary can be won by shielding judges from published criticism wrongly appraises the character of American public opinion. For it is a prized American privilege to speak one's mind, although not always with perfect good taste, on all public institutions. And an enforced silence, however limited, solely in the name of preserving the dignity of the bench, would probably engender resentment, suspicion, and contempt much more than it would enhance respect.[32]

Similarly, in *Landmark Communications, Inc.* v. *Virginia*,[33] the Supreme Court explained: "[S]peech cannot be punished when the purpose is simply to protect the court as a mystical entity or the judges as individuals or as anointed priests set apart from the community and spared the criticism to which in a democracy other public servants are exposed."[34] The Supreme Court's flat denial of any validity in repressing speech regarding the judiciary solely to preserve perceived judicial integrity in both *Landmark Communications* and *Bridges* directly contradicts the core rationale for punishing attorney speech critical of the judiciary.[35]

Preserving the Actual Integrity of the Judiciary

The democratic method to promote public confidence in the judiciary is not to make everyone clap or to punish those who refuse to do so. Instead, the only political safety lies in allowing people to actually raise and address grievances or problems with the judiciary.

One of the main arguments opposing Locke's ideas was that his "Hypothesis lays a *ferment* for frequent Rebellion."[36] That is, if people were free to criticize the government and to resist the government when it breached the trust given to it, it would lead to constant rebellion, anarchy, and war – it would destroy stable governments. Locke responded by arguing that resistance is a difficulty that will confront any government where the people "are persuaded in their Consciences, that their Laws, and with them their Estates, Liberties, and Lives are in danger."[37] In other words, you can clap all you like, but if people are miserable or feel

---

[32] *Id.* at 270–71.

[33] 435 U.S. 829 (1978).

[34] *Id.* at 842 (internal citations omitted).

[35] Nevertheless, the Supreme Court in *Williams-Yulee* v. *Florida Bar*, 135 S.Ct. 1656, 1666–68, 1673 (2015), found that the Florida Bar's asserted interest in "public confidence in judicial integrity" was a compelling state interest. However, in *Williams-Yulee*, the Florida Bar was not suppressing speech by other citizens about the judiciary, but speech *by judges* to solicit money for their own election campaigns. The idea that what a judge herself does or says (including asking lawyers and parties directly for campaign contributions) is proscribable because it may show favoritisms or partiality is an entirely different concept from silencing critics and prohibit-ing speech *about* the judiciary to protect judicial reputation – as soundly condemned in *Bridges*, *Landmark Communications*, *Sullivan*, and *Garrison*.

[36] LOCKE, *supra* Note 22, at ¶ 224.

[37] *Id.* at ¶ 209.

oppressed, there will be civil unrest. Requiring people to speak with reverence and praise of government will not prevent unrest. In Locke's words, you can "cry up their Governours, as much as you will, for Sons of Jupiter; let them be Sacred and Divine, descended, or authoriz'd from heaven; give them out for whom or what you please, the same will happen."[38] Because "when the *People* are made *miserable*, and find themselves *exposed to the ill usage of Arbitrary Power*," there will still be civil unrest and rebellion.[39]

Requiring praise will not – and cannot – fix the problem. Instead, "*the best fence against Rebellion,* and the probablest means to hinder it," Locke posits, is giving the people the power to remove and replace government officials who breach their trust.[40] Thus, it is not the recognition of people's right to criticize, resist, and even change government that leads to rebellion and unrest; instead, "the most dangerous state which [governors] can possibly put themselves in"[41] is created by allowing government abuse or oppression to go unremedied while insisting that the public must nevertheless swear allegiance to that government. Further, for Locke, the most likely "rebels" are *not* citizens who rise up in the face of injustice, but government agents who breach their trust in the first place and subject people to arbitrary power or abuse (which in turn leads to people rising up).[42] Locke analogizes: "They may as well say, upon the same ground, that honest Men may not oppose Robbers or Pirates, because this may occasion disorder or bloodshed."[43]

Established First Amendment theory (outside of caselaw regarding attorney speech critical of the judiciary) is in complete accord with these views from Locke. Justice Brandeis, in his powerful concurrence in *Whitney* v. *California*, explained the overarching democratic theory embraced by the founders in the adoption of the First Amendment, which will be referenced throughout this book:

> Those who won our independence believed that the final end of the state was to make men free to develop their faculties, and that in its government *the deliberative forces should prevail over the arbitrary.* They valued liberty *both as an end and as a means* ... They believed that *freedom to think as you will and to speak as you think are means indispensable to the discovery and spread of political truth;* that without free speech and assembly discussion would be futile; that with them, *discussion affords ordinarily adequate protection against the dissemination of noxious doctrine* ...
>
> They recognized *the risks to which all human institutions are subject.* But they knew that *order cannot be secured merely through fear of punishment for its infraction;* that

---

[38] *Id.* at ¶ 224.

[39] *Id.*

[40] *Id.* at ¶ 226.

[41] *Id.* at ¶ 209.

[42] *Id.* at ¶¶ 226–28.

[43] *Id.* at ¶ 228. Locke says he will leave to "impartial history" whether disobedience (by subjects) or oppression (by rulers) has been the more common cause of civil unrest. *See id.* ¶ 230.

it is hazardous to discourage thought, hope and imagination; that *fear breeds repression*; that repression breeds hate; that *hate menaces stable government*; that *the path of safety lies in the opportunity to discuss freely supposed grievances and proposed remedies*; and that *the fitting remedy for evil counsels is good ones*. Believing *in the power of reason* as applied through public discussion, *they eschewed silence coerced by law – the argument of force in its worst form*. Recognizing the occasional tyrannies of governing majorities, they amended the Constitution so that free speech and assembly should be guaranteed.[44]

Brandeis embraces – as inherent in the First Amendment – several of the concepts that Locke had posited, and which are directly relevant in examining what powers and rights to speech attorneys should have.

As both Locke and Brandeis understood, the Tinkerbell solution is fundamentally flawed because forcing attorneys to clap by employing fear of severe punishment and artificially inflating one side of the debate is actually itself likely to create a greater hazard to judicial power. Repression, fear, and hate – including repression of speech through fear of severe punishment – is the very thing that "menaces stable government." As Locke said "the best fence against rebellion" is allowing people power and oversight over their government agents, and Brandeis agrees that "*the path of safety lies in the opportunity to discuss freely supposed grievances and proposed remedies.*"

Never is that path of safety to raise grievances and seek remedies more essential than in the context of muzzled speech by lawyers – and especially speech made by lawyers in their capacity as lawyers on behalf of clients. It is essential to our system of government for attorneys to have a right, as a lawyer, to assert all colorable claims on behalf of their clients to protect client life, liberty, and property. Lawyers are integral, not only to the protection of client rights but also to the invocation and exercise of the judicial power in our system of government. Although the judiciary is the branch of government constitutionally designed to provide remedies and pun- ishment for law violation and legal injury, it cannot perform this function on its own. Because the judiciary only has power to adjudicate cases and controversies that are brought before it, the judiciary relies on lawyers to enable the exercise of its government powers. The judiciary cannot protect or enforce rights and it cannot check the other branches of government or even abuse in its own branch without attorneys who bring cases before it. Again, in theory, this function could be performed by litigants acting pro se, but lawyers are essential to the meaningful and effective invocation of judicial power.

Thus the great irony of the Tinkerbell solution – along with the constitutional conditions theory and the categorical approach – is that by smothering attorney speech, the judiciary actually limits its own power to address the problems that attorneys would have raised. The only path of safety for preserving the proper

---

[44] *Whitney v. California*, 274 U.S. 357, 375–76 (Brandeis, J., concurring) (emphasis added).

functioning *of the judicial power* is for attorneys to have protectable speech, association, and petition rights to raise all colorable claims on behalf of clients in protecting client life, liberty, and property – including where those claims involve assertions of judicial corruption, abuse, incompetence, bias, or the appearance of bias. The only way that the judiciary can properly address and remedy such problems is for lawyers to raise them.

Of Reverence and Resistance

Several courts, including the Supreme Court, have indicated that they do not object per se to lawyers criticizing the judiciary or exposing judicial abuse, incompetence, etc., but that any such exposure or criticism must be done in a respectful tone. In *In re Snyder*,[45] the Supreme Court reversed the suspension of a lawyer who had written a letter to a United States District Court expressing his dismay at the administration of the Criminal Justice Act and the payment of attorneys who represented indigent defendants. The Court did not reach the issue of whether the attorney had a First Amendment right to write the letter; instead, the Court reversed the case because suspension was not warranted under federal disciplinary standards. Importantly, the Supreme Court stated that it "did not consider a lawyer's criticism of the administration of the Act or criticism of inequities in assignments under the Act as cause for discipline or suspension."[46] However, the Court then went on to say that the letter could be read as "ill-mannered" and "[a]ll persons involved in the judicial process – judges, litigants, witnesses, and court officers – owe a duty of courtesy to all other participants," and thus "members of the bar [should] cast criticisms of the system in a professional and civil tone."[47]

Numerous courts cite this dicta from *Snyder*, and many more similarly purport to allow attorneys to criticize the judiciary but threaten (or actually discipline) attorneys for not being respectful enough in their tone. Seven states include in their Rules of Professional Conduct a prohibition that attorneys shall not "engage in undignified or discourteous conduct degrading to a tribunal"[48] and other states require attorneys on admission to promise to "maintain the respect due to courts and judicial officers."[49]

In 2007, the Kansas Supreme Court suspended E. Thomas Pyle from the practice of law for three months, explaining that while "[a]ttorneys have wide latitude in differing with, and criticizing the opinions of the courts," yet "[u]pon admission to

---

[45] 472 U.S. 634 (1985).
[46] *Id.* at 646.
[47] *Id.* at 647.
[48] Delaware, Kansas, Michigan, North Carolina, Ohio, and Vermont have added this requirement to their Rule of Professional Conduct 3.5, while New York has added it to New York Rule of Professional Conduct 3.3(f).
[49] *In re Simon*, 913 So.2d 816, 826–27 (La. 2005).

the bar of this state, attorneys assume certain duties as officers of the court," including "the duty to *maintain the respect due to the courts of justice and to judicial officers.*"[50] Thus attorneys could only "attack the integrity or competence of a court or judge" if they did so "*in a proper tone* and through appropriate channels."[51] Similarly, the Utah Supreme Court admonished attorneys that "[a]ny allegation that a trial judge became biased … *should be made in a reserved, respectful tone,* shunning hyperbole and name-calling."[52] And the Iowa Supreme Court has similarly explained: "An attorney has the right to criticize the courts of this state, so long as his criticisms are made in good faith and *in respectful language* and with *no design to* willfully or maliciously misrepresent the position of the courts, or *bring them into disrepute or lessen the respect due them.*"[53] This of course begs the question of how an attorney can criticize the courts without bringing them into disrepute or lessening the respect due them.

Locke noted a similar conundrum about reverence owed to the absolute sovereign. Locke explains that William Barclay – a proponent of absolute monarchy – would allow resistance to the king in very limited instances where the king is literally pillaging subjects en masse. But even then, Barclay maintains that any such resistance had to be done "with reverence." Locke's witty response is worth the read:

> How to *resist Force without striking again,* or how to *strike with Reverence,* will need some Skill to make intelligible. He that shall oppose an Assault only with a Shield to receive the Blows, or in any more Respectful Posture, without a Sword in his hand … will quickly be at an end of his *Resistance,* and will find such a defence serve only to draw on himself the worse usage. This is [a] ridiculous [] way of *resisting* … [Defeat] will always be the event of such an imaginary *Resistance,* where Men may not strike again. He therefore *who may resist, must be allowed to strike.* And then let our Author, or any Body else, joyn a Knock on the Head, or a Cut on the Face, with as much *Reverence* and *Respect* as he thinks fit. *He that can Reconcile Blows and Reverence,* may, for ought I know, deserve for his pains, a Civil, Respectful Cudgeling where-ever he can meet with it.[54]

Although Locke was dealing with physical force, the problem persists in the verbal context as well. How can attorneys aptly claim that a client has been denied due process because of apparent judicial bias, while still "maintain[ing] the respect due to the courts" and without being "discourteous" or otherwise "lessening the respect due" them? What if an attorney has evidence of corruption or actual bias, or bribery, or abuse, or racism, or incompetence, or other illegality? How can an attorney raise such issues without *lessening* the public's respect for the courts? How can it be that

---

[50] *In re Pyle,* 283 Kan. 807, 824 (2007) (emphasis added).
[51] *Id.* (emphasis added).
[52] *State v. Santana-Ruiz,* 167 P.3d 1038, 1044 (Utah 2007) (emphasis added).
[53] 130 N.W.2d 672, 676 (Iowa 1964) (emphasis added).
[54] LOCKE, *supra* Note 22, ¶ 235 (final italics added).

lawyers have a right to criticize the judiciary, and perhaps more importantly, have a right to assert claims on behalf of clients to check judicial power and to assert their clients' constitutional rights to an impartial judiciary, and yet can be severely disciplined if not done with enough respect tossed in toward the errant judge? The lawyer's ability to check judicial power, the ability to resist, becomes, as Locke said, "imaginary resistance" if it must be done in a way that doesn't ruffle any judicial feathers and doesn't negatively affect public opinion regarding the judiciary. If all that people have is a shield to respectfully deflect unwarranted judicial blows, but no sword to vindicate rights of people against judicial incompetence, bias, abuse, or corruption, then there really is not an effective check on judicial power.

Oath of Allegiance

The Rehnquist construction of the constitutional conditions theory – where complete emasculation of attorney First Amendment rights is accomplished by the fiat of requiring attorneys to take an oath of allegiance to anything the judiciary has or will impose as a regulation or rule – is utterly contrary to the political theory that undergirds the establishment of the United States. Locke maintained that because the people are "always the Supream Power," they actually lack the power to bind themselves "to the Absolute Will and arbitrary Dominion of another."[55] Yet Rehnquist's constitutional conditions theory requires attorneys to do exactly that – take an oath that a ruler has absolute and arbitrary power over them. According to Locke, that is not political power at all, but is the definition of despotical power.[56] Locke asserts that such absolute and arbitrary power is one "which neither Nature gives ... nor Compact can convey."[57] Whether compact, covenant, or oath – none can convey arbitrary power to a ruler. People who swear to it are not bound by it, as such oaths are void.

According to Locke, despotical power is maintained by governors through the use of force rather than through reason – "Reason" being what "God hath given to be the Rule betwixt Man and Man."[58] Locke thus asserts that force is the rule of right in despotic power and any oath of allegiance to such a power is a nullity. Justice Brandeis, quoted earlier in this chapter, explained that "silence coerced by law" was "the argument of force in its worst form." Brandeis contends that the founders created a system not based on force or fear, but instead a system that exalted the "deliberative powers" (reason and discussion), "over the arbitrary" (force).[59] Nevertheless, attorneys are arbitrarily forced into silence when it comes to impugning judicial integrity – it is "silence coerced by law" as to the integrity and qualifications

---

[55] *Id.* at ¶ 149.
[56] *Id.* at ¶ 172.
[57] *Id.*
[58] *Id.*
[59] *Whitney*, 274 U.S. at 375–76 (Brandeis, J., concurring).

of government actors to artificially inflate public confidence in judicial integrity. Yet the First Amendment requires instead that reason and discussion be the rule as to government actors – the deliberative powers must prevail over the arbitrary.

Hobbes maintained that the only injustice in society was the breaking of the subject's covenant of loyalty to the absolute sovereign – precisely because Hobbes viewed such oath-breaking as *the cause* for the downfall of government.[60] Yet for Locke, government's downfall was not brought about by the breaking of subjects' oaths to absolute power but by governors "act[ing] contrary to their Trust" – whether "by Ambition, Fear, Folly or Corruption," whenever governors "endeavour to invade the Property of the Subject, and to make themselves, or any part of the Community, Masters, or Arbitrary Disposers of the Lives, Liberties, or Fortunes of the People."[61]

Additionally, and significantly, the core of the lawyer's oath is not an oath of allegiance to any particular government official or judge or even allegiance to a specific branch of government (like the judiciary). In this way it is very different from the oath of allegiance to an absolute sovereign. Instead, when an attorney is admitted to practice law in a United States jurisdiction, the attorney swears to uphold the Constitution of the United States as well as the constitution of the state in which that attorney is being admitted.

Under both the constitutional conditions theory and the categorical approach, attorneys are deemed by this oath to have relinquished their personal liberty interest (guaranteed by the Free Speech Clause) to speak contrary to the regulations imposed by the judiciary and bar. However, the idea is flawed. Even assuming attorneys can waive their own personal liberty interest of free speech in exchange for a license to practice law, attorneys cannot waive providing speech essential to the fair administration of justice. Attorneys cannot waive fulfilling their essential role in our system of justice or providing access to law to clients in the protection of their lives, liberty, and property. Lawyers are not solely officers of the specific court of which they are admitted, but more importantly are officers of the overall United States justice system – a justice system founded in democratic political theories repositing the ultimate sovereign power in the people and guaranteeing the ability of the people to check the power of their governmental servants whether executive, legislative, or judicial.

Rather than extinguishing their right to free speech, the attorney's role as an officer of the court and their oath to uphold the Constitution instead require that attorneys assert their constitutional right to free speech on behalf of clients in invoking and avoiding the power of government and securing the rights of their clients to life, liberty, and property. The ultimate sovereign in the United States is the people, and when attorneys represent an individual, they are representing the ultimate sovereign – a sovereign which retained a right to check the power it had

---

[60] *See* HOBBES, *supra* Note 2, Chap. 21, 148.
[61] LOCKE, *supra* Note 22, at ¶¶ 221–22.

delegated to the judiciary. Moreover, the judiciary is not an independent sovereign; its power comes from the people. And the people retain a right to check the use of the power delegated to the courts. Locke maintained that the only proper purpose of government power was in protecting citizen life, liberty, and property.[62] And that is precisely the power that is delegated to attorneys as officers of the court.

---

[62] *Id.* at ¶ 171 (Political power "can have no other *end or measure* . . . but to preserve the Members of that Society in their Lives, Liberties, and Possessions.").

PART II

Toward a Proper Methodology

5

Core Ideals of the First Amendment

Although the regular doctrines of the First Amendment often do not properly identify which attorney speech should be protected and which should not, there are core ideals and theories underlying the First Amendment that elucidate the proper scope of First Amendment protection for attorneys.

THE "CENTRAL MEANING" OF THE FIRST AMENDMENT

In 1964, the Supreme Court decided *New York Times* v. *Sullivan*[1] – the seminal case regarding defamation of public officials. The Court held that a police commissioner of Montgomery, Alabama, could not recover a half million dollar jury verdict against the *New York Times* for an advertisement that contained relatively minor inaccuracies about the civil rights movement in Montgomery.[2] The Court added a constitutional gloss to the common law tort of defamation, ruling that public officials cannot recover for defamation unless they can show that an allegedly defamatory statement was false and was made with "actual malice" – meaning that the speaker knew that the statement was false or made it with reckless disregard as to its truth or falsity.[3]

But *Sullivan*'s importance reaches far beyond the defamation context because the Court identified what it termed "the central meaning of the First Amendment." As Harry Kalven expounds, in *Sullivan*, "[t]he theory of the freedom of speech clause was put right side up for the first time." Instead of examining exceptions to speech protection – what speech is at the outside periphery of the

---

[1]   376 U.S. 254 (1964).

[2]   The inaccuracies leading to the jury's award included statements in the ad that Martin Luther King, Jr., had been arrested seven times and the police had ringed a college campus, when, in fact, King had only been arrested four times and the police had not "ringed" the campus, but just been deployed near the campus three times. *See id.* at 258–59.

[3]   *Id.* at 279–80.

First Amendment – the Court defined the core of protection that the First
Amendment safeguards. Again, Kalven explains:

> The Amendment has a "central meaning" – a core of protection of speech *without
> which democracy cannot function* ... This is not the whole meaning of the
> Amendment. There are other freedoms protected by it. But *at the center* there is
> no doubt *what speech* is being protected and no doubt *why* it is being protected.[4]

The *Sullivan* Court identified as the Amendment's central meaning the rejection of
seditious libel in the United States and the recognition of the unconstitutionality
of the Sedition Act of 1798. As the Court recounted, the Sedition Act had made it a
crime for a person to "write, print utter or publish ... any false, scandalous and
malicious writing or writings against the government of the United States, or either
house of the Congress ... or the President ... or to bring them or either of them,
into contempt or disrepute ... "[5]

Thomas Jefferson and James Madison both decried the Act as unconstitutional,
and the *Sullivan* Court embraced their sentiments. These founders joined the
Virginia Resolutions of 1798, which resolved that the Sedition Act was "expressly
and positively forbidden" by the First Amendment because the Act "is levelled
against the [people's] right of *freely examining public characters and measures* and
of free communication among the people thereon, which has ever been justly
deemed the *only effectual guardian of every other right.*"[6] Madison further relied
on the American concept of popular sovereignty and the rejection of monarchy –
"the censorial power is in the people over the Government, and not in the
Government over the people."[7] The *Sullivan* Court summarized Madison's
and Jefferson's views: "The right of *free public discussion of the stewardship
of public officials* was ... a fundamental principle of the American form of
government."[8]

The *Sullivan* Court relied on the work of Alexander Meiklejohn in his 1948
masterpiece, FREE SPEECH AND ITS RELATION TO SELF-GOVERNMENT.
Meiklejohn proffered a democratic theory of the First Amendment. Specifically,
the purpose of the First Amendment is to protect the ability of US citizens to govern
themselves.[9] In his own words, "[t]he First Amendment does not protect a 'freedom
to speak.' It protects the freedom of those activities of thought and communication

---

[4] Harry Kalven, *The New York Times Case: A Note on "The Central Meaning of the First
    Amendment,* 1964 SUP. CT. REV. 191, 208 (emphasis added).
[5] *Sullivan*, 376 U.S. at 273–74 (internal citations omitted).
[6] *Id.* at 274 (internal citations omitted; emphasis added).
[7] *Id.* at 275 (internal citations omitted).
[8] *Id.* (emphasis added).
[9] *See generally,* ALEXANDER MEIKLEJOHN, FREE SPEECH AND ITS RELATION TO SELF-
    GOVERNMENT (1948).

by which we 'govern.'"[10] The central idea is that free speech is essential for democracy to function. Under the social contract created by the Constitution, "We the People of the United States" established a democratic form of government. Consequently, free speech must exist so that all citizens can fully participate in the privilege and responsibility of self-government.[11]

Further, Meiklejohn contends that in a democracy, the people are the ultimate sovereigns: "All constitutional authority to govern the people of the United States belongs to the people themselves, acting as members of the corporate body politic."[12] Through the constitutional compact, the people delegated limited powers to "subordinate agencies, such as the legislature, the executive, [and] the judiciary."[13] However, "[t]he people do not delegate all their sovereign powers."[14] Consequently:

> Public discussions of public issues, together with the spreading of information and opinion bearing on those issues, must have a freedom *unabridged by our agents.* Though they govern us, *we, in a deeper sense, govern them.* Over our governing they have no power. *Over their governing we have sovereign power.*[15]

Thus, as Cass Sunstein has reiterated, "the American tradition of free expression" and its "extraordinary protection" for "political speech can well be understood as an elaboration of the distinctive American understanding of sovereignty."[16] This is so because "[r]estrictions on political speech have the distinctive feature of impairing the ordinary channels for political change" and thus "are especially dangerous."[17] For "if the government forecloses political argument, the democratic corrective is unavailable"[18] – the citizens lose their sovereignty over the government.

This "central meaning" of the First Amendment has important implications in the context of attorney speech. It of course demonstrates, as shown in Chapters 4 and 11, that attorneys must have First Amendment rights to openly discuss judicial behavior – but it has far greater implications.

Just as the central meaning of the First Amendment is that speech and assembly essential to democracy must be protected, so too, the central meaning of the First Amendment as to attorneys is that speech, association, and petitioning that are essential to the ability of attorneys to fulfill their functions in our justice system must be protected. As noted in Chapter 2, attorney speech, association, and

---

[10]   Alexander Meiklejohn, *The First Amendment Is an Absolute*, 1961 SUP. CT. REV. 245, 252 ("The freedom that the First Amendment protects is not, then, an absence of regulation. It is the presence of self government.").

[11]   MEIKLEJOHN, *supra* Note 9, at 15.

[12]   Meiklejohn, *supra* Note 10, at 253.

[13]   *Id.* at 254.

[14]   *Id.*

[15]   *Id.* at 257 (emphasis added).

[16]   Cass R. Sunstein, *Free Speech Now*, 59 U. CHI. L. REV. 255, 257 (1992).

[17]   *Id.* at 306.

[18]   *Id.*

petitioning are essential to enabling the judicial power. Attorneys associate with clients and then petition the government by properly invoking the jurisdiction and power of the courts. Further, it is only by associating with attorneys that clients are able to effectively invoke the power of the law to secure their legal rights, including protecting their life, liberty, and property. As will be shown throughout this book, attorney speech, association, and petitioning made by attorneys in their capacity as attorneys are essential to the fair administration of the laws and the protection of life, liberty, and property. And it is that very speech, association, and petitioning that should comprise the core of attorney First Amendment protection.

THE CHECKING VALUE

Closely related to Meiklejohn's democratic theory is Vincent Blasi's demonstration that "the checking value" of free speech "was uppermost in the minds of the persons who drafted and ratified the First Amendment."[19] The checking value is *the value that free speech*, a free press, and *free assembly can serve in checking the abuse of power by public officials.*"[20] As Blasi notes, for political thinkers at the time of the founding, one of the most important aspects of free speech was its value in "checking the inherent tendency of government officials to abuse the power entrusted to them."[21]

As Blasi points out, "the abuse of official power is an especially serious evil."[22] Government officials can commandeer the police power of the state and full weight of government to their selfish ends if abuse of their power is not checked. Blasi contends that "the power of public opinion" can check such abuse – by either leading to the ouster of the abusive government officers or to other needed changes. Indeed, Blasi contends that public opinion holds within it the ultimate threat of the power of the populace "to withdraw the minimal cooperation required for effective governance."[23] The United States government already has a structural system of checks and balances; nevertheless, Blasi observes that this system breaks "down in certain political contexts" and is reliant on public opinion to operate effectively. He explains, "the system of checks and balances usually functions only when an aroused populace demands that one segment of the government perform its checking function."[24] Thus free speech and association not only provide a means

---

[19] Vincent Blasi, *The Checking Value in First Amendment Theory*, AM. B. FOUND. RES. J. 521, 527 (1977).

[20] *Id.*

[21] *Id.* at 538.

[22] Blasi argues that official power is a particularly serious evil for several reasons, including that much human suffering "is caused by persons who hold public office." *Id.* at 541. Thus persons should "value free expression primarily for its modest capacity to mitigate the human suffering that other humans cause." *Id.*

[23] *Id.* at 539.

[24] *Id.*

whereby the populace can check official abuse, but also act as a catalyst for the other branches of government to perform their checking functions.

Again, the checking value has direct relevance to attorney First Amendment rights. Attorney speech, association, and petitioning play a critical role in checking power and ensuring compliance with legal obligations. Attorneys directly challenge the exercise of government power. Suits against federal, state, and local government and government officials are a crucial aspect of lawyering in the United States. As the Supreme Court explained in *Button*, "[i]n the context of NAACP objectives, *litigation* is not a technique of resolving private differences; *it is a means for achieving the lawful objectives of equality of treatment by all government, federal, state and local* . . . It is thus a form of political expression."[25] The Court emphasized that "litigation may well be *the sole practicable avenue open to a minority to petition for redress of grievances.*"[26] Civil rights lawyers and other cause lawyering are perhaps the quintessential examples of lawyer speech, association with clients, and petitioning that perform this checking function.

As a nation we expect and rely on this checking activity from lawyers. When President Donald Trump signed Executive Order 13769 on Friday, January 27, 2017, at 4:42 pm EST, creating a three-month ban on entry into the United States by immigrants and nonimmigrants from seven countries – Iraq, Syria, Sudan, Iran, Somalia, Libya, and Yemen – travelers with valid green cards and visas were detained by federal officials from Friday evening and throughout Saturday and Sunday. Over that weekend, hundreds of lawyers throughout the United States went to international airports and offered to represent people who were being detained. Lawyers knew how to invoke the law on behalf of those detained – how to intervene between people (even noncitizens) and government. Lawyers invoked the power of the ancient common law Writ of Habeas Corpus – which the American founders had touted as "the Great Writ of Liberty" – and which reached its ancient hand out of the thirteenth century into the twenty-first and brought the original travel ban to a halt. But that only happened because lawyers spoke with, associated with, and petitioned on behalf of the noncitizen detainees.[27] Imagine if, in addition to creating the travel ban, President Trump had ordered that lawyers were prohibited from speaking, associating with, or acting on behalf of those

---

[25] *NAACP v. Button*, 371 U.S. 415 (1963).

[26] *Id.*

[27] *See, e.g.,* Jennifer Peltz and Frank Eltman, *Volunteer Lawyers Have Descended on Major Airports after Trump's Immigration Order*, TIME, Jan. 31, 2017, *available at* http://time.com/4656131/trump-immigration-lawyers-airports/; Jonah Engel Bromwich, *Lawyers Mobilize at Nation's Airports after Trump's Order*, N.Y. TIMES, Jan. 29, 2017, *available at* www.nytimes.com/2017/01/29/us/lawyers-trump-muslim-ban-immigration.html; *See* Orin Kerr, *Four Federal Judges Issue Orders Blocking Parts of Trump's Executive Order on Immigration*, WASH. POST, Jan. 29, 2017, *available at* www.washingtonpost.com/news/volokh-conspiracy/wp/2017/01/29/four-federal-judges-issue-orders-blocking-parts-of-trumps-executive-order-on-immigration/?utm_term=.aa7baf87c657.

detained. That is the type of regulation that the Virginia legislature attempted in *Button*, and that Congress successfully imposed as to designated foreign terrorist organizations in *Holder v. Humanitarian Law Project*.[28]

The amount of checking of government power performed by attorneys is vast. It happens in lawsuits against local law enforcement for exceeding their powers up to the US President and everyone in between. It occurs on behalf of citizens, noncitizens, immigrants, and even alleged terrorists. Further, in every criminal prosecution where there is a potential punishment of imprisonment and thus an accused's liberty is at stake, an attorney is assigned to the accused to protect the rights of the accused and to act as a check against abuse of the prosecutorial power.

Yet attorneys are not merely a check against *government* power. They also act as a check against abuse of other types of power – including economic and social power. Lawyers act as consumer advocates – protecting consumers from fraudulent, predatory, and abusive business practices and improving the safety of products through products liability lawsuits (and even the threats of such lawsuits, which keep companies from releasing harmful products or induce them to recall). Lawyers protect shareholders and business entities from securities fraud and mismanagement by corrupt officers and directors. Environmental lawyers protect our nation's and even the world's, environment, natural resources, endangered species, clean water, and air – and they seek the enforcement of laws created to protect these environmental interests. Lawyers represent employees against employers who fail to pay wages, pay overtime, provide benefits, create safe work environments, or who are abusive, harassing, or discriminatory. Lawyers protect people in securing fair housing and in obtaining benefits to which they are entitled by law. They protect both individuals and society at large through associating with clients who have been harmed and invoking the power of the law in protecting their clients' interests.

Certainly attorneys are not always heroes (although I'd love them to be such). Attorneys also – and, invariably, because they work for money – represent the empowered, and use the law to reinforce and solidify the state of the powerful against those without. The fact that the empowered can obtain the advice, counsel, and assistance of lawyers enables them to structure their conduct and the conduct of their businesses and activities in a way to minimize liability.

While there certainly is a serious problem in the United States with a huge disparity in access to legal counsel based on wealth,[29] appropriately recognizing attorneys' First Amendment rights does not alter that problem in a negative way and, in fact, is likely to protect speech, association, and petitioning among those without power. Historically it has been disfavored groups and minorities that have been negatively affected – and even targeted – by laws that restrict lawyers' First Amendment rights. The point here is that lawyer speech, association, and petitioning play a

---

[28] 561 U.S. 1 (2010).
[29] *See, e.g.,* Deborah Rhode, Access to Justice (2004).

major role in checking the use of governmental and nongovernmental power in the United States – and must be protected.

THE PROPER REMEDY FOR EVILS

In FREE SPEECH AND ITS RELATION TO SELF-GOVERNMENT, Meiklejohn eloquently poses the following problem: If the government "has both the right and the duty to prevent certain evils," then is the government "authorized to take whatever action is needed for the preventing of those evils"?[30] Meiklejohn explains that "our plan of government by limited powers" flatly forbids such a conclusion.[31] Rather:

> The Bill of Rights ... lists, one after the other, forms of action which, however useful they might be in the service of the general welfare, the legislature is forbidden to take. And that being true, *the 'right to prevent evils' does not give unqualifiedly the right to prevent evils.* In the judgment of the Constitution, *some preventions are more evil than are the evils from which they would save us.* And the First Amendment is a case in point. If that amendment means anything, it means that certain substantive evils which, in principle, Congress has a right to prevent, must be endured *if the only way of avoiding them is by the abridging of that freedom of speech upon which the entire structure of our free institutions rests.*[32]

So what is the remedy to evils and societal problems? Repeatedly, the Supreme Court has declared the answer: more speech, not less. As Justice Brandeis wrote, "the fitting remedy for evil counsels is good ones."[33] Brandeis explained, "If there be time to expose through discussion the falsehood and fallacies, to avert the evil by the processes of education, the remedy to be applied is more speech, not enforced silence."[34]

It is not just that more speech is a "nicer" path – it is actually the only safe path for the stability of our government. As the Court explained in *Sullivan*, free discussion of public, social, and political issues is essential precisely so that "the government may be responsive to the will of the people and that *changes may be obtained by lawful means*" – which the Court said was "an opportunity essential to the security of the Republic" and "a fundamental principle of our constitutional system."[35] Again, as Justice Brandeis observed, "the path of safety lies in the opportunity to discuss freely supposed grievances and proposed remedies."[36]

---

[30] *See* MEIKLEJOHN, *supra* Note 9, at 48.
[31] *Id.*
[32] *Id.* (emphasis added).
[33] *Whitney v. California*, 274 U.S. 357, 375–76 (Brandeis, J., concurring).
[34] *Id.* at 377.
[35] *New York Times v. Sullivan*, 376 U.S. 254, 269 (1964) (internal citations omitted; emphasis added).
[36] *Whitney*, 274 U.S. at 375–76 (Brandeis, J., concurring).

The idea that the First Amendment enables changes to be wrought "by lawful means" is imperative in considering the First Amendment rights of lawyers. Lawyers are the primary instrument through which individuals and entities obtain access to government power in the protection of life, liberty, and property. They are the principal conduit through which grievances are raised, remedies are sought, and ultimately, changes are "obtained by lawful means." If lawyers can be thwarted in their abilities to raise grievances or seek remedies or petition on behalf of aggrieved clients or constituencies – if they can be prohibited from bringing specific claims or from representing certain persons – then change for those people cannot be brought about by "lawful means" because their access to government power has been obstructed.

SILENCE COERCED BY LAW

In his *Whitney* concurrence, Justice Brandeis maintained that the founders "eschewed silence coerced by law, the argument of force in its worst form."[37] Thus, another important First Amendment principle is the idea that the force of law should not be used to coerce silence – to shut down unpopular (or, as discussed in the next section, even allegedly "dangerous") ideas. According to Brandeis, the First Amendment demonstrated the founders' understanding that in our government "the *deliberative force* should prevail over the *arbitrary*." Deliberative force – the power of free thought, assembly, and discussion, "the freedom to think as you will and to speak as you think" – "are means indispensable to the discovery and spread of political truth."[38]

Silence coerced by the force of law is, in contrast, a completely arbitrary force – entirely dependent on the political views of whichever parties or persons happen to be in political control. As Zechariah Chafee explained in FREEDOM OF SPEECH, "once force is thrown into the argument it becomes a matter of chance whether it be thrown on the false side or the true – and truth loses all its natural advantage."[39] Chafee was writing in 1920 – during the first red scare – at a time when people were in fact serving significant prison sentences for espousing socialist viewpoints. Chaffee explained that when he was "loafing around on my boat," or playing golf, he would "occasionally think of these poor devils who won't be out [of prison] for five or ten years" for exercising their First Amendment rights.[40]

---

[37] *Whitney v. California*, 274 U.S. 357, 375–76 (Brandeis, J., concurring).

[38] *Id.*

[39] ZECHARIAH CHAFEE, FREEDOM OF SPEECH, 34–35 (1920).

[40] Letter from Zechariah Chafee to Sayre MacNell (Oct. 9, 1923), *quoted in* DONALD L. SMITH, ZECHARIAH CHAFEE, JR., DEFENDER OF LIBERTY AND LAW 2 (1986).

The *Sullivan* Court reiterated this principle, quoting Judge Learned Hand, that our system of government renounces "any kind of authoritative selection" of "right conclusions" – but instead relies on "a multitude of tongues." Learned Hand concluded in momentous terms: "To many this is, and always will be, folly; but we have staked upon it our all."[41]

These ideas find expression in the standard First Amendment doctrines regarding content-based and viewpoint-based laws. Under standard First Amendment doctrines, content-based laws are generally subject to strict scrutiny. The idea is that the regulator is trying to eradicate specific content, rather than just making a reasonable regulation about the time, place, or manner of specific speech. As problematic as content-based restrictions on speech are, even more suspect are viewpoint-based restrictions on speech. Viewpoint-based restrictions on speech are those that only punish a specific viewpoint on a matter. Thus, for example, regulations in the 1920s that punished those who advocated communism and socialism were viewpoint-based restrictions because people were able to freely condemn those same ideas. Only one point of view or one side of an issue was allowed to be discussed, while the opposing side was censored.

In its 2017 opinion, *Matal* v. *Tam*,[42] the Supreme Court held unconstitutional the antidisparagement clause for trademark registration, which forbids federal registration of a trademark if it "disparage[s] ... or bring[s] ... into contemp[t] or disrepute" any "persons, living or dead."[43] An Asian-American dance-rock band had been denied a federal trademark because their name, "The Slants," "is a derogatory term for persons of Asian descent."[44] The Supreme Court reaffirmed that – even as to hateful or offensive speech – the First Amendment does not allow viewpoint discrimination. The Court explained: "[T]he First Amendment forbids the government to regulate speech in ways that favor some viewpoints or ideas at the expense of others."[45] Both Justice Alito's opinion for 4 and Kennedy's concurrence for 4 (Justice Gorsuch did not participate) declared that the First Amendment does not allow speech to be proscribed because it is offensive – such a law is unconstitutional viewpoint discrimination. Alito broadly declared that "Speech that demeans on the basis of race, ethnicity, gender, religion, age, disability, or any other similar ground is hateful; but the proudest boast of our free speech jurisprudence is that we protect the freedom to express 'the thought that we hate.'"[46] Justice Kennedy similarly explained, that "[a] law that can be directed against speech found offensive to some portion of the public can be turned against minority and dissenting views to the

---

[41] *New York Times* v. *Sullivan*, 376 U.S. 254, 270 (1964) (quoting *United States* v. *Associated Press*, 52 F. Supp. 362, 372 [S.D.N.Y. 1943]).

[42] *Matal* v. *Tam*, 137 S. Ct. 1744 (June 19, 2017).

[43] 15 U. S. C. §1052(a).

[44] *Matal*, 137 S. Ct. at 1751 (Alito, J.).

[45] *Id.* at 1751 (Alito, J. for majority).

[46] *Id.* at 1764 (Alito, J.).

detriment of all." Kennedy concludes that "[t]he First Amendment does not entrust" such power to government.[47]

In the context of attorney speech and association, the idea that there should not be authoritative selection or silence coerced by law has great significance in considering attorney speech, association, and petitioning. As will be discussed further in Chapter 8, in some sense judges do make authoritative selection as to what lawyers can present in court, as they can exclude evidence that is irrelevant, cumulative, nonresponsive, or otherwise inadmissable. However, even in that context, it is essential to the very idea of an adversary system that both sides of an issue be fully presented – that there is not viewpoint-based discrimination, and that certain views, certain rights, or certain classes of persons are not excised from the courts or from accessing law.

The concern that such could happen is not theoretical. Particular people (generally the unpopular or the impoverished) and the bringing of particular claims (most notably claims impugning judicial integrity) have been targeted by regulation or punishment of attorney speech, association, or petitioning. For example, in *Velazquez v. Legal Services Corp.*,[48] Congress attempted to forbid attorneys who were paid by the Legal Services Corporation and represented welfare recipients from bringing any claims that challenged the constitutionality or validity of welfare laws. This is patently viewpoint discrimination. Lawyers could make arguments that assumed or stated that the laws were valid and constitutional, but could not make contrary arguments. Similarly, in the area of impugning judicial integrity, lawyers are free to praise the wisdom, competence, impartiality, rightness or any other good characteristic of judges. However, as discussed in Chapter 11, if lawyers criticize judges as being incompetent, abusive, biased, etc. – whether inside or outside of court – they open themselves up to possible severe punishment.

DANGEROUS AND UNPOPULAR IDEAS

Relatedly, our national experience of two red scares has concluded with the recognition that speech and assembly cannot be suppressed constitutionally on the basis that they involve allegedly "dangerous ideas." In Justice Brandeis's words, "Fear of serious injury cannot alone justify suppression of free speech and assembly. Men feared witches and burnt women. It is the function of speech to free men from the bondage of irrational fears."[49] During both national red scares in the twentieth century, the Supreme Court allowed punishment of those who advocated communism or socialism or who associated with such advocates.[50] Yet

---

[47] *Id.* at 1769 (Kennedy, J.).
[48] 531 U.S. 533 (2001).
[49] *Whitney v. California*, 274 U.S. 357, 375–76 (1927) (Brandeis, J., concurring).
[50] *See, e.g., Debs v. United States*, 249 U.S. 211 (1919); *Abrams v. United States*, 250 U.S. 616 (1919); *Dennis v. United States*, 341 U.S. 494 (1951).

ultimately, in *Brandenburg* v. *Ohio*, the Court noted that those decisions had been discredited by the test of time and held that a State cannot forbid even subversive advocacy – "advocacy of the use of force or of law violation" – unless that advocacy "is directed to inciting or producing imminent lawless action *and* is likely to incite or produce such action."[51] If a person is advocating "use of force" or "law violation," then the appropriate responses, as Justice Brandeis had admonished, are "the deterrents ordinarily to be applied to prevent crime" – namely, "education and punishment for violations of the law, not abridgment of the rights of free speech and assembly."[52] We don't silence the speaker, but we educate people (more speech) – and if people actually violate the laws or break out into riots, then we punish those actual violations of law.

The fact that a majority of people think that particular ideas are "dangerous," "un-American," wrong-headed, evil, unscientific, backward, bigoted, inaccurate, hateful, intolerant, or any other terrible-sounding adjective is *not* a basis to silence speech. Even if the majority is technically right – a specific idea is in fact dangerous, un-American, and wrong-headed – that is not a basis to silence speech. The *Sullivan* Court explained, "constitutional protection does not turn upon 'the truth, popularity, or social utility of the ideas and beliefs which are offered.'"[53] As Zechariah Chafee explained, "[W]e are more especially called upon to maintain the principles of free discussion in case[s] of unpopular sentiments or persons, as in *no other case will any effort to maintain them be needed.*"[54] If the First Amendment is only for popular or majoritarian ideas and persons, if it is only for those who toe the ideological line, then we simply don't need it. People whose ideas are popular or are viewed as "correct" by social or political powers-that-be do not need the shield of the First Amendment because no one is going to punish or censor their speech or association. As Justice Holmes explained in his famous *Abrams* dissent, we must "be eternally vigilant against attempts to check the expression of opinions *that we loathe* and believe *to be fraught with death.*"[55]

The First Amendment is not for the timid. Yet it is and has been "the first article of our faith," as Justice Douglas beautifully reminded us during the second red scare:

> We have founded our political system on it. It has been *the safeguard of every religious, political, philosophical, economic, and racial group amongst us* ... This has been the one single outstanding tenet that has made our institutions the symbol of freedom and equality. We have deemed it *more costly to liberty to suppress a*

---

[51] *Brandenburg* v. *Ohio*, 395 U.S. 444, 447 (1969).
[52] *Whitney*, 274 U.S. at 378 (Brandeis, J., concurring).
[53] *New York Times* v. *Sullivan*, 376 U.S. 254, 271 (1964) (internal citations omitted).
[54] CHAFFEE, *supra* Note 39, at 3.
[55] *Abrams*, 250 U.S. at 630 (Holmes, J., dissenting) (emphasis added).

despised minority than to let them vent their spleen. We have *above all else feared the political censor.* We have wanted a land where our people can be exposed to all the diverse creeds and cultures of the world.[56]

Chafee noted the extreme irony in the idea that we can secure liberty by suppressing speech. Liberty must be both the means and the ends – because the means inevitably transforms and defines the ends achieved.[57] One simply cannot create a free society by forbidding free speech and association. At a time when people were being silenced from expressing allegedly "un-American" communist ideas, Chafee remarked:

> The only way to preserve "the existence of free American institutions" is *to make free institutions a living force.* To ignore them in the very process of purporting to defend them, as frightened men urge, will leave us little worth defending. We must choose between freedom and fear – we cannot have both.[58]

As a nation, we have not always done very well in choosing between freedom and fear. Fear turns out to be a pretty convincing motivator. Unfortunately, this appears just as true in recent times with the threat of terrorism as it was during the twentieth-century red scares. And, as noted in Chapter 4, fear that the public might lose faith in the judiciary is the primary justification for punishing attorney speech impugning judicial integrity.

Fear has also underwritten nonjudicial regulations infringing on attorneys' First Amendment rights. After the terrorist attacks in Manhattan on September 11, 2001, Congress enacted the USA PATRIOT Act and the Intelligence Reform and Terrorism Prevention Act (IRTPA),[59] which make it a crime to "knowingly provide material support or resources"[60] to any group designated by the Secretary of State as a "foreign terrorist organization [FTO]."[61] In June 2010, the Supreme Court in *Holder* v. *Humanitarian Law Project* interpreted these statutes as prohibiting

---

[56] *Dennis* v. *United States,* 341 U.S. 494, 584–85 (1951) (Douglas, J., dissenting) (emphasis added).

[57] "Those who won our independence believed that the final end of the state was to make men free to develop their faculties ... They valued liberty both as an end as a means." *Whitney,* 274 U.S. at 375–76 (Brandeis, J., concurring).

[58] Zechariah Chafee, The Blessings of Liberty 142, 156 (1956).

[59] *See* 18 U.S.C. 2339A and 2339B. The prohibition on providing "material support" to foreign terrorist organizations was initially enacted in 1996 with the Anti-Terrorism and Effective Death Penalty Act, yet those provisions did not clearly include within their scope attorney speech and advice. In 2001, as part of the USA PATRIOT Act, 115 Stat. 377, Congress amended the material support statute by additionally prohibiting "expert advice or assistance." Finally, in IRTPA in 2004, Congress "added the term 'service' to the definition of 'material support or resources' and defined 'training' to mean 'instruction or teaching designed to impart a specific skill, as opposed to general knowledge,'" and "also defined 'expert advice or assistance' to mean 'advice or assistance derived from scientific, technical or other specialized knowledge.'" *See Holder* v. *Humanitarian Law Project,* 561 U.S. 1, 8–14 (2010); *see also* 18 U.S.C. § 2339A and 2339B.

[60] 18 U.S.C. § 2339B.

[61] *See* 8 U.S.C. § 1189.

attorneys from providing legal assistance and legal advice regarding lawful non-violent conduct to FTOs – and held that such restrictions did not violate the First Amendment rights of speech or association. The plaintiffs, Ralph Fertig and the Humanitarian Law Project, wished to assist two such FTOs by advising them on how "to use humanitarian and international law *to peacefully resolve disputes*," "to petition various representative bodies," including the United Nations and the United States Congress, to obtain recognition under the Geneva Conventions, and other peaceful, lawful activities aimed at securing human rights.[62] As explained by counsel for the Plaintiffs at oral argument, the Humanitarian Law Project sought to advise these groups regarding "how to pursue their goals in a lawful, rather than a terrorist way."[63] The Supreme Court held that the restrictions clearly prohibited plaintiffs' proposed activities,[64] yet did *not* violate the First Amendment because the attorneys could still engage in "independent advocacy" of any political or other message they wished to promote.[65] Allegedly, the plaintiff attorneys' First Amendment rights were not infringed because the law merely *criminalized* (with a potential fifteen-year prison sentence[66]) their "speech to, under the direction of, or in coordination with" their proposed clientele.[67]

The *Humanitarian Law Project* case acutely illustrates how a fearful majority or regulator can cut off access to law itself as to a disfavored minority. Notably, the FTOs themselves were not forbidden (and Congress lacks the ability to forbid them) from seeking the protections of international law or petitioning the United Nations – or even from petitioning Congress. Rather, the goal of denying access to the law for these groups – even for peaceful and legitimate purposes – is accomplished by restricting speech and association of US citizen attorneys. The threatened punishment for

---

[62] *See Humanitarian Law Project*, 561 U.S. at 14–15; *see id.* at 42, 54 (Breyer dissenting) (noting that plaintiffs wanted to petition the United States Congress and seek "recognition under the Geneva Conventions").

[63] *See Holder v. Humanitarian Law Project*, Nos. 08–1498, 09–89, Oral Arg. Trans. at 46 (Feb. 23, 2010) (Ginsburg, J., clarifying); *see also id.* ("They want to engage in advocacy of peaceful means of achieving the goals of these groups."). *See also* David Cole, *The Roberts Court's Free Speech Problem*, NYRblog, June 28, 2010. Cole was counsel to the Humanitarian Law Project, and summarizes the Court's opinion thus: The Court "ruled that the First Amendment permits Congress to imprison human rights activities for up to fifteen years merely for advising militant organizations on ways to reject violence and pursue their disputes through lawful means." *See id.*

[64] *Humanitarian Law Project*, 561 U.S at 21 (holding that "the statutory terms are clear in their application to [and thus prohibition of] plaintiffs' proposed conduct").

[65] *See id.* at 25–26 (explaining that "plaintiffs may say anything they wish on any topic" because "[t]he statute does *not* prohibit *independent advocacy or expression* of any kind." [emphasis added; internal quotations omitted]); *see also id.* at 36 (in explaining why statute is constitutional, concluding that "*most importantly*, Congress *has avoided any restriction on independent advocacy*, or indeed any activities *not directed to, coordinated with, or controlled by* foreign terrorist groups").

[66] *See id.* at 8, n. 1.

[67] *Id.* at 26.

the attorney is severe enough that the scheme works. As stated by the lawyer for the Humanitarian Law Project: "The government has spent a decade arguing that our clients cannot advocate for peace, cannot *inform about international human rights.*"[68] "We think it's our right, but we're not going to risk going to jail for 15 years to do it."[69]

---

[68] *Holder* v. *Humanitarian Law Project*, Nos. 08–1498, 09–89, Oral Arg. Trans. at 60 (Feb. 23, 2010).

[69] *Id.*

6

Cognate Inseparable Rights

The First Amendment enumerates a list of rights that it protects against abridgment – freedom of religion, speech, press, assembly, and petition.[1] The Supreme Court has called these "the great, the indispensable democratic freedoms secured by the First Amendment."[2] These rights are great and indispensable to democracy because each right guarantees individuals freedom of mind and conscience – and forbids government domination or control thereof. But the First Amendment is not solely about the freedom to think as you will and speak as you think – although it certainly guarantees that. It "extends to more than abstract discussion, unrelated to action," as the Supreme Court explained, because the Amendment is, importantly, "a charter for government."[3]

The rights to speech, press, association, assembly, and petition are "a charter for government" in that they work together to preserve democratic processes and institutions. In order to participate in self-government, citizens must be able to freely speak about issues, to join together in their speech, to meet together to discuss concerns, to publish their views, and to petition governmental bodies and use legal processes to achieve their goals and redress grievances. These rights are cognate inseparable rights that are interrelated and must be considered together. As the Supreme Court explained in *Thomas* v. *Collins*:

> It was not by accident or coincidence that the rights to freedom in speech and press were coupled in a single guaranty with the rights of the people peaceably to assemble and to petition for redress of grievances. All these, though not identical,

---

[1] Some material contained in this chapter was previously published in Margaret Tarkington, *Freedom of Attorney-Client Association*, 2012 UTAH L. REV. 1071.

[2] *Thomas v. Collins*, 323 U.S. 516, 530 (1945).

[3] *Id.* at 537.

are inseparable. They are cognate rights, and therefore are united in the First Article's assurance.[4]

Although not listed in the First Amendment, the Supreme Court has additionally recognized, as derived from the other enumerated rights in the First Amendment, the freedom of association.[5]

Recognizing the interconnectedness of these rights is crucial when considering the First Amendment rights of lawyers. Indeed, these essential rights can easily be "divided and conquered" as aptly illustrated by the *Humanitarian Law Project* and *Button* decisions.

Again, in *Holder v. Humanitarian Law Project*[6] the Supreme Court rejected the attorneys' freedom of speech and association claims and held that Congress could constitutionally prohibit attorneys from providing legal assistance and advice regarding lawful nonviolent conduct and international human rights to designated foreign terrorist organizations (FTOs). While the Court discussed the plaintiffs' Speech Clause claims at length, the Court rejected their freedom of association claim cursorily.[7] The Court explained that the constitutional right to association protected membership in an organization, yet the challenged provisions did not prohibit plaintiffs from membership in any organization.[8]

On the flip side, in resolving the plaintiffs' free speech claims, the Court created a dichotomy between protected and unprotected speech that directly relied on a lack of freedom of association. Specifically, the Court held that the statute did not abridge the right to free speech because the plaintiffs were still free to engage in "independent advocacy."[9] Allegedly, they were still free to "say anything they wish on any topic" because the statute only prohibited "a narrow category of speech": namely, "speech to, under the direction of, or in coordination with" their desired clientele.[10] In other words, the Court indicated that there was no violation of the plaintiff attorneys' right to free speech because they were only prohibited from speaking *in association with* their desired clientele.

In stark contrast, in *Button*, the Court held that Virginia could not constitutionally prohibit NAACP attorneys from meeting with parents of school children, explaining their legal rights, and offering representation. The Supreme Court held

---

[4] *Id.* at 531.

[5] *See, e.g., Healy v. James*, 408 U.S. 169, 181 (1972) ("Among the rights protected by the First Amendment is the right of individuals to associate ... While the freedom of association is not explicitly set out in the Amendment, it has long been held to be implicit in the freedoms of speech, assembly and petition."); *Elfbrandt v. Russell*, 384 U.S. 11, 18 (1966) ("This Act threatens the cherished freedom of association protected by the First Amendment ... ").

[6] 561 U.S. 1 (2010).

[7] Compare the *Humanitarian Law Project* Court's discussion of the free speech claim, *see id.* at 25–39, with its couple-paragraph treatment of the free association claim, *see id.* at 39–40.

[8] *See id.* at 39.

[9] *Id.* at 26.

[10] *See id.* at 25–26.

that lawyers' rights of "expression and association" were infringed by the law, as well as their right to petition the government for redress of their clients' grievances through litigation.[11] Although the *Button* Court did not directly discuss the right to peaceably assemble, that right was also implicated and protected by the Court's holding. In a subsequent case, the Supreme Court recognized that "[w]hatever the precise limits of the holding in *Button*, the Court at least found constitutionally protected the activities of NAACP members and staff lawyers in '*advising* Negroes of their constitutional rights, urging them to institute litigation of a particular kind, recommending particular lawyers and financing such litigation.'"[12] These are the activities that were undertaken by the NAACP staff lawyers at their meetings with African American parents, which also could have easily been said to come within the protected right of assembly as defined in the Court's caselaw – the right of "peaceable assembly for lawful discussion."[13] In *Button*, the Court recognized that a lawyer's right to associate with clients was essential to protect "vigorous advocacy … of lawful ends."[14] By protecting attorney association with clients, the *Button* Court also protected the NAACP lawyers' inseparable rights to free speech, assembly, and petition.

While there are several differences in the facts underlying the *Button* and *Humanitarian Law Project* cases, there are essential similarities. First, both legislative schemes worked by separating attorneys from their proposed clientele. In *Button*, if attorneys of the NAACP could be separated from African American parents and children, desegregation would in large part be defeated.[15] The *Button* Court recognized such implications of legislatively imposed attorney–client separation, and thus repeatedly stated that the statute unconstitutionally infringed the attorneys' right to *associate* with clients.[16] To fail to recognize such a right would allow representative bodies to defeat unpopular judicial constitutional rulings by restricting lawyer association with the affected group.

Second, in both cases the attorneys sought only to pursue lawful ends through lawful means to accomplish their clients' goals. Indeed, it was necessary for attorneys and clients to pursue these objectives together because the attorney could not bring suit or seek relief without the specific client, and the client could not obtain effective access to government power without the attorney. The key to both cases is that attorney–client association for legal advice, assistance, and representation was essential to preserve effective attorney speech and advocacy, peaceable assembly to discuss wrongs, and petitioning of governmental bodies (including through litigation)

---

[11] *See NAACP v. Button*, 371 U.S. 415, 428–30 (1963).
[12] *In re Primus*, 436 U.S. 412, 425 n. 16 (1978).
[13] *De Jonge v. Oregon*, 299 U.S. 353, 365 (1937).
[14] *See Button*, 371 U.S. at 429.
[15] Indeed, as Justice Douglas documented, the purpose of the law was to defeat desegregation. *See Button*, 371 U.S. at 445–46 (Douglas, J., concurring).
[16] *See Button*, 371 U.S. at 428, 430, 431, 437, 444, 445.

for redress of grievances. Although, in both contexts, association was essential to preserve the other express rights of the First Amendment, the *Humanitarian Law Project* Court denied the right to associate, and thus thwarted the effective realization of these other First Amendment rights. Moreover, the Court in *Humanitarian Law Project* nowhere alludes to *Button* or to the stark disconnect between the *Button* holding and the Court's cursory rejection of the Humanitarian Law Project's association claim.[17]

THE INTERRELATED RIGHTS

As *Button* and *Humanitarian Law Project* demonstrate, failure to recognize one right – such as the freedom of association – inures to the detriment and even defeat of other First Amendment rights. To a certain extent that is simply common sense. If lawyers cannot associate with specific clients, they cannot speak with them or advise them regarding their rights, invoke the law or petition the government on their behalf, or otherwise work to protect their life, liberty, or property. All the other First Amendment rights crumble at the defeat of one. Similarly, if lawyers don't have a right to speak as a lawyer, then that defeats their right to associate and assemble with clients (why associate and assemble if you cannot speak) and their right to petition. Contrary to the *Humanitarian Law Project* Court's cursory dismissal of an attorney's right to associate with clients, such a right is indispensable and is not only guaranteed by the First Amendment but additionally undergirded by the Fifth and Sixth Amendment rights to counsel. Indeed, one of the primary rationales for recognizing a right of freedom of association was to protect the other enumerated rights of the First Amendment.

FREEDOM OF ASSOCIATION

Freedom of association was initially recognized as a constitutional right in *NAACP v. Alabama ex rel. Patterson*, where Alabama had ordered the NAACP to disclose the

---

[17] This omission cannot be placed fully at the Supreme Court's feet. Although the activities discussed in the briefing, oral arguments, and the court's opinion were attorney activities, the petitioners did not rely strongly on *Button*, and their cites to it do not emphasize the protection of attorney association (as opposed to association in general). In the Humanitarian Law Project's opening brief, the only citation to *Button* is for the proposition that "Criminal prohibitions affecting speech demand 'precision of regulation.'" *See* Brief of Humanitarian Law Project, *Holder v. Humanitarian Law Project*, 561 U.S. 1 (2010) (Nos. 08–1498, 09–89), 2009 WL 3865433, at *18. In its Reply Brief, the Humanitarian Law Project, in objecting to the contention that only membership is protected by association, lists the prior types of association protected by the Court, including "litigat[ing] for social and political purposes." *See* Reply Brief of Humanitarian Law Project, 2010 WL 302209, at *39. Yet the Reply Brief does not point out the similarities between the activities protected by the attorneys' right to association in *Button* (including providing expert legal advice, meeting with potential clients, and litigating on their behalf) and the proposed activities of the Humanitarian Law Project itself.

names of its Alabama members and agents.[18] The NAACP was manifestly unpopular in 1958 Alabama, and disclosure of membership in that organization would certainly impede the NAACP's ability to attain members and support (even among those who favored its cause) and would likely create serious negative consequences for existing members. The Court held that Alabama's law unconstitutionally abridged the NAACP members' "right to freedom of association."[19]

Although *Patterson* was the first case to expressly recognize the constitutional right to freedom of association, the right had been emerging in the Court's jurisprudence in two other contexts, namely, (1) cases involving punishment for association or membership with the Communist Party, which initially was the primary context for protecting the right of association, whether or not it was officially termed such[20] and (2) cases involving limitations on soliciting membership in unions and organized labor.[21] All three of these contexts deal with the same ultimate associational problem: Can the government punish people for associating with a specific unpopular group (be it the Communist Party, a labor union, or the NAACP)? Notably, that is the precise type of association claim raised by both *Button* and *Humanitarian Law Project*. Also notable is that in each of these contexts, the unpopular group had political aims and goals and was engaged in some type of political advocacy. Even for groups like the Communist Party, strains of which resorted to violence and unlawful conduct, those individuals whose associational interests were found constitutionally protected only pursued lawful means to obtain political change. Thus government prohibition or punishment for associating with such disfavored groups was aimed at forestalling political change.

The Court's recent freedom of association jurisprudence has focused on the separate issue of whether a private association has a constitutional right to preclude someone from membership and, relatedly, whether government can forbid associations from engaging in certain forms of discrimination, as addressed in *Roberts v. United States Jaycees*[22] and progeny.[23] Nevertheless, the extent of the right of private associations to discriminate was not the context in which the constitutional right to association was officially recognized,[24] nor the sole or even primary context for associational protection.[25]

---

[18] 357 U.S. 449, 451 (1958).

[19] *See id.* at 462.

[20] *See, e.g., De Jonge,* 299 U.S. 353; *Schneiderman v. United States,* 320 U.S. 118, 136 (1943); *Schware v. Bd. of Bar Examininers of New Mexico,* 353 U.S. 232 (1957); *Scales v. United States,* 367 U.S. 203 (1961).

[21] *See, e.g., Thomas v. Collins,* 323 U.S. 516 (1945).

[22] 468 U.S. 609 (1984).

[23] *See Christian Legal Society v. Martinez,* 561 U.S. 661 (2010).

[24] Freedom of association, although implied and protected in prior cases, such as *De Jonge v. Oregon,* 299 U.S. 353, and *Thomas v. Collins,* 323 U.S. 516, was officially given constitutional status in *NAACP v. Alabama ex rel. Patterson,* 357 U.S. 449 (1958).

[25] As Jason Mazzone has categorized the Supreme Court's cases, the right to associate protects several types of associational interests, including forbidding government from imposing

As revealed in the Court's own association cases and explored by commentators, the constitutional right of association has several purposes, including three that are strongly implicated when examining the right of attorney–client association. Namely, the right of association (1) is essential to secure the other rights expressly guaranteed by the First Amendment; (2) promotes self-government and provides essential access to government and democratic process; and (3) is intended to ensure that guilt is personal.

Freedom of Association Secures Speech, Assembly, and Petition

In the context of attorney association with clients, the need for a right of association to secure effective rights of free speech, peaceable assembly, and petitioning the government are compelling. The *Humanitarian Law Project* case illustrates this poignantly. In that case, the Court adopted a categorical approach to attorney First Amendment rights – basically, lawyers are viewed as not having First Amendment rights when acting in their "official" capacity as attorneys or "officers of the courts." Thus the Court concluded that the plaintiffs' free speech rights were not abridged because they were still free to "say anything they wish on any topic" and "may speak and write freely" about their concerns regarding their proposed clients.[26] As characterized by the Court, the plaintiff attorneys were forbidden from engaging in "only a narrow category of speech": namely, "speech to, under the direction of, or in coordination with" their desired clientele.[27] Having endowed attorneys with speech but denied them the ability to speak *in association with* those who needed to hear what they had to say and needed their assistance, the Court went on to find, in a very cursory passage, that there also was no violation of the plaintiffs' right of association.[28]

In essence, the Court held that attorneys could say, on their own and independently, anything they wanted. What they could not do was associate with (by providing speech to, under the direction of, or in coordination with) their clients.

---

burdens or criminal sanctions on certain associations. Jason Mazzone, *Freedom's Associations*, 77 WASH. L. REV. 639, 651–70 (2002) (examining holdings of Supreme Court cases and identifying, nonexclusively, that freedom of association can be abridged (1) "by imposing burdens on certain associations"; (2) "by burdening individuals or denying them benefits because of their associational ties, thereby increasing the costs associated with membership"; (3) "by requiring membership in an association in order to receive a governmental benefit"; (4) by forbidding organized labor; (5) by forcing members to support the political speech of nonvoluntary associations, like certain unions and state bar associations; (6) by interfering with a political party's right to identify their delegates and candidates; and (7) by requiring expressive associations to admit members through antidiscrimination laws where the presence of the person affects in a significant way the group's ability to advocate public or private viewpoints).

[26] *Humanitarian Law Project*, 561 U.S. at 25–26.
[27] *See id.*
[28] *Id.* at 39.

The dichotomy created by the Supreme Court to "save" the statute from violating the Free Speech Clause – allowing independent speech but denying associated speech or speech made in the capacity of attorney – is to directly deny freedom of association.

Moreover, by denying freedom of association, the Court robbed the plaintiffs of the effectiveness of their speech, thereby abridging their free speech rights. By separating speech and association, the court undermined both rights. It should seem absurd that attorneys' rights to free speech are protected because they can "say anything they wish" and yet at the same time can be denied the ability to speak "to, in coordination with, or under the direction of" their proposed clientele.[29] In essence, the Court held that the attorneys could say whatever they wanted; they just could not speak or act *as attorneys*. In order to provide any kind of legal assistance, attorneys must be able to speak effectively, which requires that they advise their clients of their legal rights, assist their clients in invoking those legal rights, and in petitioning the government for redress of grievances, including engaging in formal representation. Thus, the Court's dichotomy also undermined the rights of assembly and petition, discussed in the next section.

A lawyer's very function is to speak *to and on behalf of others*, to provide effective access to judicial power, and to otherwise invoke or avoid government power through speech (both written and spoken in the forms of advice, legally binding documents, court filings, etc.) – all of which is done to secure the individual and collective life, liberty, or property of others. This type of speech should be the core of protected attorney speech, and yet it is the very speech that the *Humanitarian Law Project* Court's dichotomy prohibits. Lawyers cannot fulfill their function nor effectively advocate on behalf of a client if they can be prohibited from speaking to or in coordination with that client. As the Supreme Court has previously acknowledged, "[u]rgent, important, and *effective speech* can be no less protected than impotent speech, lest the right to speak be relegated to those instances when it is least needed."[30] By separating speech from association, the court protected impotent lawyer speech, while prohibiting effective lawyer speech.

Attorneys cannot bring lawsuits on their own; they cannot create legally binding documents for nonclients, and they cannot provide confidential legal advice if they cannot speak to their proposed clients. Thus, contrary to the Court's conclusion in *Humanitarian Law Project*, the plaintiff attorneys cannot act in the capacity of attorney without *associating* with their desired clientele. The idea that attorney free speech rights are preserved by allowing attorneys to engage in "independent advocacy" but prohibiting *associated* advocacy is laughable. Legal advocacy *is* associated

---

[29] *See id.* at 25–26.

[30] *McIntyre* v. *Ohio Elections Comm'n*, 514 U.S. 334, 347 (1995) (emphasis added). Rather than lessening the protection provided, the *McIntyre* Court recognized that the urgency, importance, and effectiveness of speech "*only strengthens the protection* afforded to [the] expression." *See id.* (emphasis added).

advocacy. Lawyers act with and on behalf of others – that is their very role and the method by which they invoke and avoid government power to protect client life, liberty, and property.

The right of attorney–client association is also undergirded by clients' reciprocal Fifth Amendment due process right to retain hired legal counsel in civil proceedings,[31] and clients' Fifth and Sixth Amendment rights to counsel in criminal proceedings. The Supreme Court explained that it "would be a denial of a hearing, and therefore of due process" if "in any case, civil or criminal" in "state or federal court," litigants were prohibited from obtaining and employing attorneys to represent their interests.[32]

Freedom of Association Protects Access to Government Processes

Separation of attorney and client, and failure to recognize a right of association between them, works to defeat access to law, and thus access to government power and processes. To the extent that such is denied only to specific groups of people, it creates unequal access to law and to government power. It is not just the separation discussed in many association cases where the person is not able to combine their voice with other like-minded persons to make an impact in a democracy; rather, the separation deprives people of access to law and to government itself.

The *Button* Court explained that for minority and unpopular groups *"association for litigation* may be the most effective form of political association"[33] and "may well be the sole practicable avenue open to a minority to petition for redress of grievances."[34] Significantly, as demonstrated by *Button*, the protectable right of attorney–client association for litigation and legal redress is required not solely for the minority group or proposed clientele but also for attorneys who wish to represent them. The NAACP and its lawyers could not pursue their own political goals, or effectively challenge government law and policy, without associating with clients.

For those on the losing side of majoritarian politics, access to courts, as well as to other governmental entities and processes, is essential to preserve their rights and to counter majoritarian overreaching.[35] This antimajoritarian purpose is one of the cornerstones of our Constitution. As Amanda Frost and Stefanie Lindquist explained: "Constitutionalism may be viewed as the antithesis of democracy because

---

[31] *See Potashnick v. Port City Constr. Co.*, 609 F.2d 1101, 1104 (5th Cir. 1980).

[32] *Powell v. Alabama*, 287 U.S. 45, 69 (1932).

[33] *NAACP v. Button*, 371 U.S. 415, 431 (1963).

[34] *Id.* at 429.

[35] *See, e.g., id.* ("Groups which find themselves unable to achieve their objectives through the ballot frequently turn to the courts. Just as it was true of the opponents of New Deal legislation during the 1930's, for example, no less is it true of the Negro minority today. And under the conditions of modern government, litigation may well be the sole practicable avenue open to a minority to petition for redress of grievances.").

the very existence of a constitution presumes that some choices are to be withheld from the majority."[36] Court access and other legal processes that challenge majoritarian laws as exceeding constitutional bounds implement these underlying constitutional purposes of protecting minorities in a democracy and checking government power.

Freedom of Association Ensures Guilt is Personal

The right to association, particularly as defined in the cases involving punishment for membership in or affiliation with the Communist Party, ensures that one who is prosecuted or punished for associating with a group is punished for their own guilty acts and intent and not for merely associating with others who themselves are engaged in illegal conduct. In establishing this principle, the Court accepted congressional findings that the organization at issue, the Communist Party, "was engaged in illegal activity, including terrorism and espionage, toward the end of overthrowing the United States by force and violence."[37] Yet the Court prohibited the imposition of guilt based on association with that organization rather than on the personal intent and actions of the accused. Indeed, David Cole argues that the prohibition against guilt by association is the "bedrock principle" of the right to associate.[38]

The Court elaborated on this principle in the seminal case, *Scales v. United States*:

> In our jurisprudence *guilt is personal*, and when the imposition of punishment on a status or on conduct can only be justified by reference to the relationship of that status or conduct to other concededly criminal activity . . . *that relationship must* be sufficiently substantial to *satisfy the concept of personal guilt*.[39]

Thus, as established in a number of cases,[40] in order to prohibit or punish membership, association, or affiliation with an organization, it must be demonstrated that the

---

[36] Amanda Frost and Stefanie A. Lindquist, *Countering the Majoritarian Difficulty*, 96 VA. L. REV. 719, 729 (2010).

[37] *See* David Cole, *Hanging with the Wrong Crowd: Of Gangs, Terrorists, and the Right of Association*, 1999 SUP. CT. REV. 203, 218 (1999).

[38] *Id.* at 215. David Cole served as legal counsel for the Humanitarian Law Project.

[39] *Scales v. United States*, 367 U.S. 203, 224–25 (1961).

[40] *See, e.g., id.* at 226 (stating that prosecution is constitutional where "one actively and knowingly works in the ranks of that organization, *intending* to contribute *to the success of those specifically illegal activities* "); *NAACP v. Claiborne Hardware Co.*, 458 U.S. 886, 920 (1982) ("For liability to be imposed by reason of *association* alone, it is necessary to establish that the group itself possessed unlawful goals and that the individual held a specific intent to further those illegal aims." [emphasis added]); *Healy v. James*, 408 U.S. 169,186 (1972) ("The government has the burden of establishing a knowing *affiliation* with an organization possessing unlawful aims and goals, and a specific intent to further those illegal aims." [emphasis added]); *Keyishian v. Bd. of Regents of the Univ. of the State of New York*, 385 U.S. 589, 606–08 (1967) (holding that

person associating both (1) knows of the illegal activities of the organization and (2) has "the 'specific intent' to further the illegal aims of the organization."[41] A law prohibiting or punishing association with a group that omits this specific intent requirement "rests on the doctrine of 'guilt by association'" and thus violates the constitutional right of association.[42]

In *Humanitarian Law Project*, the plaintiffs' association claim was based on this body of association cases.[43] The Humanitarian Law Project not only "ha[d] *no interest* in furthering terrorism" or the illegal activities of any of the FTOs, but they instead encouraged such organizations to "*disavow violence* and engage in *lawful peaceful means* of resolving their disputes."[44] Under the Supreme Court's prior association precedents forbidding guilt by association absent specific intent to further illegal activities, the Humanitarian Law Project's association claim should have been quite strong. Yet the Court cursorily rejected the claim in a couple of paragraphs, explaining that plaintiffs were still free to become *members* of an FTO – which the Court indicated was protected by its prior association cases – but the plaintiffs were *not* free to associate with an FTO for the purpose of providing legal advice and assistance once Congress labeled such advice and assistance "material support."[45]

Indeed, one of the oddities of the *Humanitarian Law Project* opinion is the Court's indication that the right of association protects solely membership in an organization and not other associational ties with an organization.[46] Any such suggestion turns the communist membership cases on their heads. The right of association was at issue in the communist membership cases because people were subject to criminal and other sanctions based solely on their association with an organization (which organization was itself engaged in criminal activity). Similarly, the Humanitarian Law Project was threatened with criminal sanctions if they associated with FTOs. In the communist cases, that association happened to take

---

"[m]ere knowing membership without a specific intent to further the unlawful aims of an organization" violates constitutional limits); *Elfbrandt* v. *Russell*, 384 U.S. 11 (1966) 17–19 ("A law which applies to *membership* without the 'specific intent' to further the illegal aims of the organization infringes unnecessarily on protected freedoms. It rests on the doctrine of 'guilt by association' which has no place here." [emphasis added]).

[41] *Elfbrandt*, 384 U.S. at 19.

[42] *Id.*

[43] *See Holder* v. *Humanitarian Law Project*, 561 U.S. 1, 39 (2010).

[44] *See Holder* v. *Humanitarian Law Project*, Nos. 08–1498, 09–89, Oral Arg. Trans. at 22 (Feb. 23, 2010) (emphasis added).

[45] *Humanitarian Law Project*, 561 U.S. at 39.

[46] The *Humanitarian Law Project* Court does not expressly hold that association protects only membership – an argument put forth by the government – but the Court implies acceptance of this position both by its statement "[t]he statute does not prohibit being a member of one of the designated groups" and by its cursory treatment of the plaintiffs' association claim. *See Humanitarian Law Project*, 561 U.S. at 39–40. Yet the *Humanitarian Law Project* Court also did not overturn or even address its multiple prior cases where it expressly recognized that more than membership is protected by the right of association.

the form of membership, but membership is not the only type of association that could be used as a basis for imposing guilt by association. The Court in *Scales* did not limit its explanation of the overarching principle to membership: "when the imposition of punishment on *a status* [such as membership] *or on conduct* [any other form of association] can only be justified by reference to the relationship of that status *or conduct* to other concededly criminal activity . . . that relationship must be sufficiently substantial to satisfy the concept of personal guilt."[47] The problem was not that "membership" was at issue, but that the statute imposed guilt solely by association.

The Supreme Court itself has repeatedly extended the right of association beyond solely protecting membership in an organization. For example, in *NAACP v. Claiborne Hardware Co.*,[48] the Court held that those joining in a boycott could not be held liable for the illegal activities of some boycotters unless they specifically intended to further those illegal activities.[49] The Court explained: "The First Amendment . . . restricts the ability of the State to impose liability on an individual solely because of his association with another."[50] Similarly, in *Healy v. James*, the Court held that a local student organization could not be denied recognition based on its affiliation with a national organization and other local chapters who were engaged in violent and even criminal activity.[51] Thus, "the right of association . . . includes the right to express one's attitudes or philosophies by membership in a group *or* by affiliation with it *or by other lawful means*."[52]

Providing lawful advice and legal assistance to a client is a "lawful means" of associating with others that deserves constitutional protection. Like the communist membership cases, the "material support" statute as applied to the *Humanitarian Law Project* plaintiffs can be said to "quite literally establish . . . guilt by association alone."[53] The Humanitarian Law Project wanted to help FTOs cease acting unlawfully (using terrorism) and instead pursue their goals through peaceful and lawful means.[54] How can such association be deemed criminal? How can legal advice to cease criminal behavior and act lawfully create culpability for the attorney and "satisfy the concept of personal guilt"?[55] As will be discussed in Chapter 8, basing

---

[47] *Scales v. United States*, 367 U.S. 203, 224–25 (1961).

[48] 458 U.S. 886 (1982).

[49] *Id.* at 920.

[50] *Id.* at 918–19.

[51] *Healy v. James*, 408 U.S. 169 (1972).

[52] *Griswold v. Connecticut*, 381 U.S. 479, 484 (1965).

[53] *United States v. Robel*, 389 U.S. 258, 265 (1967).

[54] *See Holder v. Humanitarian Law Project*, Nos. 08–1498, 09–89, Oral Arg. Trans. at 22 (Feb. 23, 2010).

[55] Justice Breyer expressed his dismay at the majority's reasoning, asking: "What is one to say about these arguments – *arguments that would deny First Amendment protection to the peaceful teaching of international human rights law* on the ground that a little knowledge about 'the international legal system' is too dangerous a thing . . . What might be said of these claims by

guilt upon association is particularly problematic in the attorney–client context and undermines the attorney's role in the system of justice.

THE RIGHT TO ASSEMBLY

In *De Jonge* v. *Oregon*,[56] one of the earliest cases indicating a constitutional right of association, the Supreme Court held that "peaceable assembly for lawful discussion cannot be made a crime."[57] Attorneys engage in peaceable assembly for lawful discussion, for example, when they meet with clients to provide legal advice – including to discuss the meaning, contours, and reach of the law, sanctions for law violation, avenues for legal redress, and the benefits of pursing lawful rather than unlawful behavior.

David Cole argues that the right of association should be understood "as the modern-day manifestation of the right to assembly."[58] He contends that at the time the Constitution was drafted, and "in the absence of modern communications, it was difficult if not entirely impossible to associate effectively without physically assembling."[59] Thus the reason for providing express constitutional protection for assembly had "little to do with the physical act of gathering together in a single place, and everything to do with the significance of coordinated [that is, associated] action to a republican political process."[60] In protecting freedom of association, the Supreme Court has recognized that "by collective effort individuals can make their views known, when individually, their voices would be faint or lost."[61]

De Jonge exemplifies the rights of association and peaceable assembly. Dirk De Jonge had been convicted and sentenced to seven years of imprisonment for violating Oregon's Criminal Syndicalism Law because he helped conduct a meeting of the Communist Party.[62] The Oregon Supreme Court held that because the Communist Party in Multnomah County advocated criminal syndicalism and sabotage, the prosecution was not required to prove that such unlawful conduct was advocated at the specific meeting in which De Jonge assisted.[63] The Supreme

---

those who live, as we do, in a Nation committed to the resolution of disputes through 'deliberative forces'?" *Id.* at 52 (Breyer, J., dissenting).

[56] 299 U.S. 353 (1937).

[57] *Id.* at 365.

[58] Cole, *supra* Note 37, at 226–28.

[59] *See id.* at 226.

[60] *See id.*; *see also id.* ("This is not to denigrate the value of face-to-face encounters and public demonstrations and meetings, but simply to acknowledge that *what was sought* to be furthered by protecting assembly *was not assembly for its physical sake, but for the association and collective action* that it made possible."[Emphasis added.]).

[61] *Claiborne Hardware*, 458 U.S. at 907; *see also id.* at 908 ("emphasizing 'the importance of freedom of association in guaranteeing the right of people to make their voices heard on public issues'").

[62] *See De Jonge*, 299 U.S. at 356–58.

[63] *See id.* at 361–62.

Court reversed and held that De Jonge should have been allowed to prove that the meeting was "orderly and lawful" and "was not called or used for the advocacy of criminal syndicalism or sabotage or any unlawful action."[64] As interpreted by the state courts, the statute would criminalize assisting in a meeting "[h]owever innocuous the object of the meeting, however lawful the subjects and tenor of the addresses, however reasonable and timely the discussion ... if the meeting were held by the Communist Party."[65] The Court emphasized that "[t]he holding of meetings for peaceable political action cannot be proscribed"[66] because "[t]he very idea of a government, republican in form, implies a right on the part of its citizens *to meet peaceably for consultation* in respect to public affairs and to petition for redress of grievances."[67] The fact that there were organizations, such as the Communist Party, that advocated overthrowing our government, created an increased need for protecting our communities from violence, but, according to the Court:

> The greater the importance of safeguarding the community from incitements to the overthrow of our institutions by force and violence, *the more imperative* is the need to preserve inviolate the constitutional rights of free speech, free press and free assembly *in order to maintain the opportunity for free political discussion, to the end that government may be responsive to the will of the people* and that *changes*, if desired, *may be obtained by peaceful means*. Therein lies the security of the Republic, the very foundation of constitutional government.[68]

De Jonge provides a powerful reiteration of the right of peaceable assembly. By assisting in a meeting "at which nothing unlawful was done or advocated,"[69] De Jonge had been sentenced to seven years in prison – clearly a punishment for merely associating with the Communist Party. The Court held that punishment for engaging in peaceable assemblies to discuss political grievances and how they could be redressed violated the rights secured by the First Amendment. As Jason Mazzone has argued, association must be understood and must protect the ability of people to peaceably discuss their grievances (assemble) and to petition the government for redress. In short, association should protect the ability of people to influence government.[70]

This understanding of peaceable assembly has strong implications for the right of attorney–client association, counseling, and advocacy. The rights of association and assembly protect people who "meet peaceably for consultation" to discuss political grievances and to seek to obtain redress – and this is so even if the assembly occurs with a group, such as the Communist Party, that seeks to overthrow our government

---

[64] *See id.* at 362.
[65] *Id.*
[66] *Id.* at 365.
[67] *Id.* at 364.
[68] *Id.* at 365.
[69] *Id.* at 357.
[70] Mazzone, *supra* Note 25, at 645–47, 743.

by violence. Consequently, these freedoms of assembly and association evince a right of attorneys to meet with clients (even clients who have acted or are acting unlawfully) to discuss their legal grievances, avenues for redress and recourse, and other peaceable and lawful advice and advocacy on their behalf. Thus, assembly and association secure an attorney's right to associate with others for the purpose of providing legal advice. As the Court stated in *De Jonge*, "peaceable assembly for lawful discussion cannot be made a crime."[71]

The *Humanitarian Law Project* plaintiffs explained that they wanted to help FTOs "disavow violence and engage in lawful peaceful means of resolving their disputes."[72] Thus illustrating the reality that attorneys who meet with clients – even clients engaged in illegal or criminal conduct – can point out and encourage *superior legal alternatives* to otherwise attractive illegal conduct. Attorneys swear an oath to uphold the law and are prohibited from advising or assisting clients in criminal or fraudulent conduct.[73] Consequently, protection of attorney–client assembly and association works to "*promote the observance of law* and administration of justice"[74] and to help ensure that changes in society "if desired, may be obtained by peaceful means."[75]

THE RIGHT TO PETITION THE GOVERNMENT FOR REDRESS

In the Supreme Court's Petition Clause jurisprudence, the Court has recognized that the right to petition includes a protectable right to bring nonfrivolous claims in litigation – whether based on state or federal law.[76] This Petition Clause right is often called the *Noerr-Pennington* doctrine after the leading cases on the matter.[77] Thus, under the Petition Clause, in order for someone to be punished for filing civil claims, the claims must be a "sham" – that is, the claims must be "so baseless that no

---

[71] *De Jonge*, 299 U.S. at 365.

[72] *See Holder v. Humanitarian Law Project*, Nos. 08–1498, 09–89, Oral Arg. Trans. at 22 (Feb. 23, 2010).

[73] *See, e.g.*, MODEL RULES OF PROF'L CONDUCT R. 1.2 (prohibiting attorneys from counseling a client to engage, or assisting a client "in conduct that the lawyer knows is criminal or fraudulent").

[74] *Upjohn v. United States*, 449 U.S. 383, 389 (1981) (discussing the purposes underlying evidentiary protection of attorney–client communications under the attorney–client privilege).

[75] *De Jonge*, 299 U.S. at 365.

[76] *See, e.g., Christopher v. Harbury*, 536 U.S. 403, 414–15 (2002); *Prof'l Real Estate Investors, Inc. v. Columbia Pictures Indus., Inc.*, 508 U.S. 49, 62–63 (1993); *Bill Johnson's Rests., Inc. v. NLRB*, 461 U.S. 731, 743 (1983); *see generally*, Carol Rice Andrews, *A Right of Access to Court under the Petition Clause of the First Amendment: Defining the Right*, 60 OHIO STATE L. J. 557 (1999); *see also* MONROE H. FREEDMAN AND ABBE SMITH, UNDERSTANDING LAWYERS' ETHICS 25–28 (4th edn. 2010) (explaining that "civil litigation is part of the First amendment right to petition, through the courts, for redress of grievances").

[77] *Eastern R. Presidents Conference v. Noerr Motor Freight, Inc.*, 365 U.S. 127, 138 (1961); *United Mine Workers v. Pennington*, 381 U.S. 657 (1965).

reasonable litigant could realistically expect to secure favorable relief."[78] An attorney or litigant is required to have *"no more than a reasonable belief* that there is a chance *that a claim may be held valid* upon adjudication" to obtain protection under the Petition Clause from being punished for instituting civil proceedings.[79]

The ability of people and organizations to effectively petition the government through litigation and court access requires attorney association and speech. Although, in theory, individuals can proceed pro se, their right to petition in an effective manner is severely undercut if attorneys can be foreclosed from assisting in such litigation.[80] Additionally, for organizations and associations, which generally cannot appear pro se, litigation requires appearance by counsel – if an attorney cannot appear on behalf of an organization or association, then the organization's right to petition through litigation is defeated.[81] Thus, a right to attorney–client association and a right to speech as an attorney work to protect the right of individuals and organizations to exercise effectively their right to petition for redress through litigation.

It bears repeating that the Supreme Court in *Button* relied on *Noerr* in protecting attorneys *from professional discipline* in filing cases.[82] Thus, the Petition Clause of the First Amendment protects attorneys from professional discipline for the filing of a lawsuit unless the lawsuit is "objectively baseless."[83] Further, in *Legal Services Corporation v. Velazquez*,[84] the Supreme Court also recognized an attorney's own First Amendment right to make relevant claims and arguments in court proceedings on behalf of a client. The *Velazquez* Court noted that attorneys' First Amendment rights are essential, not only to the vindication of their clients' rights but also to the proper functioning of the judiciary itself. The Court explained that attorneys engage in "speech and expression *upon which the courts must depend* for the proper exercise of the judicial power."[85]

---

[78] *Prof'l Real Estate*, 508 U.S. at 62.

[79] *Id.* at 62–63.

[80] *See, e.g., Powell v. Alabama*, 287 U.S. 64, 68–69 (1932) ("The right to be heard would be, in many cases, of little avail if it did not comprehend the right to be heard by counsel.").

[81] *See, e.g., D-Bean Ltd. Partnership v. Roller Derby Skates Inc.*, 366 F.3d 972 (9th Cir. 2004) (stating that corporations and unincorporated associations must appear through counsel in court); *Michael Reilly Design, Inc. v. Houraney*, 835 N.Y.S.2d 640 (N.Y.A.D. 2d Dept. 2007) (explaining that "a corporation or a voluntary association" must appear in court through counsel); *Prunte v. Universal Music Group*, 484 F. Supp. 2d 32, 38 (D.D.C. 2007) ("[A]ny artificial entity, whether a corporation, partnership or association cannot proceed in federal court without counsel."). *But see Vermont Agency of Natural Resources v. Upper Valley Regional Landfill Corp.*, 621 A.2d 225 (Vt. 1992) (explaining that in Vermont, courts have discretion to allow an organization to appear without counsel if interests are not threatened and enforcement of the rule would preclude appearance of the organization).

[82] *See NAACP v. Button*, 371 U.S. 415, 430–31 (1963).

[83] *Prof'l Real Estate*, 508 U.S. at 60.

[84] 531 U.S. 533 (2001).

[85] *Id.* at 545.

Attorneys' First Amendment rights are interrelated. The *Button* Court protected the rights of the NAACP lawyers to associate with clients, to advise them, to represent them, and bring litigation on their behalf – thus protecting all of these inseparable essential First Amendment rights. On the other hand, the *Humanitarian Law Project* Court denied the attorney plaintiffs' right of association, and by so doing, the Court completely undermined all of their other First Amendment rights – the right to speak to clients, to peaceably assemble for lawful discussion, and to petition for redress of grievances.

7

The Access to Justice Theory

Horace Hunter is an attorney in Virginia, who in 2013 maintained a blog detailing his completed criminal defense cases without obtaining client permission to disclose information about the representations.[1] Such information falls squarely within the attorney's duty of confidentiality, which, under nearly every state's professional conduct rules, absolutely prohibits an attorney from divulging information regarding a representation without client consent or without falling within a very narrow range of exceptions (for example, an attorney can disclose information to prevent reasonably certain death or serious bodily injury).[2] Although Virginia's rule on confidentiality is somewhat more lenient than many states, the Virginia rule still prohibits attorneys from disclosing any client information that "would be embarrassing or would be likely to be detrimental to the client unless the client consents after consultation."[3] Disciplinary proceedings were brought against Hunter for violating both the rules regarding confidentiality and advertising, and Hunter defended against the charges by arguing that he had a First Amendment right to publish the material because it had been revealed in court filings and proceedings, and thus was public.

The Virginia Supreme Court genuinely tried its hand at protecting attorneys' First Amendment rights but ultimately produced a gaffe of an opinion. Although counsel for the Virginia State Bar argued for a constitutional conditions approach,[4] the court rejected that argument and instead stated that "the disciplinary rules governing the legal profession cannot punish activity protected by the First Amendment."[5] So far,

---

[1] See *Hunter v. Virginia State Bar*, 285 Va. 485 (2013). Some material contained in this Chapter was previously published in Margaret Tarkington, *A First Amendment Theory for Protecting Attorney Speech*, 45 UC Davis L. Rev. 27 (2012).

[2] See generally Model Rules of Prof'l Conduct R. 1.6.

[3] Virginia Rules of Prof'l Conduct R. 1.6.

[4] *Hunter*, 285 Va. at 501–02 (noting the bar's argument "that lawyers, as officers of the Court are prohibited from engaging in speech that might otherwise be constitutionally protected").

[5] *Id.* at 503 (internal citations omitted).

so good. But the court then proceeded to rely on traditional First Amendment doctrines to decide Hunter's case. Citing the facts (1) that speech regarding what transpires in a court proceeding is public information under the First Amendment, (2) that a reporter or others would be protected in disseminating the exact same information if they had it, and (3) that punishing "the publication of truthful information can rarely survive constitutional scrutiny," the court held that the First Amendment protected Hunter from discipline for disclosing information regarding clients without their permission.[6] The court formally held that the First Amendment *forbids* states from "prohibit[ing] an attorney from discussing information about a client or former client" without client consent unless the information is protected by the attorney–client privilege.[7] Indeed, according to the court, as to information revealed in court proceedings (either through court filings or in open court), "a lawyer is *no more prohibited than any other citizen* from reporting" such information – even if the lawyer's client does not want the lawyer to publish that information and the information is embarrassing and/or detrimental to the client.[8]

Notably, if the Virginia Supreme Court got it right in *Hunter*, then the First Amendment demands that *no state* can punish or prohibit lawyers from revealing client confidences without client permission unless the information falls within the attorney–client privilege – which protects only a narrow category of communications. Most of the information that attorneys receive from clients does *not* fall within the privilege, as will be discussed in Chapter 9. Thus, if the First Amendment really allows – and, in fact, absolutely protects from punishment – attorney revelation of client confidences, that would fundamentally alter the attorney–client relationship and the duties owed to clients in the United States.

But the *Hunter* case is even worse than appears at first blush, because Hunter was a criminal defense attorney. Further, because his blog was also used for commercial purposes, in all but one of his cases that he decided to showcase on his blog – complete with his clients' names – he basically won the case. The clients "were either found not guilty, plea bargained to an agreed upon disposition, or had their charges reduced or dismissed."[9] Further, at the disciplinary hearing, a former client testified that the information posted about him was "embarrassing" and "detrimental to him," and an investigator for the bar testified that "other former clients" had reported that they "felt similarly."[10] So we have a criminal defense attorney who successfully advocates for his clients by getting acquittals and other very favorable results – thus protecting them and their reputations from damaging convictions and vindicating the presumption of innocence – only to then *reveal* embarrassing and detrimental confidential information about these

---

[6] *Id.* at 502–03.
[7] *Id.* at 502.
[8] *Id.* at 503 (emphasis added).
[9] *Id.* at 492.
[10] *Id.*

clients publicly on his blog. The role of the criminal defense attorney, as will be discussed in Chapter 12, does not countenance such actions.

WHERE DID THE *HUNTER* COURT GO WRONG?

The Virginia Supreme Court in *Hunter* sincerely attempted to protect the First Amendment rights of lawyers, but they did not have a workable methodology to do so. Once they rejected the constitutional conditions and categorical approaches and declared that lawyers – even as lawyers – had protectable First Amendment rights, they were in deep, open waters. They had no method to then protect the near sacrosanct duty of confidentiality because normal First Amendment doctrines are not adapted to account for it. Consulting the normal doctrines of the First Amendment, the Virginia Supreme Court would find that what occurs in court cases is speech of public concern, and arguably political speech. Additionally, the restriction on disclosure is content-based – information relating to a representation – and it is patently *not* merely a permissible time, place, or manner restriction that allows speech to take place at a different, more appropriate time. The duty of confidentiality forbids lawyers from revealing information relating to the representation of a client continually, even outlasting the death of the client. The *Hunter* Court was also correct that information submitted in open court proceedings (whether through court filings or in open court) is public information protected by the First Amendment in its dissemination by the media and citizens and that the dissemination of truthful information is nearly always protected speech. In light of all of this – and having rejected the constitutional conditions and categorical approaches – how could the Virginia Supreme Court find other than it did?

In March 2018, the ABA responded to the *Hunter* case by issuing Formal Opinion 480, and opining that attorneys can be prohibited from revealing client confidences absent client consent. Unfortunately, the ABA reached that result by ascribing to the constitutional conditions theory, thus undermining lawyer and client access to essential First Amendment rights.[11]

What cries out from the *Hunter* case and the ABA's response is the blatant need for a methodology of analyzing and protecting attorney First Amendment rights that attunes those rights to the lawyer's function in the justice system. Normal First Amendment doctrines are ineffective in the context of regulating attorneys. These doctrines fail to protect attorney speech and association that is essential to the attorney's role in the justice system (as seen in *Humanitarian Law Project*), and they also fail to identify what restrictions on attorney speech and association are necessary for the proper functioning of the attorney in the justice system (as seen in *Hunter*). Just as the Supreme Court has adopted a role-specific method for

---

[11] *See* Am. Bar Ass'n, Standing Comm. on Ethics and Prof'l Responsibility, Formal Op. 480, at 4–5 and n. 18 (2018).

examining speech rights of public employees, a specialized method is necessary to properly protect and restrict attorney speech, association, and petitioning.[12]

THE ACCESS TO JUSTICE THEORY AND THE CORE OF ATTORNEY FIRST AMENDMENT PROTECTION

I propose the access to justice theory of the First Amendment as a methodology for examining the First Amendment rights of lawyers.[13] As used herein, "access to justice" indicates access to law and legal processes *by anyone* – it encompasses the work of a lawyer (whether paid or not, transactional or litigation, civil, administrative, or criminal) that serves to invoke or avoid the power of the government in securing individual or collective life, liberty, or property. It also includes attorney speech, association, petitioning (or other First Amendment activities) that are essential to the fair administration of the laws or the attorney's role in the justice system – including the attorney's role in invoking the judicial power.

This approach is grounded in established free speech theories and philosophy. Ludwig Wittgenstein posits that speech itself can only be understood as part of the "form of life" in which it exists.[14] Thus, viewing the justice system as a desirable "form of life," attorney speech must be understood as part of, and as securing, the proper and constitutional functioning of the justice system.

More specifically, the access to justice theory is modeled on a democratic theory of the First Amendment, as propounded by Alexander Meiklejohn.[15] Just as citizen free speech is essential to the proper functioning of a democratic government,[16] so too, under the access to justice theory, are certain species of attorney speech essential to the proper functioning of our justice system and so must be protected. The same is true of other First Amendment rights – certain attorney association and petitioning is likewise essential to the proper working of the justice system and requires protection.

Attorneys – through their speech, association, and petitioning – play a key role in our justice system. They provide to clients speech that has the force of law, speech

---

[12] *See, e.g., Pickering v. Board of Ed. of Tp. High School Dist.* 205, 391 U.S. 563, 538 (1968) (creating standard specific for analyzing cases involving the speech rights of public employees).

[13] The term "access to justice" as used herein should not be confused with the idea of access to justice as meaning providing legal services to those with low or moderate incomes. To avoid such confusion, one could use the term "legal access theory" instead of "access to justice theory." However, because it is justice itself that is at stake, I have used the phrase "access to justice."

[14] LUDWIG WITTGENSTEIN, PHILOSOPHICAL INVESTIGATIONS 11 (trans. G. E. M. Anscombe; 1958) ("[T]he speaking of language is part of an activity, or of a form of life."); *see also* Frederick Schauer, Formalism, 97 *Yale L. J.* 509, 548 (1988) (arguing that advantages of formalist interpretations of language depend on the domains in which they are used).

[15] *See generally* ALEXANDER MEIKLEJOHN, FREE SPEECH AND ITS RELATION TO SELF-GOVERNMENT (1948).

[16] *See id.*

necessary for effective access to the judiciary, and speech that is intended to invoke or avoid the power of government in securing life, liberty, or property. Through attorney association and petitioning, attorneys and clients are able to counsel regarding the meaning and application of the law before acting, to invoke the law's protection through the creation of enforceable legal documents, and to petition the judiciary and thereby enable the judicial power. The access to justice theory proposes that where attorney speech, association, or petitioning is key to providing or ensuring access to justice or the fair administration of the laws, it is entitled to protection under the First Amendment – akin to political speech. Moreover, where the role of the attorney includes challenging and checking government or other institutional power, the access to justice theory protects the attorney's speech, association, and petitioning in making such a challenge. This "checking value" of the attorney in our system of justice is a primary justification for protecting certain types of attorney First Amendment activities and resonates with the fore-most purposes underlying the creation of the First Amendment as expounded by Vincent Blasi.[17]

The Supreme Court in *Garrison* v. *Louisiana*[18] recognized that political speech "was more than self-expression" but constituted "the essence of self-governance"[19] and thus required protection. So too attorney speech – particularly speech made in their capacity as attorney on behalf of or to clients – is far more than self-expression, and instead provides access to the invocation or avoidance of government power. Thus, unlike the constitutional conditions ideas, the categorical approach or the analogies to limited speech protection discussed in Chapter 1, the access to justice theory places its primary protection on attorney speech made in the capacity of attorney. Indeed, the protected core of *attorney* speech should generally not be "*self-expression*" in a normal sense of that word. Rather, the protected core of attorney speech is representative, associative, and/or communicative by nature. Even attorneys committed to a cause can only bring cases to courts involving real parties in interest who have suffered a legally cognizable harm and hire the attorney to represent them. Attorney First Amendment activity creates effective access to the third branch of government, enables the judicial power, advises people regarding their rights so that they can structure their conduct and protect their life, liberty, and property, and provides access to law itself both outside and through official court proceedings. It is this speech, association, and petitioning that constitute the essential role of attorneys in our system of justice and which deserve core protection under the access to justice theory of the First Amendment.

---

[17] *See* Vincent Blasi, The Checking Value in First Amendment Theory, 1977 *Am. B. Found. Res. J.* 521, 527, 538 (1977).
[18] 379 U.S. 64 (1964).
[19] *Id.* at 74–75.

Thus, the access to justice theory focuses on what should be at the core of protected attorney First Amendment activities. What speech, association, and petitioning are essential to the proper functioning of the justice system and must be protected? The remaining chapters will clarify this core of First Amendment protection, which protects (1) the attorney–client relationship and client counseling; (2) the ability of the lawyer to invoke the law, preserve client rights, and petition for relief; (3) the attorney's ability to safeguard judicial integrity; and (4) the integrity of criminal processes. As in *Sullivan* with political speech, First Amendment protection for attorneys is placed "right side up" – we begin by understanding and defining the core of what requires protection.[20]

Necessary Restrictions

A corresponding part of the access to justice theory is that there also are *restrictions* on attorney speech that are essential to preserve the integrity of the justice system. Alexander Meiklejohn uses the town meeting as an example of a major "paradox" found in the First Amendment. He notes that political speech in the traditional town meeting is *absolutely* protected by the First Amendment.[21] People who attend come as "political equals" and each has a duty and right to think and speak as they will and to listen to the arguments of others. Nevertheless, despite being within the First Amendment's core of absolute protection for political speech, the speech at the town meeting is and must be abridged – for example, through rules and regulations about who speaks when, limits on how much of the available time each person can take, and order by the chair, etc.[22] The abridgment is necessary to accomplish the governmental purpose in holding the town meeting.[23] As Meiklejohn explains, "The town meeting, as it seeks for freedom of public discussion of public problems, would be wholly ineffectual unless speech were thus abridged."[24] While manipulation of the process cannot be allowed – for example, through abridging just one side of an issue – abridgment through creating rules of the game is essential to preserve the process itself.[25]

In like manner, certain restrictions on attorney speech are essential to preserve the judicial process and overall justice system in which attorneys work. As in the town meeting, there are "rules of the game" that are essential to preserve the processes of the justice system. Thus, the access to justice theory does *not* protect attorney speech that would frustrate the American system of justice, including the trial process itself,

[20] Harry Kalven, *The* New York Times *Case: A Note on "The Central Meaning of the First Amendment,* 1964 SUP. CT. REV. 191, 208.
[21] MEIKLEJOHN, *supra* Note 15, at 19.
[22] *Id.* at 25–26.
[23] *Id.* at 23.
[24] *Id.*
[25] *Id.* at 26–27.

the right to jury trial, the right against compelled self-incrimination, the right to effective assistance of counsel, the right to confront and to call witnesses, the presumption of innocence, the duty of confidentiality, and other constitutional and otherwise essential components of our justice system.[26]

Schauer attempts to illustrate how problematic it would be to apply the First Amendment to attorney speech, with a hypothetical situation where a trial court rules that evidence of a drug deal should be excluded.[27] Schauer's hypothetical prosecutor decides in opening argument to describe to the jury the excluded evidence and the fact of its exclusion by the judge.[28] Schauer asserts: "Now we all know what would happen to the trial and the prosecutor at this point were this to happen. And we know as well what would happen if the prosecuting attorney were to claim a denial of his or her First Amendment right to speak to the jury – unmitigated laughter."[29]

Schauer seeks to show the inapplicability of the First Amendment to the "speech of law." Yet employing the access to justice theory does not create his hypothetical problem. The idea of the access to justice theory is to create First Amendment protection for attorney speech that is attuned to the United States justice system and the role of the attorney therein. Thus if a "restriction" (like the exclusionary rule or the rule prohibiting ex parte communications to jurors) is aimed at, for example, securing the criminal defendant's right to a fair trial before an impartial jury or right against compelled self-incrimination, then that restriction would clearly be constitutionally permissible.

Thus, under the access to justice theory, attorneys cannot invoke the First Amendment's shield for attorney speech or activities that frustrate or undermine the justice system or that interfere with the core rights protected thereby. This is true regardless of whether citizens would enjoy protection for the same speech. The Virginia Supreme Court in *Hunter* relied, erroneously, on the fact that if the media and other citizens could disclose the information if they had it, then so could attorneys. But the court was mistaken – attorneys can be forbidden from revealing client confidences even if nonattorneys cannot. Similarly, attorneys can be forbidden from referring to inadmissible evidence in court. They can also be forbidden from using government power – in the form of law invocation or legal advice – to

---

[26] *See* Monroe H. Freedman and Abbe Smith, Understanding Legal Ethics 15–17 (4th edn. 2010). ("The rights that comprise the adversary system include personal autonomy, the effective assistance of counsel, equal protection of the laws, trial by jury, the rights to call and to confront witnesses, and the right to require the government to prove guilt beyond a reasonable doubt and without the use of compelled self-incrimination. These rights, and others, are also included in the broad and fundamental concept that no person may be deprived of life, liberty, or property without due process of law – a concept which itself has been substantially equated with the adversary system.").

[27] Frederick Schauer, *The Speech of Law and the Law of Speech*, 49 Ark. L. Rev. 687, 693 (1997).

[28] *See id.*

[29] *See id.*

perpetrate crimes or frauds.[30] It is immaterial that other citizens enjoy free speech rights under *Brandenburg v. Ohio*[31] to advocate even the most unlawful actions. Because of their role in the system of justice and their tie to government power, attorneys do not have such a right when assisting and advising clients, as further explored in Chapter 9.

Schauer's example of an attorney trying to undermine the exclusionary rule by invoking the First Amendment is accurate in demonstrating that the normal doctrines and discourse of the First Amendment would not readily show when attorney speech *should be restricted* to preserve our justice system. And that is precisely why the Virginia Supreme Court in *Hunter* faltered in dealing with client confidences. However, the application of – or even Schauer's view to disregard – the normal doctrines and discourse of the First Amendment also fails to show when attorney speech *should be protected* because the speech is essential to fulfill the attorney's function and role in the justice system. The access to justice theory does both. It attunes speech protection to the role of the attorney in the justice system – providing core protection for speech, association, and petitioning essential to that role and refusing any First Amendment protection for speech or activities that undermine the justice system.

Of course, in between these two extremes there likely are categories of attorney speech that are neither essential to the proper functioning of the justice system nor do they frustrate that system. In such instances, the normal doctrines of the First Amendment may provide an appropriate framework. But where attorney speech, association, or petitioning is tied to government power and affects the workings of the justice system, the scope of appropriate protection and restriction under the First Amendment must be attuned to the attorney's role in the justice system.

SAFEGUARDING JUSTICE AND THE ROLE OF THE ATTORNEY

In discussing the punishment of people for their speech or association regarding communism, Zechariah Chafee explained, "The only way to preserve 'the existence of free American institutions' is *to make free institutions a living force*" – and thus we cannot "ignore them in the very process of defending them."[32] Chafee was making the point that we cannot protect our democratic institutions by undermining our own freedoms, such as the First Amendment. Similarly here, in protecting and promoting the integrity of our justice system, it is essential to make "free institutions a living force." Rather than denying or ignoring the First Amendment rights of lawyers when acting in their capacity as lawyers, we must protect our justice system and the essential role that attorneys play therein. The access to justice theory

---

[30] *See* MODEL RULES PROF'L CONDUCT R. 1.2(d).
[31] 395 U.S. 444, 447 (1969).
[32] ZECHARIAH CHAFEE, THE BLESSINGS OF LIBERTY 142, 156 (1956).

calls upon the First Amendment to make essential attorney speech, association, and petitioning that secures life and liberty "a living force" – one that cannot be undermined by regulation or legislation.

The access to justice theory, consequently, is not only aimed at providing a workable First Amendment theory for examining regulations of attorney speech but, more importantly, is aimed at preserving the role of the attorney in our system of justice – regardless of the regulating entity. The theory realizes the supposed benefit of self-regulation; namely, that regulations will be properly attuned to the role of the attorney and the protection of the integrity of the justice system. Under self-regulation, this benefit allegedly would materialize simply by having regulation come from members of the profession or the judiciary.

The access to justice theory does not leave the preservation of the essential functions that attorneys perform in our justice system to the good graces of regulators – be they the judiciary, a state bar, the ABA, Congress, state or federal legislatures, administrative agencies, global entities, or anyone else. The role of the lawyer in the justice system to invoke or avoid government power in the protection of life, liberty, and property is instead protected by the powerful shield of the First Amendment. The First Amendment is the hook that protects from disruptive regulation these core attributes of attorney speech, association, and petitioning essential to justice itself.

Schauer also expressed a justifiable concern that if the First Amendment were applied to attorney speech then that may harm the First Amendment itself because the protections of the First Amendment would have to be watered down to ensure that regulations essential to the justice system (like forbidding lawyers from referring to inadmissible evidence in trial) survive constitutional attack.[33] The Supreme Court's 2015 decision in *Williams-Yulee* v. *Florida Bar*[34] appears to validate those concerns, as noted in Chapter 2, where the Court applied a relatively lenient form of strict-scrutiny to ultimately uphold restrictions on solicitations of campaign donations by Florida candidates for judicial office.

But under the access to justice theory, the dilution effect of applying the First Amendment to lawyers would not materialize because the theory (1) recognizes that certain restrictions are essential to the proper functioning of the justice system and denies resort to the First Amendment to defeat such essential regulations – thus dilution of traditional doctrines is not needed to uphold the constitutionality of such regulations, and (2) does not apply to nonlawyers and thus does not modify First Amendment doctrines outside of the lawyer context. By tailoring First Amendment protection to the role of the lawyer in the justice system, both the essential role of the lawyer and the First Amendment are preserved.

---

[33] Schauer, *supra* Note 27, at 691.
[34] 135 S. Ct. 1656 (2015).

LET'S KILL ALL THE LAWYERS

Geoffrey Stone has commented that attorneys "play and have played, a critical role in opposing, and sometimes, moderating" abuses to civil liberties, particularly during times of war or conflict.[35] Stone puts the historical Shakespeare quote, "The first thing we do, let's kill all the lawyers," in its literary and historical context. The reason the lawyers needed to be killed was to make it possible for conspirators to "destroy the rights and liberties of the English people."[36] In the lines immediately following the directive to kill lawyers, the conspirators demonstrate their intent to deprive citizens of life and liberty when they unjustly put to death the Clerk of Chatham for being able to write his name.[37]

But an alternate to "killing" lawyers could be accomplished through the abridgment of attorney speech in such a way as to inhibit or block the attorneys' ability to fulfill their function in invoking the law to preserve rights to life, liberty, and property. While initially sounding extreme and unlikely, both *Humanitarian Law Project* and *Button* illustrate that one way to destroy or unjustly harm an undesirable group is to restrict lawyers from providing speech, association, or petitioning that assists the group from pursuing even lawful and peaceful ends. The purpose of the restriction in *Humanitarian Law Project* was to eliminate the organization.[38] But this purpose is accomplished not by directly denying the organization access to law, but by prohibiting attorneys from speaking – specifically from assisting the organization in invoking either domestic or international law. The organization is killed by "kill[ing] [] the lawyers." In *Button*, the purpose was to deprive African Americans from realizing their constitutional rights as announced in *Brown v. Board of Education*.[39] Justice would be killed by "kill[ing] [] the lawyers." In both cases, regulation of attorney speech, association, and petitioning is used by a majority to destroy or undermine the rights of a disfavored minority by keeping the minority powerless to effectively invoke or avoid the power of government.

---

[35] Geoffrey Stone, *A Lawyer's Responsibility: Protecting Civil Liberties in Wartime*, 22 WASH. U. J. L. & POL'Y 47, 53 (2006).

[36] *Id.* at 47.

[37] WILLIAM SHAKESPEARE, THE SECOND PART OF HENRY THE SIXTH, Act IV, Scene 2, Lines 81–114.

[38] The *Humanitarian Law Project* Court repeatedly asserts that the plaintiff attorneys' speech "importantly helps lend legitimacy to foreign terrorist groups – legitimacy that makes it *easier for those groups to persist.*" See Holder v. *Humanitarian Law Project*, 561 U.S. 1, 30–31 (2010). The purpose of the statute is to destroy any such organization, which is accomplished in part by denying them legal advice and access to the law. As summarized by Justice Scalia: "The end that Congress seeks to proscribe is the existence of these terrorist organizations." *Holder* v. *Humanitarian Law Project*, Nos. 08–1498, 09–89, Oral Arg. Trans. at 17 (Feb. 23, 2010). *See also id.* at 34, 39–40 (statements of Solicitor General).

[39] *See NAACP v. Button*, 371 U.S. 415, at 445–46 (Goldberg, J., concurring).

Again, as Schauer recognized, speech is *all* the lawyer has – it is the lawyer's sole tool to protect clients, to invoke the law on their behalf, to protect individual and collective life, liberty, and property, to check government and other institutional power, and to enable the judicial power. If attorneys can be silenced in any of these aspects of their essential role, then justice itself is undermined. The access to justice theory does not allow any regulator to undermine justice so simply – but instead invokes the impervious shield of the First Amendment to safeguard the justice system and the lawyer's role therein.

PART III

Protecting the Role of the Attorney

8

Freedom to Form an Attorney–Client Relationship

The essential and defining attribute of nearly all lawyering is the relationship between attorney and client. Lawyers work as agents for a client-principal – they work in a representative capacity acting on behalf of other people or entities.[1] This agency relationship entails fiduciary duties of the lawyer on behalf of the client. The lawyer owes the client core duties of loyalty, confidentiality, competence, and communication. The lawyer must protect the client's interests and must pursue the client's objectives within the boundaries of the law.

One of the most alarming features of both *Button* and *Humanitarian Law Project* is that if regulators (in both of those cases, legislatures) can separate attorneys from representing specific clients, then the whole attorney–client relationship and all rights attendant thereto collapse. There is simply nothing left. The rights of the attorneys who wished to undertake the representation and the legal rights and objectives of clients are extinguished. Lawyers who cannot associate with a client cannot protect that client's interests or fulfill their role in invoking or avoiding government power in the protection of life, liberty, and property. Nor can clients effectively protect their own legal interests without associating with an attorney.

The initial aspect of protecting the First Amendment rights of lawyers under the access to justice theory is to safeguard the attorney–client relationship itself and the central features of that relationship. The attorney must have a right to associate with clients – a right undergirded by the client's concomitant Fifth and Sixth Amendment rights to counsel. That right cannot be extinguished by a client's prior bad acts unless the lawyer is assisting the client in criminal or fraudulent conduct. There is literally no place for guilt by association in the realm of attorney–client associations; it is antithetical to our justice system and the constitutional requirements of due process of law. Nevertheless, because attorneys owe clients a core duty of loyalty,

---

[1]   Some material contained in this chapter was previously published in Margaret Tarkington, *Freedom of Attorney-Client Association*, UTAH L. REV. 1071 (2012).

which entails conflict avoidance, attorneys can be prohibited from associating with clients where such conflicts of interest exist that undermine the attorney's ability to loyally and competently undertake the representation. This chapter will focus on the attorney's right to form an attorney–client relationship. As discussed in the next chapter, once the attorney–client relationship is formed, that relationship must be protected by attuning lawyers' First Amendment rights to safeguard their central duties to their clients – including both the duties of communication and confidentiality.

FREEDOM OF ATTORNEY–CLIENT ASSOCIATION

A protectable right for attorneys to associate with clients is essential for the realization of access to law, to government power, and to government processes by individuals and entities. Without association, attorneys cannot invoke (or inform their clients how to invoke) law that would benefit and protect their clients. In *Humanitarian Law Project*, for example, the attorneys sought to associate with the FTOs in part to inform them how to invoke law, including international law and recognition under the Geneva Conventions.[2] If lawyers can be kept from associating with a particular group of people, then the protection of the law for that group can be nullified in large part – even if, in theory, the law is applicable and available to them.

As the *Button* Court recognized in protecting attorney association, a lawyer's right to associate with clients is essential to the proper vindication of legal rights – particularly for minority and unpopular groups.[3] Without such protection regulators and governmental entities subject to majoritarian control may be able to deprive minorities of access to the law's protections, and can do so without even changing the substantive law, but simply by limiting attorney association with an unpopular group. This undermines concepts of equal protection of the laws, as well as due process.

The Attorney's Right to Associate Is Undergirded by the Client's Rights to Counsel

The attorney's right to associate with clients is undergirded by the client's Fifth and Sixth Amendment rights to counsel. The Sixth Amendment to the Constitution declares that "[i]n all criminal prosecutions, the accused shall ... have the Assistance of Counsel for his defence." This constitutional guarantee for criminal

---

[2]   *Holder* v. *Humanitarian Law Project*, 561 U.S. 1, 14–15 (2010); *see id.* at 42, 54 (Breyer dissenting) (noting that plaintiffs wanted to petition the United States Congress and the United Nations, and wanted to seek "recognition under the Geneva Conventions").

[3]   *See* NAACP v. *Button*, 371 U.S. 415, 429–31 (1963).

processes is a distinctive aspect of the American concept of justice. The Sixth Amendment guarantee was a break from eighteenth-century criminal procedure in England, where a defendant accused of a felony was *prohibited* from having or employing counsel to assist in their defense, and instead was required to "speak for yourself."[4] Yet in the American Colonies, the English rule had been rejected even before the federal Constitution's creation. Nearly every colony had provided by law that accused individuals had a right to have counsel for their defense – and thus the right to counsel in criminal proceedings was an integral part of American conceptions of justice at the time of the creation of the Bill of Rights.[5]

This history underlying the Sixth Amendment was recited by the Supreme Court in *Powell* v. *Alabama*,[6] wherein the Supreme Court held that states were required by the Due Process Clause of the Fourteenth Amendment to provide effective assistance of counsel to an accused in certain cases. In *Powell*, nine African American teens (commonly referred to as the "Scottsboro boys") had been convicted of gang-raping two Caucasian women on a slow-moving train. The defendants were tried within days of the alleged incident. Immediately before their trials were to begin, the defendants were appointed counsel – characterized by the Supreme Court as being "pro forma [rather] than zealous and active." The trials were completed quickly with all defendants convicted and all but one sentenced to death.[7] The Supreme Court reversed the convictions, noting that the appointment of counsel and trials had gone forward not in the "spirit of regulated justice but ... with the haste of the mob":

> The defendants, young, ignorant, illiterate, surrounded by hostile sentiment, haled back and forth under guard of soldiers, charged with an atrocious crime regarded with especial horror in the community where they were to be tried, were thus put in peril of their lives within a few moments after counsel for the first time charged with any degree of responsibility began to represent them.[8]

Moreover, the Court noted that defendants had not been provided with any counsel "during perhaps the most critical period of the proceedings against these defendants,

---

[4] *See* John H. Langbein, *Shaping the Eighteenth-Century Criminal Trial: A View from the Ryder Sources*, 50 U. Chi. L. Rev. 1, 123–30 and nn. 515–16 (1983). In the first half of the eighteenth century, the accused could not have any assistance of counsel, although later in the century the accused could employ counsel to cross-examine witnesses and address points of law. Nevertheless, defense counsel could only speak as to issues of law (and not fact), and defense "counsel was forbidden to 'address the jury,' that is, to make opening and closing statements." Thus the accused could not use an attorney "for his 'defense'" – instead the accused had to speak for himself. *See id.*

[5] *See Powell* v. *Alabama*, 287 U.S. 45, 60–64 (1932).

[6] *Id.*

[7] The jury was hung as to the appropriate sentence for Roy Wright who was thirteen years of age. The prosecution had recommended life in prison, but eleven jurors held out for death, leading to a mistrial. *See* Jay Bellamy, *The Scottsboro Boys: Injustice in Alabama*, Prologue, 29 (Spring 2017), *available at* www.archives.gov/files/publications/prologue/2014/spring/scottsboro.pdf.

[8] *Powell*, 287 U.S. at 59–60.

that is to say, from the time of their arraignment until the beginning of their trial, when *consultation, thorough-going investigation and preparation were vitally important*" – indeed, the Court emphasized, "they were *as much entitled to such aid during that period* as at the trial itself."[9] Ultimately, the Court held that "in a capital case, where the defendant is unable to employ counsel . . . it is the duty of the court, whether requested or not, to assign counsel for him *as a necessary requisite of due process of law*; and that duty is not discharged by an assignment at such a time or under such circumstances as to preclude the giving of *effective aid* in the preparation and trial of the case."[10] The Supreme Court thus indicated the need for effective assistance of counsel. In making its determination, the Court explained:

> The *right to be heard* would be, in many cases, *of little avail if it did not comprehend* the right to be heard *by counsel*. Even the intelligent and educated layman has small and sometimes no skill in the science of law. If charged with crime, he is incapable, generally, of determining for himself whether the indictment is good or bad. He is unfamiliar with the rules of evidence. Left without the aid of counsel he may be put on trial without a proper charge, and convicted upon incompetent evidence, or evidence irrelevant to the issue or otherwise inadmissible. He lacks both the skill and knowledge adequately to prepare his defense, even though he have a perfect one. He *requires the guiding hand of counsel at every step in the proceedings* against him. Without it, though he be not guilty, he faces the danger of conviction because he does not know how to establish his innocence. If that be true of men of intelligence, how much more true is it of the ignorant and illiterate, or those of feeble intellect?[11]

The court subsequently expressly incorporated the Sixth Amendment's guarantee of assistance of counsel as applying to the states through the Fourteenth Amendment in *Gideon v. Wainwright*.[12]

But even outside of the criminal context, clients have a right to employ counsel in civil matters based in the Fifth and Fourteenth Amendments' guarantee of due process of law. Again, as the Supreme Court explained in *Powell*, if "in any case," whether "civil or criminal, a state or federal court were arbitrarily to refuse to hear a party by counsel, employed by and appearing for him, it reasonably may not be doubted that *such a refusal would be a denial of a hearing*, and, therefore, *of due process* in the constitutional sense."[13]

In fact, attorneys have an enforced monopoly on effective access to the judiciary. Unauthorized practice of law restrictions forbid nonlawyers from representing other people in court. Although individuals can proceed pro se, such judicial access is often ineffective, and organizations generally are prohibited from proceeding pro se

[9] *Id.* (emphasis added).
[10] *Id.* (emphasis added).
[11] *Id.* at 68–69 (emphasis added).
[12] 372 U.S. 335 (1963).
[13] *Powell*, 287 U.S. at 69 (emphasis added).

in judicial proceedings.[14] Yet, the attorney cannot represent a client in a court or other legal proceeding without associating with that client. In both civil and criminal matters, attorney–client association is essential to provide *effective* access to the judiciary for individuals and *all* access to the judiciary for organizations and associations.

This role of attorneys – providing access to the judiciary – is *as essential* to our justice system *as is* the judiciary itself. The *Velazquez* Court recognized that to allow blanket prohibitions on attorney representation would not only distort the role of attorneys in our justice system but would thereby undermine the constitutional role of the judiciary itself by limiting the cases that could be brought before it.[15] Thus access to the judiciary, which itself is constitutionally protected by the Due Process and Petition Clauses as discussed in Chapter 9, is defeated to the extent that attorneys can be forbidden from associating with clients.

The concern of distortion of the legal system is at its height for restrictions on attorney representation created by representative bodies subject to majoritarian capture. For minorities and unpopular groups at the mercy of majoritarian politics, court access through counsel is essential to protect their rights of life, liberty, and property.[16] If Congress (as it did in *Humanitarian Law Project* and as attempted in *Velazquez*) or a state legislature (as attempted in *Button*) can single out an unpopular or minority group for separation from attorneys, that group loses effective recourse to the judiciary against legislation imposed and unlawful actions taken against them. One of the judiciary's primary functions – indeed, the central theory underlying the salary and tenure protections for federal judges created in Article III of the Constitution[17] – is to protect minorities and constitutional rights from majoritarian politics and pressures. As Ralph Temple summarized, "a healthy legal system requires that the courts have the power to declare unlawful those acts of the majority, through its legislature or its executive, which are abusive."[18] Our constitutional system of justice, including the role of attorneys therein, adheres to this principle.

Although court access, which itself is constitutionally guaranteed, is obviously hampered or extinguished by prohibitions on attorney–client association, access to other governmental entities, processes, and powers is also inhibited by such prohibitions. Notably, the Humanitarian Law Project wanted to petition Congress and the United Nations on behalf of certain FTOs.[19] Even mildly competent legal counsel

---

[14] *See, e.g., D-Bean Ltd. Partnership v. Roller Derby Skates Inc.*, 366 F.3d 972 (9th Cir. 2004).
[15] *Legal Services Corp. v. Velazquez*, 531 U.S. 533, 544–46, 548–49 (2001).
[16] *See NAACP v. Button*, 371 U.S. 415, 429–31 (1963).
[17] U.S. Const. art. III.
[18] Ralph Temple, *In Defense of the Adversary System*, 2 A.B.A. Litig., at 43, 47 (Winter 1976), at 43, 47 *as quoted in* Monroe H. Freedman and Abbe Smith, Understanding Legal Ethics 23 (4th edn. 2010)).
[19] *See Holder v. Humanitarian Law Project*, 561 U.S. 1, 22 (stating that plaintiffs wished to teach FTOs "how to petition various representative bodies such as the United Nations"); *see id.* at 42

should generally improve the efficacy of petitioning governmental bodies, particularly for change in law or law-imposed status (such as being designated an FTO). In the *Humanitarian Law Project* litigation before the Court of Appeals, the government maintained that "ask[ing] Congress to grant [a specific FTO] exemption from the statute" would constitute criminal activity.[20]

Association Is Essential to an Attorney's Ability to Improve the Quality of Justice

Protecting attorney–client association does not solely protect the client's rights. It also protects the rights of attorneys to pursue cause lawyering, political ends, and otherwise work to improve the quality of justice. Attorneys, who have sworn an oath to uphold the Constitution and who are made instruments of state power, have a "special responsibility for the quality of justice."[21] This ethical duty includes within it an obligation to "seek improvement of the law, access to the legal system," and "to ensure equal access to our system of justice for all those who because of economic or social barriers cannot afford or secure adequate legal counsel."[22]

Attorneys cannot pursue these obligations – or their own personal or political goals – of remedying injustice, seeking for equal protection of the laws, and challenging even our own government's policies through court processes if attorneys can be prohibited from associating with clients.[23] This is a major feature of the *Button* holding: The NAACP could not pursue its civil rights goals without associating with the clients affected by the governmental actions the NAACP opposed.[24] It is simply ludicrous to claim, as did the *Humanitarian Law Project* Court, that attorneys can say whatever they want, if they cannot speak to, on behalf of, or in coordination with those affected by laws and policies they believe are unjust and wish to change.[25] As the *Button* Court held, "litigation . . . is a means for achieving

(Breyer, J., dissenting) (noting that plaintiffs wanted to petition the United States Congress); *id.* at 54 (Breyer, J., dissenting) (noting that declarations below showed that the "relief" sought would *not* be monetary, but would include seeking "recognition under the Geneva Conventions").

[20] At oral argument before the Court of Appeals, the government maintained "that if plaintiffs filed an amicus brief for the LTTE [Liberation Tigers of Tamil Eelam] in this lawsuit, advocated on the group's behalf before the United Nations, asked Congress to grant the LTTE an exemption from the statute, or provided advice on how to mediate disputes, they would be engaged in criminal activity under the statute." *See* Brief of Humanitarian Law Project, *Holder v. Humanitarian Law Project*, 561 U.S. 1 (2010) (Nos. 08–1498, 09–89) 2009 WL 3865433, at *12.

[21] MODEL RULES OF PROF'L CONDUCT pmbl. ¶ 1.

[22] *See id.* ¶ 6.

[23] *See, e.g., Humanitarian Law Project*, 561 U.S. at 42 (Breyer, J., dissenting) ("We cannot avoid the constitutional significance of these facts on the basis that some of this speech takes place outside the United States and is directed at foreign governments, for the activities also *involve advocacy in this country directed to our government and its policies.*" [Emphasis added.]).

[24] *NAACP v. Button*, 371 U.S. 415, 429 (1963).

[25] *Humanitarian Law Project*, 561 U.S. at 25–26.

the lawful objectives of equality of treatment by all government" and "is thus a form of political expression."[26] For attorneys wishing to remedy injustice against minority and unpopular groups, as did the NAACP, "association for litigation may be the most effective form of political association."[27] It is essential to the attorney's own political expression and ability to challenge unjust laws, as well as to the attorney's role in the justice system and the constitutional role of the judiciary itself.

Guilt by Association is Antithetical to the Role of the Attorney

An extremely problematic aspect of the *Humanitarian Law Project* case is the Court's apparent imposition of guilt by association on attorneys based on the unlawful acts of clients. The "material support" statute in *Humanitarian Law Project* not only *frustrates* the attorney–client relationship but in fact *criminalizes* the attorney–client relationship and imputes culpability for unlawful conduct of clients onto the attorney who advises them. As with red scare statutes aimed at eradicating communism, the "material support" statute as applied to the *Humanitarian Law Project* plaintiffs can be said to "quite literally establish ... guilt by association alone"[28] because it criminalizes association even if the associating attorney "dis-agree[s] with th[e] unlawful aims"[29] of the FTO. Reliance on the government's war power does not change this principle: "Even the war power does not remove constitutional limitations safeguarding essential liberties."[30] If attorneys advise and help clients to violate law or engage in criminal or fraudulent conduct, then it would seem fair to hold them civilly or criminally responsible for such actions. But where an attorney is only advising a client on how to pursue peaceful and lawful conduct, how can that speech be criminalized? Again, as established from our era of convicting communists as a central tenet of the right of association:

> In our jurisprudence *guilt is personal*, and when the imposition of punishment on a status or on conduct can only be justified by reference to the relationship of that status or conduct to other concededly criminal activity ... *that relationship must* be sufficiently substantial to *satisfy the concept of personal guilt.*[31]

The Humanitarian Law Project wanted to help FTOs cease their unlawful activities and instead pursue their goals through peaceful and lawful means. How could such advice "satisfy the concept of personal guilt"?[32]

---

[26] *Button*, 371 U.S. at 431.
[27] *Id.*
[28] *United States* v. *Robel*, 389 U.S. 258, 265 (1967).
[29] *See id.* at 267.
[30] *See id.* at 264.
[31] *Scales* v. *United States*, 367 U.S. 203, 225 (1961).
[32] In *Humanitarian Law Project*, the Court determined that even providing peaceful advice could be criminalized because it could "legitimize" the group and the group could find ways to use such advice to further their unlawful activities. *See Holder* v. *Humanitarian Law Project*, 130

The best the *Humanitarian Law Project* majority could do in arguing that the plaintiffs' advice might somehow further terrorism was to assert that by providing legal advice regarding human rights and international law that itself "promot[es] peaceable, lawful conduct," the Humanitarian Law Project nevertheless "helps lend legitimacy" to these FTO groups. Such "legitimacy" might in turn influence others to support a terrorist organization and its unlawful terrorist ends.[33] The Court expressly relied on the idea of guilt by association in explaining that it was the "taint" of the FTOs' bad acts that made the attorney's association criminal, explaining: "It is not difficult to conclude, as Congress did, that the taint of [a designated FTO's] violent activities is so great that working in coordination with them or at their command legitimizes and furthers their terrorist means."[34]

If the Humanitarian Law Project wished to advise or assist an FTO to act unlawfully, or provided legal assistance that was likely to promote or assist the FTO's terrorist activities, then punishing such conduct would *not* be based on guilt by association and, instead, would be based on the attorney's own intents and actions. But it is completely contrary to the role of the lawyer in our system of justice to hold, as did the *Humanitarian Law Project* Court, that an attorney can be criminally punished for providing "peaceable, lawful" advice to a client (including advice on how to cease acting unlawfully) based on the "taint" of the client's bad acts.[35]

One of the central features of our legal system is the provision of counsel for even the guiltiest of criminals, regardless of the heinous nature of the crime. Again, contrary to English practice, the American colonies had provided for a right to counsel in all criminal proceedings, which was then enshrined in the Sixth Amendment. Further, in the civil context, attorneys represent and defend

---

S.Ct. 2705, 1725–26 (2010) Specifically, the Court said if shown how to petition the United Nations or how to negotiate for peace, an FTO could feign interest in peace negotiations and gain time and position. *See id.* at 2729 ("The PKK could, for example, *pursue peaceful negotiation as a means of buying time* to recover from short-term setbacks, lulling opponents into complacency, and ultimately preparing for renewed attacks." [Emphasis added.]). Justice Breyer's response is provoking:

"What is one to say about these arguments – *arguments that would deny First Amendment protection to the peaceful teaching of international human rights law* on the ground that a little knowledge about 'the international legal system' is too dangerous a thing; that an opponent's subsequent willingness to negotiate might be faked, so let's not teach him how to try? What might be said of these claims by those who live, as we do, in a Nation committed to the resolution of disputes through 'deliberative forces'?"

Id. at 2738 (Breyer, J., dissenting) (emphasis added); *see also id.* ("Moreover the risk that those who are taught will put otherwise innocent speech or knowledge to bad use is omnipresent, at least where that risk rests on little more than (even informed) speculation.").

[33] *See Humanitarian Law Project*, 561 U.S. at 30 ("Material support meant to 'promot[e] peaceable, lawful conduct' ... importantly helps lend legitimacy to foreign terrorist groups – legitimacy that makes it easier for those groups to persist, to recruit members, and to raise funds – all of which facilitate more terrorist attacks.").

[34] *Id.* (internal citations omitted).

[35] *See id.*

clients seeking the fullest extent of legal protection from liability despite the inhumanity of their client's action.

Lawyers understand that a central aspect of their role in the American adversary system is to provide due process and to promote equal protection and the fair administration of the laws through legal representation even of the alleged "bad apples" of society. As Monroe Freedman and Abbe Smith have explained, the lawyers' "respect for the rights even of the guilty individual, are a significant expression of the political philosophy that underlies the American System of Justice."[36] They note that such protection, even for the guilty or culpably liable, works to (1) affirm our respect for and treatment of "the accused as a human being," which "remind[s] [the accused] and the public about the sort of society we want to become and, indeed, about the sort of society we are"[37]; (2) protect the innocent from the possibility of an unjust conviction by encouraging defense lawyers to fiercely defend their clients and thus keep prosecution in check and require observance of constitutional processes[38]; and (3) "preserve the integrity of society itself ... [by] keeping sound and wholesome the procedure by which society visits its condemnation on an erring member."[39]

Ironically, the Court's argument that attorney provision of lawful peaceful advice could be proscribed because it could lend "legitimacy" to the FTOs is itself at complete odds with these central themes of our justice system. The provision of legal advice and assistance (including advice on how to change one's conduct to conform to the law and avoid further government condemnation) arguably provides "legitimacy" to people and to groups who receive such advice and assistance. Such legitimacy makes members of FTOs (or of the Communist Party from earlier association cases) appear human rather than solely "an object of purposes and policies."[40] Yet the creation of this specific type of legitimacy is not only an insufficient basis on which to impose guilt but, instead, is a central feature of our justice system, and preserving that type of legitimacy is actually part of the lawyer's role in our form of government.

Moreover, if the creation of legitimacy is a sufficient state interest to restrict rights of association, it is puzzling how membership in an organization is quintessentially

---

[36] FREEDMAN AND SMITH, *supra* Note 18, at 20.

[37] *See id.* at 21 (quoting Laurence H. Tribe, *Trial by Mathematical Precision and Ritual in the Legal Process*, 84 HARV. L. REV. 1329, 1391–92 (1971)).

[38] *See* FREEDMAN AND SMITH, *supra* Note 18, at 20–21. Freedman and Smith quote Jethro K. Lieberman, *Book Review*, 27 N.Y.L. SCH. L. REV. 695 (1981), in pointing out: "The singular strength of the adversary system is measured by a central fact that is usually deplored: The overwhelming majority of those accused in American courts are guilty. Why is this a strength? Because its opposite, visible in many totalitarian nations ... is this: Without an adversary system, a considerable number of [innocent] defendants are prosecuted."

[39] *See* FREEDMAN AND SMITH, *supra* Note 18, at 21 (quoting Lon Fuller, *The Adversary System*, in TALKS ON AMERICAN LAW 35 (Berman ed., 1960)).

[40] *See* FREEDMAN AND SMITH, *supra* Note 18, at 20 (quoting Bostjan M. Zupancic, *Truth and Impartiality in Criminal Process*, 7 J. CONTEMP. L. 39, 133 (1982)).

protected by the right of association. Membership lends legitimacy to an organization's policies and purposes by showing popular support for at least some of the organization's ideals. Nevertheless, the *Humanitarian Law Project* Court indicated that membership in an organization would be protected, apparently agreeing with established association cases that to punish membership would impose guilt solely by association.[41] Yet, the Court saw no such problem with imposing guilt based on association for legal advice and assistance that was entirely peaceable and lawful.

The Court's understanding is entirely backward. Legal representation and assistance for lawful ends should have a far lesser associational tie (for purposes of imposing guilt) than membership. Membership generally accurately indicates that the member agrees with at least some of the organization's principles or goals. Representation or assistance by an attorney has and should have no such implications. Attorneys represent people accused of – and sometimes utterly guilty of – the gravest and most inhumane crimes. This does not mean that the attorney agrees with, has advised, or wants to assist the client's crime or assents to anything their client believes, thinks, or does. Rather, attorneys provide representation because they understand the need for such representation in our justice system and are committed to principles of due process, equal protection, fair administration of the laws, and adherence to constitutional and other legal requirements.

Further, attorneys have an ethical duty to provide access to justice to unpopular causes and clients. As stated in the Model Rules of Professional Conduct, lawyers have a responsibility to accept "a fair share of unpopular matters or indigent or unpopular clients" and "may also be subject to appointment by a court to serve unpopular clients or persons unable to afford legal services."[42] Loyal and competent representation of unpopular clients has a long and honored tradition in the United States, beginning at least with John Adams and his representation of the British Soldiers tried for murder after the Boston Massacre. Although Adams personally supported the revolution, he recognized the need to provide effective representation to these alleged enemies to his cause. In his own words, Adams experienced "popular suspicions and prejudices," "anxiety and obloquy," yet he declared his representation of the British soldiers to be "one of the most gallant, generous, manly and disinterested Actions of my whole Life, and one of the best Pieces of Service I ever rendered my Country."[43]

How could representing a country's alleged enemy be "one of the best Pieces of Service I ever rendered my Country"? Because, as Adams the lawyer could see, "[a]s the evidence was," a "Judgment of Death against those Soldiers would have

---

[41] *See Holder v. Humanitarian Law Project*, 561 U.S. 1, 39 (2010).
[42] MODEL RULES OF PROF'L CONDUCT R. 6.2, cmt. 1.
[43] *See* JOHN ADAMS, DIARY AND AUTOBIOGRAPHY OF JOHN ADAMS 2:79 and 3:291–96 (ed. 1961).

been as foul a Stain upon this Country as the Executions of the Quakers or Witches, anciently."[44] In short, Adams the revolutionary aligned himself with British soldiers for legal representation precisely to preserve the *legitimacy* of our emerging United States' justice system. He did not agree with the British soldiers' actions or beliefs, but he did understand the need for due process, for the fair administration of the law, and for exertion of government power to be based on "evidence" (which he found wanting in this prosecution) – rather than being based on "suspicions and prejudices," a hallmark of tyrannical legal systems.[45]

Attorneys today continue to recognize that the legitimacy of our justice system is not solely based on what process and protection is provided to the clearly innocent, deserving, or popular but especially to the accused and to the unpopular. Consequently, despite their client's alleged bad acts, attorneys associate with clients to provide legal advice, assistance, and representation to lawfully protect life, liberty, and property – and thereby promote the legitimacy of our justice system.

Moreover, the imposition of guilt by association can work to thwart political movements and social change. If guilt could be imposed by association with those who acted unlawfully, entire political movements could be foreclosed by the bad acts of a few proponents of the movement. *NAACP v. Claiborne Hardware* provides a poignant example. In 1966, African American citizens of Claiborne county gave the Caucasian elected officials a list of demands for racial equality (including desegregation of schools and public facilities).[46] After failing to receive a favorable response, several hundred African Americans voted at a local NAACP meeting to boycott Caucasian merchants in the area.[47] The boycotted merchants later sued 146 individuals involved in the boycott as well as the NAACP and the Mississippi Action for Progress (MAP).[48] The state trial court imposed joint and several liability for lost business earnings and lost goodwill during the seven-year period of the boycott for a total of $1.25 million, plus interest and costs.[49] The Mississippi Supreme Court affirmed the liability as to most of the individuals sued, holding that the entire boycott was unlawful because of a few instances of violence and threats during the boycott.

The Supreme Court reversed, noting that the few instances of violence all occurred in 1966[50] and only involved a very few participants in the boycott.[51] Thus,

---

[44] *Id.* at 2:79.
[45] *See, e.g.,* FREEDMAN AND SMITH, *supra* Note 18, at 18–20 (reviewing legal systems in totalitarian regimes and the lack of process and protection for the accused).
[46] *NAACP v. Claiborne Hardware Co.,* 458 U.S. 886, 889, 899–900 (1982).
[47] *See id.*
[48] *See id.* at 889–90.
[49] *See id.* at 893.
[50] *See id.* at 906.
[51] *See id.* at 905–06.

while the people who engaged in violence could be held liable for the injuries they caused,[52] the entire boycott could not be declared illegal based on the illegal actions of a few participants.[53] The Court relied on the freedom of association principle prohibiting guilt by association: Each of the participants could not be held liable based on their continued association with and participation in the boycott in light of the few instances of violence by some other participants.[54] To impose liability on all who continued to participate in the boycott once there had been incidents of violence would be to impose guilt by association alone. Rather, the government was required to prove that the group itself possessed unlawful goals and that each individual held liable had the "specific intent to further those illegal aims."[55]

Importantly, if the *Claiborne Hardware* Court had held that all those who participated in the boycott could be held liable because a few participants engaged in violent conduct, entire political movements could be undermined whenever some involved in a political or social movement acted unlawfully. In nearly all major political movements there is some unrest and some people who resort to violence or unlawful activities – and this would certainly be true of the American Revolution, the Black Lives Matter movement, organization of labor, the civil rights movement, or abolition of slavery. It is these very kinds of contexts where the right to associate is most essential; indeed, the right of association was born in the context of majoritarian attempts to squelch such political movements. It would stifle political change and the redress of political grievances if all people associating together in a common movement could be punished based on the illegal conduct of others seeking the same ends. Thus, the *Claiborne Hardware* Court correctly held: "The right to associate does not lose all constitutional protection merely because some members of the group may have participated in conduct or advocated doctrine that itself is not protected."[56]

Even in the communist membership cases, red scare legislation was exactly that: fear that communist political theory would influence our country and ultimately succeed. Yet the First Amendment protects such political views and advocacy at its very core. What constitutionally could be forbidden was sabotage and terrorism, but that did not mean that the political ideals behind communism could be foreclosed just because some, or even many, communists were engaged in illegal conduct or even because the international communist movement sought the violent overthrow of the United States government. Those espousing communist ideals saw true

---

[52] *See id.* at 926 (stating that individuals who engaged in violence or threats could be held liable for the injuries caused by such violence and threats).

[53] *See id.* at 915 ("We hold that the nonviolent elements of petitioners' activities are entitled to the protection of the First Amendment.")

[54] *See id.* at 907–12, 918–20; *see also id.* at 920 ("For liability to be imposed by reason of association alone, it is necessary to establish that the group itself possessed unlawful goals and that the individual held a specific intent to further those illegal aims.")

[55] *Id.* at 920.

[56] *Id.* at 908.

injustice in our capitalist system, and should have been (and eventually were) protected in advocating the alleviation of such injustices. They should not be foreclosed from discussing their grievances and seeking political change because of imposition of guilt by association with violent factions of the Communist Party.

This problem is exacerbated to the extent it is applied to forbid attorney association based on the bad acts of proposed clients seeking political change. Particularly problematic is the aspect of *Humanitarian Law Project* that prohibits attorneys from advising FTOs on how to change their conduct to conform to the law and achieve their goals in a lawful and peaceable manner. Such an application of guilt by association forestalls political change by prohibiting certain groups from even finding out how to conform their conduct to the law. Further, if an attorney were to agree with some of the group's lawful political goals or aims, the attorney would be unable to associate for the purpose of informing the group how to cease their unlawful activities and assert those same political ends in a lawful and peaceful manner. As long as the attorney does not counsel or otherwise assist a client in engaging in unlawful activities, the attorney's fundamental role in the administration of justice requires that attorneys have a protected right to associate with and represent clients despite a client's bad acts.

LIMITS ON THE RIGHT OF ATTORNEY–CLIENT ASSOCIATION

Appropriate limitations exist for the constitutionally protected right of attorney–client association. The access to justice theory attunes lawyers' First Amendment rights to safeguard their central duties to their clients and their role in the justice system. There are two basic ways that attorney–client association can frustrate the role of the attorney in the justice system and thus fall outside the protection of the First Amendment: (1) where attorneys are using the powers given them by the state to undermine their role in the justice system by assisting in crime or fraud or taking advantage of clients and (2) where association with a client is prohibited by the attorney's core duties of loyalty, confidentiality, and/or competence.

Misuse of State Powers

As discussed in Chapter 4, attorneys are delegates of state power, and while the power delegated is that which inheres in a democracy – a vitally important point in many contexts – it also contains within it essential limitations on abuse of government powers. The state can prohibit lawyers from using their license to practice law to undermine the system of justice or to harm those over whom lawyers are given power. As with all delegates of state power in a democratic system of government, the lawyer's use of government power contains limitations congruous to the attorney's role in the justice system.

Consequently, it is elemental that attorneys can be prohibited from using the power of the state that they receive through their license to engage in crime or fraud. Lawyer association and speech is tied to accessing government power. States provide to lawyers the ability to invoke law on behalf of clients and obtain the protection of the courts and other governmental processes. It would absolutely frustrate the justice system if lawyers could freely use this grant of government power to commit or conceal crimes or fraud. Thus states are free to forbid lawyers from using the power of the state entrusted to lawyers to advise or assist clients in committing crimes or frauds.[57] Lawyers simply do not have a constitutional right to associate with clients for criminal or fraudulent ends. Notably, such a restriction does not create guilt by association because it is the lawyer's own acts in advising or assisting the client in criminal or fraudulent conduct that makes the association (or speech) proscribable.

Thus, for example, in *Humanitarian Law Project*, even under the access to justice theory, the attorneys could be prohibited from advising or assisting FTOs in any terrorism or other crimes. That is, if the attorneys solely provided legal advice regarding how to engage in peaceable lawful conduct in compliance with law, then that advice could not be proscribed or punished under the access to justice theory. On the other hand, if the attorney provides advice or assistance that is likely to further terrorism, then that advice or assistance is absolutely proscribable. Notably, such proscribable advice or assistance would have been foreclosed by Justice Breyer's limiting construction of the material support statute, which complies with general constitutional restrictions on association by requiring that an attorney know or intend to further the FTO's unlawful terrorist aims. Under his construction, a "person acts with the requisite knowledge if he is aware of (or willfully blinds himself to) a significant likelihood that his or her conduct will materially support the organization's terrorist ends."[58]

Similarly, in endowing the attorney with power, the state may also proscribe uses of that power that deceive, harm, or take advantage of clients – including through solicitation of clients. Notably, in *Button*, the Supreme Court had recognized a right of the NAACP to solicit in person African American parents of children in segregated schools as part of the attorney's freedom of association. But that does not mean that lawyers are free to engage in deceitful practices or take advantage of clients. The state, having given power to the attorney, can protect clients and can forbid the attorney from using that power to exploit people.

This view comports with the Supreme Court's primary holdings regarding restrictions on in-person solicitation, which the Court examined in the companion cases, *Ohralik* v. *State of Ohio*[59] and *In re Primus*.[60] In *Ohralik* the Court held that a state

---

[57] *See, e.g.,* MODEL RULES OF PROF'L CONDUCT R. 1.2(d).
[58] *Holder* v. *Humanitarian Law Project*, 561 U.S. 1, 56 (2010) (Breyer, J., dissenting).
[59] 436 U.S. 447 (1978).
[60] 436 U.S. 412 (1978).

bar could prohibit and punish in-person solicitation undertaken by a lawyer for pecuniary gain – but only "under circumstances likely to pose dangers that the State has a right to prevent."[61] *Ohralik* involved a rather stereotypical ambulance-chaser-style attorney who solicited two young women who had been in a car accident, one of whom was hospitalized when he contacted her.[62] Although he ultimately did not represent either (both fired him), he sued each to recover the one-third contingency fee they had orally agreed to give him and which he had recorded via concealed tape recorder.[63] The Court held that the state "may discipline a lawyer for soliciting clients in person, for pecuniary gain, under circumstances likely to pose dangers that the State has a right to prevent."[64]

In *Primus*, the ACLU was asked by Gary Allen, an officer of a group serving indigent clients in Aiken, South Carolina, to have an ACLU representative come talk to some African American women who had been sterilized as a condition of their continued receipt of Medicaid.[65] Edna Primus, a lawyer working with the ACLU, went down to Aiken and met with Allen and with Mary Etta Williams, one of the women who had been sterilized.[66] Later, Primus learned that the ACLU was willing to provide representation in a case against the doctor and those involved in the sterilization, and Primus sent a letter to Williams informing her of the offer of free legal representation.[67] Nevertheless, Williams settled her claims against the doctor at an appointment for her sick child.[68] Primus was reprimanded by the South Carolina Bar for engaging in prohibited solicitation by sending the letter to Williams.

The Court held that Primus's letter, including the legal advice therein and the offer of free legal representation constituted "a form of political expression and political association."[69] The Court relied strongly on the *Button* case, and reaffirmed that the *Button* "Court at least found constitutionally protected, the activities of NAACP members and staff lawyers [1] *in advising* Negroes *of their constitutional rights*, [2] urging them to institute litigation of a particular kind, [3] recommending particular lawyers and [4] financing such litigation."[70] The Court

---

[61] *Id.* at 449.

[62] *Id.*

[63] *See id.* at 450–53.

[64] *Id.* at 449.

[65] *Primus*, 436 U.S. at 415–16.

[66] *See id.*

[67] *See id.* at 416–17.

[68] As recounted in the Court's opinion, "shortly after receiving appellant's letter … Williams visited Dr. Pierce to discuss the progress of her third child, who was ill. At the doctor's office, she encountered his lawyer and at the latter's request signed a release of liability in the doctor's favor." *See id.*

[69] *Id.* at 428.

[70] *Id.* at 425 n. 16.

also reaffirmed that the right of association protects litigation itself,[71] as well as "collective activity undertaken to obtain meaningful access to the courts."[72]

The *Primus* Court recognized the need for attorney association with potential clients (even if technically in the form of traditional solicitation) for effective civil liberties protection. Those whose civil liberties are infringed often are unaware of the infringement or unable to pursue remedies on their own. On the flip side, attorneys who wish to devote their time and talents to protection of civil liberties (like those members of the NAACP, the ACLU, and the Humanitarian Law Project) cannot instigate litigation on their own. They must have a client who has suffered a legally cognizable injury and has standing to sue. The Court in *Primus* thus noted that "the efficacy of litigation as a means of advancing the cause of civil liberties often depends on the ability to make legal assistance available to suitable litigants."[73] Because both the NAACP and the ACLU in the respective cases solicited prospective litigants "for the purpose of furthering the civil-rights objectives of the organization and its members," such activity fell within the constitutional right of association.[74]

The access to justice theory comports with the basic results in *Primus* and *Ohralik*. *Primus* demonstrates that attorney–client association and solicitation – especially for political or cause lawyering – is strongly protected by the First Amendment rights of expression and association. *Ohralik* indicates that if an attorney is merely trying to make money, then the state can prohibit certain types of in-person solicitation – but *only* "under circumstances likely to pose dangers that the State has a right to prevent,"[75] such as "undue influence, overreaching, misrepresentation, invasion of privacy, conflict of interest, and lay interference."[76]

Undermining Core Duties to Clients

Additionally, attorneys lack a constitutional right to undermine their core duties to their clients, including the duty of loyalty or conflict avoidance. States can prohibit lawyers from violating their duty of loyalty – as well as competence and confidentiality – to a client by engaging in a representation where the lawyer has a conflict of interest. As the Model Rules indicate, attorneys with a conflict of interest generally risk "materially limit[ing]" a representation (thus undermining their duty of competence as well as loyalty) and/or risk the revelation or use of confidential information

---

[71] *See id.* at 431 ("The ACLU engages in litigation as a vehicle for effective political expression and association").

[72] *Id.* at 426.

[73] *Id.* at 431.

[74] *Id.* at 423–24.

[75] *Id.* at 449.

[76] *Primus*, 436 U.S. at 426.

adversely to the client (thus undermining confidentiality as well as loyalty).[77] Consequently, lawyers do not have a First Amendment right to associate with clients where they are affected by a conflict of interest. Regulators are free to prohibit conflicted representations.

Limitations Still Allow for Representation by Counsel

Overarchingly, regulators may prohibit certain forms of solicitation (such as in-person solicitation for pecuniary gain or deceptive advertising) or association (such as conflicted representations) to enforce the attorney's duties of loyalty, competence, and confidentiality. Such prohibitions on association either enforce attorney's duties of confidentiality, competence, and loyalty or protect clients from misuse of state power by undue influence and invasion of privacy from self-dealing attorneys. Importantly, under such restrictions the client can obtain another attorney – restrictions based on conflict of interest or prohibitions on certain forms of solicitation do not cut off all attorney association with a particular client or class of clients. The client is still free to hire a different attorney in the conflicts scenario, and the attorney can use other less intrusive forms of solicitation to obtain clients. In contrast, the restriction upheld in *Humanitarian Law Project* is particularly pernicious in that it prohibits all attorneys from associating with a particular class of clients.

A SAFETY VALVE FOR STABLE GOVERNMENT

David Cole has argued that freedom of association "serves as a safety valve" for the stability of our government and society.[78] Protecting association with others "makes it less likely that individuals and groups will go underground and adopt violent means."[79] Attorney–client association is particularly important in serving this end. For example, in *Button*, if the NAACP lawyers could not pursue desegregation litigation by associating with African American parents of school children, both lawyers and clients would lose recourse to law to vindicate constitutional rights for African Americans and to oppose unjust and illegal practices. By cutting off lawyers from those affected by unjust practices and policies, lawful recourse that would check official power is also effectively cut off. Without recourse to law, violence and unlawful means are left as the only means to oppose government oppression and excess or to instigate change. Thus, as the *De Jonge* Court explained regarding

---

[77] *See* MODEL RULES OF PROF'L CONDUCT R. 1.7(b).
[78] *See* David Cole, *Hanging with the Wrong Crowd: Of Gangs, Terrorists, and the Right of Association*, 1999 SUP. CT. REV. 203, 231 (1999).
[79] *Id.*

association in general, the right to attorney–client association helps ensure that changes in government and society, "if desired, may be obtained by peaceful [and lawful] means," – for "[t]herein lies the security of the Republic, the very foundation of constitutional government."[80]

[80] *De Jonge v. Oregon*, 299 U.S. 353, 365 (1937).

9

Safeguarding Client Counseling and Confidences

Once freedom to form an attorney–client relationship is established, that relationship must be protected by attuning lawyers' First Amendment rights to safeguard their central duties to their clients – including both the duties of communication and confidentiality. Thus, attorneys must have a protected First Amendment right to counsel with clients. Although the attorney–client privilege protects confidential client counseling from compelled disclosure in court proceedings, it does not protect attorney–client counseling from regulation. Attorneys must have the right to advise clients about the lawfulness or unlawfulness of both proposed and past client conduct.

Additionally, the First Amendment must *not* be contorted to undermine the attorney's vital duty of confidentiality. As agents of the client, attorneys only receive information relating to the representation because of their tie to government power and resultant ability to assist the client in achieving the client's legal objectives and to protect the client's interests. They must use that information accordingly – to pursue the client's objectives and to protect the client's interests. Thus the Virginia Supreme Court in *Hunter* erred in holding that the First Amendment defeats a regulation requiring lawyers to maintain client confidences.[1] The state has endowed the attorney with power to protect the client's interests, and thus the state can prohibit the attorney from using information obtained solely by virtue of the attorney's license to practice law to the detriment of the client. Additionally, the duty of confidentiality is one of the core duties lawyers owe to clients – duties that have been understood as part of the lawyer's role for centuries. Confidentiality is tied to the duty of loyalty – lawyers have a duty to *not* betray clients who provide information to lawyers for the sole purpose of protecting their legal interests, including life, liberty, and property.

---

[1] *Hunter v. Virginia State Bar*, 285 Va. 485 (2013).

THE BASICS OF THE ATTORNEY–CLIENT PRIVILEGE AND THE DUTY OF CONFIDENTIALITY

Before delving into the appropriate shaping of attorney First Amendment rights to the lawyer's role as relating to client communication and confidentiality, it is important to briefly set out the contours of the separate, but interrelated, duty of confidentiality and attorney–client privilege. Unfortunately, even lawyers sometimes conflate the two or seem to think that if something isn't covered by the attorney–client privilege, then they are free to reveal it. Indeed, in the *Hunter* case, the Virginia Supreme Court ultimately appeared to constitutionalize that line of thinking by holding that the First Amendment *forbids* states from "prohibit[ing] an attorney from discussing information about a client or former client *that is not protected by attorney-client privilege* without express consent from that client."[2] In other words, according to the Virginia Supreme Court, the First Amendment forbids states from punishing lawyers for disclosing client confidences without client consent unless those confidences are covered by the attorney–client privilege.

It is true that both the attorney–client privilege and the duty of confidentiality fall within the lawyer's overarching duty not to reveal certain information relating to a representation. But they are not the same at all – they cover different information and they perform different functions. As to coverage, the duty of confidentiality is exceptionally broad, while the attorney–client privilege only covers a narrow category of communications. In general, the attorney–client privilege only covers (1) confidential, (2) communications, (3) between the attorney and client, (4) made for the purpose of receiving or giving legal advice. Moreover, it is only the "communication" between the attorney and client that is covered by the privilege and *not* the underlying facts or any preexisting documents or other evidence that reveal the information.

For example, if a client confidentially tells their attorney that they knew certain products were defective and, moreover, that company documents reveal as much, the privilege only covers the communication of this fact to the attorney. The privilege does *not* cover either the documents demonstrating the knowledge (these are discoverable even though the client told the attorney about them) or the *fact* that the client knew about the defect. If the client is asked in a deposition or court proceeding, "Did you know that the products were defective?" the client cannot assert the attorney–client privilege based on the fact that they told their attorney that same information. What is protected by the privilege is just the communication. If the client is instead asked, "What did you tell your attorney?" or the attorney is asked, "What did your client tell you?" that is where the attorney–client privilege applies and neither the lawyer nor the client can be compelled to reveal the communication.

---

[2]   *Id.* at 502.

Thus the attorney–client privilege only covers confidential *communications* between attorneys and clients – and there is a whole world of information in a given representation that is not covered by that privilege. The underlying facts are not covered by the privilege, documentary evidence is not covered by the privilege (unless a document is itself a communication to the lawyer, such as emails or letters from the client to the lawyer or vice versa), and information obtained from third parties or witnesses is not covered by the privilege.

In stark contrast to the attorney–client privilege's narrow scope of protection, the duty of confidentiality covers everything. As the Model Rules of Professional Conduct state, the duty covers "*all* information relating to the representation, *whatever its source*."[3] Comment 2 to Model Rule 1.6 asserts: "A fundamental principle in the client-lawyer relationship is that, in the absence of the client's informed consent, the lawyer must not reveal information relating to the representation."[4] Lawyers are allowed to reveal confidences as impliedly authorized to accomplish the representation, but otherwise the duty of confidentiality absolutely forbids lawyers from revealing *any* information relating to the representation without client consent unless it falls within one of several very narrow exceptions to the duty. Those exceptions include disclosure made to prevent a substantial risk of death or serious bodily injury, to prevent or rectify crimes or fraud in which the lawyer's services were used, and for lawyer self-defense.[5] The narrowness of these exceptions is telling – lawyers are to be trusted guardians of client information.

The precise contours of the duty of confidentiality differ among states – with most following a variant on the Model Rules. Nevertheless, a few states follow the approach created by the 1969 Model Code of Professional Responsibility, which forbids attorneys from revealing "confidences or secrets" of the client. Confidences are defined to mean attorney–client privileged materials, and secrets are defined to mean "other information gained in the professional relationship that the client has requested be held inviolate or the disclosure of which would be embarrassing or would be likely to be detrimental to the client."[6] Lawyers are then prohibited from revealing either confidences or secrets, and additionally are prohibited from using confidences or secrets either to the disadvantage of the client or to the advantage of the lawyer or a third party without client consent.[7]

This idea that lawyers have a near inviolable duty to keep confidences goes back to the birth of the legal profession in England. Carol Rice Andrews traces the duty of confidentiality (and loyalty) to the thirteenth century, the very century where lawyers

---

[3] MODEL RULES OF PROF'L CONDUCT R. 1.6, cmt. 3 (emphasis added).
[4] *Id.* R. 1.6, cmt. 2.
[5] *Id.* R. 1.6(b).
[6] *See, e.g.*, MICH. RULES OF PROF'L CONDUCT R. 1.6(a).
[7] *See id.* R. 1.6(b).

started to appear as a profession in England.[8] She even cites a case from 1282 where lawyer William of Wells was punished for disloyalty and for revealing client confidences in violation of a 1275 statute.[9] Nearly four hundred years later, in 1648, Lord Whitelocke enumerated the duties of lawyers – including three overarching duties of "secrecy, diligence, and fidelity"[10] – what we would call today core duties of confidentiality, competence, and loyalty. As to confidentiality, Whitelocke explained:

> [A]dvocates are *a king of confessors*, and ought to be such, to whom the client may with confidence lay open his evidences, and the naked truth of his case, *sub sigillo*, and he ought not to discover them to his client's prejudice; nor will the law compel him to it.[11]

And approximately 400 years later, we still are at the same place – with narrow exceptions, lawyers are forbidden from revealing confidential information, be that defined as both "confidences and secrets" of the client or as "any information relating to the representation, whatever its source." Under either version, the duty of confidentiality is vast, and it outlasts the representation and even the death of the client.

The attorney–client privilege and the duty of confidentiality also perform very different functions, despite both falling under the umbrella of an overarching duty not to reveal. The attorney–client privilege protects attorney–client communications from compelled disclosure – but the duty of confidentiality does not. In other words, an attorney cannot be put on the witness stand and asked, "What did your client tell you?" The attorney–client privilege protects the lawyer from having to reveal that information even under compulsory court processes. Similarly, in discovery, the attorney and client are protected from turning over attorney–client privileged materials (such as emails from the client to the attorney). However, the duty of confidentiality has no such protection from compulsory court processes. If a non-privileged document falls within the scope of discovery and is appropriately requested, the lawyer cannot resist the compulsory process and must turn over the materials – even though the lawyer is under a duty of confidentiality not to *volunteer* that same information on their own.

Thus, the duty of confidentiality keeps a lawyer from *volunteering* information outside of the context of compulsory court processes. If a lawyer is reviewing documents and determines that his client is liable based on the documentary evidence, the attorney cannot call up the other side and say, "I've looked at this,

---

[8] Carol Rice Andrews, *Standards of Conduct for Lawyers: An 800-Year Evolution*, 57 S.M.U. L. REV. 1385, 1395 (2004).
[9] *See id.* at 1395 and n. 80.
[10] *Id.* at 1400 (quoting LORD WHITELOCKE, MEMORIALS OF THE ENGLISH AFFAIRS OF THE KING CHARLES THE FIRST (1625–1649), 352 (1732).
[11] *Id.* at 1400 n.117 (quoting WHITELOCKE, *supra* Note 10, 355).

and my client violated the law." Importantly, the attorney–client privilege does *not* prevent the lawyer from volunteering this information – because the information was never covered by the privilege (the attorney is *not* revealing a privileged communication from his client). Nevertheless, the duty of confidentiality absolutely prohibits the lawyer from volunteering this nonprivileged information without client consent.

In short, the duty of confidentiality is expansive in scope, and it keeps lawyers from volunteering information about a representation of a client, but it does not protect information from compelled disclosure through compulsory court processes. The attorney–client privilege, on the other hand, protects information from compelled disclosure, but it only covers a very narrow category of materials – confidential communications between an attorney and client for the purpose of obtaining or receiving legal advice. Understanding this distinction is essential for considering both counseling with clients and confidentiality.

COUNSELING WITH CLIENTS

Lawyers have a duty to communicate and counsel with clients. Eli Wald has explained that "[c]ommunications between clients and attorneys are the cornerstone of the attorney-client relationship."[12] Wald notes that because most cases settle or plea, "many clients never actually enter the courtroom, interact with a judge or a jury, or meet the opposing party or its attorney" and thus "for a good number of Americans, communicating with their own lawyers will constitute most, if not all, of their exposure to law and the legal system."[13]

A lawyer's communication with a client is the method whereby a client knows what is going on in a given representation, including in lawsuits in which the client is a party and in which their interests to life, liberty, and property are being finally determined by government power. For many clients a lawsuit implicates intimately important personal interests that weigh heavily and constantly on the client's mind (criminal charges, housing, child custody, employment, medical benefits, disability, social security, probate, etc.).

In addition to the client's need to hear from the attorney about their case, it is critically important for the attorney to hear from and communicate with the client in order for the attorney to ascertain the client's objectives and the underlying facts of the case. Again, Wald observes:

> [T]he attorney-client relationship is an agency relationship in which a lawyer-agent serves the interests of a client-principal. Communications are the mechanism by which the client controls the agency relationship, informs the attorney about his

[12] Eli Wald, *Taking Attorney-Client Communications (and Therefore Clients) Seriously*, 42 UNIV. SAN FRANCISCO L. REV. 747 (2008).

[13] *Id.* at 747–48.

goals and objectives, and provides the lawyer with necessary and relevant information about the representation. *Successful representation requires effective communications*, without which the attorney-agent cannot know, understand, or represent the client's goals.[14]

The lawyer's ability to communicate with clients and vice versa is absolutely essential to the fulfillment of the lawyer's role in the justice system. Lawyers cannot effectively represent the client's interests at all (they cannot ascertain either the underlying facts or the client's objectives) without effective communication. A particularly important aspect of lawyer–client communications, additionally, is the ability of the client to seek and the lawyer to provide full and frank advice about the lawfulness or unlawfulness of proposed or past client conduct.

As noted, attorney–client *communications* are protected by perhaps the most enduring and protective of privileges recognized by law: the attorney–client privilege. The purpose of the attorney–client privilege is often regarded as the need for full and frank communication from the client to the attorney so the attorney will know how to best serve the client's needs.[15] This purpose even has constitutional underpinnings found in the Fifth Amendment right against self-incrimination – the government should not be able to obtain from an attorney what they constitutionally are unable to obtain from the client.[16] However, the purpose of the privilege is not solely to allow the client to fully and frankly communicate with the lawyer, but it is equally essential for the attorney to be able to fully and frankly advise the client, particularly regarding the lawfulness or unlawfulness of proposed or past conduct. Thus, as explained by the Supreme Court, the purpose of the privilege "is to encourage full and frank *communication between attorneys and their clients* and *thereby promote* broader public interests in *the observance of law and administration of justice.*"[17]

Thus it is not just full and frank *disclosure* by the client that is essential but full and frank *communication* on the part of both the attorney and the client.[18] The ability of the client to obtain full and frank advice from an attorney is essential, again, to the attorney's role in invoking or avoiding the power of the government in the protection of life, liberty, and property. When a person consults an attorney about proposed conduct – whether in a transactional context, criminal context, or civil liability context – the attorney serves an important legitimizing and fairness function for governmental civil and criminal power that deprives individuals of life, liberty, and property. Just as the client should be able to fully and frankly explain the facts to the attorney, the attorney should likewise be able to fully and frankly explain

---

[14] *Id.* at 748 (emphasis added).
[15] *See, e.g., Upjohn* v. *United States*, 449 U.S. 383, 389 (1981).
[16] Monroe H. Freedman and Abbe Smith, Understanding Legal Ethics 172–81 (4th edn. 2010); Thomas D. Morgan, The Vanishing American Lawyer 57 n. 137 (2010).
[17] *Upjohn*, 449 U.S. at 389 (emphasis added).
[18] *See* Restatement (Third) of the Law Governing Lawyers § 68 cmt. c (2000).

the contours of the law, its purpose and function, and the potential for and extent of liability or criminal sanctions for violations thereof. As recognized in Model Rule of Professional Conduct 1.2(d), lawyers should "discuss the legal consequences of any proposed course of conduct with a client" and may "counsel or assist a client to make a good faith effort to determine the validity, scope, meaning or application of the law."[19]

The ability of the individual to obtain such advice and interpretation of law before acting (or even after acting in order to determine the potential scope of liability or other consequences of violation) improves the fairness of government-imposed liability and sanctions, which in turn improves the legitimacy of our entire system of justice. Part of "keeping sound and wholesome the procedure by which society visits its condemnation on an erring member"[20] must include fair notice and warning through the ability of the "erring member" to obtain assistance in understanding the potential "condemnation" they may receive for their actions and thus to help them structure their conduct in such a way to avoid such criminal and civil government-backed condemnation.

In fact, one of the premises underlying the attorney–client privilege is that "vindicating rights and complying with obligations under the law and under modern legal processes are matters often too complex and uncertain for a person untrained in the law, so that clients need to consult lawyers."[21] If this assumption is true, justice and fairness require that a person be able to consult with an attorney regarding the reach and extent of the law. As the New York Court of Appeals has explained, the privilege is intended to "foster *uninhibited dialogue between lawyers and clients* in their professional engagements, thereby ultimately *promoting the administration of justice.*"[22] Gregory Sisk has argued that by protecting the attorney–client "*dialogue* from outside intrusion," the privilege allows "lawyers and clients to engage with difficult problems by *considering the full spectrum of legal and moral dimensions*" and thus "also promotes the public interest in obedience to the rule of law and advancement of the common good."[23] Again, the fact that large segments of the population lack access to such legal advice does not undermine the importance of the availability of such access to as many people as can either pay for it or otherwise obtain it.

---

[19] *See* MODEL RULE OF PROF'L CONDUCT 1.2(d). However, Rule 1.2(d) prohibits a lawyer from engaging or assisting a client in engaging "in conduct that the lawyer knows is criminal or fraudulent."

[20] *See* FREEDMAN AND SMITH, *supra* Note 16, at 18 (quoting Fuller, *The Adversary System*, in TALKS ON AMERICAN LAW **35** (H. Berman ed., 1960)).

[21] RESTATEMENT (THIRD) OF THE LAW GOVERNING LAWYERS § 68(c) (2000).

[22] *Rossi v. Blue Cross & Blue Shield*, 540 N.E.2d 703, 705 (N.Y. 1989) (emphasis added); *see also* RESTATEMENT (THIRD) OF THE LAW GOVERNING LAWYERS § 68(c) (2000) ("It is assumed that, in the absence of such frank and full *discussion between client and lawyer*, adequate legal assistance cannot be realized."[Emphasis added.]).

[23] Gregory C. Sisk, *The Dynamic Attorney-Client Privilege*, **23** GEO. J. LEGAL ETHICS 201, 217 (2010) (emphasis added).

Nevertheless, while the existing attorney–client privilege serves to protect communications from *compelled disclosure*, it does not protect attorney advice from *regulation or restriction* – an imperative point. *Humanitarian Law Project* and *Milavetz* are cases in point. In *Milavetz, Gallop & Milavetz v. United States*,[24] Congress had passed a law forbidding attorneys (and others falling within the rubric of "debt relief agencies") from advising clients to incur debt in contemplation of bankruptcy. The law appeared to forbid attorneys from even advising clients regarding lawful conduct – such as selling a home and entering into a lease (which would be a new debt obligation, but is legal and may be prudent in some situations).[25] Importantly, the debtor herself was not prohibited from undertaking new debt obligations under the law, but the attorney was prohibited from *advising* clients that they could lawfully incur such a debt. The Supreme Court in large part avoided the problem by interpreting the statute in such a way that the attorney was only prohibited from providing particular advice that would abuse the bankruptcy system.[26] The Court acknowledged that without this narrowing interpretation, the statute "would seriously undermine the attorney-client relationship"[27] through its "inhibition of frank discussion."[28]

The *Milavetz* Court recognized that a regulation forbidding attorneys from advising clients in accordance with the actual state of the law would "seriously undermine the attorney-client relationship." The Court strove to preserve the attorney–client relationship by narrowly interpreting the statute, and not through application of the First Amendment. Indeed, no First Amendment doctrine or theory accounted for the fact that the restriction frustrated the essential role of attorneys in the fair administration of justice. Rather, the best argument available was that the statute was vague – and not only vague for attorneys, but vague as applied to anyone.[29] Vagueness was similarly one of the primary challenges used in the *Humanitarian Law Project* case. The important point is that no First Amendment doctrine was presented, in either case, that could effectively recognize and address the frustration of core attributes of the attorney–client relationship.

---

[24] 559 U.S. 229 (2010).

[25] Indeed, this was how the Eighth Circuit had interpreted the statute, as "'broadly prohibit[ing] a debt relief agency from advising an assisted person ... to incur any additional debt when the assisted person is contemplating bankruptcy,' even when that advice constitute[d] prudent [and legal] prebankruptcy planning not intended to abuse the bankruptcy laws." *See id.* at 235.

[26] The Court specifically held that the statute "prohibits a debt relief agency only from advising a debtor to incur more debt because the debtor is filing for bankruptcy, rather than for a valid purpose." *See id.* at 243, 248 n. 6.

[27] *See id.* at 246 n. 5.

[28] *See id.* at 1338.

[29] *Milavetz, Gallop & Milavetz v. United States*, Nos. 08–119, 08–1225, Oral Arg. Trans. at 20 (Dec. 1, 2009) ("[D]on't bring in the fact that, well, and moreover, if it's applied to attorneys, it's unconstitutional ... [b]ecause if it's applied to anybody it's unconstitutional, according to your [vagueness] argument.") (Scalia, J.)

Unlike its *Milavetz* decision, the *Humanitarian Law Project* Court did not interpret the "material support" statute in such a way as to avoid the frustration of the attorney–client relationship. In fact, the Court specifically noted that under its interpretation, the statute "barred" plaintiffs from "*speak[ing] to* the PKK and LTTE" – the FTOs the Humanitarian Law Project wanted to assist – if their "speech to those groups imparts a 'specific skill' or *communicates advice derived from 'specialized knowledge'* – for example, training on the use of international law or advice on petitioning the United Nations."[30] Thus, in *Humanitarian Law Project*, the law prohibited, among other things, the provision of any legal advice to groups designated as foreign terrorist organizations. As the Court noted, the goal of the statute is eradication of the groups – and in pursuit of that goal, the statute forbids attorneys from advising members of the group regarding the contours and reach of the law, how to begin acting in a lawful manner, how to petition our own United States government (to perhaps change its policy about specific groups), and how to seek international assistance from the United Nations and under the Geneva Conventions. As argued by the dissent, not only did the *Humanitarian Law Project* plaintiffs want to advise the FTOs regarding international law but also to advocate on their behalf "in *this* country directed to *our* government and *its* policies."[31] The government's goal is to eradicate these groups, and yet the statute forbids attorneys from providing their legal expertise to these groups on how to change their methods and act lawfully and peacefully, on how to petition *our* government to avoid eradication, or even how to petition the United Nations for human rights relief and recognition under the Geneva Conventions.

The Court's decision allows our government to enact a policy of destroying particular groups and, then, on top of that, to threaten citizen attorneys with imprisonment if they provide the targeted group with any legal advice – even legal advice on how to act peacefully and lawfully. While the Court explains that it does "not suggest that Congress could extend the same prohibition on material support at issue here to domestic organizations," the Court's analysis does not rely on that distinction.[32] Rather, the Court relies on the superficial distinction that the plaintiffs can independently say whatever they want; they just cannot speak to or in coordination with the FTOs.[33]

The ability of the attorney to provide full and frank legal advice to clients plays an essential role in our system of justice. It legitimizes the government's criminal and

---

[30] *Holder v. Humanitarian Law Project*, 561 U.S. 1, 27 (2010) (emphasis added). PKK stands for Partiya Karkeran Kurdistan and LTTE stands for the Liberation Tigers of Tamil Eelam.

[31] *Id.* at 42 (Breyer, J., dissenting).

[32] *Id.* at 39 (majority opinion).

[33] *See id.* at 25–26; *id.* at 36 (listing reasons why Court concludes statute is constitutional, "*most importantly*, Congress *has avoided any restriction on independent advocacy*, or indeed any activities *not directed to, coordinated with, or controlled by* foreign terrorist groups" [emphasis added]).

civil power by providing a means for the lay individual or organization to structure their conduct to avoid prosecution or liability and to protect their life, liberty, or property – particularly in the face of laws and legal processes that are difficult to understand without legal training. Such advice greatly increases the fairness of the administration of the laws by providing people with notice of the content and reach of the law. Consequently, under the access to justice theory, full and frank advice from attorney to client regarding the lawfulness and unlawfulness of proposed or past conduct, the reach and purpose of the law, and liability or punishment under the law would be subject to core speech protection.

The ability to provide such legal advice is guaranteed not only by the speech clause but also by the rights of association and assembly. Recall that in *De Jonge v. Oregon*,[34] the Supreme Court held that "peaceable assembly for lawful discussion cannot be made a crime."[35] Attorneys engage in peaceable assembly for lawful discussion when meeting with clients to provide legal advice – including the meaning, contours, and reach of the law, sanctions for law violation, avenues for legal redress, and the benefits of pursing lawful rather than unlawful behavior.

Nevertheless, there are limits to the appropriate scope of First Amendment protection. Justice Breyer, in dissent in *Humanitarian Law Project*, argued that existing First Amendment doctrine "permit[s] pure advocacy of *even the most unlawful activity* – as long as that advocacy is not 'directed to inciting or producing imminent lawless action and . . . likely to incite or produce such action.'"[36] However, that rule, as initially announced in *Brandenburg v. Ohio*,[37] should *not* be the standard for attorney speech. The access to justice theory provides core speech protection for speech essential to providing access to justice and the fair administration of the laws. It is patently *not* essential to the fair administration of the laws to constitutionalize attorney speech advising their clients to engage in "even the most unlawful activity"[38] – regardless of whether or not it would "incite or produce imminent lawless action."[39]

The dichotomy of alternatives argued in *Humanitarian Law Project* demonstrates, again, the need for a First Amendment theory attuned to the attorney's function in the system of justice and the attorney's tie to government power and processes. The divergence between the majority and the dissent reflect the typical alternative methods for examining restrictions on attorney speech: either no protection for attorney speech or the application of traditional First Amendment doctrine (which is not attuned to the attorney function in the administration of justice). The *Humanitarian Law Project* majority provides attorney speech, including lawful

---

[34] 299 U.S. 353 (1937).
[35] *Id.* at 365.
[36] *Humanitarian Law Project*, 561 U.S. at 51 (Breyer, J., dissenting) (emphasis added).
[37] 395 U.S. 444, 447 (1969).
[38] *Humanitarian Law Project*, 561 U.S. at 51 (Breyer, J., dissenting).
[39] *Brandenburg*, 395 U.S. at 447.

advice, no protection. But the application of *Brandenburg* v. *Ohio*, as indicated by the dissent, to attorney speech would make unconstitutional rules such as Model Rule of Professional Conduct 1.2(d), which forbids an attorney from counseling or assisting a client to engage in criminal or fraudulent activities.[40]

The access to justice theory provides core speech protection for attorney communications to clients regarding the representation of the client and any other legal advice about proposed or past client conduct and the interpretation, application, validity, or reach of law – speech that is essential to the role of the attorney in our justice system.[41] However, it would not provide First Amendment protection for attorney advice intended to further or assist client crimes or fraud. Attorneys are delegates of state power – the state gives them a license that allows them to harness the force of law in protecting their clients' interests. As noted in Chapter 8, it would frustrate the justice system if attorneys could use their knowledge of the law to advise clients to engage in unlawful activity. States do and should be able to prohibit lawyers from advising or assisting clients in criminal or fraudulent conduct.

THE DUTY OF CONFIDENTIALITY

The lawyer's duty of confidentiality is as old as the English ancestor to the American profession of lawyering – going back to the thirteenth century – and is recognized as an essential component of the attorney–client relationship and the role of the lawyer in the justice system.[42] As explained in the Ethical Considerations of the 1969 Model Code of Professional Responsibility, "*Both the fiduciary relationship* existing between lawyer and client and *the proper functioning of the legal system* require the preservation by the lawyer of confidences and secrets of one who has employed or sought to employ him."[43] Why is this so? Because a lawyer, in order to be an effective agent who properly invokes and avoids government power in the protection of his client's life, liberty, and property, must have full access to the facts. People often need lawyers in situations involving embarrassing or detrimental information. If the client hides this information from the attorney – in the fear that the lawyer will reveal it to others and cause the client harm or embarrassment – then the lawyer cannot appropriately handle the client's case.

Every good lawyer knows that it is essential to any representation – be it civil, criminal, or transactional – for the lawyer to gain as full an understanding of the facts as practicable. Lawyers cannot properly perform their role without the facts. Without an accurate picture of the facts, lawyers will not know what legal arguments to make, what claims or defenses to assert, what contract clauses to draft, what course of

---

[40] MODEL RULE OF PROF'L CONDUCT R. 1.2(d).
[41] *See id.*
[42] *See* Andrews, *supra* Note 8, at 1395–1400.
[43] MODEL CODE OF PROF'L RESPONSIBILITY EC 4–1.

action to advise, and so on. The practice of law is, in large part, the application of law to fact – and a misunderstanding of either law or fact critically undermines any representation. Thus, to enable lawyers to fulfill their role in the legal system, lawyers must have the means to know the facts, which happens primarily through two methods: client disclosure of information (both privileged and nonprivileged) and the use of government compulsory processes to discover information.

As to client disclosure, it is imperative that clients feel free to fully discuss and disclose *all* information relating to a representation to their attorney – even (or especially) highly damaging and detrimental information. A client will only provide detrimental information if the client is convinced that the lawyer is completely loyal to the client and will not use the information in any way other than in protecting the client's interests. This is a central rationale underlying the duty of confidentiality.

Nevertheless, attorneys do not receive information solely from their clients through attorney–client communications and disclosures, attorneys are also able to employ state power – compulsory processes – to obtain information. Lawyers are delegates of state power and are enabled through their license to use that power on the client's behalf in the protection of client life, liberty, and property. Thus the state provides to lawyers means by which lawyers are able to obtain information relating to a representation so that attorneys can fulfill their role. Attorneys use discovery devices – such as depositions, document requests, interrogatories, requests for admissions, and medical examinations – and have access to the subpoena power to obtain information from third parties. These processes are backed by court-imposed sanctions for refusing to comply or unreasonable resistance thereto. Many government attorneys, such as prosecutors, have even greater access to information. They are able to harness the police powers of the state to investigate crimes and provide them information.

Having given attorneys the power to access information through compulsory processes, the state can require the attorney not to abuse those processes or the purposes for which lawyers were given that power. This point is different from the argument that having given lawyers power, the state is free to define or revoke that power however it wants. Instead, the state has delegated power to attorneys to perform a specified role in the justice system – to act as an agent of a client in invoking and avoiding government power. In granting attorneys that power and providing attorneys with government compulsory processes to obtain necessary information to fulfill that role, the state can restrict the attorney's use of that information consistent with the attorney's role as advocate for the client.

The Supreme Court recognized this basic concept in its 1984 decision, *Seattle Times Co. v. Rhinehart.*[44] In *Rhinehart*, the Seattle Times had published stories about a religious group, the Aquarian Foundation, that believed in communication with the dead through a medium – Rinehart being their primary medium.

---

[44] 467 U.S. 20 (1984).

The Foundation and Rhinehart responded by filing suit for defamation and invasion of privacy, claiming that the articles published were false and had caused a reduction in both membership and monetary contributions. In discovery, the defendants sought membership records and information relating to the finances of the Foundation in order to dispute the alleged damages. The Foundation resisted discovery, claiming that such information was private and protected by the Foundation members' First Amendment rights. The trial court ordered the Foundation to produce the materials but also entered a protective order that prohibited the defendants "from publishing, disseminating, or using the information in any way except where necessary to prepare for and try the case."[45] The defendants argued that the restriction on dissemination was a classic prior restraint forbidden by the First Amendment and that the information being suppressed was speech of public concern.

The Supreme Court upheld the constitutionality of the protective order. The Court explained that the "critical question" presented in *Rhinehart* is whether a litigant has a First Amendment "right to disseminate information that he has obtained pursuant to a court order that both granted him access to that information and placed restraints on the way in which the information might be used."[46] The Court emphasized that the defendants "gained the information they wish to disseminate *only* by virtue of the trial court's discovery process."[47] Further, the Court noted that the state provides liberal discovery processes "for the *sole purpose* of assisting in the preparation and trial, or the settlement, of litigated disputes."[48] The Court held that Washington could prevent "abuse of its processes," explaining that the protective order was justified by Washington's substantial government interest in "the prevention of the abuse that can attend the coerced production of information under a State's discovery rule."[49] The Court emphasized that the order only prohibited dissemination of "information obtained through use of the discovery process," and that parties could still disseminate "identical information ... gained through means independent of the court's processes."[50]

Rhinehart is not about the First Amendment rights of lawyers at all. The case involved the rights of the *parties* (not the attorneys, specifically) to disseminate information obtained through discovery in contravention of a court protective order prohibiting dissemination. However, *Rhinehart* is about the relationship of the First Amendment to court processes. Relevant to the issue of attorney confidentiality is the *Rhinehart* Court's recognition that the government in creating a process like discovery that allows for compelled disclosure of information – a process essential for

---

[45] *Id.* at 27.
[46] *Id.* at 32.
[47] *Id.* (emphasis added).
[48] *Id.* at 34.
[49] *Id.* at 35–36.
[50] *Id.* at 34.

the proper adjudication of cases – can limit the use of disclosed information to that purpose. A court can prevent "abuse of its processes." The Supreme Court also noted that if courts could not appropriately protect sensitive information obtained in discovery from dissemination "individuals may well forgo pursuit of their just claims," frustrating the right of court access.[51]

Similarly, in the client confidentiality context, the lawyer has received information solely because of his license to practice law. It is because of the lawyer's license from the state and tie to government power that the client has come to the lawyer for help and has provided the lawyer access to the client's information (both privileged and nonprivileged). It is for this purpose – to assist the client in invoking and avoiding government power in protection of the client's rights – that both the client and the state (through compulsory processes) have provided the attorney access to information in a given representation. It would undermine this purpose if the attorney could then use that information in ways that would embarrass or injure the client – either through loss of reputation or otherwise.

Moreover, as the agent of a client-principal, lawyers owe their clients a duty of loyalty and attendant fiduciary obligations to protect the client's interests. The idea that an attorney could disclose detrimental or embarrassing information about a client without client consent (as the *Hunter* Court held) undercuts both core ideals of loyalty and the lawyer's fiduciary duties to protect the client's interests. Clients give attorneys information for a very specific purpose: to protect their legal interests. The information is given to attorneys in trust. Just as a client may give an attorney money or property to hold in trust for the client, so too the information that the client gives to the attorney and provides access to is also to be held in trust by the attorney as the client's fiduciary. Being held in trust, the attorney is *only* to use the information as impliedly authorized to accomplish the client's legal objectives or as otherwise authorized through client consent after consultation. Notably, even the information obtained through compulsory processes is made available only by the client's engagement of the attorney. If the client fires the attorney, the attorney will no longer be able to use those processes to continue to obtain information about that client or representation.

Clients understand the attorney's related duties of loyalty and confidentiality – that the lawyer will not divulge information obtained except as necessary to accomplish the representation and protect the client's interests. They trust that attorneys will not betray them by using the information provided in any way that would harm them or their interests. As Geoffrey Hazard and William Hodes surmise, "It is probably only a slight exaggeration to say that in the public mind, lawyers are

---

[51] *Id.* at 35–36 and n. 22

regarded as people who know how to keep secrets, as much as they are regarded as litigators or advisors or draftsmen of contracts and wills."[52]

Overall, the duty of confidentiality inheres in several key aspects of the lawyer's role and fundamental duties to clients, including the duty of loyalty, the agency relationship and duty to act as the client's fiduciary, the attorney's need to obtain all information relating to a representation in order to effectively secure the client's legal interests, the use of state power in obtaining the information, and the client's expectations in providing information to the attorney for the sole purpose of protecting the client's interest. All of these indicate that the duty of confidentiality is an essential aspect of the attorney–client relationship, and of the role of the lawyer in the justice system in protecting the client's interests.

It would seriously frustrate the attorney–client relationship and the attorney's ability to fulfill their role if the First Amendment protected from regulation attorney revelation of client confidences. Again, under the access to justice theory, restrictions on attorney speech that are essential to the system of justice are not protected by the First Amendment. The duty of confidentiality is a restriction on attorney speech that is central to both the attorney–client relationship (and has been for nearly 800 years) and to our system of justice. Consequently, it is constitutionally permissible for states to restrict and punish attorneys for revealing client confidences without client consent.

There are two potential readings of the Virginia Supreme Court's holding in *Hunter*. Under the broad reading, and as the court actually stated, any information not covered by the attorney–client privilege is protected by the First Amendment, and a lawyer cannot be prohibited or punished for revealing such information without client consent.[53] The broad reading undermines the duty of confidentiality as understood in every state. Lawyers have access to a manifold of information regarding a representation outside of attorney–client privileged information. Such information includes everything obtained through discovery processes and from the client through nonprivileged sources (such as documents or witnesses for the attorney's client). If litigants can be prohibited from disclosing information obtained in discovery under *Rhinehart* in order to protect against abuse of discovery processes, attorneys can be prohibited from revealing such information in order to prevent abuse of both the attorney–client relationship (and trust of the client) and the court's compulsory processes.

Under the narrow reading, Hunter was only protected by the First Amendment because the information he posted had previously been disclosed in court filings or proceedings. Our justice system is one of open courts, and the Virginia Supreme Court cited the Supreme Court's caselaw establishing that what is said in open court

---

[52] 1 GEOFFREY C. HAZARD, JR. AND W. WILLIAM HODES, THE LAW OF LAWYERING §1.7, at 1–14 (3d edn. 2004 and Supp. 2009).

[53] *Hunter v. Virginia State Bar*, 285 Va. 485, 502 (2013).

is public property, which people can freely disseminate. Similarly, in *Rhinehart*, the Supreme Court noted that materials obtained through civil discovery, such as pretrial depositions and interrogatories, are not open to the public and are "not public components of a civil trial."[54] Further, the Court explained that restrictions "on discovered, but *not yet admitted information* are not restrictions on a tradition-ally public source of information."[55] These statements from *Rhinehart*, as well as the Supreme Court's holdings about the public nature of court proceedings, indicate that a party can disseminate information that has been admitted into open court or has been disclosed in publicly available court filings. But that still does not answer the question of whether the narrow reading of *Hunter* is an appropriate interpret-ation of the First Amendment. Is an attorney free to disseminate detrimental infor-mation about the attorney's *own client*, without client permission, that is available in a public source, such as a court filing, but that is not general knowledge?

Renee Newman Knake appears to favor such a proposition, arguing that the narrow reading of the *Hunter* decision is in accord with the Supreme Court's recent emphasis in other nonlawyer contexts on free-flowing access to information.[56] Knake argues that by blogging about his completed cases, Hunter is assisting in the free flow of legal information to the public, including performing the following valuable functions: "advertising and marketing, education about legal entitlements and obligations, news reporting, and criticism of the legal system."[57] Knake asserts that it is precisely because the information may *not* be "known by the public" – even though contained in a public source – that Hunter's speech is valuable, as he providing "legal information … to those who currently lack it."[58]

Despite Knake's arguments, Hunter was not just passing along "legal information … to those who currently lack it." He was exposing embarrassing and detrimental facts about his own former clients to the public. The fact that the information was contained in a public source does not change the fact that Hunter obtained those facts and knew those facts solely because a criminal defendant hired him as a licensed lawyer to undertake the representation. The California State Bar issued an ethics opinion highlighting this important aspect of the lawyer's duty of confidentiality. The California Bar reviewed a case where an attorney disclosed detrimental information about a former client, a hedge fund manager. Some of the information was publicly available, yet the California Bar opined that it was still a violation of the lawyer's duty of confidentiality to disclose information – precisely

---

[54] *Rhinehart*, 467 U.S. at 33.

[55] *Id.*

[56] *See* Renee Newman Knake, *Legal Information, the Consumer Law Market, and the First Amendment*, 82 FORDHAM L. REV. 2843, 2856–61 (2014).

[57] *Id.* at 2858.

[58] *Id.*

because the information had been *"acquired by virtue of the [attorney-client] rela-tionship."*[59] The California Bar correctly understood that information that attorneys receive solely by virtue of their license to practice and that is provided in trust by the client for the purpose of protecting the client's interests can be safeguarded from dissemination by lawyers.

States differ somewhat as to what they consider covered by the duty of confidenti-ality, but several, like the California opinion, have interpreted that duty to forbid attorneys from disclosing information contained in public sources, such as court filings. Courts cite to the duty of loyalty, asserting that revelation by the attorney of detrimental information about a client is a betrayal of trust, even if the information can be found in a public source.[60] Notably, in March 2018, the ABA issued Formal Opinion 480, specifically opining that "information about a client's representation contained in a court's order, for example, although *contained in a public document or record, is not exempt from the lawyer's duty of confidentiality."*[61]

Knake argues, nevertheless, that Hunter improved the free flow of information, arguing that "[r]ather than sitting in some obscure court file, the information is now curated, pieced together with the most relevant and interesting facts, posted in a targeted way for a mass audience."[62] But Knake's point cuts exactly the opposite way under the access to justice theory and demonstrates that the First Amendment emphatically does not protect lawyers from discipline for disseminating information obtained in a representation about their clients – even information that is contained in a public source.

As courts have recognized, there is a significant difference between information that can be "found" in a public source and information that is "generally known" to the populace.[63] The Indiana Supreme Court explained that "the Rules contain no exception allowing revelation of information relating to a representation *even if a diligent researcher could unearth it* through public sources."[64] The truth is that most

---

[59] State Bar of California, Standing Committee on Prof'l Responsibility & Conduct, Formal Op. No. 2016–195, at *4 (emphasis added).

[60] *See, e.g., Iowa Supreme Court Disciplinary Bd.* v. *Marzen,* 779 N.W.2d 757, 766 (2010) (holding that information found in public sources was still covered by duty of confidentiality and explaining, "the sanctity of the lawyer-client relationship is necessary to ensure free and unrestrained communication without fear of betrayal").

[61] AM. BAR ASS'N, STANDING COMM. ON ETHICS AND PROF'L RESPONSIBILITY, Formal Op. 480, at 3 (2018); *see also id.* at 4 (stating that Rule 1.6 "does *not* provide an exception for information that is 'generally known' or contained in a 'public record'"). Unfortunately, the ABA relied on a constitutional conditions theory when addressing whether enforcement of the duty of confi-dentiality violated the First Amendment. *See id.* at 4–5 and n. 18. The access to justice theory results in protection of both the duty of confidentiality as an essential component of the lawyer's role and duties to clients, but does not jettison lawyer First Amendment rights.

[62] Knake, *supra* Note 56, at 2857–58.

[63] *See, e.g.,* State Bar of California, Standing Committee on Prof'l Responsibility & Conduct, Formal Op. No. 2016–195, at *3 n. 4.

[64] *In re Anonymous,* 932 N.E. 2d 671, 674 (Ind. 2010).

legal cases are *not* covered by the media and are *never* generally known to the public. Literally no one other than the attorneys and parties shows up to most court hearings or knows of the information contained in court filings. For someone other than one of the attorneys to find information from court filings may take serious research and effort. On the other hand, the attorney *knows* the information – and knows it solely because he was hired by the client who gave him the information to represent the client's interests. Thus if attorneys are free to publicize any information without client permission that is contained in a court submission, such publications could seriously work to the detriment of the client – as other people are very unlikely to discover the information without the attorney pointing it out.

If Hunter had not disclosed the embarrassing and detrimental information about his criminal defense clients, the information would most likely have remained, as Knake observes, "sitting in some obscure court file." But instead, Hunter took embarrassing information that clients entrusted to him to protect their interests, and "curated" it, "pieced [it] together with the most relevant and interesting facts," and "posted in a targeted way for a mass audience."[65]

Hunter's clients did not come to him – did not disclose to him and authorize him to discover humiliating facts about themselves – so that he could turn it into a juicy story "for a mass audience." Instead they came to him, and they entrusted information to him, so he could serve his role in the system of justice as a criminal defense attorney and discover all the necessary facts to protect their lives, liberty, and property, including their reputations, in the face of the full weight of state criminal power.

While it is imperative that courts remain open – as the openness of courts performs a critical checking function as to the judiciary and the justice system – the fact that people other than the client's attorney can disclose information without the client's consent that is contained in a court filing or stated in open court does not determine whether an *attorney* can disclose that same information without client consent under the access to justice theory. Under the access to justice theory, attorneys' First Amendment rights are attuned to their role in the justice system and must be defined in a manner to allow attorneys to fulfill their essential duties to clients and the justice system.

Again, one of the primary purposes underlying the duty of confidentiality is to encourage full and frank disclosure by the client – not only as to privileged information, but in providing access to nonprivileged information. The concern is that clients will not reveal information to their attorney if the attorney can publicize that information without the client's consent or otherwise use it to the detriment of the client. Just as the Court in *Rhinehart* was concerned people may avoid the judicial system if sensitive information obtained in pretrial discovery cannot be protected from dissemination, thus frustrating court access, allowing attorneys to disclose

---

[65] Knake, *supra* Note 56, at 2857–58.

information without the client's consent frustrates the attorney–client relationship, and ultimately deters clients from full disclosure to attorneys.

Hunter is a case in point. Hunter received information from his clients in trust – to use for the sole purpose of protecting their legal interests, which in criminal cases certainly includes clients' reputational interests. He then used that information in a manner contrary to the purpose for which the clients gave it to him, betraying his clients' trust in giving him the information and ultimately working to the clients' detriment. Such actions undermine the attorney's duty of loyalty and obligation to act as a fiduciary of client information. His role in the system of justice is to protect client life, liberty, and property, not to undermine client reputation – an aspect of liberty. Without the license given to him by the state, he simply would not have ever received the information from his clients or from government processes. Thus, the state is not prohibited by the First Amendment from punishing him for divulging client confidential information on his blog.

10

Invoking Law and Processes to Protect Client Interests

An attorney's primary function is to invoke and avoid government power on behalf of their client in the protection of life, liberty, and property. This is equally true for the transactional attorney as it is for the civil litigator and the criminal lawyer, although the function is performed through somewhat different methods. The attorney performs this core function through (1) invoking the law on behalf of the client; (2) petitioning the courts and other bodies by bringing lawsuits; and (3) presenting the client's legal claims, defenses, and arguments in court and other proceedings. Each of these core functions are protected by the attorney's First Amendment rights to speech, association, and petition – and each requires protection under the access to justice theory.

INVOKING THE LAW

A key element to a proper understanding of the access to justice provided by lawyers through their speech is the lawyer's ability (through legal training and knowledge) to use speech that will invoke the protection or power of the law. As discussed in Chapter 2, clients hire lawyers not so much for their command of language or eloquence but because lawyers know what language to use to properly invoke the law on the client's behalf and thus gain access to or protection from government power.

Consider the example of a client hiring a lawyer to write a will – the client is hiring a lawyer because the lawyer knows what to say to effectively invoke the law and to protect the client's legal interests. The lawyer knows what is required to make the will legally enforceable and devisable according to the client's wishes. Similarly, when a client hires a lawyer to write a contract, it is not because the lawyer is particularly articulate but because the lawyer knows what elements must be included to make the contract legally enforceable and because the lawyer knows what clauses to include to protect the client's interests in the event of a deal gone awry.

What clients want from their lawyers' speech is access to the force of law to protect the client's life, liberty, and property. If a lawyer is competent, then a will or contract or business association will be recognized as valid under law – and its terms can and will be enforced through government power if necessary. Indeed, the full weight of government power can be invoked to protect that legally enforceable interest – wages can be garnished, titles to property can be changed, and people can be restrained, enjoined, held in contempt, and even imprisoned. Similarly, if a corporation is created competently for individuals, the individuals will not be held personally liable for their corporate dealings – they are effectively shielded from government imposition of individual liability. The lawyer is consulted to obtain this legally enforceable shield from liability.

While the litigator provides this service as well, it is the transactional attorney's very function to use speech that will have the force of law and will protect the client's interests. The transactional attorney drafts documents that create business organizations and contractual relationships, invoking the force of law by complying with legal requirements – and thus protecting the client's life, liberty, or property. Examples include multifarious contracts across all areas of commercial activity, estate planning, creating business organizations, issuing securities, and mergers and acquisitions. In each instance lawyers are hired because lawyers have the knowledge and training to make the speech legally enforceable, to understand how the speech is likely to be interpreted by courts, and to protect the client's interests should a dispute arise.

Lawyers thus serve an essential role in our system of justice by providing individuals with the necessary language and process to invoke or avoid government power, including future liability. By forbidding such speech – even though allegedly only a restriction on attorney speech – individuals would in large part be unable to invoke the law to protect their life, liberty, or property.[1] Thus attorney speech that invokes the protections of existing law is essential for access to justice and the fair administration of the laws and deserves core Free Speech Clause protection under the access to justice theory.

Humanitarian Law Project exemplifies this category of speech. The plaintiffs, all of whom were United States citizens or organizations,[2] wanted to assist two FTOs in invoking the law – specifically obtaining recognition under the Geneva Conventions and advising them on how to invoke international human rights law and petition both the United Nations and the United States Congress. The statute prohibits (and is aimed at prohibiting) attorney speech that is politically and legally effective. The Court held that the statute was constitutional and "cover[ed] *only a narrow category* of speech *to, under the direction of, or in coordination with*" FTOs,

---

[1] *See Gideon v. Wainwright*, 372 U.S. 335 (1963).
[2] *See Humanitarian Law Project*, 561 U.S. 1, 10 (2010).

and thus Congress did not "suppress ... 'pure political speech.'"[3] Yet, the statute prohibits them from speaking *as attorneys* to assist others by providing legal advice or access to international human rights law. The plaintiffs cannot "say anything they wish," as the majority claimed,[4] because they are deprived of speaking in the manner and context in which the speech will effectively create desired legal and political results. Speech loses its value if it can be prohibited in the context in which it matters. As noted, the Supreme Court has recognized "the urgency, importance, and effectiveness of speech *"only strengthens the protection* afforded to [the] expression."[5]

The ends of the statute are achieved by prohibiting *attorneys* from providing designated people with access to the power of the law – even international human rights law through international entities such as the United Nations. Notably, the FTOs themselves are not forbidden (and Congress lacks the ability to forbid them) from seeking the protections of international law. Rather, the goal of denying access to the law for these groups – even for peaceful and legitimate purposes – is accomplished by restricting speech of United States citizen attorneys. The threatened punishment (15 years' imprisonment) for the attorney is severe enough that the scheme works.

Invoking law on behalf of clients is one of the primary methods through which attorneys protect their clients' rights to life, liberty, and property. It is very problematic if regulators can keep a group of people from invoking law, not by changing the substantive law but by forbidding lawyers from speaking to or on behalf of certain clients, and thus foreclosing access to law by specified groups.

COURT ACCESS AND PETITIONING FOR REDRESS

In the very context of professional discipline of lawyers, the Supreme Court recognized in *Button*: "[A]bstract discussion is *not* the only species of communication which the Constitution protects"; rather, the First Amendment also protects *"vigorous advocacy*, certainly of lawful ends, against governmental intrusion" – and specifically the amendment protects *"litigation ... [as] a form of political expression."*[6] Thus, in *Button*, the Supreme Court held that Virginia could not redefine its professional responsibility regulations in such a way as to prohibit the NAACP's solicitation and instigation of desegregation lawsuits. In so holding, the Court relied on the bundle of cognate First Amendment rights of "speech, petition, [and] assembly" at stake in the case – First Amendment rights of both the attorneys and their clients "to petition for the redress of grievances" as well as the regulated

---

[3] *Id.* at 25–26 (emphasis added).
[4] *Id.*
[5] *McIntyre v. Ohio Elections Comm'n*, 514 U.S. 334, 347 (1995) (emphasis added).
[6] *NAACP v. Button*, 371 U.S. 415, 429 (1963) (emphasis added).

attorneys' rights to engage in "political expression and association."[7] In recognizing that the Petition Clause protected the NAACP attorneys from regulation or discipline by the Virginia Bar for instituting litigation, the *Button* Court cited to the *Noerr* case, one of the cornerstone decisions giving rise to the *Noerr-Pennington* doctrine.[8]

As noted in Chapter 6, according to the *Noerr-Pennington* doctrine, under the Petition Clause of the First Amendment, a litigant cannot be sanctioned or punished for bringing a nonbaseless claim in court – unless the lawsuit is a mere "sham."[9] Furthermore, an improper motive will not divest a nonbaseless claim of Petition Clause protection. Thus, the Petition Clause of the First Amendment protects attorneys from punishment or discipline for filing a lawsuit unless the lawsuit is "objectively baseless."[10]

Moreover, the lawyer's ability to file lawsuits is not only essential to protecting client's legal rights and interests, such as the interests of African American parents in *Button* in obtaining desegregation, but is also essential to enabling the judicial power itself. The judiciary has no power to act unless there is a case or controversy filed before it.[11] To the extent to which lawyers can be prohibited from bringing colorable claims to the judiciary, the power of the judiciary to adjudicate such claims is lost. Thus, the Petition Clause right of lawyers to bring lawsuits is an essential component of our justice system – both in invoking and avoiding government power to protect life, liberty, and property, and in preserving the proper functioning of the judicial process.

Notably, even if the Petition right were considered the client's, the attorney would have a concomitant right to invoke the client's right because a litigant's right to petition through litigation is effectively meaningless if it does not protect petitioning through counsel.[12] Attorneys are essential to providing clients with effective access to the judiciary and to petition the judiciary for relief – for "[t]he right to be heard would be, in many cases, of little avail if it did not comprehend the right to be heard by counsel."[13]

Because the Petition Clause protects the attorney's petitioning of the judiciary as a government entity, it applies not only to the filing of lawsuits but also to the filing of appeals (as long as not objectively baseless). The Second Circuit has also expressly

---

[7] The *Button* Court emphasized that the racial setting of the lawsuit was "irrelevant to the ground of our decision" and that the First Amendment protections recognized by the Court would apply equally in other circumstances. *See id.* at 444.

[8] *See id.* at 430–31; *see also Eastern R. Presidents Conference* v. *Noerr Motor Freight, Inc.*, 365 U.S. 127, 138 (1961); *United Mine Workers* v. *Pennington*, 381 U.S. 657 (1965).

[9] *Prof'l Real Estate Investors, Inc.* v. *Columbia Pictures Indus., Inc.*, 508 U.S. 49, 62 (1993).

[10] *Id.* at 60.

[11] U.S. Const. art. III § 2.

[12] *See, e.g., Freeman* v. *Lasky, Haas, and Cohler*, 410 F.3d 1180, 1186 (9th Cir. 2005) ("*Noerr-Pennington* immunity *is not limited to [protecting] lawyers*: The First Amendment petition right *belongs to the defendants* in the original case, *through their* employees, *law firms and lawyers*, as their agents in that litigation, get to benefit as well." [emphasis added]).

[13] *Powell* v. *Alabama*, 287 U.S. 45, 68–69 (1932).

noted that the Petition Clause and *Noerr-Pennington* doctrine protect certain activities incident to filing lawsuits, including writing and sending demand letters and settlement offers.[14]

Further, the lawyer's petitioning right is essential to protect clients' rights to court access. Although the Supreme Court has been unclear regarding the precise source for the right to court access,[15] the Court has recognized a constitutional right to access the courts arising from the Due Process Clauses for criminal defendants,[16] civil rights litigants,[17] and people denied fundamental rights over which the state courts have a monopoly.[18] Moreover, the Due Process Clauses prohibit the state and federal governments from depriving individuals of life, liberty, or property without due process of law. The Due Process Clauses thus require "a meaningful opportunity to be heard."[19] These rights to due process and court access belong to the client, but if the attorney can be punished or prohibited from bringing claims, the underlying rights of clients to court access are all but lost.

As noted in Chapter 8, attorneys have an enforced monopoly on effective access to the judiciary – nonlawyers are prohibited from representing other people in court. Although individuals can proceed pro se, such judicial access is often ineffective,[20] and organizations generally are prohibited from proceeding pro se in judicial proceedings.[21] Attorneys provide *effective* access to the court system, and to the extent that individuals have a right to raise a claim or defense in court proceedings, attorneys should have corresponding speech, association, and petition rights to effectuate the client's court access and due process rights.

Petitioning is also essential for serving the central First Amendment value of checking power – both governmental power and other forms of economic and

---

[14] *See, e.g., Primetime 24 Joint Venture v. Nat'l Broadcasting Co., Inc.*, 219 F.3d 92, 100 (2d Cir. 2000) ("Courts have extended *Noerr-Pennington* to encompass concerted efforts incident to litigation, such as prelitigation 'threat letters' ... and settlement offers."); *Matsushita Electronic Corp. v. Loral Corp.*, 974 F. Supp. 345, 359 (S.D.N.Y. 1997) (holding that Petition Clause "protects those acts reasonably and normally attendant upon effective litigation," including demand letters even though no lawsuit was ever filed because the underlying threatened lawsuit "itself was not sham litigation").

[15] *See Christopher v. Harbury*, 536 U.S. 403, 415, n. 12 (2002) ("Decisions of this Court have grounded the right of access to courts in the Article IV Privileges and Immunities Clause, the First Amendment Petition Clause, the Fifth Amendment Due Process Clause, and the Fourteenth Amendment Equal Protection and Due Process Clauses." (Citations omitted)).

[16] *See, e.g., Bounds v. Smith*, 430 U.S. 817, 821 (1977) ("It is now established beyond doubt that prisoners have a constitutional right of access to the courts.").

[17] *See, e.g., NAACP v. Button*, 371 U.S. 415 (1963).

[18] *See, e.g., M.L.B. v. S.L.J.*, 519 U.S. 102, 116–19 (1996); *Boddie v. Connecticut*, 401 U.S. 371, 380–81 (1971).

[19] *See Boddie*, 401 U.S. at 377; *see also Matthews v. Eldridge*, 424 U.S. 319, 335 (1976) (creating three-factored balancing test to determine what process is due and whether there has been a meaningful opportunity to be heard).

[20] *Powell v. Alabama*, 287 U.S. 45, 68–69 (1932).

[21] *See, e.g., D-Bean Ltd. Partnership v. Roller Derby Skates Inc.*, 366 F.3d 972 (9th Cir. 2004).

social power. By bringing lawsuits against government officers and agencies on behalf of clients, attorneys directly check the abuse of government power. For example, whenever a controversial law, executive order, or agency regulation is issued, lawyers inevitably test the constitutionality of that law in the courts – bringing cases on behalf of those negatively affected by the new law or policy. In so doing, lawyers actually enable the judicial power to consider and address the constitutionality of such laws. Without lawyers bringing such cases, the judiciary would be powerless to protect those harmed by unconstitutional and abusive actions of those in power. In a related vein, lawyers have brought lawsuits against economically powerful corporations and individuals who use that power to abuse and harm the weak. The lawyer's right to petition on behalf of clients is central to the checking value of the First Amendment as propounded by Vincent Blasi.

Indeed, the bringing of lawsuits or other adjudicative proceedings on behalf of clients implicates all three of the cognate rights of speech, association, and petition – these three rights work together to protect access to judicial and adjudicative processes. *Button* amply illustrates the point. The NAACP lawyers were themselves devoted to a cause, but in order to pursue their own political goals and devotion to improving equality in our country, they had to bring lawsuits. The Supreme Court had spoken in *Brown v. Board of Education*,[22] but the Southern states were not voluntarily complying. In order to secure desegregation, these lawyers – committed to bring about political change in the United States – had to litigate from school district to school district to effectuate desegregation. Nevertheless, the NAACP lawyers simply could not engage in this political speech and petitioning without clients. They could not litigate without clients, and clients couldn't effectuate desegregation without lawyers. The Virginia statute prohibited lawyers from soliciting clients, from advising those clients, and from offering to represent them in litigation (even for no cost) – thus attacking the lawyers' rights to association, speech, and petitioning. The Supreme Court recognized that the lawyers had all three First Amendment rights, which were essential to bring these lawsuits – and that by protecting association with clients, speech, and petitioning, the First Amendment protected *"litigation, ... [as] a form of political expression."*[23]

Under the access to justice theory – as an essential component of the attorney's role – attorney speech, association, and petitioning are all protected by the First Amendment and build on each other to protect the bringing of lawsuits or invocation of other governmental processes in the protection of client life, liberty, and property.

---

[22] 347 U.S. 483 (1954).
[23] *NAACP v. Button*, 371 U.S. 415, 429 (1963).

RIGHT TO ASSERT CLIENT RIGHTS IN COURT PROCEEDINGS AND
OTHER GOVERNMENTAL PROCESSES

Importantly, once a lawsuit is instituted, attorneys, like litigants, "do not surrender their First Amendment rights at the courthouse door."[24] Nevertheless, understanding the appropriate speech protection in court proceedings can be difficult. Speech made in conjunction with formal court proceedings (including administrative and traditional court processes) is perhaps among the most highly regulated speech. Between the applicable rules of evidence, procedure, and professional conduct, attorneys work in an environment where their speech is subject to multiple levels of highly restrictive regulation.

Frederick Schauer describes attorney speech in court proceedings as containing an "omnipresence of speech regulation."[25] Moreover, and rightly so, Schauer contends that "the speech of the law – in court and out – owes its effectiveness and its very possibility to rules that restrict and prohibit certain forms of speaking and writing."[26] Schauer argues that "something like a courtroom trial" is both "rule-dependen[t] and enforcement-dependen[t]."[27] A trial (or really any courtroom proceeding) simply cannot proceed without "elaborate rules about who goes when, about who speaks, and about who does not speak," "rules about how to speak," and "rules about what not to say."[28] Schauer argues that "the First Amendment has, [] *properly never been thought to apply*" to "a vast array of lawyer and legal system activity" and thus the "omnipresence of speech regulation" is (and should remain) "unencumbered by either the doctrine or the discourse of the First Amendment."[29] Inherent in Schauer's conclusion is an assumption that (outside of "extrajudicial utterances") the application of the First Amendment to attorney speech would necessarily interfere with the role of attorneys and legal processes.[30] The Supreme Court has seemed to agree with Schauer's conclusion by stating in dicta in *Gentile* v. *State Bar of Nevada*: "It is unquestionable that in the courtroom itself, during a judicial proceeding, whatever right to 'free speech' an attorney has is extremely circumscribed."[31] The statement is dicta because *Gentile* dealt with pretrial publicity to the press – no statements made in the courtroom were ever at issue in the case. But in so stating, the Court leaned toward approving a categorical approach where

[24] *Seattle Times* v. *Rhinehart*, 467 U.S. 20, 32 n. 18 (1984).
[25] Frederick Schauer, *The Speech of Law and the Law of Speech*, 49 ARK. L. REV. 687, 691 (1997).
[26] *Id.* at 688.
[27] *Id.* at 689.
[28] *Id.*
[29] *Id.* at 702 and 691 (emphasis added). Notably, Schauer argues that the First Amendment may apply to attorney speech when "the justifications for the First Amendment's existence, in particular the distrust of the self-protective activities of government itself, apply to that activity." *See id.* at 702.
[30] *See id.* at 695.
[31] *Gentile* v. *State Bar of Nev.*, 501 U.S. 1030, 1071 (1991) (citations omitted).

attorneys do not have First Amendment rights as attorneys, or at least, as attorneys litigating in court proceedings.

Nevertheless, after *Gentile*, the Supreme Court, in its 2001 case *Legal Services Corporation v. Velazquez*,[32] recognized a free speech right belonging to attorneys to express and raise arguments in court proceedings and filings. *Velazquez* involved restrictions placed on attorneys who accepted funds from the congressionally created Legal Services Corporation (the "LSC"). At issue were congressionally imposed restrictions on recipients of LSC funds, specifically prohibiting attorneys from providing any representation that "involves an effort to amend or otherwise challenge existing welfare laws," including challenges as to their validity or constitutionality.[33] The Supreme Court struck down the regulations as violative of the First Amendment, explaining that the restrictions were "inconsistent with the proposition that attorneys *should present all the reasonable and well-grounded arguments necessary for proper resolution of the case*."[34] The Court further explained that by "[r]estricting LSC attorneys in advising their clients and in presenting arguments and analyses to the courts," the regulation "distorts the legal system by altering the traditional role of the attorneys."[35] As with the access to justice theory, the *Velazquez* Court recognized that the First Amendment rights of lawyers must be defined in a way that would not "alter" the role of the lawyer in the system of justice and thus "distort the legal system."

Further, the *Velazquez* Court recognized that by prohibiting lawyer speech and the ability of attorneys to raise certain arguments, the regulation also distorted the judicial power itself. The Court explained: "By seeking to *prohibit the analysis of certain legal issues* and *to truncate presentation to the courts*, the enactment under review *prohibits speech and expression upon which the courts must depend* for *the proper exercise of the judicial power*."[36] If lawyers cannot raise certain arguments to the judiciary, then the judiciary cannot hear or adjudicate those claims. Thus it is essential that lawyers be protected in raising colorable claims and making nonfrivolous arguments in court proceedings; because if they are not, then the judicial power itself can be undermined.

Further, the regulator seeking to "truncate presentation to the courts" of certain arguments was also the entity whose laws lawyers were forbidden from challenging. The *Velazquez* Court explained that Congress had designed the restriction "to *insulate* current welfare laws *from constitutional and certain other legal challenges*," which the Court held "implicat[ed] central First Amendment concerns."[37] The Court reasoned that Congress *could not* "impose rules and conditions which in

---

[32]   531 U.S. 533 (2001).
[33]   *Id.* at 537.
[34]   *Id.* at 545 (emphasis added).
[35]   *Id.* at 544.
[36]   *Id.* at 545 (emphasis added).
[37]   *Id.* at 545–47 (emphasis added).

effect *insulate its own laws from legitimate judicial challenge,*" nor could it "*exclude from litigation those arguments and theories Congress finds unacceptable* but which by their nature are within the province of the courts to consider."[38] The Supreme Court concluded: "The Constitution does not permit the Government to confine litigants and their attorneys in this manner."[39]

Notably, the gist of the *Velazquez* Court's concern has underpinnings in traditional First Amendment theory and doctrine. Recall that Alexander Meiklejohn used the town meeting as his quintessential example of the "paradox" of political speech and self-government. Meiklejohn contended that political speech was absolutely protected under the First Amendment, yet in a town meeting speech had to be abridged in order to "get business done."[40] These limitations included having a chair who moderated the meeting and limiting speakers to a share of the available time. Meiklejohn argued that these rules of the game are essential to the success of governmental processes.

But Meiklejohn does not conclude, as does Schauer, that therefore the First Amendment's protections are inapplicable in town meetings. To the contrary, Meiklejohn contends that as to such speech, the First Amendment's prohibition on abridgement is *absolute*. Meiklejohn explains his "paradox" thus: "These speech-abridging activities of the town meeting indicate what the First Amendment to the Constitution does not forbid. When self-governing men demand freedom of speech they are not saying that every individual has an unalienable right to speak whenever, wherever, however he chooses."[41] Rather, in the town meeting, the First Amendment allows citizens, as "free and equal men" and women, to "cooperat[e] in a common enterprise, and us[e] for that enterprise responsible and regulated discussion. It is not a dialectical free-for-all. It is self-government."[42] In this system, citizens "meet as political equals" and every person has "a right and a duty" to speak how they think and "to listen to the arguments of others." Meiklejohn states: "*The basic principle is that the freedom of speech shall be unabridged.* And yet the meeting cannot even be opened unless, by common consent, speech is abridged."[43]

In like manner, the court systems are created as part of our constitutional government and all individuals are free to access the courts and seek legal redress (assuming they have suffered an injury and have a legally cognizable right). Litigants "meet as political equals" and are able to raise their own arguments and respond to the arguments of others. But this free speech is only possible because of the agreement to abridge speech so that court business can get done.

[38] *Id.* at 548, 547 (emphasis added).
[39] *Id.* at 548.
[40] Alexander Meiklejohn, Free Speech and Its Relation to Self-Government 23 (1948).
[41] *Id.* at 23–24.
[42] *Id.* at 23.
[43] *Id.* at 22 (emphasis added).

Meiklejohn, of course does not end there. Having illustrated permissible speech regulation of political speech, he then examines the impermissible restriction. "[T]he vital point" according to Meiklejohn is that no idea is "denied a hearing because it is on one side of the issue rather than another."[44] Consequently, while citizens may be prohibited from speaking out of turn and in violation of the rules, "they may not be barred because their views are thought to be false or dangerous."[45] Thus "unwise ideas must have a hearing as well as wise ones, unfair as well as fair, dangerous as well as safe, un-American as well as American."[46] Meiklejohn contends that "[t]hese conflicting views may be expressed, *must be expressed*, not because they are valid, but *because they are relevant*."[47]

Thus, while the First Amendment does not safeguard "unregulated talkativeness" in political processes like the town meeting or the courtroom, that does not mean that the First Amendment plays no role in those settings. To the contrary, such settings are where the First Amendment plays its most central role. What Meiklejohn argues the First Amendment prohibits in these structured political processes is the mutilation and manipulation of self-government and of our democratic processes: "It is that mutilation of the thinking process of the community against which the First Amendment to the Constitution is directed."[48] Thus each side (and multiple sides and views) of an issue must be heard.

In the context of courtroom speech, what is vital, as Meiklejohn stated, "is that no suggestion of policy shall be denied a hearing because it is on one side of the issue rather than another"[49] and that "conflicting views ... [are] *expressed ... because they are relevant*."[50] This idea comports with the standard First Amendment prohibition on viewpoint discrimination. If one view can be stated, then so can a differing viewpoint. And the prohibition on viewpoint discrimination is particularly compelling – and, in fact, essential – to the integrity of the adversary system. The underlying premise of the adversary proceeding is that truth is more likely to be found if multiple points of view are heard. As the Fourth Circuit explained:

> Our adversary system for the resolution of disputes rests on the unshakable foundation that truth is the object of the system's process which is designed for the purpose of dispensing justice. However, because *no one has an exclusive insight into truth*, the process *depends on the adversarial presentation of evidence, precedent and custom*, and argument to reasoned conclusions – all directed with unwavering effort to what, in good faith, is believed to be true on matters material to the disposition.[51]

---

44 *Id.* at 26.
45 *Id.*
46 *Id.*
47 *Id.* at 27 (emphasis added).
48 *Id.* at 26; *see also id.* at 8 ("But the manipulation of men is the destruction of self-government").
49 *Id.* at 100.
50 *Id.* at 27 (emphasis added).
51 *United States v. Shaffer Equipment Co.*, 11 F.3d 450 (4th Cir. 1993) (emphasis added).

Thus forbidding particular viewpoints and arguments is especially problematic in the adversary system because it undermines the entire theoretical basis for which we have an adversary system. It assumes that the regulator in forbidding a lawyer from making certain arguments in fact has "an exclusive insight into truth." But as recognized in other First Amendment contexts, "silence coerced by law is the argument of force in its worst form"[52] – as it is only happenstance that force will be placed on the right, just, or true side.[53] Further, arguments should not be forbidden because the argument or idea is considered "dangerous." Instead, in our governmental processes, we rely on deliberation rather than force, which requires a presentation of all available views of those represented in the proceeding. If the arguments that a lawyer is allowed to make are distorted in the adversary system, then the outcome of adjudication is also distorted, as is, ultimately, justice itself.

The *Velazquez* Court's holding is precisely consonant with Meiklejohn's arguments and the access to justice theory regarding lawyer speech in court proceedings. Essentially, the Court recognized two categories of attorney in-court speech (including written and oral communications to a court) that must be protected: (1) attorneys must be free to "present all the reasonable and well-grounded arguments necessary for proper resolution of the case"[54]; and (2) regulators cannot restrict attorney speech in order to "insulate the Government's laws" or government action "from judicial inquiry" and scrutiny.[55]

As with Meiklejohn's arguments regarding self-government, what regulators must be forbidden from doing in restricting attorney in-court speech (both written and oral) is manipulating the judicial system by manipulating the substantive arguments that may be presented. To the extent that such manipulation is allowed, justice itself is manipulated and access to justice is thwarted for those on the losing side of the regulation. A potent example of this manipulation of judicial processes by forbidding the presentation of one side of an issue is found in the punishment of attorney speech critical of the judiciary, as discussed in the next chapter.

---

[52] *Whitney v. California*, 274 U.S. 357, 375–76 (1927) (Brandeis, J., concurring).
[53] ZECHARIAH CHAFEE, FREEDOM OF SPEECH, 34–35 (1920).
[54] *See Legal Services Corp. v. Velazquez*, 531 U.S. 533, 545 (2001).
[55] *See id.* at 546.

11

Safeguarding and Impugning Judicial Integrity

Jacob A. Atanga was an African American criminal defense lawyer practicing in Indiana in 1994 when he was suspended from the practice of law for making the following statement about Judge Donald C. Johnson, which was published in an ACLU newsletter: "I think he is ignorant, insecure, and a racist."[1] Although Atanga's choice of language at first glance seems extreme, Atanga had reason to complain about Judge Johnson. Atanga was handling a criminal matter in a case before Johnson, when Johnson rescheduled a hearing in the case for a day that Johnson knew Atanga could not attend – because Atanga had informed Johnson that he would be appearing in court in another county at that same time.[2] Judge Johnson held Atanga in contempt for missing the hearing, had Atanga arrested at his office and jailed, had Atanga brought before the court, and forced him to represent his client while Atanga was dressed in prison clothes.[3] Atanga was interviewed by an editor of an ACLU newsletter about the episode, which is when Atanga said that he thought Johnson was "ignorant, insecure, and a racist."[4]

The Indiana Supreme Court suspended Atanga from the practice of law for thirty days for making the statement about Johnson, which allegedly violated Indiana's Rule of Professional Conduct 8.2.[5] The Indiana bar never proved Atanga's statement to the press was false (that Johnson was *not* ignorant, insecure, and a racist) and indeed excluded as irrelevant Atanga's proffered testimony from witnesses in support of his statement (he apparently found people who were willing to testify that his

---

[1] *In re Atanga*, 636 N.E.2d 1253, 1256 (Ind. 1994). Some material contained in this chapter was previously published in Margaret Tarkington, *The Truth Be Damned: The First Amendment, Attorney Speech, and Judicial Reputation*, 97 Geo. L. J. 1567 (2009), and Margaret Tarkington, *A Free Speech Right to Impugn Judicial Integrity in Court Proceedings*, 51 B.C. L. Rev. 363 (2010).

[2] *Atanga*, 636 N.E.2d 1253, 1255 (Ind. 1994).

[3] *Id.* at 1255–56.

[4] *Id.* at 1256.

[5] *Id.* at 1257.

characterization of Johnson was accurate).[6] In suspending Atanga, the Indiana Supreme Court downplayed the horrendous conduct of Judge Johnson – characterizing it as "not represent[ing] contemporary jurisprudence in this state" and as being a "questionable practice"[7] – yet cracked down on Atanga. The Court explained that "the judicial institution is greatly impaired if attorneys choose to assault the integrity of the process and the individuals who are called upon to make decisions" and thus, "[t]his *court must preserve the integrity of the process* and impose discipline."[8] The Indiana Supreme Court apparently believed that punishing speech about Judge Johnson and Atanga's opinion of him for what was clearly outrageous judicial conduct is the best way to "preserve the integrity of the process."[9]

As discussed in Chapter 4, the Indiana Supreme Court's approach represents the strong majority view among state and federal courts – that it is necessary to punish and chill attorney criticism of judges as essential to preserve "the integrity" of the judiciary, which I call in Chapter 4 the Tinkerbell solution to judicial integrity.[10] The Tinkerbell solution asserts that the judiciary is only able to keep its power if public confidence in the judiciary is kept alive (just as Tinkerbell was kept alive by the audience clapping to demonstrate belief in fairies), and public confidence is undermined if attorneys disparage the judiciary. Thus, in order to instill public confidence – to save public faith and belief in the judiciary – attorneys are required to clap. Indeed, the Indiana Supreme Court had earlier asserted – in oft-quoted language – that attorneys who disparage the judiciary commit a "wrong ... against society as a whole, the preservation of a fair, impartial judicial system, and the system of justice as it has evolved for generations."[11]

Indiana is far from being an outlier. The Kentucky Supreme Court has stated in similarly momentous terms: "Every lawyer, worthy of respect, realizes that *public confidence in our courts is the cornerstone of our governmental structure*."[12] That

---

[6] *See id.*

[7] *Id.* at 1257.

[8] *Id.* at 1258 (emphasis added). Notably, the hearing officer had recommended to the Indiana Supreme Court that Atanga receive no discipline because he "ha[d] already been adequately punished." *See id.* But the Supreme Court determined that it "must preserve the integrity of the process and impose discipline," and thus suspended him from the practice of law. *Id.*

[9] The Indiana Supreme Court publicly reprimanded Judge Johnson for the episode in a matter-of-fact decision that simply stated agreed-upon facts and concluded that those facts constituted violations of various codes of judicial conduct. *See In re Johnson*, 658 N.E.2d 589 (Ind. 1995). Entirely missing from the opinion is any of the rhetoric of the kind used about Atanga's conduct, for example that Atanga "greatly impaired" the "judicial institution."

[10] As noted in Chapter 4, the analogy to Tinkerbell originated with New York attorney Frederick Oberlander. *See supra* Chapter 4, Note 20.

[11] *In re Terry*, 394 N.E.2d 94, 95 (Ind. 1979); *Lawyer Disciplinary Bd. v. Hall*, 234 W. Va. 298, 308 (2014) (same, quoting *Terry*); *In re Cobb*, 445 Mass. 452, 470–71 (2005) (same, quoting *Terry*); *In re Graham*, 453 N.W.2d 313, 322 (Minn. 1990) (same, quoting *Terry*); *In re Holtzman*, 78 N.Y.2d 184, 192 (1991) (same, quoting *Terry*); *Bd. of Prof'l Responsibility, Wyo. State Bar v. Davidson*, 205 P.3d 1008, 1015–16 (Wyo. 2009) (same, quoting *Terry*).

[12] *Ky. Bar Ass'n v. Heleringer*, 602 S.W. 2d 165, 168 (Ky. 1980).

"cornerstone" of "public confidence in our courts" is assertedly crippled by lawyer free speech regarding the judiciary. The Supreme Court of Delaware expounded: "Adherence to the rule of law keeps America free. Public respect for the rule of law requires the public trust and confidence that our legal system is administered fairly . . ."[13] An attorney's statement to the press regarding a court's decision to hold a politically sensitive hearing ex parte was characterized as "chip[ping] away at the public confidence in the integrity of the judicial system" and bringing "the judicial system into discredit in the public mind."[14] As noted by the Supreme Court of Missouri, "[m]any courts disregard a claim of [F]irst [A]mendment protection in disciplinary proceedings, holding that free speech does not give a lawyer the right openly to denigrate the court in the eyes of the public."[15] Not to be outdone rhetorically, the Supreme Court of Florida has reaffirmed, post-*New York Times v. Sullivan*, its "belief in the essentiality of the chastity of the goddess of justice," which "demands condemnation and the application of appropriate penalties" for attorney speech that brings the judiciary into disrepute.[16]

The speech being sanctioned runs the gamut of criticism and derogation. In some cases, the statements have been as mild as accusing the judiciary of being result-oriented or politically motivated.[17] At the other end of the spectrum are accusations of widespread judicial corruption and conspiracy.[18] Rarely do attorneys resort to crude language or expletives.[19] Rather, the best descriptor for the typical verbal excess by attorneys in these cases is rhetorical hyperbole.

The punishment imposed for impugning judicial reputation has often been severe, with suspension from the practice of law not uncommon[20] and, in at least

---

[13] *In re Abbott*, 925 A.2d 482, 488 (Del. 2007); *see also In re Shimek*, 284 So.2d 686, 688 (Fla. 1973) (stating, post-*Sullivan*, that "[n]othing is more sacred to man, and particularly to a member of the judiciary than his integrity" and "[o]nce the integrity of a judge is in doubt the efficacy of his decisions are [sic] likely to be questioned").

[14] *Heleringer*, 602 S.W. 2d at 168. Notably, the attorney's comment that the ex parte hearing was "highly unethical and grossly unfair" was, at most, an overstatement. Further, the attorney was not engaged in the underlying case, but worked for Right to Life and was politically interested in the outcome.

[15] *In re Westfall*, 808 S.W.2d 829, 833–34 (Mo. 1991) (citation omitted).

[16] *Shimek*, 284 So. 2d at 690.

[17] *Idaho State Bar v. Topp*, 129 Idaho 414, 416 (1996); *see also In re Reed*, 716 N.E.2d 426 (Ind. 1999); *Ky. Bar Ass'n v. Heleringer*, 602 S.W.2d 165 (Ky. 1980); *In re Westfall*, 808 S.W.2d 829 (Mo. 1991); *In re Raggio*, 87 Nev. 369 (1971).

[18] In *Committee on Legal Ethics of the W. Va. State Bar v. Farber*, 408 S.E.2d 274 (W. Va. 1991), the attorney accused a judge of being part of a secret Masonic plot to cover up the arson of a local establishment.

[19] *But see Grievance Administrator v. Fieger*, 719 N.W.2d 123 (Mich. 2006) (making crude remarks on radio show about judges after verdict for client was reversed on appeal).

[20] *See, e.g., In re Mire*, 197 So. 3d 656 (La. 2016) (one year and a day suspension); *Stilley v. Sup. Ct. Comm. on Prof'l Conduct*, 370 Ark. 294 (2007) (six month suspension); *In re Pyle*, 283 Kan. 807, 156 P.3d 1231 (2007) (3 month suspension); *In re Ogden*, 10 N.E.3d 499, 502 (2014) (30 day suspension); *U.S. Dist. Ct. for E.D. of Wash. v. Sandlin*, 12 F.3d 861 (9th Cir. 1993) (six month suspension).

one state, mandatory.[21] Moreover, courts have sanctioned attorneys regardless of the forum where the speech has occurred. Attorneys are punished for allegations in briefs and filings with courts,[22] statements to the press,[23] letters to the judiciary,[24] communications with an authority to complain about a judge,[25] pamphlets or campaign literature,[26] blogs,[27] emails to case participants,[28] and even correspondence with friends, family, and clients.[29] Attorneys have been punished when the statements made could not have affected a pending proceeding[30] and when the

---

[21] *See Office of Disciplinary Counsel v. Gardner*, 793 N.E.2d 425, 433 (Ohio 2003) ("Unfounded attacks against the integrity of the judiciary require an actual suspension from the practice of law.").

[22] *In re Wilkins*, 777 N.E.2d 714 (Ind. 2002); *Peters v. Pine Meadow Ranch Home Ass'n*, 151 P.3d 962 (Utah 2007); *In re Abbott*, 925 A.2d 482 (Del. 2007); *Office of Disciplinary Counsel v. Gardner*, 99 Ohio St.3d 416, 793 N.E.2d 425 (2003).

   Attorneys have been punished for statements about the judiciary in briefs to the court even when the suit is filed against judges, and the question at issue is whether an exception to judicial immunity exists. *See Ramirez v. State Bar of Cal.*, 28 Cal.3d 402 (1980).

[23] *Westfall*, 808 S.W.2d 829; *Raggio*, 87 Nev. 369; *Heleringer*, 602 S.W.2d 165; *Topp*, 129 Idaho 414; *In re Atanga*, 636 N.E.2d 1253 (Ind. 1994); *Kentucky Bar Ass'n v. Nall*, 599 S.W.2d 899 (Ky. 1980); *In re Holtzman*, 78 N.Y.2d 184 (1991); *Fieger*, 719 N.W.2d 123; *Ramsey v. Board of Professional Responsibility of the Supreme Court of Tennessee*, 771 S.W.2d 116 (Tenn. 1989).

[24] *In re Arnold*, 274 Kan. 761 (2002) (letter sent to judge by attorney who had been disqualified); *In re Guy*, 756 A.2d 875 (Del. 2000) (letter sent to judge); *Fla. Bar v. Ray*, 797 So.2d 556 (Fla. 2001) (three letters sent to Chief Immigration Judge complaining about another immigration judge); In re *Evans*, 801 F.2d 703 (4th Cir. 1986); (letter sent to magistrate after case was on appeal).

[25] *Ray*, 797 So.2d at 560 and n. 2 (letter sent to Chief Immigration Judge, complaining about another immigration judge, a method which had been local practice for "seek[ing] redress when an attorney is having difficulties with an immigration judge"); *U.S. Dist. Ct. for E.D. of Wash. v. Sandlin*, 12 F.3d 861 (9th Cir. 1993) (statements made to FBI and appropriate authorities at United States Attorney's office regarding judge's editing of transcripts); *In re Graham*, 453 N.W.2d 313, 315 (Minn. 1990) (statements in letter to the U.S. Attorney, in a judicial misconduct complaint, and in an affidavit in support of a motion to recuse, although court indicates that also released to public).

[26] *See, e.g., In re Charges of Unprofessional Conduct involving File No. 17139*, 720 N.W.2d 807 (Minn. 2006) (statements made in campaign literature by judicial candidate about incumbent judge); *In re Glenn*, 256 Iowa 1233 (1964) (leaflet circulated in community).

[27] *Florida Bar v. Conway*, 996 So. 2d 213 (2008) (blogged that judge was an "Evil Unfair Witch"); *see* John Schwartz, *A Legal Battle: Online Attitude vs. Rules of the Bar*, N.Y. TIMES, Sep. 12, 2009.

[28] *In re Ogden*, 10 N.E.3d 499, 502 (Ind. 2014) (email sent to opposing counsel and case participants explaining why attorney had sought a change of judge).

[29] *In re Pyle*, 283 Kan. 807, 808–10 (2007) (letter sent to family, friends, and clients).

[30] *See, e.g., Pyle*, 283 Kan. 807 ("explanatory" letter regarding discipline sent to family, friends, and clients); *Glenn*, 256 Iowa 1233 (1964) (pamphlet after cases decided with no appeal pending). There are several cases where statements are made to the press after an appellate decision has been handed down. *See, e.g., In re Westfall*, 808 S.W.2d 829 (Mo. 1991); *In re Raggio*, 87 Nev. 369 (1971); *In re Lacey*, 283 N.W.2d 250 (S.D. 1979); *Fieger*, 719 N.W.2d 123.

   Nevertheless, some courts have verbally recognized a right of an attorney to criticize the judiciary after a case is no longer pending. *See In re Cobb*, 445 Mass. 452, 467 (Mass 2005); *In re Graham*, 453 N.W.2d 313, 321 (Minn. 1990).

statements are made by attorneys who are not engaged in a representative capacity before the criticized court.[31]

Traditional First Amendment doctrines and theories, particularly those espoused in *Sullivan*, soundly condemn as unconstitutional the punishment of attorney speech critical of the judiciary. Such prohibitions and punishment are not just content-based; they are viewpoint-based. Attorneys are free to praise the courts and specific judges, but may very well face discipline for criticism. The alleged justification is an entirely hypothesized and speculative fear of a "dangerous idea" – if attorneys speak ill of the judiciary, the public will lose confidence in the judiciary, and consequently will stop complying with the rule of law and judicial decisions, resulting in the collapse of the judicial system. The solution is to keep the public in ignorance by prohibiting attorney speech critical of judges. This paternalistic protection of government from the public is antithetical to the First Amendment and to self-government, where "the censorial power is in the people over the Government, and not in the Government over the people."[32] Further, by silencing the very group of people with the requisite knowledge of and exposure to the judiciary to make informed judgments, the judiciary has shielded itself from effective criticism, allowing for judicial self-entrenchment and clogging the wheels of political change. In short, Courts are enforcing a self-serving prophylactic viewpoint-based restriction on political speech regarding the qualifications and integrity of government officials – speech at the core of First Amendment protection.

It was in the very context of attorney speech impugning the integrity of the judiciary that the Supreme Court explained:

> Speech concerning public affairs is more than self-expression; it is *the essence of self-government*. The First and Fourteenth Amendments embody our "profound national commitment to the principle that debate on public issues should be uninhibited, robust, and wide-open, and that it may well include vehement, caustic, and sometimes unpleasantly sharp attacks on government and public officials."[33]

In *Garrison* v. *Louisiana*, the Supreme Court overturned the conviction of a district attorney for criminal defamation after holding a press conference where he attributed "a large backlog of pending criminal cases to the inefficiency, laziness, and excessive vacations" of particular judges and mused about possible "racketeer influences on our eight vacation-minded judges."[34] Recalling the evils of seditious libel in England, and of the Sedition Act in the United States, the Court held that "*only* those false statements made with the high degree of

---

[31] *Idaho State Bar* v. *Topp*, 129 Idaho 414 (1996); *Ky. Bar Ass'n* v. *Heleringer*, 602 S.W.2d 165 (Ky. 1980); *Pyle*, 283 Kan. 807 (2007).
[32] *New York Times* v. *Sullivan*, 376 U.S. 254, 275 (1964) (citations omitted).
[33] *Garrison* v. *Louisiana*, 379 U.S. 64, 74–75 (1964) (quoting *Sullivan*, 376 U.S. at 270).
[34] *Garrison*, 379 U.S. at 66.

awareness of their probable falsity demanded by *New York Times* may be the subject of *either civil or criminal sanctions.*"[35]

After *Garrison*, the American Bar Association (ABA) expressly adopted the *Sullivan* standard in Model Rule of Professional Conduct 8.2 for regulating lawyer speech regarding the judiciary, which rule has been adopted by most states.[36] Thus Model Rule 8.2 only prohibits attorneys from making "a statement that the lawyer *knows to be false or with reckless disregard as to its truth or falsity* concerning the qualifications or integrity of a judge."[37] Despite disciplining attorneys under a rule that on its face adopts the *Sullivan* standard, state and federal courts interpret that rule to require an "objective reasonableness" standard – the very standard expressly rejected by the Supreme Court in *Garrison*. This creates a trap for the unwary lawyer. Every lawyer is familiar with the *Sullivan* standard – it is tested on the multistate portion of the bar exam. Thus, when a lawyer is considering making a statement about a judge, the lawyer may consult the rule, recognize that it codifies the *Sullivan* standard and assume that *Sullivan* will shield the lawyer from punishment – only to find out that despite the rule's actual language, the standard to be applied is a far cry from *Sullivan*.

The objective reasonableness standard that courts apply comes in one of two variants. Some courts focus on whether the attorney had an "objectively reasonable factual basis for making the statements."[38] Other courts examine "what the reasonable attorney, considered in light of all his professional functions, would do in the same or similar circumstances."[39] Some courts combine these tests,[40] or do not expressly adopt either while rejecting the subjective *Sullivan* standard and instead adopting a reasonableness or objective approach.[41]

An objective reasonableness approach was expressly rejected by the Supreme Court in *Garrison* in the precise context of *lawyer speech regarding judges*. Louisiana

---

[35] *Id.* at 74.

[36] The drafters of the Model Rules intentionally incorporated the *Sullivan* standard. In the proposed final draft, the drafters cited both *Sullivan* and *Garrison* and explained that "[t]he Supreme Court has held that false statements about public officials may be punished only if the speaker acts with knowledge that the statement is 'false or with reckless disregard of whether it is false or not.'" *See* Proposed Final Draft: Model Rules of Professional Conduct, Am. Bar Ass'n, May 30, 1981 (legal background explanation for Rule 8.2).

[37] MODEL RULES OF PROF'L CONDUCT R. 8.2(a).

[38] *Fla. Bar Ass'n v. Ray*, 797 So. 2d 556, 559 (2000); *see also, e.g., In re Cobb*, 445 Mass. 452 (2005).

[39] *In re Graham*, 453 N.W.2d 313, 322 (Minn. 1990); *see also, e.g., In re Westfall*, 808 S.W.2d 829, 837 (Mo. 1991); *Idaho State Bar v. Topp*, 129 Idaho 414, 417 (1996); *In re Holtzman*, 78 N.Y.2d 184, 192–93 (1991); *Ky. Bar Ass'n v. Heleringer*, 602 S.W.2d 165 (Ky. 1980); *In re Simon*, 913 So.2d 816 (La. 2005).

[40] *See, e.g., Office of Disciplinary Counsel v. Gardner*, 793 N.E.2d 425, 431 (2003) (looking at "what the reasonable attorney in light of all his professional functions, would do in the same or in similar circumstances ... [and] focus[ing] on whether the attorney had a reasonable factual basis"); *Iowa Sup. Ct. Att'y Disciplinary Bd. v. Weaver*, 750 N.W.2d 71, 80–81 (Iowa 2008).

[41] *See, e.g., In re Terry*, 271 Ind. 499, 502 (1979); *Grievance Administrator v. Fieger*, 719 N.W. 2d 123, 141 (Mich. 2006).

had convicted Garrison because his statement was "not made in the *reasonable belief* of its truth," on the theory that it was "inconceivable" that he "had a reasonable belief, that not one but all eight of these Judges ... were guilty of what he charged them with."[42] The Supreme Court's response is direct:

> This is *not* a holding applying the *New York Times* test. The *reasonable-belief* standard applied by the trial judge *is not the same as the reckless-disregard-of-truth* standard. According to the trial court's opinion, a reasonable belief is one which 'an ordinarily prudent man might be able to assign a just reason for'; the suggestion is that under this test the immunity from criminal responsibility ... disappears on proof that *the exercise of ordinary care would have revealed that the statement was false*. The test which we laid down in *New York Times* is not keyed to ordinary care; defeasance of the privilege is conditioned, not on mere negligence, but on reckless disregard for the truth.[43]

The *Sullivan* standard for determining whether a statement is made with reckless disregard is *not* an objective or reasonableness-based standard, but instead is determined by examining the speaker's subjective intent, which requires "that the defendant *in fact entertained serious doubts* as to the truth or falsity of his publication."[44]

Additionally, application of the objective standard is generally cursory and heavily weighted toward a finding of unreasonableness and consequent discipline. For example, in *Idaho State Bar* v. *Topp*,[45] a part-time county attorney attended a politically sensitive hearing (but was not involved in the case) about a proposed county expenditure of 4.1 million dollars. After the hearing, he was asked by the press to comment on the court's decision as compared to a similar issue that had been decided a different way by another judge. Topp responded that he thought the other judge "wasn't worried about the political ramifications."[46] Topp was publicly reprimanded for violating Idaho's Rule 8.2, as the "statement necessarily implied that Judge Michaud based his decision on completely irrelevant and improper considerations" and thus "impugned his integrity."[47] At his disciplinary hearing, Topp brought forth three pieces of evidence that supported his statement,[48] but the

---

[42] *Garrison* v. *Louisiana*, 379 U.S. 64, 78 (1964) (emphasis added).
[43] *Id.* at 79 (emphasis added).
[44] *St. Amant* v. *Thompson*, 390 U.S. 727, 731 (1968).
[45] 129 Idaho 414 (1996).
[46] *Id.* at 416.
[47] *Id.* at 418.
[48] Specifically, Topp pointed to the following facts: (1) there had been "a political frenzy" in the County on the issue, of which the judge certainly was aware, *see id.*; (2) the judge rendered an oral decision "immediately after the close of argument" and released a written decision "within minutes" of the end of the hearing, *see id.* at 415, which Topp thought supported "an inference that the case was decided prior to argument and that Judge Michaud was concerned with disseminating that decision to the public quickly," *see id.* at 418; and (3) "another district judge in a similar case had reached a different decision," *see id.*

court rejected this, summarily concluding that "a reasonable attorney in considering these facts, would not have made the statement in question."[49]

Notably, the *Topp* decision is typical in that the court and disciplinary authority garnered no evidence, standards, or testimony as to what a reasonable attorney would do or say in such a circumstance (indeed, I have yet to read such a case). The assumption in these cases appears to be either (1) that the court itself is competent to decide summarily what a reasonable attorney would or would not say or (2) that a reasonable attorney would never impugn the dignity of the court without significant conclusive evidence of misconduct.

The "reasonable basis in fact" standard also is not applied in a manner consistent with typical evaluations of that standard. In most contexts, such as Federal Rule of Civil Procedure (FRCP) 11 or Model Rule 3.1, a reasonable basis in fact sets a very low threshold of proof. Sanctions are not warranted "unless a particular allegation is utterly lacking in support."[50] Courts applying the objective reasonableness standard as to statements regarding the judiciary, in contrast, have required that the statements be supported by "substantial competent evidence" or "copious facts"[51] and eschew circumstantial evidence[52] or anything less than direct proof of the assertions.[53] Attorneys are to be "certain of the merit[s]" and "avoid petty criticisms."[54] Further, courts have taken an extremely literal (and sometimes exaggerated) reading of attorney statements regarding the judiciary, and then punished the attorney for not proving the exaggerated version.[55]

A striking example of such judicial construction occurred in *In re Westfall*.[56] Prosecutor George E. ("Buzz") Westfall made statements to the press about an appellate decision prohibiting him from pursuing a prosecution on the grounds of double jeopardy. Westfall stated in part that the decision did not follow the Supreme Court "for reasons that I find somewhat illogical and I think even a little bit less than honest" and that the opinion "distorted the statute and . . . convoluted logic to arrive at a decision that [the judge] personally likes."[57] In disciplining Westfall and finding that he lacked evidence for the statement, the court rephrased his statement each time it addressed it, claiming, for example, that Westfall "accused Judge Karohl of

[49] *Id.* at 418.
[50] *O'Brien v. Alexander*, 101 F.3d 1479, 1489 (2d Cir. 1996).
[51] *See, e.g., Ky. Bar Ass'n v. Heleringer*, 602 S.W.2d 165, 168 (Ky. 1980); *State v. Santana-Ruiz*, 167 P.3d 1038, 1044 (Utah 2007).
[52] *See, e.g., In re Wilkins*, 777 N.E.2d 714, 716–17 (Ind. 2002); *In re Glenn*, 256 Iowa 1233 (1964); *Peters v. Pine Meadow Ranch Home Ass'n*, 151 P.3d 962 (Utah 2007).
[53] *See, e.g., U.S. Dist. Ct. for E.D. of Wash. v. Sandlin*, 12 F.3d 861 (9th Cir. 1993).
[54] *In re Arnold*, 274 Kan. 761, 767 (2002) (citations omitted).
[55] *See, e.g., In re Frerichs*, 238 N.W.2d 764, 767 (Iowa 1976) (court construes attorney's statement in petition for rehearing that court was "willfully avoiding the substantial constitutional issues" as "easily" being read to "allege commission of public offences," including a misdemeanor and a felony, and thus as accusing the court of "sinister deceitful and unlawful motives and purposes").
[56] 808 S.W.2d 829 (Mo. 1991).
[57] *Id.* at 831.

deliberate dishonesty" and of "purposefully ignoring the law to achieve his personal ends" – not as "an implication of carelessness or negligence but of a deliberate, dishonest, conscious design on the part of the judge to serve his own interests."[58] The dissent pointed out that the majority's construction was "not even grammatically plausible" as the phrase "a little bit less than honest" grammatically refers to "the reasons, not the judge."[59] More importantly, the dissent explained that the majority used "at least six unsupportable paraphrases of the respondent's actual words" to support its decision, each of which, "are the words of the writer [the court], not the words of" Westfall.[60]

Another major point of departure from *Sullivan* and *Garrison* is the failure of courts to verify that the statements for which attorneys are punished are in fact false. While the Ninth Circuit has required the disciplinary authority to prove falsity,[61] which has influenced other courts to follow suit, many courts do not require the bar to prove falsity. This occurs in large part because a number of courts place the burden of proof on the disciplined attorney to bring forth evidence supporting the statement. In a 2011 disciplinary proceeding from Florida, the Referee explained that Rule 8.2, as interpreted, creates this standard: "[I]f you say it, you better be prepared to prove it." Thus, courts have held that speech is punishable because the *attorney failed* to bring forth sufficient evidence to support the statement, and no further examination is made as to whether the statement is true or not.[62]

Additionally, some courts appear to presume falsity. Applying an objective standard, they examine whether the attorney had a reasonable basis in fact for making the statement or whether a reasonable attorney would make the statement. If the answer to either of those inquiries is no, the court assumes that the assertion was therefore false.[63] Additionally, as in *In re Atanga*, a few courts have denied the attorney the opportunity to prove that the statement was true.[64] In *Kentucky Bar*

---

[58] *Id.* at 838.

[59] *Id.* at 841 (Blackmar, J., dissenting).

[60] *Id.*

[61] *Committee on Discipline for the U.S.Dist. Ct. for the Cent. Dist. Cal. v. Yagman*, 55 F.3d 1430 (9th Cir. 1995).

[62] *See, e.g., In re Glenn*, 256 Iowa 1233, 1239 (1964) (stating that attorney "offered no evidence" supporting statements, although Glenn brought significant circumstantial evidence); *Wilkins*, 777 N.E. 2d at 717 (noting that attorney "offered no evidence to support his contentions" regarding the motive of the court, even though Wilkins brought circumstantial evidence).

[63] *See, e.g., Office of Disciplinary Counsel v. Gardner* 793 N.E. 2d 425, 431 (Ohio 2003); *Wilkins*, 777 N.E. 2d at 717 (failing to examine whether false, but relying on fact that attorney, allegedly, failed to bring forth sufficient evidence in support); *In re Westfall*, 808 S.W.2d 829 (Mo. 1991) (same); *Peters v. Pine Meadow Ranch Home Ass'n*, 151 P.3d 962 (Utah 2007) (same).

At oral argument in the *Peters* case, an unidentified Justice stated in question to the offending attorney: "Would you care to address the question about [sanctions] or *is your answer simply that you were right*. That's what I hear you saying is … that your material is *not inappropriate simply because it's correct*."

[64] *See, e.g., In re Atanga*, 636 N.E.2d 1253 (Ind. 1994); *see also In re Cobb*, 445 Mass. 452, 468 (2005). In *Cobb*, the Court stated: "The Supreme Court decisions in the *Bradley, Sawyer*, and

Association v. *Waller*, the Kentucky Supreme Court denied the attorney an evidentiary hearing and rejected the argument that "truth or some concept akin to truth, such as accuracy or correctness, is a defense to the charge against him."[65]

Again, all of this is in direct conflict with *Sullivan* and *Garrison*. The *Sullivan* Court explained: "Truth may not be the subject of either civil or criminal sanctions where discussion of public affairs is concerned."[66] The Court further stated that the burden of proving truth (or the lack of it) should be on the person seeking to punish speech and *not* on the speaker because "would-be critics of official conduct may be deterred from voicing their criticism, even though it is believed to be true and even though it is in fact true, because of doubt whether it can be proved in court or fear of the expense of having to do so."[67]

Another common way around the express wording of Rule 8.2 and the *Sullivan* standard is for a court to punish attorneys for statements critical of judiciary by relying on a different catch-all professional conduct rule, such as for engaging "in conduct prejudicial to the administration of justice"[68] or in "undignified or discourteous conduct."[69] Yet *Sullivan* and the requirements of the First Amendment cannot be avoided merely by charging discipline under another rule. For example, in *Button*, Virginia argued that it was *not* prohibiting speech, association, or petitioning, but instead was just prohibiting "solicitation," to which the Supreme Court responded: "[A] state cannot foreclose the exercise of constitutional rights *by mere labels*."[70] Because the First Amendment jealously protects speech regarding public officials, including the judiciary, *Sullivan* applies regardless of the specific rule employed.

SAFEGUARDING THE INTEGRITY OF THE JUDICIARY

The majority approach is utterly unconstitutional under traditional First Amendment doctrine and theory, and none of the attempts to distinguish or carve out professional discipline withstand scrutiny, as I have previously shown.[71] Yet under the access to justice theory, the question is whether the speech is essential to the attorney's role in the justice system in invoking or avoiding government power in the protection of client life, liberty, and property, or if the speech is otherwise essential to the proper functioning of the justice system. Under this analysis, attorneys must

Gentile cases did not distinguish between true and false criticism, founded and unfounded criticism." Notably, *Bradley* and *Sawyer* were both decided before *Sullivan* and *Garrison*, and *Gentile* involved pretrial publicity rules rather than discipline for impugning judicial integrity.

[65] *Ky. Bar Ass'n v. Waller*, 929 S. W.2d 181, 182–83 (Ky. 1996).

[66] *New York Times v. Sullivan*, 376 U.S.254, 274 (1964).

[67] *Id.* at 279.

[68] *See* MODEL RULES OF PROF'L CONDUCT 8.4(d).

[69] *See* N.Y. RULES OF PROF'L CONDUCT R. 3.3(f)(2).

[70] *NAACP v. Button*, 415, 429 (1963).

[71] *See* Tarkington, *Truth Be Damned, supra* Note 1, at 1610–36.

have First Amendment rights of speech, association, and petitioning to criticize the judiciary in order to check judicial power both by informing the public and protecting the rights of their clients – and ultimately to safeguard the actual integrity of the judicial system.

Checking Judicial Power and an Informed Public

One of the most significant problems with suppressing attorney speech critical or disparaging of the judiciary is that the public loses its right to receive that information. The Supreme Court has recognized a separate, reciprocal speech right for people to receive information,[72] including information from attorneys.[73] In *Virginia Board Pharmacy*, for example, the Court held that even though the State could regulate the dissemination of prescription drug information from pharmacists, the First Amendment protection "is enjoyed by the appellees *as recipients of the information*, and *not solely, if at all*," by the speakers.[74] Thus, even if courts could constitutionally restrict attorney speech under the constitutional conditions or categorical approaches, that would not eliminate the First Amendment right of the public to receive the information.

Again, as Vincent Blasi contended, the foremost purpose for including the First Amendment in the Constitution was the "checking value" – meaning the value that free speech plays in checking official abuse of power. Attorneys play a vital role in checking abuse of power of government and nongovernment actors through bringing lawsuits and petitioning on behalf of clients as discussed in Chapter 10. Yet attorneys play a singularly important role in checking the exercise of judicial power – even when not acting in a representative capacity. Attorneys perform this role by informing the public about the qualifications and integrity of the judiciary. This role of the lawyer flows from the reality that lawyers are the class of people with both the exposure to the judiciary and the requisite legal knowledge to evaluate and comment upon judicial activity. While some courts have cited the lawyer's expertise and exposure as a justification for restricting attorney commentary on the judiciary (e.g., "[p]recisely because lawyers are perceived to have special competence in assessing judges, the public tends to believe what lawyers say about judges"[75]), in actuality, the lawyer's informed opinion cuts precisely the other way, demonstrating the need for First Amendment protection.

Lawyers have the education and training to recognize, understand, and articulate problems with the judiciary, and are exposed to and experience those problems as they bring their clients' cases before judges. This is exactly the kind of information

---

[72] *Va. State Bd. of Pharmacy v. Va. Citizens Consumer Council*, 425 U.S. 748 (1976).
[73] *Bates v. State Bar of Ariz.*, 433 U.S. 350 (1977).
[74] *Va. State Board*, 425 U.S. at 756 (emphasis added).
[75] *See, e.g., In re Pyle*, 283 Kan. 807, 831 (2007).

that the public has both the right and need to receive in order to make informed decisions about the judiciary, to fulfill their self-governing roll, and check judicial abuses and incompetence. Thirty-nine states elect their judiciary either initially or through retention elections.[76] In order to vote with informed judgment, citizens should be free to make and to obtain opinions and information regarding such candidates. Even as to appointed judges, the citizenry perform self-governance in selecting representatives responsible for appointing judges and can still employ democratic correctives through their representatives, including impeachment. If lawyers are prohibited from speaking and performing this checking function, then the judiciary is largely shielded from effective criticism and the public is left ignorant regarding the actual integrity of the judiciary.

As Justice Goldberg explained: "The effective functioning of a free government like ours depends largely on the force of an informed public opinion. This calls for the widest possible understanding of the quality of government service rendered by all elective or appointed public officials or employees."[77] But by silencing *all lawyers*, the courts have denied the public the opportunity to gain an informed opinion regarding deficiencies in the judiciary from those who know (by education, training, and exposure) – leaving relatively few other effective critics in that wake.[78] The Supreme Court of Oklahoma is one of the few courts to recognize the free speech interests of the public in obtaining informed and educated criticism about the judiciary from attorneys, stating:

> In keeping with the high trust placed in this Court by the people, we *cannot shield the judiciary from the critique of that portion of the public most perfectly situated to advance knowledgeable criticism*, while at the same time subjecting the balance of government officials to the stringent requirements of *New York Times* and its progeny.[79]

Nevertheless, in nearly all other states, public confidence in the judiciary is preserved through public ignorance. Government-coerced public ignorance regarding the qualifications of public officials is completely antithetical to democracy. It deprives the citizen of the ability to self-govern.[80] It deprives American people, who possess the ultimate sovereignty over government, including the judiciary, to exercise their power to respond to or correct government abuses. It eliminates the checking power of the people and denies them the right to define government

---

[76] See *Republican Party of Minn.* v. *White*, 536 U.S. 765, 790 (2002) (O'Connor, J., concurring).

[77] *New York Times* v. *Sullivan*, 376 U.S. 254, 304 n. 5 (Goldberg, J., concurring); *see also id.* at 281 ("It is of the utmost consequence that the people should discuss the character and qualifications of candidates for their suffrages.")

[78] As the *Sullivan* Court observed: "Criticism of [] official conduct does not lose its constitutional protection merely because it is effective criticism." *Id.* at 273 (majority opinion).

[79] *Okla. Bar Ass'n* v. *Porter*, 766 P.2d 958, 968–69 (Okla. 1988).

[80] "Popular choice will mean relatively little if we don't know what our representatives are up to." JOHN HART ELY, DEMOCRACY AND DISTRUST 125 (1980).

misconduct. To the extent that they are left in the dark, the people cannot exercise their democratic power and right to govern themselves.

Lawyers, in speaking about the judiciary, thus play an essential role in enabling the public to perform self-government and to check judicial power. This idea appears to have been understood at an earlier period in our nation's history, as Bruce Green recounts.[81] For example, the Pennsylvania Supreme Court in 1880 overturned the disbarment of two lawyers for their published statements that opined that certain acquittals were "secured by a prostitution of the machinery of justice to serve the exigencies of the Republican party" and noting that the judges were members of that party.[82] Nevertheless, Chief Justice George Sharswood, whom, as Green notes, is considered "the father of modern legal ethics,"[83] explained:

> No class of the community ought to be allowed *freer scope* in the expression or publication of opinions *as to the capacity, impartiality or integrity of judges than members of the bar.* They have the best opportunities of observing and forming a correct judgment. They are in constant attendance on the courts. Hundreds of those who are called on to vote never enter a court-house, or if they do, it is only at intervals as jurors, witnesses or parties. *To say that an attorney can only act or speak on this subject under liability to be called to account and to be deprived of his profession and livelihood by the very judge or judges whom he may consider it his duty to attack and expose,* is a position too monstrous to be entertained for a moment under our present system.[84]

Similarly, the current federal contempt statute was enacted in response to, and in order to curtail future instances of, punishment of an attorney for criticizing a judge. In 1831, James H. Peck, a United States District Court Judge for the District of Missouri, used the contempt power to imprison attorney Luke E. Lawless for one day and to suspend Lawless from the practice of law for eighteen months.[85] The reason for the contempt citation and suspension was a newspaper article that Lawless wrote in which he criticized Peck's decision in a case Lawless had argued before Peck.[86] Judge Peck's actions in disbarring a lawyer for criticizing him did not sit well with people in 1831. Peck was impeached – one of only fifteen federal court judges to be impeached in the history of the United States – as a result of punishing Lawless for his speech. The Articles of Impeachment declared it was an "abuse of

---

[81] *See* Bruce A. Green, *Lawyers' Professional Independence: Overrated or Undervalued?*, 46 AKRON L. REV. 599 (2013).

[82] *Ex Parte Steinman and Hensel*, 95 Pa. 220, 221 (1880).

[83] Green, *supra* Note 81, at 623.

[84] *Steinman and Hensel*, 95 Pa. at 238–39 (emphasis added).

[85] *See* ARTHUR J. STANSBURY, REPORT OF THE TRIAL OF JAMES H. PECK, 52 (1833) (quoting the articles of impeachment). Judge Peck published his opinion in a newspaper, and Lawless published a response noting eighteen legal errors in the opinion. When Lawless published his article, the underlying case was on appeal to the US Supreme Court. *See id.* at 1, 50–51.

[86] *See id.* at 52 (quoting the articles of impeachment).

judicial authority" and a "subversion of the liberties of the people of the United States" to punish Lawless for criticizing the judge.[87] In the Senate proceedings, soon-to-be President James Buchanan, who "had charge of the prosecution of Judge Peck,"[88] argued that Peck had in essence punished Lawless for libel of the judiciary without a jury, explaining,

> To allow the judiciary to dispense with this tribunal [a jury], whenever any publication has been made *affecting the dignity or the official conduct of a judge,* is to create a privileged order of men in the state *whose will is law,* and who are not only *judges in their own cause* [i.e. when the judges are the victims] of the guilt of the accused, but also of *the extent of his punishment.* Such a power, so far as it goes, partakes of the very essence and rankness of despotism.[89]

Although not convicted, the impeachment trial of Judge Peck also led to the enactment of a federal statute limiting the jurisdiction of federal courts in exercising the contempt power.[90] As Buchanan stated, "whatever may be the decision of the Senate upon this impeachment, Judge Peck has been the last man in the United States to exercise this power, and Mr. Lawless has been its last victim."[91] Unfortunately, Buchanan was sorely mistaken in his prediction, as attorneys today continue to be suspended by the judiciary for criticizing judges.

Although delegates of state power, lawyers can only receive the political power that the judiciary holds under our constitutional government. And the judiciary's political power has permanently embedded within it the checking power of the people over the judiciary. Lawyers in obtaining a license and becoming "officers of the court" thus retain their right as citizens to check judicial power – both on their own behalf and on behalf of clients. The lawyer's own individual right to express criticism of the judiciary should not be overlooked. Lawyers understand the justice system. Many of them went to law school and became lawyers precisely to work to improve inequities and other deficiencies in our justice system. Lawyers who find themselves practicing before a judge whom the lawyer considers incompetent, biased, or abusive absolutely have a First Amendment right to express that view to the public so that the public can be fully informed and employ democratic correctives as the public sees fit. The right of lawyers to provide their assessment of judicial behavior is an essential component of the lawyer's role and obligation to improve the quality of justice.

[87] *Id.*
[88] *Nye v. United States,* 313 U.S. 33, 46 (1941).
[89] STANSBURY, *supra* Note 85, at 426 (emphasis added).
[90] *See Nye,* 313 U.S. at 44–45 (explaining that the Act of Mar. 2, 1831, arose in response to the "impeachment proceedings against James H. Peck, a federal district judge, who had imprisoned and disbarred one Lawless for publishing a criticism of one of his opinions in a case which was on appeal").
[91] *Id.* at 46.

Lawyers are not an officer of a specific judge, or even a specific court, but of the justice system as a whole. They swear allegiance to state and federal constitutions, not to individual judges. They undertake an obligation to improve the quality of justice, which must include a right to point out deficiencies in that system and in its officers so that actual improvements to the integrity of the system can be made. The idea that the judiciary – all or part of which is elected in thirty-nine states – is somehow immune from officers of deficient caliber is ludicrous. And it will not make the judiciary immune from deficiencies to require attorneys to pretend that there are never problems and to continuously clap and express their faith in the integrity of all judicial officers. Thus, to improve the quality of justice, the judicial bad apples need to be identified and criticized by the only group with the knowledge and exposure to do so – attorneys – which will then allow the public to have the requisite information to exercise their sovereignty over their judicial agents.

Judicial Self-Entrenchment

One of the points made by Judge Sharswood and Senator Buchanan was that the judiciary should not be "judges in their own cause." In other words, one of the very problematic features of judicial discipline of attorneys for criticizing the judiciary is that the attorney, as Sharswood explained, is "called to account and to be deprived of his profession and livelihood by the very judge or judges whom he may consider it his duty to attack and expose."[92]

In *Democracy and Distrust*, John Hart Ely argued that a representative government malfunctions, not when substantive ends are achieved with which one may disagree but "when the *process* [of representative government] is undeserving of trust."[93] One way that such malfunction occurs is when "the ins are choking off the channels of political change to ensure that they will stay in and the outs will stay out."[94] In other words, a primary form of democratic malfunction occurs when those in government positions use their power to entrench themselves.

An example provided by Ely is the problem of allowing the legislature to manipulate voting rights. As Ely notes, voting is "essential to the democratic process" and its "dimensions cannot safely be left to our elected representatives, who have an obvious vested interest in the status quo."[95] In like manner, the judiciary has authority to punish attorneys, their most likely and effective critics. Public debate as to the qualifications, integrity, and impartiality of the judiciary is essential to the democratic process – which is particularly obvious where the judiciary is elected or retained by election but is also true where the judiciary is appointed because

---

[92] *Ex Parte Steinman and Hensel*, 95 Pa. 220, 238–39 (1880).
[93] ELY, *supra* Note 80, at 103 (emphasis in original).
[94] *Id.*
[95] *Id.* at 117.

institutional checks will generally only be invoked as a result of public insistence.[96] As with Ely's example, the punishment of speech critical of the judiciary "cannot safely be left to [the judiciary], who have an obvious vested interest in the status quo" and in preserving their own reputations from other would-be critics. To the extent that public debate is distorted to be rid of attorney criticism and disparagement of particular judges, the populace will not be aware of problems and will not vote them out or employ other democratic correctives. Despite the constant pitch otherwise, the current system does not actually protect the integrity of the overall judicial system – it instead protects individual judges in retaining their seats by silencing critics.

Indeed, because it is the judiciary who punishes the attorney, the situation is more suspect than the scenario presented in *Sullivan* or *Garrison*. In *Sullivan* the punishment for offensive speech had to come from a jury, and in *Garrison* the punishment for criminal defamation of the judiciary came from the executive branch. But in the scenario of attorney discipline, the punishment is made by the branch being criticized, which has an obvious interest in keeping the ins in and in avoiding negative public exposure.

An example can be found in *In re Raggio*.[97] William J. Raggio was an attorney of excellent reputation, who "was prominently mentioned as a candidate for either governor or United States senator" for Nevada.[98] Raggio made a statement in an interview with the press about a decision of the Nevada Supreme Court to rehear a death penalty case he had prosecuted, and called that decision "most shocking and outrageous" and "judicial legislation at its very worst."[99] Raggio was disciplined for his statements. The Nevada Supreme Court revealed its concern with Raggio's comments. Noting Raggio's prominence, the Court related:

> Maximum dissemination was given to his views. His initial comments were frequently repeated in the press and on television during the weeks and months to follow. *The public was quick to respond. This court became the center of controversy.* Essential public confidence in our system of administering justice may have been eroded.[100]

Certainly, the Nevada Supreme Court did not appreciate being "the center of controversy" – which is precisely why they should *not* be the entity punishing such

---

[96] *See* Vincent Blasi, *The Checking Value in First Amendment Theory*, AM. B. FOUND. RES. J. 521, 539 (1977).

[97] 87 Nev. 369 (1971). Raggio ultimately served in the Nevada State Senate from 1972 until 2011. He died in 2012. A news article written about him at his death calls him a "[p]olitical icon, statesman, the Mount Rushmore of Nevada politics, the lion of the north." Ed Vogel and Laura Myers, *Nevada Lawmaking Legend, Raggio, 85, Dies*, LAS VEGAS REVIEW-JOURNAL, Feb. 24, 2012, *available at* www.reviewjournal.com/news/nevada-lawmaking-legend-raggio-85-dies/.

[98] *Raggio*, 87 Nev. at 371.

[99] *Id.*

[100] *Id.* (emphasis added).

speech, or at the very least should not be allowed to carve out an exception to the *Sullivan* rule for itself.

Justice Goldberg argued that the *Sullivan* standard was insufficient to protect critics of the government because of the possibility of "friendly juries" who would protect government and find that the requisite mental state had been met.[101] Thus Goldberg argued that "the First and Fourteenth Amendments to the Constitution afford to the citizen and to the press an absolute, unconditional privilege to criticize official conduct despite the harm which may flow from excesses and abuses."[102] The possibility of a government-friendly jury is hard to quantify. But in cases involving attorney discipline for statements regarding the judiciary, Goldberg's hypothetical problem of a judiciary-friendly "jury" is a reality. As Justice Boehm of the Indiana Supreme Court stated in a dissenting opinion, "[t]his Court acts as judge, jury, and appellate reviewer in a disciplinary proceeding," and, "[w]here the offense consists of criticism of the judiciary, we become the victim as well."[103]

Judges understand that what is sauce for the goose is sauce for the gander. Thus they protect each other from attorney disparagement. The standard assumption in these cases is that attorney criticism of a specific judge (even a pretty awful judge) constitutes an attack on the integrity of the entire judiciary. This idea was expressed by the Indiana Supreme Court in *Atanga* – that by calling Judge Johnson "ignorant, insecure, and a racist," Atanga had somehow insulted the entire judiciary and the judicial process itself.[104] In fact, courts have justified their departure from the *Sullivan* standard by arguing that defamation protects a personal interest in reputation while professional discipline of lawyers protects the public interest in the reputation (or integrity) of the judicial system as a whole. Yet the comments for which attorneys are sanctioned invariably regard the actions of a specific judge or panel and not the judicial system as a whole. Certainly, a comment about one senator cannot be read as being subject to suppression because it brings all of Congress into disrepute and thus can shake the foundation of the entire legislative branch. Even if comments regarding an individual judge (or senator or other government official) could be seen as affecting the public's perception of the overall integrity of the system, how does that make it speech worthy of suppression under *Sullivan* and *Garrison*? If speech can be punished as long as one can characterize comments made about one government official as affecting the reputation of that entire branch of government, then the *Sullivan* rule can never be applied to statements about any government officials.

Unfortunately, the problems surrounding self-entrenchment are more than the malfunction of the democratic process and the ins staying in. Rather,

---

[101] *New York Times v. Sullivan*, 376 U.S. 254, 300, 304 (Goldberg, J., concurring).
[102] *Id.* at 298 (Goldberg, J., concurring).
[103] *In re Wilkins*, 777 N.E.2d 714, 720–21 (Ind. 2002).
[104] *In re Atanga*, 636 N.E.2d 1253, 1258 (Ind. 1994).

self-entrenchment and the protection of one's own dignity leads to additional abuses of power made in pursuit of that end. Again, as Justice Goldberg argued in his *Sullivan* concurrence:

> The American Colonists were not willing, nor should we be, to take the risk that "[m]en who injure and oppress the people in their administration [and] provoke them to cry out and complain" will also be empowered to "make that very complaint the foundation for new oppressions and prosecutions."[105]

Unfortunately, Goldberg's scenario has occurred in the context of punishing speech critical of the judiciary, including in the suspension of Jacob Atanga after having been forced to represent his client in criminal garb. Atanga was "injure[d] and oppress[ed]" by Judge Johnson, and then when Atanga spoke "out and complain[ed]," "that very complaint [became] the foundation for new oppressions and prosecutions."

Similarly, Gene Glenn – the author of the leaflet claiming that Judge Willard Dullard had proven that justice is "DEAF and DUMB!" – was actually criticizing a suspicious set of circumstances regarding the arrest and forfeiture of bail bonds of seventy-nine people for patronizing a bootlegging establishment in violation of a city ordinance, while letting the establishment out on a plea with almost no penalties and without forfeiting its bond. The Supreme Court of Iowa disciplined Glenn, while admitting that the plea agreement "does little credit to those who participated in it," including the criticized judge.[106] Rather than be concerned that something fishy was going on in the arrest and forfeiture of the bonds of seventy-nine citizens, the court suspended Glenn for one year for questioning and trying to expose it.

The checking power of attorney speech is not the antithesis of preserving judicial integrity; instead, checking government power is the primary method *for* preserving government integrity. It is through attorney criticism that judicial incompetence, corruption, abuse, bias, or other deficiencies come to light. Bringing such information to light – and then dealing with it and taking appropriate action – is how we preserve the actual integrity of the judiciary. The only "path of safety," as Brandies said, is to discuss grievances and propose remedies – not silence speech that exposes problems with our government agents or processes.

While the "perceived" integrity of the judiciary may be promoted by silencing attorney criticism and thus keeping the public in ignorance, that does absolutely nothing to protect the *actual* integrity of the judiciary. In fact, it does the opposite. It results in entrenchment of judges who are incompetent, abusive, or biased. Such judges – who probably should lose their seats – may be very inclined to file grievances against attorneys for exposing their weaknesses or malfeasance. Unfortunately, rather than consider that possibility, disciplinary authorities and courts

---

[105] *Sullivan*, 376 U.S. at 301 (Goldberg, J., concurring).
[106] *In re Glenn*, 256 Iowa 1233, 1236 (1964).

instead protect judges, allegedly to protect the integrity of the entire judiciary. It emphatically does not protect or promote the integrity of the judiciary as a whole to allow bad judges to keep their seats by silencing and punishing any exposé regarding them.

Curtailing the ability of government officials to engage in self-entrenchment and to insulate themselves from criticism is one of the primary purposes underlying the First Amendment – a purpose that goes hand-in-hand with the attorney's role in checking judicial power. As Cass Sunstein explained, "There can be little doubt that suppression by the government of political ideas that it disapproved, or found threatening, was *the central motivation for the [speech] clause*. The *worst* examples of unacceptable censorship involve efforts by government to *insulate itself from criticism*."[107]

Consequently, under the access to justice theory, it is part of the attorney's role in improving the quality of justice and checking judicial power to provide the public with informed opinions based on the attorney's experience and knowledge regarding the qualifications and integrity of the judiciary. Thus, when acting outside of court proceedings, attorneys should be protected by the First Amendment for their speech critical of the judiciary unless the attorney acted with actual malice, as defined in *Sullivan*, *Garrison*, and progeny. Speech regarding judicial qualifications and integrity by lawyers is far "more than self-expression; it is *the essence of self-government*" – and it is essential to the preservation of the actual integrity of the judiciary.

SAFEGUARDING JUDICIAL INTEGRITY IN COURT PROCEEDINGS

The access to justice theory rejects the constitutional conditions and categorical approaches and maintains that the core of First Amendment rights is the ability of the attorney to speak, associate, and petition *in the capacity of attorney* in the protection of clients' rights. This central tenet of the access to justice theory requires that attorneys have First Amendment protection to engage in speech critical of the judiciary in court proceedings by bringing claims or making motions or arguments to protect client rights and preserve the integrity of judicial processes. Importantly, protecting this area of speech is not only essential to the attorney's role in securing clients' rights; it is essential to the proper functioning of the judicial power. Nevertheless, even in this context, courts impose severe sanctions against attorneys advocating for their clients and petitioning for relief from judicial incompetence or malfeasance.

A salient example is found in the Louisiana Supreme Court's 2016 case, *In re Mire*.[108] Christine Mire is an attorney in Louisiana who had multiple family law matters before Judge Phyllis Keaty. At a hearing on July 20, 2009, Judge Keaty

---

[107] Cass R. Sunstein, *Free Speech Now*, 59 U. CHI. L. REV. 255, 305 (1992) (emphasis added).
[108] 197 So. 3d 656 (La. 2016).

disclosed on the record her relationship with the opposing party. However, later Mire learned of additional ties between Keaty and the opposing party and moved for Keaty's recusal – claiming Keaty had failed to make a full disclosure. In response, Judge Keaty insisted that that she had previously disclosed the full extent of her ties at the July 20 hearing. Mire requested the transcript of the July 20 hearing, which transcript contained a disclosure by Judge Keaty that neither Mire nor her client remembered Keaty making at the hearing. Mire then requested the audio recordings and was given a CD, which she had analyzed by an expert and which showed that the recording had been spliced – and, in fact, "material was added in a recording format that was not available with the court's recording software."[109] In a different family law matter that had also initially been before Judge Keaty and had been affirmed by the appellate court (in an opinion that misstated what materials were in the record), Mire filed a writ application to the Supreme Court of Louisiana, attached the July 20 audio CD, and asserted the "incompetence and/or corruption" of judicial members.[110] She further surmised that perhaps the appellate court was acting "to cover up the egregious actions of the trial court so it could not be used in the current election" – as Judge Keaty was at that time running (and ultimately succeeded in obtaining) a seat on the appellate court.[111] In 2016, the Louisiana Supreme Court suspended Mire from the practice of law for a year and a day (with six months deferred followed by two years of probation and required attendance at "Ethics School").[112]

The *Mire* majority adopted an "objectively reasonable" approach in interpreting Louisiana's Rule 8.2 and held that Mire lacked a reasonable basis for her statements because "[o]rdinary experience suggests that equipment can often malfunction without any underlying incompetence or intentional corruption."[113] Justices Weimer and Hughes wrote strident dissents. Justice Weimer argued that "a reasonable person could justifiably *disbelieve* that the court's recording equipment went haywire at the exact moment of Judge Keaty's purported disclosure."[114] Indeed, the hearing had been recorded by three redundant recording devices. Justice Weimer opined: "The odds of all three redundant systems malfunctioning simultaneously during the district judge's disclosure defies belief and 'ordinary experience.'"[115] In his dissent, Justice Weimer marshalled the evidence brought by Mire demonstrating an "objective basis" for her accusations, which included, in addition to the evidence already mentioned, that the court reporter was very defensive about turning over the audio recordings and even filed suit to enjoin Mire from getting them, and that

---

[109] *See id.* at 670 (Weimer, J., dissenting); *see also id.* at 661–62.
[110] *See id.* at 659–70 (majority opinion).
[111] *Id.*
[112] *Id.* at 669.
[113] *Id.* at 668.
[114] *Id.* at 671 (Weimer, J., dissenting).
[115] *In re Mire*, 190 So. 3d 705 706 (La. 2016) (Weimer, J., dissenting from denial of rehearing).

Judge Keaty initially testified that the reason for the splice was to remove material from other hearings held that same day, but then recanted when shown court records proving that there were no other hearings held that day.[116] Justice Hughes' pithy dissent simply states:

> Alteration of the transcript of a recorded judicial proceeding is a serious, perhaps criminal, matter. *This court does justice no favor by punishing the whistle-blower.* As pointed out by Justice Weimer, the majority manages to avoid the hard evidence that the alteration in this case was no accident or "malfunction."[117]

Importantly, Mire's accusations came in the form of a court filing – a writ application – petitioning for relief from the Louisiana Supreme Court. As Justice Weimer pointed out, the standards for obtaining a writ from the Louisiana Supreme Court include "gross departure from proper judicial proceedings." Consequently, an attorney's *"[q]uestioning and/or criticizing judges is inherently expected* as part of this court's writ consideration process."[118] In order to invoke a court's own processes to protect their clients' interests, attorneys, such as Mire, require protected First Amendment rights of speech and petitioning to impugn judicial integrity in court proceedings.

The Right to an Unbiased Judiciary

The Supreme Court has repeatedly recognized that "[t]rial before 'an unbiased judge' is essential to due process"[119] – and this is so in both criminal[120] and civil proceedings.[121] As elaborated in *In re Murchison*: "A fair trial in a fair tribunal is a basic requirement of due process. Fairness of course requires an absence of actual bias in the trial of cases. But our system of law has always endeavored to prevent even the probability of unfairness."[122] In 2009, the Supreme Court in *Caperton v. A.T. Massey Coal Co., Inc.* held that an objective "potential" or "probability of bias" by a judge or decision maker can reach unconstitutional proportions and deny a litigant due process.[123]

The right to an unbiased judiciary is particularly compelling in criminal cases, where a person's life or liberty is placed in the hands of a judge as an instrument of state power. Consequently, "[n]o matter what the evidence [is] against [a criminal

---

[116] *Mire*, 197 So. 3d at 672 (Weimer, J., dissenting).

[117] *Id.* at 676 (Hughes, J., dissenting) (emphasis added).

[118] *Id.* at 674 (Weimer, J., dissenting) (emphasis added).

[119] *Johnson v. Mississippi*, 403 U.S. 212, 216 (1971).

[120] *See Bracy v. Gramley*, 520 U.S. 899 (1997); *Ward v. Village of Monroeville*, 409 U.S. 57 (1972); *In re Murchison*, 349 U.S. 133 (1955); *Tumey v. Ohio*, 273 U.S. 510 (1927).

[121] *See, e.g., Caperton v. A.T. Massey Coal Co., Inc.*, 556 U.S. 868 (2009).

[122] *Murchison*, 349 U.S. at 136; *see also Caperton*, at 876 (quoting *Murchison* in stating, "It is axiomatic that '[a] fair trial in a fair tribunal is a basic requirement of due process.'").

[123] *Caperton*, 556 U.S. at 868, 878, 887.

defendant], he ha[s] the right to have an impartial judge."[124] Further, due process is not satisfied by invoking an assumption that judges are above common failings of other men and women. As the Supreme Court explained,

> the requirement of due process of law in judicial procedure is *not* satisfied by the argument that men of the highest honor and the greatest self-sacrifice could carry it on without danger of injustice. Every procedure which would offer *a possible temptation to the average man* as a judge to forget the burden of proof required to convict the defendant, or which might lead him not to hold the balance nice, clear, and true between the state and the accused denies the latter due process of law.[125]

The Supreme Court in *Caperton* reaffirmed this statement as "the controlling principle."[126] Although the *Caperton* Court repeatedly noted that the criteria for finding a violation of due process "cannot be defined with precision,"[127] it held that the inquiry is "objective," does "not require proof of actual bias" (although "actual bias, if disclosed no doubt *would* be grounds for appropriate relief"[128]), and requires "under a realistic appraisal of psychological tendencies and human weakness,"[129] a determination of "whether the average judge in his position is 'likely' to be neutral, or whether there is an unconstitutional 'potential for bias.'"[130]

The Court noted that its objective test "may sometimes *bar* trial by judges *who have no actual bias* and who *would do their very best to weigh the scales of justice equally* between contending parties."[131] It is important to recognize that if due process will sometimes actually *bar* an unbiased, upright judge from hearing a case, then certainly *challenges* to judges in papers filed with courts will include challenges against judges who are in fact unbiased and upright. Attorneys should and must be able to assert and preserve their clients' due process rights – even when doing so results in attacking the neutrality or integrity of a judge who in actuality is unbiased and fair. Nevertheless, courts have required attorneys to prove the truth of allegations of bias or improper purpose – often extremely strictly[132] and with an exaggerated view of the assertions made by attorneys.[133]

---

[124] *Tumey*, 273 U.S. at 535.

[125] *Id.* at 532 (emphasis added).

[126] *Caperton*, 556 U.S. at 878.

[127] *Id.* at 879.

[128] *Id.* at 883 (emphasis added).

[129] *Id.* (quoting *Withrow v. Larkin*, 421 U.S. 35, 47 (1975)).

[130] *Id.* at 881.

[131] *Id.* at 886 (internal citations omitted) (explaining that "objective standards may ... require recusal whether or not actual bias exists or can be proved") (emphasis added).

[132] *See, e.g., Burton v. Mottolese*, 835 A.2d 998 (Conn. 2003); *In re Wilkins*, 777 N.E. 2d 714 (Ind. 2002).

[133] *See, e.g., In re Frerichs*, 238 N.W.2d 764, 765 (Iowa 1976). In *Frerichs*, a criminal defense attorney wrote in petition for rehearing that the court "willfully avoided" and "refuse[d] to address themselves to the merits of a defendant's substantial constitutional claims" and thus

Notably, not all questions regarding judicial qualification violate or even implicate due process.[134] While due process "establishes a constitutional floor,"[135] both Congress and the States have imposed more stringent requirements for judicial disqualification.[136] Under 28 U.S.C. § 455, for example, disqualification of a federal judge or magistrate is required "in any proceeding in which his *impartiality might reasonably be questioned*" – in addition to requiring judicial disqualification in specified circumstances involving impediments such as personal bias or prejudice, personal knowledge of evidentiary facts, or pecuniary interest in or certain familial or professional connections with a particular proceeding.[137] Further, the ABA's Model Code of Judicial Conduct, applicable in the majority of states, requires disqualification under similar circumstances.[138] Additionally, attorneys who seek reassignment of a case to a different judge on remand may need to show under the standards set by appellate courts that reassignment is necessary to "preserve not only the reality but also the appearance of the proper functioning of the judiciary as a neutral, impartial administrator of justice"[139] or that "impartiality might reasonably be questioned by the average person on the street who knows all the relevant facts of a case."[140]

---

violated the defendant's "rights to due process and equal protection of the laws." *Id.* The court construed this statement as "easily" being construed to "allege commission of public offenses," including a specific misdemeanor and felony identified by the court, and as "attribut[ing] to this court sinister, deceitful and unlawful motives and purposes." *Id.* at 767.

[134] *See, e.g., Bracy v. Gramley*, 520 U.S. 899, 904 (1997) ("Of course, most questions concerning a judge's qualifications to hear a case are not constitutional ones ... "); *see also Caperton*, 556 U.S. at 876 ("most matters relating to judicial disqualification [do] not rise to a constitutional level" [quoting *FTC v. Cement Institute*, 333 U.S. 683, 702 (1948)]).

[135] *Bracy*, 520 U.S. at 904.

[136] *Cf. Aetna Life Ins. Co. v. Lavoie*, 475 U.S. 813, 829 (1986).

[137] 28 U.S.C. § 455 (2000). In *Liteky v. United States*, 510 U.S. 540 (1994), the Supreme Court interpreted § 455(a)'s requirement of disqualification "in any proceeding in which [a judge's] impartiality might reasonably be questioned" to generally be limited by the "extrajudicial source doctrine," which requires that the impartiality come from some factor or source outside of the judicial proceeding itself. Attorneys whose clients (or who themselves) are abused by judicial hostility and seek disqualification of the judge under § 455, thus generally have to show that the source of that hostility came from something other than what the judge learned or heard in the pending matter. As the *Liteky* majority elaborated, "Not establishing bias or partiality, however, are expressions of impatience, dissatisfaction, annoyance, and even anger, that are within the bounds of what imperfect men and women, even after having been confirmed as federal judges, sometimes display." *See id.* at 555–56.
   The four-justice dissent in *Liteky* argued that "[t]he statute does not refer to the source of the disqualifying partiality." *Id.* at 558 (Kennedy, J., dissenting). Thus, regardless of whether the source is "extrajudicial or intrajudicial," disqualification should be "triggered by an attitude or state of mind so resistant to fair and dispassionate inquiry as to cause a party, the public, or a reviewing court to have reasonable grounds to question the neutral and objective character of a judge's rulings or findings." *Id.* at 557–58 (Kennedy, J., dissenting).

[138] MODEL CODE OF JUDICIAL CONDUCT, R. 2.11 (2007).

[139] *Alexander v. Primerica Holdings*, 10 F.3d 155, 167 (3d Cir. 1993).

[140] *Sentis Group v. Shell Oil Co.*, 559 F.3d 888, 904 (8th Cir. 2009).

Of course, in order for litigants to meaningfully assert any of these rights, attorneys must be afforded the speech and petition rights to express and bring such claims. Again, under the Petition Clause attorneys have a right to bring claims without fear of punishment unless those claims are objectively baseless. The necessity of these rights is essential to the attorney's ability to protect client life, liberty, and property. Yet, in 2007, the Utah Supreme Court admonished criminal defense attorneys to remember "the pitfalls that may accompany the pursuit of" an argument of judicial bias resulting in a denial of due process.[141] The court cited a prior civil case where the Utah Supreme Court had stricken the briefs of an attorney and summarily affirmed a lower court's decision that was factually and legally erroneous because the attorney questioned the motives of the lower court judge.[142] The court went on to explain that any arguments regarding judicial bias must be "supported by copious facts and record evidence" and "made in a reserved, respectful tone, shunning hyperbole and name-calling."[143] By citing a case where the court had summarily affirmed an erroneous decision as a sanction for impugning judicial integrity, the court demonstrated its intention to chill attorney speech made in court filings regarding judicial bias – even when made on behalf of criminal defendants.

Criminal defense attorneys should not be admonished to be wary of making *any* colorable constitutional claim on behalf of their clients whose liberty or lives are at stake. Protecting the accused's constitutional rights is a central feature of their role in the criminal justice system and criminal defense attorneys must have First Amendment rights of speech and petition to fulfill that role under the access to justice theory. Nor should there be extra judicially imposed "pitfalls" (namely, sanctions or other punishment) that "accompany" arguments made by attorneys that a criminal defendant was denied due process because of a biased judge. It is shocking that a court would be more concerned with ensuring respectful rhetoric regarding the judiciary than with ensuring, whenever there is any question, that criminal defendants are afforded due process by impartial judges before losing their liberty.

The only way that the due process rights afforded to all criminal defendants can be vindicated is if their attorneys actively seek their enforcement during the actual criminal proceedings and subsequent judicial review. If the attorney fails to raise such arguments, they are generally waived and lost forever – even on habeas review. For courts to chill (as did the Utah Supreme Court in *Santana-Ruiz*) and/or to punish attorney speech raising such claims all but denies the existence of the right for the criminal defendant. Thus, under the access to justice theory, attorneys have First Amendment rights to make such arguments, when colorable, on behalf of their clients without threat or fear of punishment.

---

[141] *State v. Santana-Ruiz*, 167 P.3d 1038, 1044 (Utah 2007).

[142] *See id.; see also Peters v. Pine Meadow Branch Home Ass'n*, 151 P.3d 962, 963, 967–68 (Utah 2007).

[143] *Santana-Ruiz*, 167 P.3d at 1044.

Finally, it is the very function of appellate attorneys in our system of justice to highlight the failings of the lower court's handling of and decision in the case in order to obtain a reversal for their clients. While a number of cases indicate that some appellate attorneys go further than they need (or than is wise) by attributing nefarious motives to the lower court or exaggerating the error,[144] the question becomes whether they and/or their clients should be punished for so doing. As will be discussed later in this chapter, where the error of the attorney is something that would be punished if the speech regarded a nonjudicial actor or assertion, then the judiciary should punish the speech – but only to the extent that they would punish it if it regarded another actor. To the extent that the standard applied or the sanction imposed is more stringent than it would be in another context, then the judiciary is merely protecting its own reputation, and the *Sullivan* standard should apply.

Again, the Supreme Court's decision in *Legal Services Corporation* v. *Velazquez*[145] sets the basic contours of the attorney's free speech right to express and raise arguments in court proceedings and filings. Recall that the *Velazquez* Court invalidated restrictions placed on attorneys funded by the Legal Services Corporation that prohibited attorneys from challenging the validity or constitutionality of existing welfare laws. In expounding on the attorney's First Amendment rights, the Court explained that "attorneys *should present all the reasonable and well-grounded arguments necessary for proper resolution of the case*," noting that Congress had designed the restriction "to insulate current welfare laws from constitutional and certain other legal challenges."[146] The *Velazquez* Court, citing "central First Amendment concerns," held that Congress *could not* "impose rules and conditions which in effect *insulate its own laws from legitimate judicial challenge*," nor could it "*exclude from litigation those arguments and theories Congress finds unacceptable* but which by their nature are within the province of the courts to consider."[147] The Supreme Court concluded: "The Constitution does not permit the Government *to confine litigants and their attorneys* in this manner."[148]

Applying these principles from *Velazquez* to the suppression or punishment of speech critical of the judiciary made in court filings, courts should *not* be able to "impose rules ... which in effect *insulate [judicial actions] from legitimate judicial challenge*" and "*exclude from litigation those arguments and theories [that the judiciary] finds unacceptable* [or insulting] but which by their nature are within the province of the courts to consider."[149] Threat of professional discipline for

---

[144] *See, e.g., In re Wilkins*, 777 N.E. 2d 714 (Ind. 2002) (per curiam); *Peters* v. *Pine Meadow Ranch Home Ass'n*, 151 P.3d 962 (Utah 2997); *In re Graham*, 453 N.W.2d 313 (Minn. 1990).
[145] 531 U.S. 533, 545 (2001).
[146] *Id.* at 545, 547 (emphasis added).
[147] *Id.* at 547–48 (emphasis added).
[148] *Id.* at 548 (emphasis added).
[149] *Id.* at 545 (emphasis added).

impugning judicial integrity can foreclose and certainly chills "analysis of certain legal issues," encouraging attorneys to "truncate [their] presentation to the courts" when raising arguments regarding judicial abuse, corruption, incompetence, or bias – thereby denying attorneys and their clients their constitutionally protected "speech and expression."[150]

Invoking the Judicial Power

The *Velazquez* Court also noted that the regulation at issue "distorts the legal system" and ultimately undermined the judicial power itself.[151] The Court explained that "[b]y seeking to *prohibit the analysis of certain legal issues* and *to truncate presentation to the courts*, the enactment under review prohibits speech and expression *upon which the courts must depend* for *the proper exercise of the judicial power*."[152]

The judiciary only has power to the extent that lawyers bring cases and controversies before it, properly invoking its jurisdiction. Lawyers are "officers of the court" in large part because attorneys file cases, invoking the court's jurisdiction and *enabling the judiciary to exercise its governmental powers* as the third branch of government. The judiciary is absolutely powerless – it cannot protect or enforce rights; it cannot check the use government power (including its own) – without attorneys who bring cases before it.[153] By punishing and suppressing attorney speech critical of itself, the judiciary actually limits its own power.

And that limitation is particularly important in considering the preservation of the actual integrity of the judiciary. To the extent that lawyers are and can be silenced in what they are allowed to present to courts regarding judicial malfeasance, bias, incompetence, or other failings, courts lose power to address and correct those problems. Not only are judicial deficiencies hidden from the public – the problem addressed earlier – but the judiciary loses its own power to fix them and provide remedies to those harmed by the judiciary. Thus, the only path of safety for preserving both the integrity and the proper functioning *of the judicial power* is for attorneys to have protectable speech, association, and petition rights to raise all colorable claims on behalf of clients in protecting client life, liberty, and property – even where those claims involve assertions of judicial corruption, abuse, incompetence, bias, the appearance of bias, or other malfeasance.

---

[150] *Id.* at 545, 547–48.

[151] *Id.* at 544–45.

[152] *Id.* at 545 (emphasis added).

[153] In theory individuals – but not business entities – could still bring cases pro se, but it is a fact that attorneys are essential to the meaningful invocation of court processes to vindicate legal rights.

The Problem with the Sullivan *Standard for Speech in Court Proceedings*

Courts have raised legitimate concerns with applying a subjective *Sullivan* standard in punishing statements that appear in court filings. For example, in *In re Cobb*, the Massachusetts Supreme Court adopted an objective standard for its Rule 8.2 in a case where, in court filings, an attorney accused a judge of being involved in a criminal conspiracy. The court explained that the objective standard "is essential to the orderly and judicious *presentation of cases*," explaining that courts are "not a place for groundless assertions, whatever their nature."[154]

In public debate, speech regarding government officials – including speech by attorneys regarding the judiciary – must be "uninhibited, robust, and wide open" for democracy to function[155]; yet, that same amplitude for speech would entirely frustrate court proceedings, the goal of which is to determine the truth and dispense justice. It would impede the proper adjudication of court cases if the judiciary were required to rely on assertions of "fact" that were supported only by the *Sullivan* standard. If the *Sullivan* standard applied to in-court speech, then any statement by an attorney would be permissible as long as the attorney *did not know that it was false* or did not subjectively entertain serious doubts as to its truth or falsity. Yet the proper administration of justice requires that attorneys have some basis in fact in making assertions on which the court is asked to rely in ruling on a case. This is so because "[o]ur adversary system for the resolution of disputes rests on the unshakable foundation that truth is the object of the system's process which is designed for the purpose of dispensing justice."[156] Under the access to justice theory, attorneys lack First Amendment rights that would thwart the proper functioning of the judicial system.

Erwin Chemerinsky, in commenting on the *Mire* case, indicated that the *Sullivan* standard should have applied – even though Mire's speech occurred in court filings.[157] However, Federal Rule of Civil Procedure (FRCP) 11 and Model Rule of Professional Conduct 3.1 both appropriately require the attorney to have a reasonable basis in fact for assertions presented to a court. Other rules contain similar requirements that forbid groundless and frivolous assertions.[158] These requirements comport with the basic premise that a system of justice is aimed at adjudicating the truth and with the attorney's role in the system of justice, including their duty of candor to the court.

---

[154] *In re Cobb*, 445 Mass. 452, 472–73 (2005) (emphasis added).
[155] *New York Times v. Sullivan*, 376 U.S. 254, 270 (1964).
[156] *United States v. Shaffer Equipment Co.*, 11 F.3d 450 (4th Cir. 1993).
[157] *See* David Hudson, *How Far Can Criticism of Judges Go under Ethics Rules?* ABA J. Dec. 2016, *available at* www.abajournal.com/magazine/article/criticism_judges_ethics_rules (quoting Chemerinsky).
[158] *See, e.g.*, Fed. R. App. P. 46; Fed. R. Civ. P. 12(f).

Importantly, the fact that statements in court filings should have a reasonable factual basis does not require the rejection of the *Sullivan* standard for Rule 8.2 or other punishment based on impugning judicial integrity. Rather, where the problem with statements regarding the judiciary made in court proceedings is that the statements lack sufficient factual basis, attorneys should be sanctioned under one of the several rules (such as FRCP 11 or Rule 3.1) that require a sufficient factual basis for statements in court filings, rather than being sanctioned for impugning judicial integrity. When punishing attorneys under rules such as FRCP 11 or Rule 3.1, it is appropriate for the burden to be placed on the attorney to show what formed their reasonable factual basis for the assertions. If, however, the disciplinary authority is punishing statements regarding the judiciary made in court proceedings because the statement impugns judicial integrity or fails to accord proper respect to the judiciary, then the interest being served by the rule is protection of judicial reputation, and the subjective *Sullivan* standard should apply with the requirement that the disciplining authority prove the falsity of the statement. Of course, if it can be proven that the statements satisfy the *Sullivan* standard as well, then an attorney can be sanctioned for violating both Model Rule 8.2 *and* for failing to have a reasonable basis for assertions made in court filings under FRCP 11 or Model Rule 3.1. Thus, Chemerinsky is right that Mire, who was disciplined under Rule 8.2 for impugning judicial integrity, should have had access to the *Sullivan* standard to shield her from discipline; if the Louisiana Supreme Court was concerned about her lack of foundation for statements in court filings, they needed to discipline her for that failure, for example, under Rule 3.1.

Discipline under the proper rule and for the appropriate reason is not a mere academic nicety. There are several problems with punishing attorneys under Rule 8.2 or other rules for impugning judicial integrity where the actual problem is that the attorney lacked a reasonable factual or legal basis for statements in court filings. Notably, courts have recognized that Rule 8.2 on its face applies to any and all statements made by attorneys regardless of the capacity in which the attorney made the statement.[159] Thus, where courts interpret Rule 8.2 in the context of statements

---

[159] *See, e.g., Notopoulos v. Statewide Grievance Comm.*, 890 A.2d 509, 518–19, 521 (Conn. 2006) (holding that "the Rules of Professional Conduct apply to attorneys acting in their individual capacity unless the rule clearly indicates otherwise" and that "[n]either the language of rule 8.2(a) nor the commentary associated with it clearly suggests that the rule should apply only to attorneys' professional, as opposed to personal or pro se, statements"); *Iowa Supreme Court Attorney Disciplinary Bd. v. Weaver*, 750 N.W.2d 71, 92 (Iowa 2008) (noting, in suspending lawyer for making statements about the judiciary to the press, that the relevant "ethics rules apply to attorneys even when they are not acting in their professional capacity"); *In re Pyle*, 156 P.3d 1231, 1243 (Kan. 2007) ("Upon admission to the bar of this state, attorneys assume certain duties as officers of the court. Among the duties imposed upon attorneys is the duty to maintain the respect due to the courts of justice and to judicial officers. A lawyer is bound by the Code of Professional Responsibility in every capacity in which the lawyer acts, whether he is acting as an attorney or not and is subject to discipline even when involved in nonlegal matters . . . "); *In re Donohoe*, 580 P.2d 1093, 1096 (Wash. 1978) (holding that predecessor to

made in court filings and determine that an objective standard applies and that the attorney has the burden to demonstrate the truth or reasonableness of the statement, that same standard is then used for other applications of Rule 8.2, including for statements made by an attorney outside of court processes.

But even where the statements are made in court filings (and thus attorneys have additional duties under rules such as FRCP 11 and Model Rule 3.1 that require a reasonable basis in fact for the statements), punishment under the "objective" Rule 8.2 standard is not harmless. Courts applying the "objective reasonableness" interpretation of Rule 8.2 have required a much higher factual showing than that generally required by FRCP 11 or Rule 3.1 and impose far more severe sanctions. However, if courts use the appropriate rule and discipline attorneys under Model Rule 3.1 or sanction them under FRCP 11, then courts will employ the caselaw interpreting those rules, rather than requiring a heightened showing or imposing a more severe punishment. To the extent that courts employ FRCP 11, Model Rule 3.1 or other facially content- and viewpoint-neutral rules more harshly where the allegations regard the judiciary, courts are protecting judicial reputation and the *Sullivan* standard is applicable.

Another example of a discrepancy in application between Rule 8.2 and the trial rules deals with ascribing motives to participants' actions. In court proceedings, attorneys are expressly allowed to "allege[] generally" allegations involving "malice, intent, knowledge, and other conditions of a person's mind."[160] The basic idea is that often direct evidence does not exist of people's thoughts and motives (unless they happened to articulate them in a recorded form). While the attorney still has to have a reasonable basis in fact under Rule 11 to make an assertion, that standard is relatively easy to meet, and can be shown based on circumstantial evidence or even weak evidence.[161] Rule 11 sanctions generally will not be imposed "unless a particular allegation is utterly lacking in support"[162] or is made in "deliberate indifference to obvious facts."[163] This reality indicates that in order to fulfill their truth-seeking purposes in dispensing justice, courts do not require direct evidence of motive. Nevertheless, under 8.2 courts are quick to punish attorneys for ascribing a motive to judicial action (such as bias) in court filings without direct or even conclusive evidence of that motive. Notably, such punishment is not being imposed to preserve the truth-seeking functions of the court – because otherwise such conclusive evidence would be required as to *all* assertions of motive in court filings.

Importantly, courts don't need to resort to severe punishments (like suspension) or adopt an objective standard for Rule 8.2 in order to protect their justifiable interests

---

Rule 8.2 "permeate[s] all aspects of an attorney's life, whether he be engaged in the active practice of law" or other pursuits).
[160] *See, e.g.*, FED. R. CIV. P. 9 (b).
[161] *Baker v. Alderman*, 158 F.3d 516, 524 (11th Cir. 1998).
[162] *O'Brien v. Alexander*, 101 F.3d 1479, 1489 (2d Cir. 1996).
[163] *Baker*, 158 F.3d at 524 (internal citations omitted).

in ensuring that assertions regarding the judiciary that are made in court filings have a reasonable legal and factual basis and are relevant. Courts already have the rules and tools, including sanctions, to deal with problems of irrelevancy, lack of factual and legal basis, courtroom order, etc. It is equally important to the proper functioning of the judiciary and fair resolution of cases that assertions made in court proceedings regarding nonjudicial actors have a basis in fact and be relevant. Courts do not need extra protection or extra sanctions where statements or allegations regard the judiciary. They do not need an objective interpretation of Rule 8.2 or an exception to the *Sullivan* standard carved out for themselves in order to preserve judicial functions. Rather, courts can use the normal viewpoint-neutral rules used in other contexts if the problem with a statement is irrelevancy or legal or factual insufficiency. If and when courts are doing more – including requiring a greater showing to avoid punishment or the imposition of greater punishments – than they would do if the statements did not regard the judiciary, then they are simply protecting judicial reputation and the requirements of *Sullivan* apply.

THE CORNERSTONE OF OUR GOVERNMENTAL STRUCTURE

The "cornerstone of our governmental structure" is *not* "public confidence in the courts" – as the Kentucky Supreme Court claimed[164] – but rather self-government and its essential components such as the freedoms of speech, association, and petitioning enshrined in the First Amendment. Inflated praise of government and punishment of those who criticize it or its officers are actually essential components of absolute monarchy or totalitarian dictatorships, not of our constitutional system – and such tactics do not instill actual integrity in government officers.

The judiciary is not somehow immune from having members that abuse their power, are biased, incompetent, or corrupt, or whose actions deny citizens their constitutional rights. The Supreme Court recognized this fact in *Mitchum* v. *Foster*,[165] where the Court interpreted 42 U.S.C. § 1983 and explained that at the time of its enactment Congress found that "state *courts* were being *used to harass and injure individuals*, either because the state courts were powerless to stop deprivations or *were in league* with those who were bent upon abrogation of federally protected rights."[166] More recently, the FBI's Operation Wrinkled Robe led to the conviction of two state court judges and the impeachment and removal of federal district court judge Thomas Porteous in 2010.[167]

---

[164] *Ky. Bar Ass'n v. Heleringer*, 602 S.W. 2d 165, 168 (Ky. 1980).

[165] 407 U.S. 225 (1972).

[166] *Id.* at 240 (emphasis added).

[167] *See, e.g.*, Drew Broach, *FBI Records Shed Light on Jefferson Parish Courthouse Corruption Investigation*, THE TIMES-PICAYUNE, NOLA.COM (Oct. 31, 2011), *available at* www.nola.com/crime/index.ssf/2011/10/fbi_records_shed_light_on_jeff.html.

The vast majority of attorneys do not and will not risk the severe punishments meted out in the majority of states for impugning judicial integrity. Attorneys simply will *not* risk loss of their license and thus their livelihood to report or publicize judicial misconduct. Rather, attorneys will (and do) turn a blind eye. Because attorneys are chilled (and often frozen) from performing their checking function to safeguard judicial integrity by revealing such problems, the problems remain hidden and unremedied, making way for judicial unlawfulness or corruption to commence, persist, and grow.

An example is pointed out by Indianapolis blogger Paul Ogden.[168] As reported by the *New York Times*, in 2009, two judges in Pennsylvania, Mark A. Ciavarella and Michael T. Conahan, "pleaded guilty to tax evasion and wire fraud in a scheme that involved sending thousands of juveniles to two private detention centers in exchange for $2.6 million in kickbacks."[169] A state commission investigating the scandal questioned why attorneys, who should have recognized that proceedings were fishy in those courts, had not spoken up. Ogden reviews Pennsylvania's history of silencing lawyers for criticizing the judiciary – specifically noting that from 1999 to 2006, the Pennsylvania Supreme Court had meted out "two five year suspensions and a disbarment all for speaking out about Pennsylvania county court judges."[170] Ogden concludes that, consequently, "it is not surprising that Pennsylvania attorneys chose not to say anything" about the kickback scheme.[171] He explains:

> Any attorney who dared to lodge such allegations faced the real possibility they would lose their license. Should any of those attorneys dare[] to take that risk, that attorney would have faced a shifting burden of proof that placed the responsibility of proving substantial details of the kickback scheme. Even if the attorney can successfully [pull] that off, he might still have to spend a year or more defending himself against disciplinary charges that damage his reputation and cost him a small fortune.[172]

And Ogden would know. Because Ogden, now an inactive attorney, was suspended from the practice of law for thirty days by the Indiana Supreme Court and ordered to pay half of the disciplinary commission's bill of over $20,000 for statements he made about a probate judge in a private email sent to opposing counsel and copied to case participants.[173]

---

[168] Paul K. Ogden, *Pennsylvania Supreme Court Silenced Attorney Whistleblowers Who Could Have Reported "Kids for Cash" Judicial Scandal*, DISBARRING THE CRITICS, Jan. 9, 2014, http://disbarringthecritics.blogspot.com/2014/01/pennsylvania-supreme-court-disciplinary.html.

[169] Ian Urbina, *Despite Red Flags About Judges, a Kickback Scheme Flourished*, N.Y. TIMES, Mar. 27, 2009, *available at* www.nytimes.com/2009/03/28/us/28judges.html?pagewanted=all&_r=0.

[170] Ogden, *supra* Note 168.

[171] *Id.*

[172] *Id.*

[173] *See In re Ogden*, 10 N.E.3d 499, 502 (2014) (suspending Ogden and assessing him half of the costs and expenses); *see also* Dave Stafford, *Criticism of Judge Results in Discipline Case,*

The Tinkerbell solution is thus self-defeating. In order to promote its own integrity and shore up its legitimacy and power, the judiciary prohibits speech that exposes its weakness from the only class of persons likely to have such knowledge – attorneys. The suppression keeps the public from knowing the truth about judicial actors, frustrating democracy itself and clogging the wheels of political change. But by so doing, the judiciary undermines its actual power because the only way to remedy deficiencies in judicial integrity is not to hide them but to allow those who know of them – usually attorneys – to expose them, discuss them, and raise them to the public, to the courts, and to other governing bodies (such as judicial qualifications committees or legislatures for impeachment). Indeed, the judiciary's *own power* to address constitutional and other law violations caused by judicial conduct, abuse, incompetence, or corruption is entirely undermined by prohibiting lawyer speech and petitioning regarding it – because the only way that litigants can obtain relief from judicial abuse, error, incompetence, or corruption is by having an attorney raise it on their behalf.

Importantly, even with full First Amendment protection for their speech, the parade of horribles prophesied in court opinions is very unlikely to play out. Many lawyers will continue to remain silent. This is because the justice system already has a major built-in disincentive for attorneys to make derogatory comments about a judge. Attorneys generally focus their practice to a particular location and thus are repeat players in front of specific judges. Judges hold in their hands the attorneys' cases brought on behalf of aggrieved clients. Attorneys want the judge to like them and to want to listen to them. Attorneys also recognize that they will need discretionary accommodations from the judge from time to time – such as extensions of time for their clients. Thus, on the whole – even with the shield of the *Sullivan* standard in place – lawyers will continue to curry favor with and avoid antagonizing the judges before whom they appear. Only in extreme circumstances would most

---

INDIANA LAWYER, May 22, 2013, *available at* www.theindianalawyer.com/articles/31510-criticism-of-judge-results-in-discipline-case (disclosing contents of Ogden's email sent to opposing counsel, namely, that Judge David Coleman "should be turned in to the disciplinary commission for how he handled this case" and that "[i]f this case would have been in Marion County with a real probate court with a real judge, the stuff that went on with this case never would have happened"); Paul K. Ogden, *Goodbye to Practice of Law; Indiana Disciplinary Commission Incurred More Expenses Prosecuting Ogden Than Any Other Attorney*, DISBARRING THE CRITICS, Oct. 3, 2014, http://disbarringthecritics.blogspot.com/2014/10/incurred-more-expenses-prosecuting.html (showing over $20,000 in expenses assessed).

Ogden did not pay the costs, instead deciding to leave the practice of law by going on inactive status. The disciplinary commission sought his suspension for failure to pay. The Indiana Supreme Court denied that request because Ogden had changed his status to inactive, but noted that Ogden "need[s] to pay his outstanding costs if he seeks to return his license to active status." *See In re Failure to Satisfy Costs in Lawyer Disciplinary Case of Paul K. Ogden*, No. 49500–1303-DI-183 (Ind., Oct. 29, 2015), *available at* https://public.courts.in.gov/Docket/Document/GetOdysseyDocument?DocumentID=3998313.

lawyers consider raising publicly or in court proceedings criticism of the judges before whom they will continue to appear and plead their clients' causes.

In his *Mire* dissent, Justice Weimer asserted: "judicial efforts to squelch criticism of the judiciary can result in *worse outcomes than any criticism itself could.*"[174] Weimer specifically referred to the Supreme Court's statement in *Bridges* v. *State of California*[175] that "an enforced silence" undertaken "solely in the name of preserving the dignity of the bench, would probably engender resentment, suspicion, and contempt much more than it would enhance respect."[176] Again, "the path of safety" for preserving both the perceived and actual integrity of the judiciary is *not* to artificially inflate public opinion by suppressing lawyer speech critical of the judiciary, but is instead, as Justice Brandeis counseled, "to discuss freely supposed grievances and proposed remedies."[177]

Taking this appropriate path upholds the First Amendment rights of lawyers and allows them to both perform their checking function necessary to safeguard judicial integrity and to protect the constitutional and legal rights of their clients. Our judicial Tinkerbell will not die if attorneys stop clapping; instead, the lethal threat resides in the failure to diagnose illnesses and supply needed medical attention while forcing attorneys to ignore any symptoms and proclaim her healthy.

[174] *In re Mire*, 197 So. 3d 656, 673 (La. 2016) (Wiemer, J., dissenting) (emphasis added).
[175] 314 U.S. 252 (1941).
[176] *Id.* at 270–71.
[177] *Whitney* v. *California*, 274 U.S. 357, 375–76 (1927) (Brandeis, J., concurring).

12

Securing Criminal Constitutional Processes

Deputy District Attorney Richard Ceballos worked for the Los Angeles District Attorney's Office in 2000.[1] A criminal defense attorney called him about one of his cases, explaining that he was going to file a motion to challenge a critical search warrant. Ceballos decided to look into the search warrant – examining the affidavit that was used to obtain it and examining the location it described – and "determined that the affidavit contained serious misrepresentations."[2] Ceballos spoke with the deputy sheriff who had written the affidavit and "did not receive a satisfactory explanation." Ceballos then wrote a memorandum to his supervisors, Carol Najera and Frank Sundstedt, recommending dismissal of the case. Ceballos and his supervisors held a meeting with members of the Sheriff's office (including the affiant) about the warrant and the alleged misrepresentations, and the meeting became "heated."[3] Sundstedt decided to proceed with the prosecution, and Ceballos told Najera that he was going to turn over the memo (with his own conclusions redacted as work product) to the defense as exculpatory evidence pursuant to *Brady* v. *Maryland*. Ceballos turned over the materials and was called as a witness by the defense at the suppression hearing. According to Ceballos, Najera told Ceballos that "he would suffer retaliation if he testified that the affidavit contained intentional falsehoods."[4] Ceballos testified at the hearing, but the trial court denied suppression, finding that there were "grounds independent of the challenged material" to establish probable cause for the warrant.[5]

---

[1] *Garcetti* v. *Ceballos*, 547 U.S. 410 (2006). Some material contained in this chapter and Chapter 13 was previously published in Margaret Tarkington, *Lost in the Compromise: Free Speech, Criminal Justice, and Attorney Pretrial Publicity*, 66 FLA. L. REV. 1873 (2014).
[2] *Garcetti*, 547 U.S. at 414.
[3] *Id.*
[4] *Id.* at 442 (Souter, J., dissenting).
[5] *Id.*

Subsequently, Ceballos was reassigned to a different position, transferred to another courthouse, and denied a promotion – despite excellent performance reviews before the incident. Ceballos sued the county and his supervisors for retaliating against him for his speech in violation of his First Amendment rights. Specifically, he alleged the senior prosecutors retaliated against him for his written memo (that he turned over to the defense as exculpatory *Brady* material), his statements to his supervisors about the case, and his testimony in the criminal case.[6]

In *Garcetti* v. *Ceballos*, the Supreme Court, with a bare majority of five justices, held that Ceballos did *not* have any protectable First Amendment rights to engage in his speech (specifically addressing the memo) because he was speaking as part of his official duties as a public employee.[7] The Court did *not* analyze his speech as a lawyer *per se*, but instead analyzed the case under the Court's decisions in *Pickering* v. *Board of Education of Township High School District 205*[8] and progeny regarding the free speech rights of public employees.

The majority in *Garcetti* adopted a categorical approach, holding that public employees only have free speech rights vis-à-vis their employer when acting *as citizens*, but not when acting in their capacity as government employees. The Court elaborated: "when public employees make statements *pursuant to their official duties* the employees are *not speaking as citizens* for First Amendment purposes, and the Constitution does not insulate their communications from employer discipline."[9]

This line of demarcation is very similar to the categorical approach under which attorneys have First Amendment rights when acting as lay citizens but not when acting as lawyers. The *Garcetti* Court elaborated that Ceballos "did not act as a citizen" – and thus lacked First Amendment rights – "when he went about conducting his daily professional activities, such as supervising attorneys, investigating charges, and preparing filings."[10] Nor did he have such rights "by writing a memo that addressed the proper disposition of a pending criminal case"[11] – even though that memo was created and given to the defense as potential *Brady* material, which a prosecutor is required by the Constitution to turn over. According to the majority, when Ceballos "went to work and performed the tasks he was paid to perform" he acted as an employee rather than a citizen even if "his duties sometimes required him to speak or write."[12]

Hearkening to the corollary of the constitutional conditions theory, the Court contended that "[r]estricting speech that *owes its existence* to a public employee's

[6] *Id.* at 443 and nn.14 and 15.
[7] *Id.* at 421 (majority opinion).
[8] 391 U.S. 563, 538 (1968).
[9] *Garcetti*, 547 U.S. at 421 (emphasis added).
[10] *Id.* at 422.
[11] *Id.*
[12] *Id.*

professional responsibilities does *not infringe any liberties* the employee might have enjoyed as a private citizen. It simply reflects the exercise of employer control over *what the employer itself has commissioned or created.*"[13] This argument is precisely along the lines of the argument, discussed in Chapter 1, that lawyers have no rights when speaking as lawyers because before becoming a lawyer they did not have a right to speak on behalf of people as their legal representative.

The *Garcetti* decision is problematic on many fronts. Most notable is the Court's failure to even consider the significant and specialized concerns emanating from the fact that Ceballos did not speak primarily as a public employee but as a lawyer – and, more importantly, as a prosecutor in the criminal justice system. Only one Justice seemed to appreciate this aspect of the case. Justice Breyer in his dissent noted "special circumstances" existing in the case – specifically that Ceballos was a lawyer who believed he was required by both the Constitution (under *Brady* v. *Maryland* and progeny) and the applicable rules of professional conduct to create the memo detailing his findings and provide it to the defense.[14] Breyer notes that lawyers are sometimes required by the Constitution or professional conduct rules to engage in speech – a compelling aspect of Ceballos's speech that the majority had failed to take into account, apparently considering it immaterial to their disposition.

As disconcerting as the *Garcetti* decision is on its own facts, the expansive language in the decision is far more problematic. If accurately stating the law, the decision indicates that lawyers who are public employees lack First Amendment rights (vis-à-vis their employer certainly and perhaps *in toto*) whenever acting pursuant to their "daily professional activities," including specifically investigating cases, "preparing filings," writing memos regarding "the proper disposition" of a case, or doing anything else that is part of going "to work and perform[ing] the tasks he was paid to perform."[15] This would mean that *all* publicly employed lawyers lack such First Amendment rights – including not only prosecutors like Ceballos, but also public defenders.

And apparently, publicly employed lawyers lose not only their speech rights but other First Amendment rights too, as the *Garcetti* decision specifically purports to encompass "preparing filings,"[16] which implicates not only speech but also the petitioning rights of the lawyer. Indeed, since the *Garcetti* rule covers anything that falls under the expansive umbrella of "perform[ing] the tasks" lawyers are "paid to perform" and anything that *"owes its existence* to a public employee's *professional responsibilities,"* publicly employed lawyers have essentially been stripped of all First Amendment rights when acting in their capacity as lawyers.[17] Importantly, *Garcetti* only specifically dealt with lawyers' First Amendment rights vis-à-vis their

---

[13] *Id.* (emphasis added).
[14] *Id.* at 446–47 (Breyer, J., dissenting).
[15] *Id.* at 422 (majority opinion).
[16] *Id.*
[17] *Id.* at 421–22 (emphasis added).

government employer, and not necessarily vis-à-vis another government regulator, such as the judiciary or a legislature in enacting professional conduct rules. However, the Court speaks in broad terms that can easily be read to restrictively define the First Amendment rights of public employees regardless of the government actor punishing or restricting such speech.

The number of lawyers who are also public employees is vast. According to the ABA, they comprise one-eighth of the entire legal profession in the United States.[18] Under the access to justice theory, the First Amendment rights of publicly employed lawyers must be attuned to the specific roles that they play in the justice system. Two basic categories of publicly employed attorneys require special analysis because of their prominence and importance to the integrity of the criminal justice system: prosecutors and public defenders. Each of these publicly employed lawyers plays an essential role in the proper administration of justice and in the proper invocation and avoidance of government power in the protection or deprivation of life, liberty, and property. They are the essential players in our criminal justice system and require the requisite First Amendment rights to fulfill their respective roles therein.

It is also important to recognize at the outset that the Constitution affords more jealous protection of life and liberty than it does to property. As noted by Justice Rutledge in his *Bowles* v. *Willingham* concurrence,[19] civil proceedings generally involve "rights of property, not of personal liberty or life as in criminal proceedings."[20] While deprivations of property are "serious," Rutledge argues they "are not of the same moment under our system" of justice as criminal deprivations of life and liberty. This divergence is apparent by the fact that the Constitution itself expressly mandates specific procedural protections for criminal deprivations, which are simply not applicable in the civil context.[21] Justice Rutledge acknowledges such procedural differences and concludes: "It is in this respect perhaps that our basic law, following the common law, most clearly places the rights to life and to liberty above those of property."[22] Additionally, the Suspension Clause[23] – forbidding Congress from suspending the writ of habeas corpus absent rebellion or invasion – underscores the Constitution's preferential protection for life and liberty and for freedom from unlawful restraint or incarceration.[24]

The use of state criminal power and processes by attorneys to either secure or deprive individuals of life and liberty is therefore a particularly weighty concern.

[18] *See* AM. BAR ASS'N, GOVERNMENT AND PUBLIC SECTOR LAWYERS, www.americanbar.org/portals/government_public_sector_lawyers.html.
[19] 321 U.S. 503 (1944).
[20] *Id.* at 525 (Rutledge, J., concurring).
[21] *Id.*
[22] *Id.*
[23] U.S. CONST. Art. I, § 9, cl. 2.
[24] *See also Boumediene* v. *Bush*, 553 U.S. 723, 739 (2008) ("The Framers viewed freedom from unlawful restraint as a fundamental precept of liberty, and they understood the writ of habeas corpus as a vital instrument to secure that freedom.").

Recognizing the constitutional weight afforded to governmental deprivations of life and liberty foreshadows that in the criminal context, speech, association, and petitioning essential to securing life and liberty may call for greater protection, while speech or activities that may undermine individuals' rights to life and liberty may be subject to greater restriction.

THE ROLE AND CONCOMITANT FIRST AMENDMENT RIGHTS OF THE PROSECUTOR

Prosecutors play a very unique, specific, and important role in our justice system. As a representative of the sovereign, the prosecutor represents society collectively[25] in undertaking the sovereign's "awesome power"[26] to bring criminal charges against individuals. The central job of the prosecutor is to deprive individuals of life, liberty, and property, which must be done through just and constitutionally mandated processes.

The prosecutor's client is an amorphous entity – the sovereign. But in a democratic government, the sovereign is not an individual, or even a group of individuals; rather, the sovereign is the entire body politic. Both the prosecutor and the defendant – as well as any victims – are members of the society the prosecutor represents.[27] This feature of the prosecutor's representation alters a typical attorney–client representation in several meaningful ways.

In the traditional representation, the attorney acts as an agent who represents a client-principal. The client determines the objectives of the representation, and the attorney must obtain client consent in order to undertake certain actions – including settling a case or revealing information related to the representation. The prosecutor, in contrast, acts as both agent and principal in making such decisions about settlement or disclosing confidential information.[28] But that does not mean that prosecutors simply can do whatever they wish as if there were no principal involved. The prosecutor is not a free or rogue agent. While maintaining discretion as to specific acts taken, the prosecutor's client, the principal, is still the sovereign – and that sovereign has already determined the objectives of any criminal representation: that justice will be done.

Although the prosecutor has discretion in determining the means to be used, the ultimate objectives of the representation have been established by the client – the people – through the creation of constitutional processes and guarantees, both substantive and procedural. These include the defendant's constitutional rights to due process, to counsel, to a fair trial, to confront witnesses, and against compelled

---

[25] R. Michael Cassidy, Prosecutorial Ethics 2–3 (2005).
[26] Robert P. Mosteller, *The Duke Lacrosse Case, Innocence, and False Identifications: A Fundamental Failure to "Do Justice,"* 76 Ford. L. Rev. 1337, 1366 (2007).
[27] Cassidy, *supra* Note 25, at 2–3.
[28] *Id.*

self-incrimination. It also includes the presumption of innocence, as a component of both due process and the Sixth Amendment, for the basic "guarantee, for guilty and innocent persons alike, that the State cannot impose punishment prior to conviction."[29] As Shima Baradaran explains, quoting the Supreme Court's 2012 decision in *Southern Union Co.* v. *United States*, the "jury acts 'as a bulwark between the State and the accused,'" prohibiting state punishment until "the prosecution has proved each element of an offense beyond a reasonable doubt."[30]

Further, as the Supreme Court has recognized in recent years, the guarantee of a fair trial also includes within its ambit fairness in pleas and pretrial processes. Trials have become the rare occasion, with plea bargains as the established norm. Over 95 percent of state and federal criminal cases end in a guilty plea.[31] In *Missouri* v. *Frye*, the Supreme Court explained: "The reality is that plea bargains have become *so central* to the administration of the criminal justice system" that it "is insufficient simply *to point to the guarantee of a fair trial* as a backstop that inoculates any *errors in the pretrial process*."[32]

R. Michael Cassidy elaborates that "[u]nlike other advocates ... the prosecutor has obligations of evenhandedness precisely because he does *not* represent an individual but rather the collective good," which requires that "all of [society's] members are treated fairly and protected from governmental overreaching."[33] As explained in the ABA Criminal Justice Standards for the Prosecution Function, "[t]he prosecutor should seek to *protect the innocent* and convict the guilty, consider the interests of victims and witnesses, and *respect the constitutional and legal rights* of all persons, including *suspects and defendants*."[34] For "[t]he primary duty of the prosecutor is to seek justice within the bounds of the law, not merely to convict."[35]

Thus the prosecutor's actions should reflect society's valid criminal justice interests in ascertaining guilt and allocating punishment in accord with deterrence, incapacitation, retribution, or rehabilitation. Yet prosecutors also have an obligation – central to justice – to drop charges if not supported by probable cause. It may be that the defendant is innocent, or is guilty of a lesser offense, or that a lesser punishment or even no punishment is the just result. Overarchingly, "the prosecutor's obligation is ... to take steps to ensure an accurate result through a fair process."[36] As oft-quoted, the Supreme Court poignantly explained:

---

[29] Rinat Kitai, *Presuming Innocence*, 55 OKLA. L. REV. 257, 280–81 (2002); *see also* Shima Baradaran, *The Presumption of Punishment*, CRIM L. & PHILOS. (June 2013).

[30] Baradaran, *supra* Note 29, at *10, *quoting Southern Union Co.* v. *United States*, 567 U.S. 343, 348 (2012).

[31] JONATHAN DRESSLER AND GEORGE C. THOMAS III, CRIMINAL PROCEDURE 1016 (4th edn. 2010).

[32] *Missouri* v. *Frye*, 566 U.S. 134, 143–44 (2012) (emphasis added).

[33] CASSIDY, *supra* Note 25, at 2–3.

[34] ABA STANDARDS FOR CRIMINAL JUSTICE: PROSECUTION FUNCTION AND DEFENSE FUNCTION § 3–1.2(b) (4th edn. 2015) (emphasis added).

[35] *Id.*

[36] CASSIDY, *supra* Note 25, at 3–4.

The United States Attorney *is the representative* not of an ordinary party to a controversy, but *of a sovereignty* whose obligation to govern impartially is as compelling as its obligation to govern at all; and *whose interest*, therefore, in a criminal prosecution *is not that it shall win a case, but that justice shall be done.* As such, he is in a peculiar and very definite sense the servant of the law, *the twofold aim of which is that guilt shall not escape or innocence suffer.* He may prosecute with earnestness and vigor – indeed, he should do so. But, while he may strike hard blows, he is not at liberty to strike foul ones. It is as much *his duty to refrain from improper methods calculated to produce a wrongful conviction* as it is to use every legitimate means to bring about a just one.[37]

Prosecutors have no discretion to disregard or undermine these objectives established by their client. Consequently, under the access to justice theory, the prosecutor lacks First Amendment rights to engage in speech, association, or petitioning that undermines these basic guarantees of fairness and due process in criminal prosecutions.

Another major difference from the traditional attorney–client representation is the prosecutor's access to information and evidence. In a traditional attorney–client relationship with an individual client, the client is the initial primary source for information. If a civil court proceeding is filed, the attorney can then use the court's discovery procedures to obtain information from third parties. But until a case is filed, attorneys rely on their client and on information voluntarily provided by witnesses identified by the client. Similarly, in transactional situations, both parties to a deal are obligated to volunteer and disclose complete information relevant to the deal or contract. A failure of one side to disclose material information may lead to a rescission of the deal or even to civil liability.

In contrast, prosecutors have access to and rely on the enforcement arm of the state to obtain information and evidence before a case is filed – which access is essential for prosecutors to fulfill their charging functions. Prosecutors work with and receive information from the police obtained through coercive state power (not volunteered by a client or third party), as well as obtaining physical evidence and arrests obtained through the state's power to lawfully search and seize. Notably, there are constitutional limits on the exercise of this police power to coercively take into its possession information, evidence, and people. The prosecutor's First Amendment rights in using and disclosing this information is cabined under the access to justice theory to use and disclosure that is consistent with the purposes for which the public sovereign provided the prosecutor access and the constitutional processes attendant thereto.

Prosecutors also must have the requisite First Amendment rights to fulfill their role – to speak, associate, and petition to prosecute crime and thereby enforce the criminal laws of the state. The prosecutor plays a key role in the system of criminal

---

[37] *Berger v. United States*, 295 U.S. 78, 88 (1935) (emphasis added).

justice from the investigative stage, to the filing of charges, bargaining for pleas, pretrial processes, trials, appeals, and ultimately even to remedying wrongful convictions. In each of these aspects of the prosecutor's role, the prosecutor must have the requisite First Amendment rights to fulfill that role. Again, the access to justice theory both protects speech essential to the attorney's role and recognizes that certain restrictions on First Amendment rights are constitutionally permissible where allowing such speech would undermine the prosecutor's role and frustrate the criminal justice system.

Speech Mandated by the Constitution or the Prosecutor's Role to Do Justice

As Justice Breyer noted in his *Garcetti* dissent, prosecutors are sometimes required to engage in speech or petitioning either by the Constitution or by the applicable professional conduct rules. Ceballos believed that the memo that he wrote and delivered to the defense was mandated by his obligations under *Brady* v. *Maryland*[38] and *Kyles* v. *Whitley*[39] to learn of and disclose to the defense exculpatory evidence in the hands of the prosecution or the police.[40] Additionally, state rules of professional conduct broadly require an attorney to disclose exculpatory evidence to the defense. For example, California's Rule of Professional Conduct 5–110, which would have applied to Ceballos, requires prosecutors to "[m]ake timely disclosure to the defense of all evidence or information known to the prosecutor that the prosecutor knows or reasonably should know *tends* to negate the guilt of the accused, mitigate the offense, or mitigate the sentence."[41]

The *Garcetti* Court did not analyze whether or not the memo actually fell within *Brady* v. *Maryland* and progeny or within California's professional conduct rule requiring turnover of exculpatory materials to the defense.[42] Instead, the majority

---

[38] 373 U.S. 83 (1963).

[39] 514 U.S. 419 (1995).

[40] In *Kyles* v. *Whitley*, the Supreme Court explained that "the individual prosecutor has a duty to learn of any favorable evidence known to the others acting on the government's behalf in the case, including the police," and then, once known, to disclose it to the defense pursuant to *Brady. See Kyles*, 514 U.S. at 437–38. *See also Garcetti* v. *Ceballos*, 547 U.S. 410, 447 (2006) (Breyer, J., dissenting) ("A prosecutor has a constitutional obligation to learn of, to preserve, and to communicate with the defense about exculpatory and impeachment evidence in the government's possession.").

[41] CAL. RULES OF PROF'L CONDUCT R. 5–110 (emphasis added).

[42] Lawrence Rosenthal argues that Ceballos's speech did not qualify technically as exculpatory evidence under *Brady* v. *Maryland*. Rosenthal argues that "Ceballos learned of the circumstantial evidence suggesting police perjury from the defense counsel and his inspection of the area described in the warrant application, not as the result of any information in the exclusive possession of the District Attorney or Sheriff's office." *See* Lawrence Rosenthal, *The Emerging First Amendment Law of Managerial Prerogative*, 77 FORD. L. REV. 33, 56–57 (2008). Despite Rosenthal's argument, Ceballos additionally had access to and talked to the warrant affiant – the deputy sheriff who wrote the affidavit – arguably providing him with information and evidence not in the hands of the defense.

treated this possibility as immaterial to its disposition – apparently, even if Ceballos's speech was required by *Brady* as he contended, the First Amendment provided no protection because his speech was made "pursuant to" his "official duties" as a prosecutor.

Under the access to justice theory, prosecutors must have protected First Amendment rights to engage in speech or petitioning that is requisite to preserve the constitutional rights of the accused and thus the integrity of criminal processes. This absolutely would include a protectable right to disclose to the defense exculpatory evidence known to the government or to the police pursuant to *Brady* and progeny. Such speech is essential to the prosecutor's role in representing the sovereign and ensuring compliance with constitutional processes. Prosecutors such as Ceballos should have a protectable speech right against discipline or sanctions for engaging in speech that protects the constitutional rights of the accused or is otherwise mandated by the Constitution.

As the Supreme Court recognized in *Kyles*, the professional conduct rules generally require prosecutors to provide more disclosure than *Brady*, requiring "prosecutorial disclosures of any evidence tending to exculpate or mitigate."[43] Under the access to justice theory, prosecutors would similarly have a First Amendment right to engage in such speech and disclosure because it is speech that is integral to the prosecutor's role to do justice.

On the flip side, prosecutors lack a First Amendment right to refuse to engage in speech that is required by the Constitution – such as *Brady* material – and thus they can be punished for failing to disclose exculpatory evidence. Further, even though not constitutionally required, if a jurisdiction determines that prosecutors should have greater disclosure obligations to the defense as a component of that jurisdiction's concept of fair criminal processes, such as those found in Model Rule of Professional Conduct 3.8, the jurisdiction can require as much, and the prosecutor cannot rely on the First Amendment for protection from discipline. The prosecutor's First Amendment rights do not include the ability to hide exculpatory evidence from the defendant or engage in activities that could lead to a wrongful or unjust conviction. If a jurisdiction wants to protect against such possibilities by requiring broader disclosure (or even open file discovery), it is free to do so to preserve the integrity of their criminal processes by taking actions that will minimize wrongful convictions.

In a similar vein, prosecutors should have protected First Amendment rights to assist in remedying wrongful convictions of which they become aware. Such speech is essential to their role to ensure that justice is done – as the *Berger* Court

---

Nevertheless, Rosenthal argues against "a reading of *Garcetti* that would deny prosecutors protection even when they speak pursuant to a constitutional obligation," yet he notes that such a reading is possible. *See id.*, at 68 and n. 120.

[43] *Kyles*, 514 U.S. at 437.

maintained that the prosecutor's role includes ensuring that the innocent do not suffer.[44] Moreover, some jurisdictions provide that prosecutors have disclosure obligations when they learn of any "new, credible, and material evidence" showing a reasonable likelihood of a wrongful conviction.[45] These disclosure obligations are enforceable because the suppression of such evidence by the prosecution would directly contradict the prosecutor's role and obligation to do justice. Further, the state has provided the prosecutor with extensive access to information through the state's police arm – far more access than available to criminal convicts – and can require the prosecutor to use that information to the end that innocence will not suffer.

The *Garcetti* Court conflated caselaw dealing with the separate issues of speech rights of public employees and of government-funded speech, essentially treating the speech of public employees as government-funded speech – "speech that the government has bought with a salary and thus may control free from First Amendment scrutiny."[46] Other government-funded speech cases dealt with situations where the government decides as a policy matter whether to expend money to promote a specific message or activity that it need not fund at all. Examples include funding fine arts or the building of monuments or parks, promoting beef production and consumption, and promoting alternatives to abortion.[47] Quoting a government-funded speech case, the *Garcetti* Court asserted that "[w]hen the government appropriates public funds to promote a particular policy of its own it is entitled to say what it wishes."[48] But this is utter nonsense in the context of a prosecutor's disclosure of exculpatory information (including potential police misconduct) to the defense.

The government – and specifically, the prosecution – is not free "to say what it wishes" when doing so contravenes constitutional rights of the accused. The government speech cases deal with whether the government can promote specific discretionary messages like "Beef. It's What's for Dinner."[49] And certainly, if government wants to expend money on a program that promotes beef for dinner or bacon for breakfast or bologna for lunch, they can do so. Yet, contrary to what the *Garcetti* Court indicated, the government did not "commission" Ceballos's speech. Instead, the government hired Ceballos to deprive people of life and liberty through the

---

[44] *Berger v. United States*, 295 U.S. 78, 88 (1935).

[45] ARIZ. RULES OF PROF'L CONDUCT R. 3.8(g)–(h). Arizona's rule is modeled on MODEL RULES OF PROFESSIONAL CONDUCT 3.8(g) and (h).

[46] *See* Helen Norton, *Constraining Public Employee Speech: Government's Control of Its Workers' Speech to Protect Its Own Expression*, 59 DUKE L.J. 1, 12 (2009)

[47] *See Pleasant Grove City v. Summum*, 555 U.S. 460 (2009); *Johanns v. Livestock Mktg. Ass'n.*, 544 U.S. 550 (2005); *National Endowment for the Arts v. Finley*, 524 U.S. 569 (1998); *Rust v. Sullivan*, 500 U.S. 173 (1991).

[48] *Garcetti v. Ceballos*, 547 U.S. 410, 422 (2006) (quoting *Rosenberger v. Rector and Visitors of Univ. of Va.*, 515 U.S. 819, 833 (1995)).

[49] *Johanns*, 544 U.S. at 554.

exercise of the state's criminal powers. And when government undertakes such activities, it is the Constitution that "commissions or creates" the prosecutor's obligation to turn over exculpatory evidence.

In the criminal justice system, the government is not free to promote a message of contravening the constitutional rights of the accused. They are not free to promote processes that deprive people of due process, or a fair trial, or the presumption of innocence. That is because the sovereign – the body politic – established the prosecutor's limited powers in the Constitution by making guarantees as to the use of the state's great and terrible power to deprive citizens of their very lives and liberties. Granted, prosecutors have some expressive choice, generally referred to as prosecutorial discretion, as to whether or not to prosecute certain crimes. What prosecutorial discretion does *not* include, however, is discretion to disregard the Constitution or their obligation to do justice once a decision to prosecute is made. The only message that prosecutors can promote in representing the sovereign in exercising the power to take away life and liberty is that justice will be done and constitutional processes and rights will be adhered to.

First Amendment Rights to Bring Charges

Prosecutors certainly have First Amendment rights to fulfill their role in protecting the public's legitimate and substantial interest in the enforcement of criminal laws and punishment of the guilty. They thus have speech and petitioning rights to invoke government power on behalf of their sovereign client in protecting this public interest to initiate criminal proceedings, to access court processes and make relevant and colorable arguments therein – in addition to engaging in speech necessary to protect the constitutional and legal rights of the accused.

Monroe Freedman and Janet Starwood noted that "in at least one important respect, the prosecutor's rights of expression are broader than those of the ordinary citizen."[50] Namely, "the prosecutor is specially privileged ... to go beyond the bounds that normally restrict other citizens by publishing charges in an indictment that might otherwise constitute defamation."[51] Prosecutors, appropriately, are protected

---

[50] Monroe Freedman and Janet Starwood, *Prior Restraints on Freedom of Expression by Defendants and Defense Attorneys: Ratio Decidendi v. Obiter Dictum*, 29 STAN. L. REV. 607, 617 (1977).

[51] *Id.* Monroe Freedman and Abbe Smith departed from this argument in UNDERSTANDING LEGAL ETHICS by arguing that, pursuant to *Garcetti*, prosecutors do not have First Amendment rights in their official duties at all. *See* MONROE H. FREEDMAN AND ABBE SMITH, UNDERSTANDING LEGAL ETHICS 306 n. 99 (4th edn. 2010). According to the access to justice theory, *Garcetti* was wrongly decided, and the prosecutor has First Amendment rights to engage in speech that is essential to his role as a minister of justice – including speech that secures the rights of the accused.

in making statements as part of their advocacy function in initiating or presenting the state's case, which includes publishing charges in an indictment.[52]

Prosecutors have a related right to petition the government for redress by filing charges against individuals. Nevertheless, the right is limited because prosecutors lack a petition right to bring charges that are not supported by probable cause. It is contrary to the prosecutor's role to bring charges against people – to threaten their life and liberty and harm their reputations – when there is not even probable cause supporting such an indictment.[53] Thus, while prosecutors are generally protected in invoking court processes and petitioning on behalf of the people, they can be disciplined for bringing charges that lack a minimal level of support of probable cause.

No Liberty to "Strike Foul" Blows[54]

The prosecutor can also be limited in his speech to the criminal defendant. As a minister of justice, the prosecutor cannot take advantage of the accused in a way that is unjust or works to deprive the accused of their constitutional rights. Thus professional conduct rules that protect the accused's right to counsel from interference by the prosecution are constitutional. For example, the so-called no contact rule forbids the prosecutor from contacting a represented defendant without the defendant's lawyer or permission from that lawyer. Even though the rule prohibits prosecutorial speech to the defendant, the rule is aimed at protecting the accused's Fifth and Sixth Amendment rights to counsel. Further, rules forbidding the prosecutor from taking advantage of an unrepresented criminal defendant by seeking to obtain a waiver of important pretrial rights of the accused are similarly aimed at forbidding the prosecutor from "striking foul blows" that are contrary to the impartial and just administration of the criminal laws and protection of the constitutional rights of the accused.[55]

THE ROLE AND CONCOMITANT FIRST AMENDMENT RIGHTS OF CRIMINAL DEFENSE ATTORNEYS

As dubious as the *Garcetti* Court's holding is in the context of prosecutors, the case is ludicrous if attempted to be applied to public defenders, who are also public

---

[52] *See, e.g., Imbler* v. *Patchman*, 424 U.S. 409, 431 (1976) (absolute immunity for prosecutor's conduct "in initiating a prosecution and in presenting the State's case"); *Buckley* v. *Fitzsimmons*, 509 U.S. 259, 273 (1993) (explaining that prosecutor actions "in preparing for the initiation of judicial proceedings or for trial, and which occurred in the course of his role as an advocate for the State, are entitled to the protections of absolute immunity").

[53] *See, e.g.,* MODEL RULES OF PROF'L CONDUCT R. 3.8(a).

[54] *Berger* v. *United States*, 295 U.S. 78, 88 (1935).

[55] *See id.; see also, e.g.,* MODEL RULE OF PROF'L CONDUCT R. 3.8(c).

employees. If taken at face value, the *Garcetti* opinion indicates that because public defenders are public employees, they lack First Amendment rights when performing "official duties" of their job[56] – and thus they can be freely punished for their speech by supervising attorneys and perhaps by the government more broadly.

Even inside the public defender's office, subordinate criminal defense attorneys' obligations are to their accused clients – public defenders cannot be controlled by their employer or supervisor. The Supreme Court recognized in *Polk County* v. *Dodson*, "[A] defense lawyer is not, and by the nature of his function *cannot be*, the servant of an administrative superior."[57] Rather, the defense attorney must "advanc[e] 'the undivided interests of his client.'"[58]

It is antithetical to the role of the public defender to treat their speech and petitioning as somehow subject to government or employer control, interference, and punishment without recourse to First Amendment protection. The very role of the public defender is to check and challenge government power for the protection of the accused's life, liberty, and property in the face of the full weight of government brute force. All criminal defense attorneys must have the requisite First Amendment rights to fulfill that role. Not all criminal defense attorneys are publicly employed, but, despite *Garcetti*, the fact of public employment cannot diminish the vital First Amendment rights of public defenders. Whether or not employed by the state, criminal defense attorneys have the same First Amendment rights – those rights necessary to fulfill their essential role in the criminal justice system.

The criminal defense attorney's role in the system of justice is to be the accused's "champion against a hostile world"[59] – a status that entails heightened duties of loyalty, confidentiality, communication, and zealous representation beyond those inhering in a civil representation. As the ABA Criminal Justice Standards for the Defense Function explain, the defense attorney's role includes "furthering the defendant's interest *to the fullest extent that the law and the applicable standards of professional conduct permit*."[60] By protecting the rights of the accused and challenging the prosecution, the defense counsel is "fulfilling a necessary and important function" in the criminal justice system.[61] Monroe Freedman and Abbe Smith similarly explain that "[by] keeping sound and wholesome the procedure by which society visits its condemnation on an erring member," we "preserve the integrity of society itself."[62] The ABA Defense Function Standards concur, asserting that "[t]he primary duties that defense counsel owe to their clients, *to the*

---

[56] *Garcetti* v. *Ceballos*, 547 U.S. 410, 421 (2006).

[57] *Polk County* v. *Dodson*, 454 U.S. 312, 321 (1981) (emphasis added).

[58] *Id.* at 318–19 (quoting *Ferri* v. *Ackerman*, 444 U.S. 193, 204 (1979)).

[59] Freedman and Smith, *supra* Note 51, at 20.

[60] ABA Standards for Criminal Justice: Prosecution Function and Defense Function § 4–1.2, commentary at 122 (3d. edn. 1993) (emphasis added).

[61] *Id.*

[62] Freedman and Smith, *supra* Note 51, at 21 (quoting Lon Fuller, *The Adversary System*, in Talks on American Law 35 (Berman ed., 1960)).

administration of justice, and *as officers of the court*, are to serve as their *clients' counselor and advocate with courage and devotion*; to ensure that constitutional and other legal *rights of their clients are protected*; and to render effective, high-quality legal representation with integrity."[63]

The defense counsel's duty of providing effective representation is also constitutionally mandated – it is not "commissioned or created" by a government employer, as *Garcetti* indicates,[64] but by the Constitution. The Sixth Amendment expressly provides that criminal defendants have "the Assistance of Counsel for his defense."[65] Defense attorneys serve a constitutional function of checking the state's exertions of criminal power against individuals. As Justice Kennedy observed in *Gentile*, "the criminal defense bar ... has the professional mission to challenge actions of the State."[66] The central role of the criminal defense attorney is to check the prosecutorial power of the state. As noted, the access to justice theory protects the First Amendment rights of attorneys to check government power through speech, association, and petitioning. The checking power is precisely aligned with the role of the defense attorney.

Further, as Freedman and Smith have affirmed, the criminal defendant's right to counsel is "'the most precious' of [her] rights, because it affects one's ability to assert any other right."[67] Thus, "[t]he right to competent counsel is *central to every other right of the criminally accused*, and the denial of this right *destroys* the foundation of adversarial justice."[68]

Included in the defense attorney's role, then, is the obligation to safeguard each of the rights of the accused. Thus, the criminal defense attorney has an obligation to safeguard the presumption of innocence, the right to a fair trial and pretrial processes, including a fair plea, the right to effective assistance of counsel, the right to confront witnesses, the right against self-incrimination, rights against unlawful searches and seizures, rights against the use of excessive force, and overall rights to due process and the protection of the accused's life, liberty (including reputation), and property. These are in addition to the defense attorney's duties of

---

[63] ABA STANDARDS FOR CRIMINAL JUSTICE: PROSECUTION FUNCTION AND DEFENSE FUNCTION § 4–1.2(b) (4th edn. 2015) (emphasis added).

[64] *Garcetti* v. *Ceballos*, 547 U.S. 410, 422 (2006).

[65] U.S. CONST. amend. VI.

[66] *Gentile* v. *State Bar of Nevada*, 501 U.S. 1030, 1051 (1991) (Kennedy J. for a majority).

[67] *See* FREEDMAN AND SMITH, *supra* Note 51, at 13 (quoting *United States* v. *Cronic*, 466 U.S. 648, 654 (1984)).

[68] *See id.* at 313 (emphasis added). Freedman and Smith explain that the American "adversary system represents far more than a simple model for resolving disputes," but has been "constitutionalized by the framers" and "consists of a core of basic rights that recognize, and protect, the dignity of the individual in a free society. *See id.* at 13. Thus, "[a]n essential function of the adversary system ... is to maintain a free society in which individual human rights are central." *See id.*

confidentiality, competence, and loyalty – in acting as the criminal defendant's "champion against a hostile world."[69]

Criminal defense attorneys must have protected rights of speech and petition to perform these functions and preserve the rights of the accused. Criminal defense attorneys require rights of petitioning on behalf of their clients in raising client rights – and it must be done free of government control. Protecting these interests does not just protect the accused – it protects the integrity of criminal processes. For example, criminal defense attorney speech or petitioning that safeguards the presumption of innocence or the Sixth Amendment right to trial by an impartial jury not only protects the accused but protects bedrock principles of our criminal justice system and the constitutional reservation to the people – in the form of a jury – of the power of government to deprive individuals of life and liberty.

Confidentiality and Complete Knowledge

The interrelated duties of confidentiality and complete knowledge belonging to a criminal defense lawyer are absolutely essential to the fulfillment of the defense attorney's role in the criminal justice system; thus, under the access to justice theory, the criminal defense lawyer's First Amendment rights must be keyed to fulfilling those obligations. The lawyer's duty to obtain complete knowledge about the case requires that he obtain from the client *all* information that the client has about the case – no matter how personally embarrassing or harmful to the client. This duty is essential to the criminal defense attorney's ability to render full and competent legal advice and assistance. Without such knowledge, there is no way for the defense attorney to competently and accurately evaluate the charges, respond to or resist the prosecution, or evaluate plea offers.

The duty of confidentiality is intertwined with the duty to obtain complete knowledge. In order to obtain complete knowledge from the client – especially in criminal cases where information disclosed is likely to be very embarrassing, even horrifying, for the client to reveal or provide access to – the lawyer will have to convince the client "that it would be a violation of a sacred obligation for the lawyer to reveal a client's confidence."[70] Criminally accused clients must believe that they can trust the attorney – that the attorney is their confidant with whom disclosures are safe.

An added wrinkle to these obligations is found in the "trilemma" created in the special context of perjury by the accused testifying on their own behalf. Criminal defendants have a constitutional right to testify on their own behalf, and thus the criminal defense lawyer has a concomitant obligation to protect that right. Further, as Monroe Freedman observed, "There is a clear consensus among prosecutors and

---

[69] FREEDMAN AND SMITH, *supra* Note 51, at 20.
[70] FREEDMAN AND SMITH, *supra* Note 51, at 155.

defense attorneys that the likelihood of conviction is increased enormously when the defendant does not take the stand."[71] As Freedman famously explained, in the face of perjury (or its potential) by an accused, the criminal defense lawyer has three duties, but cannot comply with all three, creating a "trilemma."[72] The first two duties are of obtaining complete knowledge and confidentiality, as previously set forth. The third duty is candor to the court – the attorney is prohibited from presenting evidence that is false to the court, and must disclose to the court any false evidence submitted.[73]

Where criminal defendants decide to exercise their constitutional right to testify on their own behalf and then commit perjury, their lawyers must either sacrifice candor to the court or client confidentiality. Of course, if lawyers violate confidentiality and reveal perjury by an accused to the court, then criminal defendants will cease disclosing potentially incriminating information to attorneys, which will undermine the attorney's ability to obtain complete knowledge. Further, the state will obtain from the lawyer what it could not have obtained from the client, which Freedman and Smith argue violates the accused's right against compelled self-incrimination.[74]

Freedman and Smith review cases dealing with the right against self-incrimination where the Supreme Court has held that the state, after an accused has been charged and provided counsel, cannot trick a defendant into making incriminating statements by arranging a relationship of trust with someone who then discloses unwarned statements. Freedman and Smith conclude:

> Surely a defendant's own lawyer cannot do what the pretended friend in *Massiah*, the psychiatrist in *Estelle*, or the cellmate in *Henry* could not do – that is, establish a relationship of trust and confidence and then "become an agent of the state recounting unwarned statements."[75]

In disclosing to the tribunal, the lawyer has falsely indicated to the client that they will not reveal confidences. In theory, lawyers could "mirandize" criminal defendants at the outset of the representation by explaining that they may be required to reveal information to the court, but such a warning is considered unethical by the

---

[71] Monroe H. Freedman, *Professional Responsibility of the Criminal Defense Lawyer: The Three Hardest Questions*, 64 MICH. L. REV. 1469, 1475 (1966). Even if this were not a consensus and it was in fact wiser for criminal defendants to *not* testify on their own behalf, the fact remains that because criminal defendants have a constitutional right to testify on their own behalf, the criminal defense attorney must be able to preserve that right.

[72] *See id.* at 1465–78; *see also* FREEDMAN AND SMITH, *supra* Note 51, at 153–54.

[73] *See* FREEDMAN AND SMITH, *supra* Note 51, 153–54.

[74] *See id.* at 172–81.

[75] *Id.* at 176–77 (discussing *Estelle* v. *Smith*, 451 U.S. 454 (1981); *Massiah* v. *United States*, 377 U.S. 201 (1964); and *United States* v. *Henry*, 447 U.S. 264 (1980)).

ABA Criminal Justice Standards and would absolutely undermine complete know-ledge.[76] Some practicing lawyers have engaged in "intentional ignorance" at the outset of the case by not asking clients specific questions about what happened or their guilt, thus leaving the attorney free to present whatever testimony the client wishes to present (because the lawyer does not "know" it is false, and thus is not obligated to disclose to the court).[77] But intentional ignorance does *not* keep perjury from happening; it just keeps the attorney from knowing that it's perjury – and it absolutely undermines the attorney's ability to provide effective assistance of counsel or protect the client's rights because the attorney *never* obtains the requisite know-ledge of the case to offer competent assistance.[78]

Indeed, the intentional ignorance approach (which is adopted by lawyers in jurisdictions that require disclosure) does not just negatively affect cases where the client might commit perjury but every criminal case that the lawyer undertakes. The lawyer fails to learn the complete facts for *all* of their criminal clients to avoid the possibility of perjury that may (or may not) exist in some unknown number of cases – thereby undermining the core duty of competence for all clients. Every lawyer knows that they cannot competently handle a case and provide effective assistance of counsel as required by the Sixth Amendment without knowing the facts.

Freedman and Smith argue that the appropriate approach is to sacrifice candor to the court.[79] Thus the attorney can obtain complete knowledge and keep confidences. Further, the testimony provided by the client is subject to cross-examination. Moreover, the attorney is still professionally obligated to advise clients not to lie and to explain to each client that lying can increase the sentence imposed and subject the client to a perjury charge. Freedman and Smith note the "professional consensus that lawyers are frequently successful in dissuading client perjury," and that such dissuasion can only happen if the lawyer has obtained both complete information and the client's trust.[80] If the client rejects the attorney's advice, testifies on their own behalf, and gives false testimony, Freedman argues that the attorney should *not* disclose the perjury to the judge.[81]

In addition to Freedman's approach, some jurisdictions follow a narrative approach (where the attorney is not required to disclose criminal client perjury to the court but also cannot specifically elicit lies or argue them to the jury), many practicing attorneys follow intentional ignorance, and the Model Rules require

---

[76] *See* ABA Standards for Criminal Justice: Prosecution Function and Defense Func-tion § 4-3.3 (d) (4th edn. 2015) ("Defense counsel should encourage candid disclosure by the client to counsel and not seek to maintain a calculated ignorance.").

[77] *See* Freedman and Smith, *supra* Note 51, 152–53.

[78] *Id.* at 153.

[79] *See id.* at 151–54, 162–63.

[80] *Id.* at 162–63.

[81] *See id.* at 154.

disclosure to the tribunal.[82] The Model Rules approach – requiring the attorney to take remedial measures, including disclosure of the accused's perjury to the tribunal – was implicitly endorsed by the Supreme Court in *Nix* v. *Whiteside*.[83] Yet, as the concurrence emphasized, despite that endorsement, the decision left jurisdictions free to recommend approaches as they saw fit.[84] Nevertheless, the question under the access to justice theory is whether attorneys should be protected from punishment for keeping their duty of confidentiality and presenting client testimony pursuant to criminal clients' constitutional right to testify on their own behalf.

Criminal defense attorneys must have a protected First Amendment right to present client testimony when their criminal clients are exercising their constitutional right to testify on their own behalf. The decision to testify, being a constitutional right of the accused, is left to the ultimate authority of the criminal defendant, which the attorney cannot override – although the attorney is obligated to discuss with the client the advisability of so doing.[85] Additionally, the criminal defendant has a constitutional right to assistance of counsel. Thus, under the access to justice theory, criminal defense attorneys must – to fulfill their role in the system of justice and preserve their criminal clients' constitutional right to testify on their own behalf – have a First Amendment right to present the testimony of a criminally accused client.

The only question is, if that client begins to engage in perjury, can the state punish the attorney for failing to disclose the client's perjury to the court? Because the client also has a constitutional right against compelled self-incrimination, the state cannot provide the client with a lawyer in an alleged relationship of trust and then obtain unwarned incriminating statements from the lawyer. Additionally, criminal defense attorneys cannot fulfill their role in the system of justice as an "undivided agent"[86] of the accused without complete knowledge, and cannot obtain that knowledge without the complete trust of the client and guarantees of confidentiality.

Importantly, this protection is afforded to the criminal defense attorney *only* in the context of criminal defendants testifying on their own behalf based on enforcing the constitutional rights of an accused. In other situations, such as in civil cases or where witnesses are testifying, the attorney's obligation of candor to the court is essential to the truth-seeking functions of adjudicative processes. Attorneys can, and generally must, be prohibited from allowing knowingly false evidence, including perjury, to be admitted into court. The integrity of the court system requires that the evidence upon which the court makes adjudications – adjudications that are then backed

[82] *See id.* at 152–63 (explaining different approaches); MODEL RULES OF PROF'L CONDUCT R. 3.3 (a)(3).
[83] 475 U.S. 157, 169–70 (1986).
[84] *Id.* at 189–90 (Blackman, J., concurring).
[85] *See, e.g.*, MODEL RULE OF PROF'L CONDUCT R. 1.2(a).
[86] *Polk County* v. *Dodson*, 454 U.S. 312, 321 (1981).

by the full weight of government power – be based in truth as far as possible, and certainly *not* be known fabrications. A system that countenanced submission of fabrications and lies to form the basis for judicial rulings and the exercise of government power would be manifestly unjust.

The access to justice theory ties the First Amendment rights of lawyers to the protection of criminal processes, including the accused's right to testify, right to effective and independent counsel (who is not an agent of the state), and right against self-incrimination. Outside of this very narrow context – the accused testifying on their own behalf – attorneys do not have a First Amendment right to present false evidence to the court. Nevertheless, Model Rule 3.3 – by requiring disclosure to the court of even a criminal accused's perjury when testifying on their own behalf and threatening punishment for an attorney's failure to disclose – undermines the First Amendment rights of criminal defense attorneys. Criminal defense attorneys must have a right to present the testimony of a criminal defendant, while keeping strict confidence and thus protecting the accused's constitutional rights to counsel, to testify on their own behalf, and against compelled self-incrimination.

Additionally, given the criminal defense attorney's role in the justice system and the extreme gravity afforded the duty of confidentiality in the context of representing a criminal defendant, the Virginia Supreme Court's decision in *Hunter* v. *Virginia State Bar*[87] is completely unsupportable. Jurisdictions following Freedman's or the narrative approach expressly allow the presentation of false evidence to the court over breaking confidences with a criminal defendant. Lawyers in practice who employ the intentional ignorance approach choose (unwisely) to *not learn of the facts of a case* rather than have to disclose a client confidence to the judge.

Freedman and Smith describe the situation in many criminal cases that leads to client distrust of their appointed attorneys:

> The problem is particularly acute for the public defender or court-appointed lawyer, who often meets her client for the first time in jail. The defendant has not chosen the lawyer. On the contrary, the lawyer has been sent by the judge and is part of the system that is trying to convict and punish him. It is no easy matter to persuade this client that he can talk freely to his lawyer without fear of prejudice. The question in the client's mind is, "Can I really trust you?"[88]

Thus, Freedman concludes that "the truth can be obtained only by persuading the client that it would be a violation of a sacred obligation for the lawyer to reveal a client's confidence."[89]

In light of this reality, the *Hunter* decision is both astonishing and absolutely incorrect. Horace Hunter posted information about his criminal defense clients on his website without their permission – purportedly both for marketing purposes and

---

[87] 285 Va. 485 (2013).
[88] FREEDMAN AND SMITH, *supra* Note 51, at 154.
[89] *Id.* at 155.

as informative for the public.[90] Evidence from the disciplinary hearing revealed that Hunter's clients believed that the information he posted about them was embarrassing and detrimental. But perhaps the greatest irony in Hunter's decision to post arises from the fact that he "only blogged about his cases that he won" – since the blog was a marketing tool. Which means that Hunter – having successfully acted as these criminal defendants' "champion against a hostile world,"[91] having protected their life, liberty, and reputational interests – then divulged, without the clients' permission, embarrassing and detrimental information about them on his blog for all the world to read!

A criminal defense attorney does not have a general First Amendment right to divulge confidential information about his client without client consent.[92] The access to justice theory recognizes that courts may punish attorneys for violating their duty of confidentiality to clients. Criminal defendants come to a lawyer as their legal confidant to whom they can divulge the most embarrassing and even incriminating facts. They make such a disclosure with the understanding that the lawyer will keep that information in trust and use it for the sole purpose for which it was provided – so that the lawyer can know how to competently respond to the charges and protect the client's interests to the extent possible under law. The client does not divulge such information so that it can be turned over to the judge (the trilemma problem) or so that it can be used in the defense attorney's blog for "marketing" and creating "a community presence for [the lawyer's] firm."[93] Without the license given to him by the state, Hunter simply would not have received the information from his criminally accused clients. Hunter used the information that his clients confided to him in a manner contrary to the purpose for which the clients gave it to him and for which the bar licensed him. His role in the system of justice was to act in the "undivided interests" of his client.[94] Yet he betrayed his clients' trust in giving him that information – using it instead for his own benefit and self-promotion and to his clients' detriment and embarrassment. Thus, contrary to the Virginia Supreme Court's opinion, the First Amendment does not shield him from punishment for divulging the confidential information of his criminal defendant clients.

---

[90] *Hunter*, 285 Va. at 492.

[91] FREEDMAN AND SMITH, *supra* Note 51, at 20.

[92] An exception allowing disclosure is likely warranted under the narrow categories set out in MODEL RULE OF PROFESSIONAL CONDUCT 1.6(b) – attorney disclosure is permissible to protect human life and limb, or where the client is using the attorney's services to commit crimes and fraud, or for attorney self-protection. While beyond the scope of this chapter, these three traditional exceptions to the duty of confidentiality do not undermine the constitutional rights of criminal defendants and each protects significant moral interests (human life, not allowing clients to use attorneys and their license to invoke state power as an instrument of crime, and protecting lawyers from having their fiduciary duties used against them).

[93] *Hunter*, 285 Va. at 492.

[94] *Polk County v. Dodson*, 454 U.S. 312, 321 (1981).

13

Uncompromised Pretrial Publicity

Statements by Special Prosecutor Angela Corey in her April 2012 press conference regarding the decision to charge George Zimmerman with Second Degree Murder again raised questions about the appropriate limitations on pretrial publicity by attorneys, particularly prosecutors.[1] After George Zimmerman's acquittal in July 2013, the prosecutors, in turn, publicly questioned the propriety of publicity from his defense attorneys, stating: "We ... did not have media interviews every day like they did ... It was obvious they were trying to influence potential jurors."[2] Indeed, beginning soon after charges were brought, Zimmerman's defense attorneys launched a website, a Facebook page, and a twitter account devoted to the case.[3]

The appropriate scope of First Amendment protection for attorney pretrial publicity has long fostered debate and divergent viewpoints. For the media, the Supreme Court has recognized robust First Amendment protection for pretrial press coverage.[4] However, in its fractured *Gentile v. State Bar of Nevada* opinion, the Court approved as constitutional the less-protective standard found in Model Rule of Professional Conduct 3.6, which forbids attorneys from engaging in publicity that creates "a substantial likelihood of materially prejudicing an adjudicative proceeding."[5] Model Rule 3.6 also contains a safe harbor listing items a lawyer is allowed to

---

[1] *See, e.g.,* Hillary Cohn Aizenman, *Pretrial Publicity in a Post-Trayvon Martin World*, 27 FALL CRIM. JUST. (2012); Monroe H. Freedman and Jennifer Gundlach, *Unethical Pretrial Publicity by Zimmerman (Trayvon Martin) Prosecutor*, AALS PROF. RESP. NEWSLETTER (Spring 2012).

[2] *See George Zimmerman Prosecutor Prayed for Him to Testify*, ABC News.com, July 15, 2013, *available at* http://abcnews.go.com/US/george-zimmerman-prosecutor-prayed-testify/story?id= 19666346#.UeRnEoop-PM%29.

[3] Adam Hochberg, *George Zimmerman's Lawyers Hope to Win Trial by Social Media in Trayvon Martin Case*, Poynter.org, May 7, 2012, *available at* www.poynter.org/news/george-zimmer mans-lawyers-hope-win-trial-social-media-trayvon-martin-case.

[4] *See Neb. Press Ass'n v. Stuart*, 427 U.S. 539, 565–68 (1976).

[5] *Gentile v. State Bar of Nevada*, 501 U.S. 1030, 1033 (1991) (Kennedy, J.); MODEL RULES OF PROF'L CONDUCT R. 3.6.

say despite the general standard and a provision allowing a lawyer to respond to unduly prejudicial publicity "not initiated by the lawyer" or the client.[6] The comments to Model Rule 3.6 list "subjects that are more likely than not to have a material prejudicial effect on a proceeding" and thus presumptively violate the standard.[7] In a number of states, this list of presumptively prejudicial items is part of the rule proper.[8]

The *Gentile* Court, like the Model Rules drafters and many scholars, viewed restrictions on attorney pretrial publicity as a compromise between two competing constitutional mandates: "the First Amendment rights of attorneys in pending cases and the State's interest in fair trials."[9] Further, the *Gentile* Court emphasized the importance of creating a rule that was viewpoint neutral and applied equally to attorneys on opposing sides of a case.[10] Importantly, Model Rule 3.6 applies to all categories of lawyers, including defense attorneys, prosecutors, and civil litigators.

Prior to *Gentile*, Monroe Freedman and Janet Starwood had argued that a compromise was unnecessary because the free speech rights of defense attorneys aligned with the criminal defendant's Sixth Amendment rights to a fair trial – thus defense attorneys should have strong First Amendment rights.[11] On the other hand,

---

[6] MODEL RULE OF PROF'L CONDUCT R. 3.6(c) and cmt. 7.

[7] *See id.* R. 3.6 cmt. 5. The subjects "that are more likely than not to have a material prejudicial effect on a proceeding" regard the following:

(1) the *character, credibility, reputation or criminal record of a party*, suspect in a criminal investigation or witness, or the identity of a witness, or the expected testimony of a party or witness; (2) in a criminal case or proceeding that could result in incarceration, *the possibility of a plea of guilty* to the offense or the existence or contents of *any confession, admission, or statement* given by a defendant or suspect or that person's refusal or failure to make a statement; (3) the performance or *results of any examination or test* or the refusal or failure of a person to submit to an examination or test, or the identity or nature of physical evidence expected to be presented; (4) *any opinion as to the guilt or innocence of a defendant or suspect in a criminal case* or proceeding that could result in incarceration; (5) information that the lawyer knows or reasonably should know is likely to be *inadmissible as evidence* in a trial and that would, if disclosed, create a substantial risk of prejudicing an impartial trial; or (6) the *fact that a defendant has been charged with a crime, unless* there is included therein a statement explaining that the charge is merely an accusation and that the *defendant is presumed innocent until and unless proven guilty.*

See id. (emphasis added).

[8] *See* ABA, *Variations of the ABA Model Rules of Professional Conduct,* available at www.americanbar.org/content/dam/aba/administrative/professional_responsibility/mrpc_3_6.authcheckdam.pdf (showing state rules containing list of presumptively prejudicial statements, including Alabama, Indiana, Michigan, Mississippi, New Hampshire, New York, Texas, and West Virginia).

[9] *Gentile*, 501 U.S. at 1075 (Rehnquist, J., for majority).

[10] *See id.* at 1076.

[11] Monroe Freedman and Janet Starwood, *Prior Restraints on Freedom of Expression by Defendants and Defense Attorneys: Ratio Decidendi v. Obiter Dictum,* 29 STAN. L. REV. 607, 612 (1977).

they argued that prosecutors generally lacked free speech rights to engage in pretrial publicity.[12] Notably, the *Gentile* Court's emphasis on the equal regulation of defense and prosecutor pretrial publicity undermined Freedman and Starwood's approach.

Even among commentators embracing the idea of a compromise between free speech and fair trials, the appropriate outcome of that compromise is anything but obvious.[13] Moreover, post-*Gentile*, Erwin Chemerinsky forcefully argued that all lawyers should be allowed to engage in pretrial publicity freely.[14] And Peter Margulies has recently argued for extremely limited First Amendment protection for all attorneys.[15]

In the face of such divergent viewpoints, several articles that advocate new regulations on attorney pretrial publicity simply ignore the First Amendment – arguing that proposed regulations would constitute prudent policy but declining to address whether they are constitutional.[16] This highlights that the First Amendment issue is problematic. Under normal First Amendment doctrines, Chemerinsky is right: Model Rule 3.6 and other attorney pretrial publicity limitations are content-based restrictions on political speech that impose a prior restraint.[17] That equals one result: strict scrutiny and free speech for attorney pretrial publicity. Yet the scholarly community and regulators have not rallied around Chemerinsky's arguments. In the wake of cases like the Duke lacrosse prosecution[18] – where Michael Nifong gave over fifty press interviews making accusations of race-based gang rape within a week of learning of the allegations[19] – regulators are not looking to expand the free speech rights of prosecutors to the apparent detriment of the lives and liberties of criminal defendants.

The access to justice theory alleviates much of the difficulty, particularly as to pretrial publicity in the criminal justice system. Rather than viewing attorney pretrial publicity as a compromise between incompatible rights to a fair trial and lawyer free speech, the lawyer's speech right is keyed to the lawyer's role in the justice system.

---

[12] *See id.* at 617–18; *see also* MONROE FREEDMAN AND ABBE SMITH, UNDERSTANDING LEGAL ETHICS, 306 n. 99 (4th Edn. 2010) (citing *Garcetti v. Ceballos*, 547 U.S. 410, 421 (2006)).

[13] *See, e.g.*, Lonnie T. Brown, *"May It Please the Camera, … I Mean the Court" – An Interjudicial Solution to an Extrajudicial Problem*, 39 GA. L. REV. 83 116–17, 123–30 (2004).

[14] Erwin Chemerinsky, *Silence Is Not Golden*, 47 EMORY L. J. 859, 862–67 (1998).

[15] Peter Margulies, *Advocacy as a Race to the Bottom: Rethinking Limits on Lawyers' Free Speech*, 43 U. MEM. L. REV. 319, 324 (2012).

[16] *See* Judith L. Maute, *"In Pursuit of Justice" in High Profile Criminal Matters*, 70 FORD. L. REV. 1745, 1746 (2002); Gerald F. Uelmen, *Leaks, Gags and Shields: Taking Responsibility*, 37 SANTA CLARA L. REV. 943 (1997); Kevin Cole and Fred C. Zacharias, *The Agony of Victory and the Ethics of Lawyer Speech*, 69 S. CAL. L. REV. 1627, 1628–30 (1996).

[17] Chemerinsky, *supra* Note 14, at 862–67.

[18] *See, e.g.*, Susan Hanley Duncan, *Pretrial Publicity in High Profile Trials: An Integrated Approach to Protecting the Right to a Fair Trial and the Right to Privacy*, 34 OHIO N. U. L. REV. 755 (2008); Laurie L. Levenson, *Prosecutorial Sound Bites: When Do They Cross the Line*, 44 GA. L. REV. 1021, 1022–23 (2010).

[19] Robert P. Mosteller, *The Duke Lacrosse Case, Innocence, and False Identifications: A Fundamental Failure to "Do Justice,"* 76 FORD. L. REV. 1337, 1349–52 (2007).

Such an approach does not eliminate the free speech side of the traditional compromise. In fact, restricting certain pretrial publicity can frustrate the attorney's role to protect a client's life, liberty, and property.

While this chapter focuses primarily on pretrial publicity in the criminal justice system, pretrial publicity in civil litigation is similarly analyzed by considering the roles of civil litigators and the effect of pretrial publicity on the integrity of civil justice. Importantly, and contrary to Model Rule 3.6, the appropriate scope of First Amendment rights as to pretrial publicity is not a one-size-fits-all solution. It requires different and separate analyses for the criminal justice system and the civil justice system. Further, pretrial publicity in the criminal justice system must be analyzed separately for the prosecutor and the defense attorney, calling for differing rights from each other. The very nature of the criminal justice system imposes vastly differing obligations and duties for the prosecution and defense and their respective attorney-client relationships. The access to justice theory keys the First Amendment rights of defense attorneys and prosecutors to their respective roles in our criminal justice system and the effects of pretrial publicity from each on the integrity of that system.

As revealed through this analysis, what is lost in the traditional compromise is the protection of both the robust free speech rights of criminal defense attorneys and the integrity of criminal processes. Contrary to the Supreme Court's *Gentile* decision, such a compromise was unnecessary to achieve viewpoint neutrality and to recognize the essential, but limited, First Amendment rights of prosecutors to engage in speech necessary for the investigation and prosecution of crime and to respond to defense-initiated publicity. By attuning the speech rights of the attorneys to the proper functioning of the criminal justice system, both free speech and criminal justice are safeguarded rather than compromised.

THE *GENTILE* CASE

In February 1988, Dominic Gentile, a criminal defense attorney, held a press conference where he asserted both the innocence of his client, Grady Sanders, and the culpability of police officers in the disappearance of four kilograms of cocaine and approximately $300,000 in traveler's checks from a safety deposit vault used in an undercover police operation at Western Vault Corporation, a company Sanders owned.[20] Prior to charging Sanders, the police and prosecution engaged in extensive publicity, "clearing" the police officers with access to the vault, implicating Sanders, and announcing that other vault renters had lost their money.[21] In reaction to the publicity, customers terminated their rentals with Western Vault,

---

[20] *Gentile v. State Bar of Nevada*, 501 U.S. 1030, 1040 (1991) (Kennedy, J.).
[21] *Id.* at 1040–41.

which went out of business.[22] Gentile, upon learning that Sanders would be indicted, decided "for the first time in his career" to call a press conference regarding a client he was confident was innocent.[23] Gentile told the press:

> When this case goes to trial, and as it develops, you're going to see that the evidence will prove not only that Grady Sanders is an innocent person and had nothing to do with any of the charges that are being leveled against him, but that the person that was in the most direct position to have stolen the drugs and the money … is Detective Steve Scholl.[24]

Gentile also asserted that the other alleged "victims" were "known drug dealers and convicted money launderers."[25] Gentile said he couldn't elaborate, but reaffirmed, "I represent an innocent guy. All right?"[26]

At first blush, Gentile's statements seem over-the-top, and Justice Rehnquist and the Nevada Supreme Court characterized them as "highly inflammatory" in that "they portrayed prospective government witnesses as drug users and dealers, and as money launderers."[27] Yet six months later a jury acquitted Sanders, and the government's witnesses were shown to be drug users (including Detective Scholl[28]), drug dealers, and money launderers.[29] Moreover, the foreman of the jury stated that if the jury had "had a verdict form before them with respect to the guilt of [Detective] Scholl they would have found the man proven guilty beyond a reasonable doubt."[30] As summarized by Justice Kennedy, "[A]t trial, all material information disseminated during [Gentile's] press conference was admitted in evidence before the jury,"[31] which the jury apparently found credible.

The Nevada State Bar disciplined Gentile for violating Nevada's version of Model Rule 3.6.[32] The United States Supreme Court reversed the discipline five to four in fractured opinions that found part of Nevada's rule unconstitutionally vague. Justice Kennedy, for four justices, advocated full First Amendment protection for attorney pretrial publicity to the same extent as the press.[33] Justice Rehnquist, in striking contrast and also for four justices, advocated a constitutional conditions position, arguing for no First Amendment protection for attorney pretrial publicity.[34]

---

[22] *Id.* at 1040.

[23] *Id.* at 1042, 1064.

[24] *Id.* at 1059 (Kennedy, J.) and 1064 (Rehnquist, J.).

[25] *Id.* at 1059 (Kennedy, J.).

[26] *Id.* at 1064 (Rehnquist, J.).

[27] *Id.* at 1079 (Rehnquist, J.).

[28] *Id.* at 1047 (Kenney, J.) (but noting that Scholl testified that he only ingested drugs "to gain the confidence of suspects").

[29] *Id.* at 1047–48, 1040–41.

[30] *Id.* at 1048.

[31] *Id.* at 1047.

[32] *Id.* at 1033.

[33] *Id.* at 1054–56.

[34] *See id.* at 1081 (Rehnquist, J.).

Justice O'Connor provided the fifth vote, joining part of each opinion. Importantly, Justice Rehnquist modified his argument that lawyers lack First Amendment rights in the portion of his opinion joined by Justice O'Connor. Thus a majority of the Court adopted a middle position, holding that "speech of lawyers representing clients in pending cases may be regulated under a less demanding standard than that established for regulation of the press" under normal First Amendment doctrines.[35] The Court upheld the "'substantial likelihood of material prejudice' standard" from Nevada's Rule (based on Model Rule 3.6) as "a constitutionally permissible balance between the First Amendment rights of attorneys in pending cases and the State's interest in fair trials."[36] In explaining why the standard was constitutional, the Court said:

> The regulation of attorneys' speech is limited – it applies only to speech that is substantially likely to have a materially prejudicial effect; *it is neutral as to points of view, applying equally to all attorneys participating in a pending case*; and it merely postpones the attorneys' comments until after the trial.[37]

Thus, according to the majority, for the rule to be constitutional it had to apply equally to defense attorneys and to prosecutors, which I will refer to throughout this chapter as *Gentile*'s equality principle.

Justice Kennedy additionally emphasized the special concerns created by limiting the speech of defense attorneys, like Gentile, who have "the professional mission to challenge actions of the State."[38] Kennedy asserted that that defense attorneys should be allowed to "take reasonable steps to defend a client's reputation" including "attempt[ing] to demonstrate in the court of public opinion that the client does not deserve to be tried."[39]

SPECIAL CONSIDERATIONS AS TO THE CRIMINAL JUSTICE SYSTEM

There are several factors that make representation in the criminal justice system different from lawyer representation in other contexts. In determining the appropriate scope of First Amendment protection for pretrial publicity in the criminal justice system, it is important to recognize these differences and how they produce differing obligations, incentives, and duties for the prosecution and the defense.

[35] *Id.* at 1074 (Rehnquist, J., for a majority).
[36] *Id.* at 1075 (Rehnquist, J., for a majority).
[37] *Id.* at 1076 (Rehnquist, J., for a majority).
[38] *Id.* at 1051 (Kennedy J. for a majority); *see also id.* at 1055–56 (Kennedy, J.).
[39] *Id.* at 1043 (Kennedy J.).

Obligations to Undertake or Continue the Representation

One primary and publicly recognized difference between the prosecution and the defense is that the prosecution is only supposed to bring charges and pursue them through trial if they are supported by probable cause.[40] If evidence does not support bringing charges against the accused, the prosecution should drop the charges. Consequently, the very existence of charges against an individual is a public statement that the prosecutor has obtained sufficient evidence of guilt to create probable cause to charge that person. The fact that the prosecutor is undertaking or continuing the representation against the accused itself indicates to the public the prosecutor's belief at some level in the validity of the cause and the likely guilt of the defendant.

Yet, the fact of representation by the criminal defense attorney carries no such weight or implication. Criminal defendants have a constitutional right to the effective assistance of counsel.[41] The public understands (and rightly so) that even the most culpable criminal defendants guilty of the most heinous crimes have an attorney. Because representation of the defendant is constitutionally required, the public may seriously doubt that the defense attorney believes in their client's cause – indeed, for all the public knows, the defense attorney may even know their client is guilty. Thus defense attorneys may need to publicly indicate some level of belief in their client's cause because the simple fact of representation will not imply it.

Duty Not to Disclose Information Relating to the Representation

As discussed in prior chapters, the duty of confidentiality forbids a lawyer from revealing confidential information without client consent.[42] Thus, outside of extremely limited exceptions, attorneys are forbidden from disclosing information learned in the course of a representation to the press or others,[43] unless impliedly authorized for the representation.[44] Thus before disclosing information to the press, criminal defense attorneys should communicate to the client their desire to publicize information relating to the representation and receive the client's consent to the disclosure. There may be some situations where the defense attorney's public statements are impliedly authorized to carry out the representation.[45] Ideally, and

---

[40] *See* Model Rules of Prof'l Conduct R. 3.8(a) ("The prosecutor in a criminal case shall: (a) refrain from prosecuting a charge that the prosecutor knows is not supported by probable cause.").

[41] *See* U.S. Const. amend. VI; *Gideon* v. *Wainwright,* 372 U.S. 335, 342–46 (1963).

[42] Model Rules of Prof'l Conduct R. 1.6 cmt 2.

[43] *See id.* R. 1.6.

[44] *See id.* R. 1.6 cmt 5.

[45] *See, e.g., id.*

when feasible, a defense attorney will communicate with the accused and receive consent even in such situations.

Prosecutors, in contrast, do not represent individual clients, but instead represent the sovereign. In that role, the prosecution acts as agent and principal.[46] Yet, prosecutors obtain information about the accused solely because of their governmental role to exercise state criminal power. Further, the information is provided to them from the investigative arm of the state, which obtained information through the exercise of coercive state power. If prosecutors were not representing the sovereign, they simply would not have access to the personal and highly derogatory information regarding the alleged criminal conduct of others. It is the people who have granted police powers to the state in our democratic compact. The state is to exercise its investigative powers and to provide such information to prosecutors for the sole purpose of executing the criminal law and fulfilling society's interests in deterrence, incapacitation, retribution, and/or rehabilitation.

Just as defense attorneys do not have a First Amendment right to disclose confidential information, prosecutors should not have a First Amendment right to publish information relating to the representation obtained solely through the exercise of state power – except when the publication is necessary to society's purpose in granting access to such information: namely, the investigation and prosecution of a particular crime. Unnecessary publication of such information undermines the integrity of government's coercive power to obtain information despite privacy rights, and, as discussed in this chapter, can undermine the constitutional rights of the accused.

Additionally, the incentives for disclosure are often different for the prosecution than they are for the defense. The prosecutor, acting as agent and principal, is not an actor in the underlying case – her actions and the actions of the sovereign client (hopefully) are not generally part of the alleged crime or controversy. While the defendant and defense attorney may likely desire confidentiality regarding the case, the prosecutor may have no personal interest in confidentiality regarding the underlying facts of the case (unless such publicity would indicate abuse of state power, for example). This difference arises because the information learned and desired to be disclosed by prosecutors is primarily about third persons and not involving their own client. Thus, a prosecutor will often have access to horrible information about the accused, while the defense generally will not have any information that would be harmful to the prosecution or their government client. In such cases, without restrictions on publicity, prosecutors can use information obtained through state coercive power to the detriment of the accused, undermining constitutional protections, without fear of any similar harm recurring to themselves or their government client.

---

[46] R. Michael Cassidy, Prosecutorial Ethics 2–3 (2005).

The Failure to Consider Publicity's Effect on Pretrial Rights and Interests

As examined in *Gentile*, the traditional compromise for pretrial publicity is between free speech and the Sixth Amendment right to a fair trial. Similarly, the Restatement identifies as the primary concern publicity that interferes with the trial proper.[47] Yet neither the prosecutor's nor the defense attorney's role is limited to trying cases. The prosecutor plays key roles in the system of justice from the investigative stage, to the filing of charges, bargaining for pleas, to trial itself. Similarly, the defense attorney plays a role as soon as the criminal defendant is charged and hires or is appointed counsel. Pretrial publicity can affect important interests at each of these stages, including both constitutionally mandated interests and interests defined by the role of the prosecutor to seek justice and the role of the defense attorney.

The failure to recognize these other interests is not harmless. In fact, attorney discipline has often been tied to the timing of the statements in reliance on the preservation of a fair trial as the primary interest affected by publicity.[48] If the statements are made well before trial, an attorney may avoid discipline on that ground alone. As discussed later, prosecutorial pretrial publicity can undermine the presumption of innocence, interfere with an accused's ability to obtain a fair plea, and ruin a defendant's reputation and liberty – even if all charges are ultimately dropped or the defendant is ultimately acquitted. Yet because approximately 95 percent of state and federal criminal cases are not tried, but are pled,[49] prosecutors can engage in whatever publicity they wish – negatively affecting these interests of the accused – without ever risking punishment.

THE RIGHTS OF THE PROSECUTOR TO ENGAGE IN PRETRIAL PUBLICITY

Right to Publish Charges in the Indictment

As noted in Chapter 12, under the access to justice theory, prosecutors have a First Amendment right to publish the indictment. As Freedman and Starwood explained, prosecutors are "specially privileged" to publish charges even if the statements would constitute defamation if published by someone else. In this respect, they note, "the prosecutor's rights of expression are broader than those of the ordinary citizen."[50]

---

[47] RESTATEMENT (THIRD) OF THE LAW GOVERNING LAWYERS § 109 and cmts. b and d.

[48] The Restatement explains that "timing may be relevant" and thus "a statement made long before jury is to be selected presents less risk." *See id.* §109 cmt. c. The ANNOTATED MODEL RULES OF PROFESSIONAL CONDUCT for Rule 3.6 also state that "timing has proved to be an important criterion in assessing [a statement's] potential for prejudice." ANN. MODEL RULES PROF'L CONDUCT R. 3.6 annot. (8th edn. 2015).

[49] *See* JONATHAN DRESSLER AND GEORGE C. THOMAS III, CRIMINAL PROCEDURE 1016 (4th Ed. 2010).

[50] Freedman and Starwood, *supra* Note 11, at 617.

This protection for prosecutorial speech is an essential component of the prosecutor's ability to initiate and present the state's case.

No Right to Undermine the Presumption of Innocence

Prosecutorial pretrial publicity can affect the proper and constitutional functioning of the criminal justice system from the outset of a case. A notable example is the presumption of innocence – that a person is presumed innocent until proven guilty – which is a "basic rule of both criminal and constitutional law."[51]

Historically, the presumption had two separate and important components. First, it constituted "a rule of proof," namely, that the prosecution bears the burden to prove guilt at trial.[52] Second, it was a "shield against punishment before conviction," meaning that the accused could not be subjected to pretrial punishment and was to be treated with the dignity accorded to other presumptively innocent people in society.[53] In *Bell* v. *Wolfish*, the Supreme Court appeared to limit the presumption of innocence as solely creating a "rule of proof" for trial and not having application pretrial.[54] The *Bell* Court recognized a separate due process right protecting against "punish[ment] prior to an adjudication of guilt,"[55] but defined that right so narrowly as to be ineffectual.[56]

Nevertheless, some states have rejected *Bell* and still treat the presumption of innocence as applying and protecting the accused in pretrial contexts.[57] Further, recent scholarship has read *Bell* as limited to its factual context of addressing the constitutionality of conditions of confinement for those in pretrial detention.[58] Scholars have grounded the presumption of innocence in due process and the Sixth Amendment, arguing that the presumption declares fundamental constitutional law that serves the historical dual purpose to protect individuals pretrial and to provide the appropriate burden of proof at trial.[59]

---

[51] *See* Rinat Kitai, *Presuming Innocence*, 55 OKLA. L. REV. 257 (2002).
[52] *See* Francois Quintard-Morenas, *The Presumption of Innocence in the French and Anglo-American Traditions*, 58 AM. J. COMP. L. 107, 107–09 (2010).
[53] *See id.* at 107–10, 148.
[54] *Bell* v. *Wolfish*, 441 U.S. 520, 533 (1979).
[55] *Id.* at 535–36.
[56] Justice Marshall argued that the majority's test was "ineffectual" and "lacks any real content" – which Marshall found "insupportable, given that all of these detainees are presumptively innocent and many are confined solely because they cannot afford bail." *See id.* at 563–65 (Marshall, J., dissenting).
[57] *See* Shima Baradaran, *Restoring the Presumption of Innocence*, OHIO STATE L. J. 723, 766 and n. 231 (2011).
[58] *Id.* at 776.
[59] *Id.* at 727–38 (discussing due process basis for presumption); Shima Baradaran, *The Presumption of Punishment*, CRIM L. PHILOS. (June 2013) (arguing constitutional basis for pretrial presumption under historical due process and Sixth Amendment jury trial right); Quintard-Morenas, *supra* Note 52, at 107 (reviewing historical and constitutional understanding of presumption in English and American law).

Shima Baradaran has traced the constitutional history of the presumption back to the Magna Carta and to the early United States as an essential component of due process and of the constitutional compact between the individual and government.[60] Rinat Kitai has similarly argued that the presumption of innocence "operat[es] to balance the State's power against the freedom of the individual."[61] Kitai explains:

> The state's power to impose punishment on individuals is almost unlimited. Thus there is great danger in granting the State an unlimited authority to use this power against the individual prior to his conviction ... The presumption of innocence [] prevents and limits the State from acting against a person until his conviction. *It constitutes the guarantee, for guilty and innocent persons alike, that the State cannot impose punishment prior to conviction ...* [62]

Prosecutors are part of the enforcement arm of the state. They are able literally to destroy people's lives with the state power given them to charge and prosecute crime and with the damning information regarding others to which they are privy as part of their office. But the presumption of innocence checks that power – a check on power that Baradaran finds grounded in the Due Process Clauses and the Sixth Amendment: the state, including the prosecution, cannot impose punishment against a person until convicted by a jury of the accused's peers.[63] As the Supreme Court explained in *Southern Union Co.* v. *United States*, the "jury acts 'as a bulwark between the State and the accused,'" prohibiting punishment until "'the prosecution has proved each element of an offense beyond a reasonable doubt.'"[64]

Prosecutorial pretrial publicity can impose pretrial punishment on an individual. That punishment may come in the form of loss of reputation and dignity, loss of society, and loss of business (as demonstrated by the *Gentile* case itself)[65] – even when there is no pretrial incarceration.[66] Prosecutors have access to highly derogatory information about people, but that information is provided to them by the state and its investigative arm for the sole purpose of justly pursuing criminal charges against those who are guilty and not against the innocent.[67] Moreover, because the public and press are aware of the prosecutor's special access to information, any statements made by a prosecutor may be taken as especially accurate.

---

[60] Baradaran, *supra* Note 59, at *3–*5.

[61] Kitai, *supra* Note 51, at 280.

[62] *Id.* at 280–81.

[63] Baradaran, *supra* Note 59, at *10–*11.

[64] *Id.* at *10 (quoting *Southern Union Co.* v. *United States*, 567 U.S. 343, 348 (2012)).

[65] *See* Kitai, *supra* Note 51, at 284.

[66] Baradaran's arguments are aimed at curbing pretrial detention, yet she concludes that it is essential to adhere to the presumption of innocence because "the presumption protects in places that a modern understanding and application of due process procedures cannot reach." *See* Baradaran, *supra* Note 59, at *14. Prosecutorial pretrial publicity is such an area.

[67] *See Berger* v. *United States*, 295 U.S. 78, 88 (1935).

Under the access to justice theory, it is contrary to the prosecutor's role to undermine the purposes and constitutional underpinnings of the presumption of innocence. Thus the state can constitutionally prohibit any prosecutorial pretrial publicity that treats the accused as if already convicted (or with an assumption of guilt), unless the speech is *essential* to a valid investigative or trial purpose. A regulation like those contained in the Code of Federal Regulations – which categorizes specific topics that Department of Justice personnel are not to discuss with the press,[68] in addition to prohibiting them from arranging perp walks,[69] and from discussing even admissible evidence[70] – is thus constitutionally permissible. The CFR contains a short list of things that federal prosecutors can publicly say, including basic identifying information regarding an accused, but then limits even this category by concluding:

> Disclosures should include only *incontrovertible, factual matters, and should not include subjective observations.* In addition, *where background information or information relating to the circumstances of an arrest or investigation* would be highly prejudicial *or where the release thereof would serve no law enforcement function,* such information should *not be made public.*[71]

Such a standard is far more restrictive than the *Gentile* standard. But it comports with the purposes of the presumption of innocence and the role of the prosecutor in the justice system and so it is constitutionally permissible under the access to justice theory. Similarly, prohibitions on prosecutorial "heightening public condemnation of the accused" are constitutionally permissible – even if more restrictive than the normal Model Rule 3.6 standard and even if it violates *Gentile*'s equality principle by not including similar restrictions on defense publicity.

The presumption of innocence is also beneficial to the just investigation, prosecution, and resolution of criminal proceedings by checking prosecutorial overconfidence in the strength of a case.[72] Pretrial publicity by the prosecution undermines this salutary purpose of the presumption. Michael Nifong's statements about the Duke lacrosse players presents a poignant example of how a prosecutor's pretrial publicity can wed them to the charges despite even overwhelming evidence that develops to the contrary. Once prosecutors – a political actor – make public statements about a prosecution, they will be held politically accountable and feel

---

[68] *See* 28 C.F.R. § 50.2.

[69] *See id.* ("Personnel of the Department of Justice should take no action to encourage or assist news media in photographing or televising a defendant or accused person being held or transported in Federal custody.")

[70] *See id.* (prohibiting "[s]tatements concerning evidence or argument in the case, whether or not it is anticipated that such evidence or argument will be used at trial.").

[71] *Id.* (emphasis added).

[72] Kitai, *supra* Note 51, at 279–80.

political pressure to live up to those statements.[73] This can blind prosecutors to mitigating evidence and put pressure on prosecutors to achieve a particular result rather than to do their job: to seek justice.

Finally, prosecutorial pretrial publicity can undermine the interest recognized by *Bell* itself: the prosecutorial burden of proof. The *Bell* Court explained that the presumption "allocates the burden of proof" and serves to admonish the jury to determine "an accused's guilt or innocence solely on the evidence adduced at trial and not on the basis of … other matters not introduced as proof at trial."[74] As discussed later, prosecutorial pretrial publicity can negatively affect a jury's verdict and perception of the evidence, influencing a jury to have a presumption of guilt.

No Right to Coerce an Unjust Plea

Prosecutorial pretrial publicity can also affect the defendant's decision and ability to take a plea, for example, by coercing the defendant to plead in order to end continued scandal in the press.[75] While the traditional compromise focuses on pretrial publicity as it may affect the right to a fair trial, the Sixth Amendment's "public trial, by an impartial jury" has become occasional, and plea bargains occur in 95 percent of state and federal criminal cases.[76] The Supreme Court recognized that "plea bargains have become *so central* to the administration of the criminal justice system" that it "is insufficient simply *to point to the guarantee of a fair trial* as a backstop that inoculates any *errors in the pretrial process.*"[77] Pretrial publicity that can unjustly manipulate a plea is thus not inoculated by the fact that it did not undermine the actual trial. Current prohibitions on pretrial publicity are aimed at safeguarding trial and empaneling an impartial jury; they are not keyed to publicity that may affect a plea and thus they fail to protect the accused's actual interests in modern criminal process.

Scholars have examined the factors, pressures, and incentives in play for plea bargaining, but much of what occurs in plea bargaining is secretive and unknown.[78]

---

[73] *See, e.g.,* Stephanos Bibas, *Plea Bargaining outside the Shadow of Trial,* 117 HARV. L. REV. 2463, 2472 (2004) ("Prosecutors are particularly concerned about their reputations because they are a politically ambitious bunch. Most district attorneys are elected and many have parlayed their prosecutorial successes into political careers.").

[74] *Bell v. Wolfish,* 441 U.S. 520, 533 (1979).

[75] *See Neb. Press Ass'n v. Stuart,* 427 U.S. 539, 600 and n. 24 (Brennan, J., concurring) (noting prevalence of pleading and instructing judges to "guard against the danger that pretrial publicity has effectively coerced the defendant into pleading guilty")).

[76] *See* DRESSLER AND THOMAS, *supra* Note 49, at 1016.

[77] *Missouri v. Frye,* 566 U.S. 134, 143–44 (2012) (emphasis added).

[78] *See* Bibas, *supra* Note 73, at 2468 ("[P]lea bargaining is hidden from public view" and is "a secret area of law."); Stephen J. Schulhofer, *Plea Bargaining as Disaster,* 101 YALE L. J. 1979, 1987, 2002–3 (1992) ("In plea bargaining, the attorney's role is *virtually immune from scrutiny or control.*" [Emphasis added.]); *see also* H. Mitchell Caldwell, *Coercive Plea Bargaining: The Unrecognized Scourge of the Justice System,* 61 CATH. U. L. REV. 63 (2011).

Nevertheless, there are several key understandings that are important when examining the potential effect of pretrial publicity on pleas. The core premise of plea bargaining is that it approximates the result of trial while avoiding the costs of trial (that is, a plea equals the approximate trial result minus some fixed discount for saving the costs of trial). Plea bargaining, ideally, takes place in "the shadow of expected trial outcomes,"[79] with the parties' expectations regarding trial results as the central bargaining chip. Thus, for criminal defendants, the most important factor is their understanding of the strength of the prosecution's case against them.[80]

One of the core inadequacies in plea bargaining is the parties' lack of knowledge regarding the merits of the case.[81] Unlike civil proceedings, criminal procedure in most states includes extremely limited pretrial discovery.[82] Thus the defendant may have to guess at the strength of the prosecutor's case.[83] Pretrial publicity by the prosecutor can skew the defendant's view of the merits of the prosecutor's case and thus lead the defendant to plead guilty to charges that may be unwarranted by the evidence.

Plea bargaining involves acute inequities in the respective bargaining positions of the prosecution and the defense. Unlike civil proceedings, where a civil defendant can often inflict equal costs on the plaintiff through counterclaims, discovery, and other devices, the criminal defendant can do nothing to pressure or harm the prosecution.[84] This is equally true with pretrial publicity. The prosecutor can engage in pretrial publicity – affecting the defendant's reputation, employment, and association with family and friends – as one way to "exercise coercion unilaterally for the purpose of encouraging a settlement."[85]

Plea bargaining is complicated by agency costs.[86] Prosecutors represent the state and society and are obligated to seek justice. Yet, as political actors, they have incentives to enhance their own reputation, obtain high conviction rates, avoid embarrassing losses, and control workloads.[87] Overall, these incentives work to

---

[79] Bibas, *supra* Note 73, at 2654–65.

[80] See *id.* at 2470 ("The strength of the prosecution's case is the most important factor").

[81] *Id.* at 2495–96 ("The result of inadequate discovery is that the parties bargain blindfolded."); Fred Zacharias, *Justice in Plea Bargaining*, 39 WM. & MARY L. REV. 1121, 1129–32 (1998) (noting lack of "fully available information by both negotiating parties" and "[i]n most jurisdictions, bilateral discovery is limited severely" in criminal proceedings); Schulhoffer, *supra* Note 78, at 1998 (noting that the "expansion of pretrial discovery" would "directly address the flaws of plea bargaining" so parties could "accurately estimate ex ante the likelihood of conviction at trial.").

[82] Zacharias, *supra* Note 81, at 1129–31.

[83] Schulhofer, *supra* Note 78, at 2002 (stating that pleas are based on "an uninformed guess about the likelihood of conviction").

[84] Zacharias, *supra* Note 81, at 1133–34.

[85] *Id.* at 1133–35.

[86] Schulhofer notes that there are agency costs between the state's interest in criminal justice and the chief prosecutor's goals to "enhance her reputation and her political standing" as an elected official. See Schulhofer, *supra* Note 78, at 1987–88.

[87] See Schulhofer, *supra* Note 78, at 1987–88; Bibas, *supra* Note 73, at 2472; Caldwell, *supra* Note 78, at 84.

create a strong preference for pleas over trials – as pleading takes less time and every plea is a win for the prosecution (a conviction), while trials risk being a loss. While such incentives appear compatible with legitimate criminal justice ends and judicial resources, they have produced some recognized perverse results. As catalogued by many scholars, prosecutors have a strong incentive to pursue a plea when the evidence of guilt is weak – which includes some scenarios where defendants are in fact innocent.[88] Rather than dismissing charges – resulting in a "loss" for the prosecutor's conviction rate and perhaps exposing a faulty investigation that targeted innocent people[89] – prosecutors can get a "win" and avoid harming their own careers if they can instead get a defendant to plead.[90] Shockingly, both DNA exonerations and police scandals have demonstrated that a significant number of innocent people plead guilty in our criminal justice system,[91] in addition to unknown numbers who plead falsely to minor crimes.[92]

A related and recognized coercive tool available to prosecutors is to overcharge defendants – that is, prosecutors charge defendants with higher level offenses or more counts of an offense than is supported by the evidence.[93] Prosecutors are

---

[88] *See* Albert Alschuler, *The Prosecutor's Role in Plea Bargaining*, 36 U. Chi. L. Rev. 50, 59 (1968) (interviewing prosecutors in ten major metropolitan areas and reporting comments from prosecutors such as, "[w]hen we have a weak case for any reason, we'll reduce to almost anything rather than lose" and "[t]he only time we make a deal is when there is a weakness in the case"); Schulhoffer, *supra* Note 78, at 1988.

[89] Bibas, *supra* Note 73, at 2473 (noting that if prosecutors can "buy off credible claims of innocence cheaply, they [can] cover up faulty investigations that mistakenly target innocent suspects").

[90] *See* Alschuler, *supra* Note 88, at 61–62 (relating stories where innocent defendants were offered and took extraordinary reductions in charges as a plea rather than risking conviction and trial, and observing that "[w]hen prosecutors respond to a likelihood of acquittal by magnifying the pressures to plead guilty, they seem to exhibit a remarkable disregard for the danger of false conviction").

[91] Samuel R. Gross, et al., *Exonerations in the United States 1989 through 2003*, 95 J. Crim. L. & Criminology 523, 533–37 (2005) (noting several scandals in jurisdictions where scores of individuals pled guilty to false charges, one of which involved between 100 to 150 people – mostly young Hispanic males – who pled guilty to false gun or drug charges); Rodney Uphoff, *Convicting the Innocent: Aberration or Systemic Problem?* Wis. L. Rev. 739, (2006) Part III.F (countering "myth" that innocent do not plead guilty, and recounting numerous cases where later-exonerated criminal defendants pled guilty in face of pressures to plead).

[92] Gross, *supra* Note 91, at 536 (explaining from exoneration data that "nobody, it seems, seriously pursues exonerations for defendants who are falsely convicted of shop-lifting, misdemeanor assault, drug possession or routine felonies – auto-thefts or run-of-the-mill burglaries – and sentenced to probation, a $2000 fine, or even six months in the county jail or eighteen months in state prison," but concluding from pretrial detention and other indicators that "[s]ome defendants who accept [such plea] deals are innocent, possibly in numbers that dwarf false convictions in the less common but more serious violent felonies, but they are almost never exonerated").

[93] Caldwell, *supra* Note 78, at 84–85.

ethically prohibited from bringing charges that are not supported by probable cause.[94] Despite their ethical duties and the severe consequences to the life and liberty of accused persons, prosecutors have "a powerful incentive to begin the inevitable negotiating process from a position of strength, which often results in overcharging."[95] Overcharging can scare the defendant into pleading because it can work to the advantage of the prosecutor if the case goes to trial.[96] Overcharging can also convince defendants that a prosecutor is giving them a good – and perhaps irresistible – deal by reducing the charges, when the heightened charges should not have been brought in the first place.[97]

Pretrial publicity can add an extra layer of pressure to already-coercive (and unethical) overcharging. The overcharged defendant is not only publicly accused of crimes, but is publicly accused of crimes regarding which there actually was insufficient evidence for charges to have been brought. Publicity regarding an overcharged indictment may significantly increase pressures on the defendant to plead – including from friends, family, and associates who receive the publicity. Pretrial publicity regarding an overcharged indictment literally *heightens* public condemnation of the accused by bringing condemnation for crimes beyond what can be or is even expected to be proven at trial.[98] Moreover, upon hearing of a multiple-count indictment, the public may be more likely to form an opinion that the accused is guilty. As Alschuler notes about the effects of overcharging on trial, "[w]hen a jury hears an endless list of charges, they tend to think, 'The District Attorney could be wrong once, but no one could be wrong this often.'"[99] The public – from which the jury venire is selected – may have the same reaction to a publicized announcement from the prosecution that an accused has been arrested on twenty counts of a particular crime. Thus, publicity regarding an overcharged indictment may further undermine the presumption of innocence (and even a fair trial, as noted later) by creating an even stronger indication of guilt than would publicity about charges for which there is sufficient evidence.

Under the access to justice theory, the prosecutor can be forbidden from engaging in publicity as a coercive tactic to pressure the accused to plead. Prosecutors already hold all the bargaining chips; they do not need any further

---

[94] *See* MODEL RULE OF PROF'L CONDUCT R. 3.8(a).

[95] Caldwell, *supra* Note 78, at 65–66; Bibas, *supra* Note 73, at 2519.

[96] *See* Alschuler, *supra* Note 88, at 98 (explaining that "overcharging has both an economic and a psychological effect at trial, and may therefore make trial a less attractive alternative," as it increases the cost of the defense, the motions and instructions to be prepared, jury confusion, and a presumption of guilt).

[97] *See* Bibas, *supra* Note 73, at 2519; Alschuler, *supra* Note 88, at 85 ("The charge is the asking price in plea bargaining … ").

[98] *See* Alschuler, *supra* Note 88, at 61 (relating a case where defendant was offered, and accepted, a plea deal that reduced charges from kidnapping and forcible rape to one count of simple battery).

[99] *Id.* at 98–99.

tools to coerce defendants into pleading. Thus it is entirely appropriate to limit the ability of the prosecutor to further stack the deck and increase pressure through pretrial publicity. Publicity that has such an end or effect frustrates the proper functioning of the criminal justice system and can be prohibited.

No Right to Exacerbate Harm to the Accused's Reputation

Perhaps most obviously, the prosecutor can wreak serious reputational harm on the accused through pretrial publicity, particularly pretrial publicity that treats the accused as guilty, contains inculpatory information, or arouses public passions against the accused. The Duke lacrosse players were the subject of national shame when Michael Nifong publicly accused them of "gang-rape" performed with "racial hostility" and described the rape as having "a deep racial motivation" that was "absolutely unconscionable" and "totally abhorrent ... add[ing] another layer of reprehensibleness, to a crime that is already reprehensible."[100]

Although reputational harm is one of the most obvious problems associated with prosecutorial publicity, the Supreme Court has held that governmental deprivation of "reputation" alone is insufficient to create a due process violation.[101] Rather, a criminal defendant whose reputation is harmed by government actions must show "stigma-plus," meaning that the reputational harm must result in an independent constitutional violation. Indeed, in December 2012, the Fourth Circuit held that several of the Duke lacrosse players' due process claims based on harm to reputation should be dismissed because the plaintiffs had failed to establish the requisite "plus" constitutional violation.[102] While other courts have found a constitutional deprivation of liberty in a prosecutor's use of knowingly fabricated evidence to bring about an indictment, pretrial detention, and related harms,[103] the bottom line is that a due process claim against the prosecutor for depriving the accused of reputation will usually be unsuccessful.

Nevertheless, the fact that the Supreme Court has not recognized a constitutional remedy for deprivation of sheer reputation does not mean that reputation is a legally insignificant interest – nor does it mean that government must allow its prosecutors to run amok in using information provided them through the government's own investigative arm to unnecessarily destroy the reputations of its citizens.

---

[100] Mosteller, *supra* Note 19, at 1350–51.

[101] *See Paul* v. *Davis*, 424 U.S. 693, 711 (1976).

[102] *See Evans* v. *Chalmers*, 703 F.3d 636, 654–55 and n. 12 (4th Cir. 2012) (dismissing certain Fourth Amendment claims, and explaining that "the parties dispute whether a Fourth Amendment violation constitutes a cognizable 'plus'," yet because the Court held that the plaintiffs failed to state a Fourth Amendment claim, the Court does not address that question). Notably, these dismissed claims were against officers and municipalities, as Nifong had not appealed the district court's holding that Nifong did not enjoy qualified immunity for his investigatory actions. *See id.* at 645, n. 1.

[103] *See, e.g., Zahrey* v. *Coffey*, 221 F.3d 342, 355 (2000) (noting circuit conflict).

The existence of the common law tort of defamation shows the enduring societal recognition of the value of reputation as a legally protected interest. Moreover, some states have recognized reputation as an interest protected in its own right by the state's constitution.[104]

In any prosecution, the state has used its police powers to obtain access to the most damning information about people and provides that to the prosecutor for one purpose: the just prosecution of crime. While reputational harms are a concomitant part of being prosecuted,[105] the prosecution should not be able to exacerbate those harms through publicity that is unnecessary to the just investigation and prosecution of a crime, particularly with inflammatory and inculpatory publicity. Consequently, under the access to justice theory, the prosecutor lacks a free speech right to engage in pretrial publicity that is unnecessary for the investigation and prosecution of crime and which heightens reputational harm to the defendant.

Thus, the Restatement's prohibition against "heightening public condemnation of the accused" is constitutionally permissible – and this is so even though it is aimed at preserving reputation and even if it is interpreted to impose a more restrictive standard for prosecutors than defense attorneys in contravention of *Gentile*'s equality principle. Similarly, the Code of Federal Regulations restrictions forbidding federal prosecutors from engaging in nearly all inculpatory publicity and from speaking to the press to arrange a perp walk are also constitutionally permissible. A perp walk – telling the press the time and place of arrest and then having law enforcement take the accused on a long walk to the police car or station for a "photo op" of the accused in custody – harms the reputation of the accused for no just prosecutorial purpose but for the press to obtain and publish emotionally charged photos of the accused in actual custody. In 2011, Dominique Strauss-Khan was subjected to a perp walk in New York City, at a time when he was a forerunner for the 2012 French presidential election. One of the more remarkable aspects of the walk was New York Mayor Michael Bloomberg's comments to the press. While noting that the perp walk was "humiliating," Bloomberg said he didn't "have much sympathy" for Strauss-Khan, who resigned from his position as the Managing Director of the International Money Fund within days of the arrest.[106] Bloomberg explained: "if you don't want to do the perp walk, don't do the crime."[107] Apparently having forgotten about the presumption of innocence, Bloomberg agreed that it would be a "real sad thing ... if somebody is accused, does the perp walk, and turns out not to have been guilty. And then society really should look in the mirror and say

---

[104] *See, e.g., Dodd v. Reese*, 24 N.E. 995, 998 (Ind. 1940) (explaining that the Indiana State Constitution specifically protects reputation in parity with property).

[105] *See Kitai, supra* Note 51, at 284.

[106] Gerry Mullany, *Stauss-Kahn Resigns from I.M.F. in Wake of His Arrest*, N.Y. TIMES, May 19, 2011, *available at* www.nytimes.com/2011/05/19/business/19imf.html?pagewanted=all.

[107] Daniel Trotta, *NY Mayor Defends "Perp Walk" of IMF Chief*, REUTERS, May 17, 2011, *available at* www.reuters.com/article/2011/05/18/strausskahn-bloomberg-idAFN1714122920110518.

we should be more careful the next time."[108] The charges against Strauss-Khan were dismissed three months later.[109]

Indeed, the fact that federal constitutional law is unavailing in providing the accused with a remedy – combined with general hurdles of immunity for civil claims against prosecutors – increases the justification for allowing state regulators to prohibit the prosecution from using publicity to impose reputational harms on the accused that are unnecessary to the investigation and prosecution of the crime. The personal impact of reputational harms is evident in *Gentile* itself, where the prosecutor's pretrial publicity resulted in Sanders losing his business.[110] While the prosecution should and must be protected in publishing the indictment and other speech necessary to their official function in prosecuting individuals, the flip side of that protection is that the state can prohibit the prosecutor from publicizing information or engaging in publicity that exacerbates harm to the accused. It is contrary to the role of the prosecutor to use the information society provides to them through the exercise of coercive state power to inflict reputational harm on individuals that is unnecessary to the prosecution of crime. Under the access to justice theory, regulators can forbid prosecutors from engaging in such publicity as the prosecutor lacks a free speech right to do so.

No Speech Right to Undermine a Fair Trial

As recognized even in the traditional compromise, it is an essential part of the prosecutor's role to see that the accused receives a fair trial. In the American system of criminal justice, the jury trial right is "no mere procedural formality, but a fundamental reservation of power in our constitutional structure."[111] The jury is a representation of the people acting as an essential check on government power to deprive individuals of their life or liberty through the execution of criminal law. Thus the impartial jury is specifically designed to check prosecutorial power. Prosecutorial pretrial publicity can undermine – and even bias in its favor – the very check on prosecutorial power created in the Constitution as essential to protecting individual life and liberty.

The prejudicial impact of pretrial publicity on juries in criminal justice has been shown in numerous psychological studies and empirical research.[112] Studies show that the bias created by pretrial publicity is generally pro-prosecution and against the

[108] *Id.*

[109] *See* John Eligon, *Strauss-Kahn Drama Ends with Short Final Scene*, N.Y. Times, Aug. 23, 2011, *available at* www.nytimes.com/2011/08/24/nyregion/charges-against-strauss-kahn-dismissed .html?pagewanted=all&_r=0.

[110] *Gentile v. State Bar of Nevada*, 501 U.S. 1030, 1043 (1991) (Kennedy, J.).

[111] *Blakely v. Washington*, 542 U.S.296, 305–06 (2004).

[112] *See, e.g.,* Nancy M. Steblay, et al., *The Effects of Pretrial Publicity on Juror Verdicts: A Meta-Analytic Review*, 23 L. & Hum. Behavior, 219, 229 (1999) (performing a meta-analytic review of 44 empirical studies involving 5,755 participants on the effects of pretrial publicity on juries,

accused. Empirical studies have found that certain types of pretrial publicity have a statistically significant prejudicial effect on juries, including information regarding a prior criminal record of the accused,[113] a confession of the accused (even if retracted),[114] results of tests implicating the accused,[115] inadmissible incriminating evidence,[116] and statements regarding the accused's character.[117] Such information has a cumulative effect: The more of it an individual receives, the more likely they are to adjudge the accused guilty.[118]

and finding overall that "negative pretrial publicity significantly affects jurors' decisions about the culpability of the defendant," that "[j]urors exposed to publicity which presents negative information about the defendant and crime are more likely to judge the defendant as guilty than are jurors exposed to limited [pretrial publicity]," and that "the combination of data in this meta-analysis has demonstrated a convergence of the evidence across method to the conclusion that pretrial publicity has a significant impact on juror decision making"); Christine Ruva and Michelle LeVasseur, *Behind Closed Doors: The Effect of Pretrial Publicity on Jury Deliberations*, 18 PSYCH. CRIME & LAW 431 (June 2012) (arguing that jurors who were exposed to negative pretrial publicity were significantly more likely than their nonexposed counterparts to discuss ambiguous trial facts in a manner that supported the prosecution's case); Christine Ruva, Cathy McEvoy and Judith Becker Bryant, *Effects of Pre-Trial Publicity and Jury Deliberation on Juror Bias and Source Memory Errors*, 21 APPLIED COGNITIVE PSYCH. 45 (Jan. 2007) (finding that "[e]xposure to PTP [pretrial publicity] significantly affected guilty verdicts, sentence length, perceptions of defendant credibility, and misattributions of PTP as having been presented as trial evidence"); Steven Fein et al., *Can the Jury Disregard that Information? The Use of Suspicion to Reduce the Prejudicial Effects of Pretrial Publicity and Inadmissible Testimony*, 23 PERSONALITY & SOC. PSYCH. BULLETIN 1215, 1215–16, 1223 (1997) ("[r]esearch has shown that jury verdicts can be influenced by ... pretrial publicity concerning the defendant, disclosure of his or her prior record, current events in the news, incriminating testimony ruled inadmissible by the judge, hideous crime-scene images, [and] clearly coerced confessions"); Norbert L. Kerr et al., *On the Effectiveness of Voir Dire in Criminal Cases with Prejudicial Pretrial Publicity: An Empirical Study*, 40 AM. U. L. REV. 665, 695 (1991) ("Not unexpectedly, we found that exposure to certain types of highly prejudicial pretrial publicity, including information concerning the defendant's prior record, the existence of incriminating physical evidence, and defendant's implication in another crime, did bias mock jury verdicts. Such publicity, therefore, can create a threat to an impartial jury.").

[113] Amy L. Otto et al., *The Biasing Impact of Pretrial Publicity on Juror Judgments*, 18 L. & HUM. BEHAVIOR 453, 465 (1994); Kerr et al., *supra* Note 112, at 695; *see also* Joel D. Lieberman and Jamie Arndt, *Understanding the Limits of Limiting Instructions*, 6 PSYCH. PUB. POL'Y & L. 677, 681 (2000).

[114] Lieberman and Arndt, *supra* Note 113, at 681 (summarizing Tans and Chafee study finding that "a police report of a confession was the most damaging category of information").

[115] *See* Otto et al. *supra* Note 113, at 455 (failed lie detector test).

[116] *See* Kerr et al., *supra* Note 112, at 673, 695 (inadmissible incriminating physical evidence); Otto et al., *supra* Note 113, at 464–65 (finding that inadmissible evidence influenced pretrial judgments of guilt, which "directly related to final verdicts").

[117] Otto et al., *supra* Note 113, at 464–65.

[118] *See* Steblay et al., *supra* Note 112, at 231 ("Multiple indicators of a defendant's 'guilt' (confession, prior record, incriminating evidence) produced an increased effect on juror judgments of guilt"); Lieberman and Arndt, *supra* Note 113, at 680–81.

An "abundance of studies" show "that jurors who claim to be unbiased are still influenced by pretrial publicity"[119] and that people's self-evaluation of impartiality – even when sincere – fails to correlate with whether their opinion of guilt is in fact influenced by pretrial publicity. Indeed, once a person has made a pre-judgment of guilt, they will actually perceive trial evidence differently. Thus, subjects who pre-judged guilt because of pretrial publicity actually interpreted the prosecution's case as significantly stronger than nonexposed subjects.[120] Further, emotional pretrial publicity (meaning publicity arousing public passion but with no inculpatory information, such as graphic crime scene pictures[121]) has strong prejudicial effects even when completely irrelevant to determining an accused's guilt.[122]

Despite the essential role of the jury in checking prosecutorial power and the psychological literature showing prejudicial effects on juries, the Supreme Court's current caselaw makes it nearly impossible for a defendant to obtain a reversal of a conviction based on a denial of a fair trial because of prejudicial pretrial publicity. According to the Court: "Pretrial publicity – even *pervasive, adverse publicity* – does not inevitably lead to an unfair trial."[123] Thus prosecutors who fuel negative pretrial publicity have very little to lose. If their pretrial publicity happens to prejudice the jury to render a guilty verdict, the verdict will not be overturned.

Unfortunately, a number of prosecutors engage in prejudicial pretrial publicity. In a content analysis of media reports covering crimes in major American news outlets, Imrich, Mullin, and Linz found that prejudicial information (defined as material presumptively deemed prejudicial by Model Rule 3.6) appeared in 27 percent of media reports identifying criminal defendants.[124] Importantly, the

---

[119] Leiberman and Arndt, *supra* Note 113, at 682–83; Norbert L. Kerr, *The Effect of Pretrial Publicity on Jurors*, 78 JUDICATURE 120, 125–26 (1994) (summarizing studies, including Sue, Smith and Pedroza's study in which individuals exposed to publicity who indicated their own ability to be impartial "were still much more likely to convict than jurors never exposed to the publicity [53 percent guilty versus 23 percent guilty, respectively]"); Fein et al., *supra* Note 112, at 1223 (finding that pretrial publicity of inadmissible evidence biased mock jurors' verdicts despite "jurors' self-reports of how little they were influenced by the inadmissible information").

[120] Otto et al., *supra* note 113, at 463, 465 ("Subjects who believed the defendant was guilty prior to viewing the trial were more likely, after viewing the trial to think the evidence was strong."); *see also* Steblay et al., *supra* Note 112, at 231 (citing Moore study indicating "that negative publicity provides not just isolated fragments of information, but a belief framework about defendant culpability," which "then *directs the juror's attention and provides a filter through which subsequent evidence is perceived*" [emphasis added]).

[121] Kerr, *supra* Note 119, at 123–24.

[122] Kerr et al., *supra* Note 112, at 673–75.

[123] *Skilling v. United States*, 561 U.S. 358, 384 (2010) (quoting *Nebraska Press Ass'n v. Stuart*, 427 U.S. 539, 554 (1976)).

[124] D. J. Imrich et al., *Measuring the Extent of Prejudicial Pretrial Publicity in Major American Newspapers: A Content Analysis*, 45 J. COMMUNICATION 94–117 (1995), *cited in* Lieberman and Arndt, *supra* Note 113, at 680.

most frequent source of such prejudicial information was the prosecution or law enforcement.[125] Although the majority of criminal defendants do not have to face negative pretrial publicity, as Norman Kerr reports, "the absolute number is not trivial (more than 12,000 per year in the United States)."[126]

Nevertheless, even though the conviction will not be overturned as a violation of due process, states can prohibit and punish prosecutors who engage in prejudicial pretrial publicity that undermines the defendant's chances for an impartial jury. The prosecutor represents "a sovereignty whose obligation *to govern impartially* is as compelling as its obligation to govern at all."[127] It is part of the prosecutor's role to ensure that the defendant receives a fair trial with an impartial jury, and it is contrary to that role – and a violation of the prosecutor's duty to their government client – for the prosecutor to engage in pretrial publicity that has been shown to undermine juror impartiality against the accused. Under the access to justice theory, prosecutors lack a First Amendment right to engage in speech that will undermine the accused's constitutional rights, their own role in the justice system, and the jury's role as a check on prosecutorial power in our constitutional criminal justice system. Thus prosecutors can constitutionally be forbidden from engaging in pretrial publicity that can prejudice jury verdicts – especially the specific categories of highly prejudicial information that studies strongly indicate can bias potential jurors.

The studies previously cited signify a tension between the accused's right to an impartial jury and the First Amendment rights of the press to report criminal cases. Some have cited this research to argue that the press should be restricted in their reporting.[128] While a "compromise" between competing constitutional values may be appropriate when considering the accused's right to a fair trial and the *media's rights* to report under the Free Speech and Free Press Clauses, under the access to justice theory, there cannot and should not be a "compromise" between the prosecutor's free speech rights and the accused's fair trial rights. The prosecutor's free speech rights are defined by the prosecutorial role. In acting on behalf of the state in executing the full weight of its criminal powers against individuals to deprive them of life or liberty, the prosecutor lacks free speech rights to engage in pretrial publicity that undermines a criminal defendant's fair trial.

In arguing for broad free pretrial publicity rights, Chemerinsky notes the existence of less-restrictive alternatives to publicity prohibitions, such as extensive voir dire, sequestration, change of venue, and continuance.[129] Nevertheless, Freedman and Starwood note that many such "fixes" require the defendant to give up a different constitutional right in order to regain a fair trial:

---

[125] *See id.*
[126] Kerr, *supra* Note 119, at 121.
[127] *Berger v. United States*, 295 U.S. 78, 88 (1935) (emphasis added).
[128] *See, e.g.*, Giorgio Resta, *Trying Cases in the Media: A Comparative Overview*, 71 Law & Contemp. Probs. 31 (2008).
[129] Kerr et al., *supra* Note 112, at 673–75.

Apart from sequestration, the most effective alternatives for avoiding the effects of prejudicial publicity are delaying the trial, changing venue and trying the case before a judge without a jury. Yet *each of these alternatives involves the forfeiture by the defendant of a right guaranteed by the sixth amendment*: the right to a speedy trial, the right to be tried in the state and district in which the crime was committed and the right to trial by jury.[130]

The prosecutor – as the representative of the state and the person exercising government power to deprive people of life and liberty – must uphold these other constitutional rights of the accused.[131] Moreover, psychological and empirical studies indicate that at least some of these more modest remedies may be ineffectual at curbing pretrial publicity.[132] Overall there is considerable doubt as to the effectiveness of these "less restrictive alternatives" in alleviating the prejudicial effects of pretrial publicity.[133] Consequently, the prosecution should not be able to prejudice the jury venire in reliance on ineffectual fixes – several of which may also deny the defendant of other constitutional rights.

THE RIGHTS OF THE DEFENSE ATTORNEY TO ENGAGE IN PRETRIAL PUBLICITY

Because of the criminal defense attorney's constitutional role in challenging state criminal power brought against individuals, all of the interests that cut against a prosecutor having a First Amendment right to engage in pretrial publicity actually cut in favor of recognition of such a right for the defense attorney. Thus a criminal defense attorney should have a protected right to engage in pretrial publicity necessary to preserve the presumption of innocence, to obtain a fair plea, to protect the reputational and liberty interests of the accused, and to secure a fair trial.

Free Speech Right to Speak for the Accused

The criminal defense attorney represents an individual client – unlike the prosecution with its amorphous government client – and thus it could be argued that the

---

[130] Freedman and Starwood, *supra* Note 11, at 617 (emphasis added).

[131] *Id.* at 617–18.

[132] Christina A. Studebaker and Steven D. Penrod, *Pretrial Publicity*, 3 Psych. Pub. Pol'y & L. 428, 439–47 (1997) (reviewing research regarding various methods and concluding that "traditional safeguards, such as continuances, extended voir dire, jury deliberations, and judicial instructions to disregard the publicity or use it under limited conditions have been found to be ineffective" at eliminating the bias created by pretrial publicity).

[133] As Studebaker and Penrod summarize: "[I]t appears that the effects of pretrial publicity can find their way to the courtroom, can survive the jury selection process, can survive the presentation of trial evidence, can endure the limiting effects of judicial instructions, and cannot only persevere through deliberation, but may actually intensify." Studebaker and Penrod, *supra* Note 132, at 445.

following interests only demonstrate that the accused should have a free speech right to engage in pretrial publicity, and not the defense attorney on the accused's behalf. Accused individuals themselves, of course, must have a First Amendment right to engage in pretrial publicity in the face of criminal charges, which, unfortunately, not all courts have recognized.[134] It would undermine recognized and core purposes of the First Amendment if the government could bring public criminal charges against a person and could also deny that person the right to publicly respond to those charges until and only in the venue of a trial conducted by the government itself. Further, under both Blasi's checking power theory and democratic theories of the First Amendment, the accused should be able to subject the use of government criminal power to the scrutiny of the ultimate sovereign in our system, the people[135] – including, as Justice Kennedy argued in *Gentile*, "to demonstrate in the court of public opinion that the [accused] does not deserve to be tried."[136] Finally, accused individuals should have such a right as an essential component of preserving their own liberty and status as a member of society.

Although recognizing the right of accused persons to speak for themselves is essential, it is also insufficient. Defense attorneys must have their own free speech right to speak in their official capacity on behalf of the accused. Criminal defendants face the full weight of the government's brute force being brought against them to literally take away their lives and liberty. In facing "what is so much stronger than themselves,"[137] they are constitutionally provided with the assistance of counsel – someone who understands the law, defenses thereto, and the workings of the criminal justice system. That counselor can use their legal expertise to ascertain the rights of the accused and to declare to the public when the prosecution is abusing its power. It is the role of the defense attorney to protect the life, liberty, and property of the accused, and, under the access to justice theory, that includes protecting the client's constitutional and legal interests discussed herein, including through pretrial publicity.

Recognizing the right of the attorney to speak also helps to provide parity between the public spokespersons for the prosecution and the defense. The prosecution does not represent an individual who has their own speech rights; thus, the state speaks only through the prosecutor. Statements made on behalf of the state, including in the indictment and charging affidavit, are made by a professional who is trained in law, speaking, reasoning, evidence, and the art of persuasion. Criminal defendants,

---

[134] *See, e.g., State v. Grossberg*, 705 A.2d 608 (Del. 1997) (issuing gag order against criminal defendant forbidding her from making pretrial statements to the press in high-profile case regarding murder of baby born at prom); *Breiner v. Takao*, 73 Haw. 499 (1992) (reversing gag order issued by trial court against criminal defendant).

[135] *See* Vincent Blasi, *The Checking Value in First Amendment Theory*, AM. B. FOUND. RES. J. 521, 527, 538 (1977); ALEXANDER MEIKLEJOHN, FREE SPEECH AND ITS RELATION TO SELF-GOVERNMENT 253–54 (1948).

[136] *Gentile v. State Bar of Nevada*, 501 U.S. 1030, 1043 (1991) (Kennedy J.).

[137] Oliver W. Holmes, *The Path of the Law*, 10 HARV. L. REV. 457 (1897).

as a whole, are overrepresented by the poor and the uneducated. They may be inarticulate (or even non-fluent in English), uneducated, or even struggling with mental health issues. As Freedman and Smith note, "[i]t could be disastrous ... for an unskilled defendant to confront the cacophony and confusion of a press conference."[138] Moreover, any statements that could be interpreted as incriminating could be used against the accused at trial.[139] It is essential that the accused have an advocate, who categorically is equally matched with that of the state's spokesman in education and training, to protect the accused's interests.

In speaking on behalf of the defendant, however, the defense attorney is not merely a public relations specialist. The lawyer's training in the law and access to information regarding the case, including communications with the defendant, make it so the lawyer can in fact make comments to the press that are far more protective of the defendant's legal rights than if they came from another source – including from the defendant. Legal training enables lawyers to evaluate the justness of the charges brought by the prosecution and the relevant and possible defenses. This is particularly true in an age where laws are often complex and the accused may not understand the law's requirements or the legal showing necessary to establish a defense.

Importantly, because of their duty of confidentiality, defense attorneys cannot just begin revealing information about the case without the client's express or implied consent. But given that consent, criminal defense attorneys have First Amendment rights under the access to justice theory to fulfill their role in the criminal justice system to fully represent the client and protect the client's rights to life and liberty from government forfeiture – not solely to secure a fair trial, as emphasized in the traditional compromise – but also to preserve the presumption of innocence, obtain a fair plea, and protect the client's reputation and liberty interests.

Speech Right to Reinforce the Presumption of Innocence

The presumption of innocence, as constitutionally grounded in due process and in the Sixth Amendment right to jury trial,[140] encompasses two underlying purposes, both of which are consistent with (and even buttressed by) defense attorney pretrial publicity. First, defense attorney pretrial publicity can act as a "shield against punishment before conviction," shoring up the presumption's goal that accused individuals are to be treated with the dignity accorded to all other presumably innocent people in society.[141] Upon publication of even the fact of an arrest or indictment, pretrial publicity from the defense can remind the public that the

---

[138] FREEDMAN AND SMITH, *supra* Note 12, at 102.
[139] *See id.*
[140] *See supra* Notes 51–64 and accompanying text.
[141] Quintard-Morenas, *supra* Note 52, at 107–10, 148.

prosecution has yet to prove its case and that they should suspend judgment until a jury has spoken. When faced with criminal charges causing family, friends, and associates to treat the accused as guilty, the defense should be able to respond publicly to preserve the accused's right not to be subjected to punishment until a jury has found them proven guilty beyond a reasonable doubt.

Unfortunately, Model Rule 3.6 only presumptively allows the defense attorney to state the "defense involved"[142] and treats as presumptively prejudicial statements regarding the evidence, forensic tests, the character, lack of criminal record, and innocence of the accused.[143] Because the public is aware that an accused is entitled to counsel, they may not give much weight to defense attorney statements containing a vague reference to the existence of a defense. It is imperative that the defense attorney be allowed to present to the public exculpatory facts and *elaborate* on the defense. Such specific information should have a greater impact on the public in presuming innocence until trial because the public will understand that reserving judgment against the accused is not merely a legal technicality but may be justified in fact. Of course, the presumption of innocence and the Sixth Amendment right to trial by an impartial jury are in no way technicalities but are an essential reservation to the people of the power of government to deprive individuals of life and liberty. Yet, to help the public understand the constitutional weight of the presumption, defense attorneys need to be able to reinforce the presumption, including by being free pretrial to elaborate on exculpatory evidence and defenses in specific cases. Even though defense attorneys may often not wish to initiate publicity, the fact that they do in some cases may serve on the whole to reinforce the presumption of innocence for criminal defendants collectively.

Moreover, defense attorneys should be able (when not a misrepresentation) to declare to the press their belief that the accused is innocent. Such "vouching" for client innocence has been condemned by some scholars[144] and Model Rule 3.6 includes as presumptively prejudicial the lawyer's opinion as to an accused's guilt or innocence.[145] But where the defense attorney believes a client to be innocent or to be unjustly charged, there is no state justification in forbidding the attorney from so stating publicly. The attorney's statements serve to bolster the presumption of innocence. Again, the prosecution will be able to respond to such statements, for example, by noting that it has evidence sufficient to continue the prosecution. Nevertheless, in light of the presumption of innocence, the prosecution lacks a free speech right to vouch for the guilt of the accused because the prosecution, in representing the state, must abide by the presumption. Although facially unequal, continued prosecution itself implies evidence supporting guilt and the result is

---

[142] MODEL RULE OF PROF'L CONDUCT R. 3.6(b).
[143] *Id.* R. 3.6 cmt. 5.
[144] *See* Cole and Zacharias, *supra* Note 16, at 1665–74.
[145] MODEL RULE OF PROF'L CONDUCT R. 3.6 cmt. 5.

consistent with the presumption of innocence and the differing roles of the prosecutor and the defense attorney in the criminal justice system. Thus Model Rule 3.6's limitation on vouching is an appropriate limit on prosecutorial speech, but it violates the defense attorney's free speech rights.

Freedman and Starwood posit that "a situation in which a defendant could generate publicity sufficient to prejudice the case against the prosecution scarcely can be imagined."[146] While there are many possible factors in play,[147] the difficulty in prejudicing the prosecution exists in part because of the presumption of innocence. The trial is supposed to start with the jury presuming that the defendant is innocent and with the prosecution bearing a heavy burden to overcome that presumption. Thus, even were jurors to go into trial inclined to think that the defendant is innocent, that would not undermine the legal presumption that is supposed to exist.

Defense pretrial publicity can also help ensure the second purpose of the presumption of innocence, which is to establish the burden of proof for the prosecution. Where defense attorney pretrial publicity works to alleviate juror pro-prosecution bias, which at least one empirical study has indicated,[148] it sustains the presumption of innocence in requiring the prosecution to prove a case beyond a reasonable doubt.

Free Speech Right to Secure a Fair Plea

As noted by several commentators, criminal defense attorneys can be as much of a problem, if not more so, in securing fair pleas for their clients as the prosecution. Often paid by case volume or flat fee, with many facing enormous caseloads, they have strong economic incentives to encourage their clients to plead rather than take cases to trial.[149] Thus many criminal defense attorneys compound the prosecution's pressure on defendants to plead guilty regardless of the evidence in the case – indeed, the defense attorney may not have or take the time to investigate the merits, defenses, or anything at all before recommending a plea.[150]

---

[146] Freedman and Starwood, *supra* Note 11, at 607.

[147] Differing access to major media outlets is a possible reason why the defense may not be able to have as great an influence as the prosecution. In the age of the internet, some defense attorneys are posting their own publicity directly on their own websites and social media. *See* Hochberg, *supra* Note 3.

[148] Fein et al., *supra* Note 112, at 1218.

[149] *See, e.g.*, Schulhofer, *supra* Note 78, at 1988 (noting defense counsel's "powerful financial incentives ... to settle as promptly as possible."); Bibas, *supra* Note 73, at 2476; *see generally* Albert W. Alschuler, *The Defense Attorney's Role in Plea Bargaining*, 84 YALE L. J. 1179 (1975) (study of defense attorneys showing overwhelming incentive to pressure defendants to plead).

[150] *See, e.g.*, Bibas, *supra* Note 73, at 2479–82 ("[M]any public defenders are overburdened. They handle hundreds of cases per year, far more than privately retained attorneys do. This volume ordinarily means that pleas become the norm ... [and] overburdened defense attorneys cannot spend enough time to dig up all possible defenses. The result is fewer plea-bargaining chips and less favorable plea bargains.")

Nevertheless, criminal defense attorneys should be able to speak to the press to alleviate the inequities favoring the prosecution in the plea bargaining process. One of the problems in plea bargaining is its secretive nature. Where evidence is weak or defendants have a credible claim of innocence, the prosecutor can hide the cases from public scrutiny with sweet deals that make the cases go away[151] – and, in fact, still result in a "win" for the prosecution's record. Yet prosecutors are "a politically ambitious bunch," who are often beholden to an electorate and thus will care about negative press they may receive.[152] Where a defendant is charged who is innocent, who has a strong defense, or who is significantly overcharged, the defense attorney should be able to publicly state as much to the press. Such press may put political pressure on the prosecution. The prosecution does have a right to respond to such publicity, but where the evidence and information indicates that a prosecution is unwarranted, publicity may help pressure the prosecution to lower or drop charges.

An example may be found in the 2012 prosecution of Bei Bei Shuai, who was charged for murder and attempted infanticide and faced a potential punishment of 45 to 65 years imprisonment. Shuai, at eight-months pregnant, ingested rat poison in a suicide attempt after her boyfriend left her. A friend found Shuai, took her to the hospital – where the baby was taken by C-section and died three days later.[153] Linda Pence, the attorney for Bei Bei Shuai undertook considerable publicity on Shuai's behalf, including creating a website, a Facebook Page, and a Twitter account. Included on Pence's website was an invitation to the public to express their dissatisfaction with the charges to the prosecutor, complete with a link to the prosecutor's office address and phone number. The prosecution eventually offered and Shuai accepted a plea to criminal recklessness, a misdemeanor, and was given credit for her entire sentence of 178 days.[154] Although it is impossible to know whether or not the defense attorney's publicity influenced the prosecutor in deciding to offer the plea, it very well may have. The issue is whether the defense attorney should have a constitutionally protected speech right to freely engage in such publicity on behalf of a defendant. As an attorney, Pence was able to frame the issues in a way to protect Shuai's interests,[155] to note Shuai's lack of criminal history, and to elaborate on the applicable law and precedent that could be set by a conviction in the case.

---

[151] *See id.* at 2473.

[152] *Id.* at 2472.

[153] *See* Diana Penner, *Woman Freed after Plea Agreement in Baby's Death*, USA TODAY, Aug. 2, 2013 *available at* www.usatoday.com/story/news/nation/2013/08/02/woman-freed-after-plea-agreement-in-babys-death/2614301/.

[154] *See id.*

[155] For example, Pence did not state or imply on her website that the rat poison was the cause of death. Ultimately, Pence successfully undermined the prosecution's cause of death evidence. The prosecutor noted in interviews about the plea that rulings from the court had hurt their case, including that "Dr. Jolene Clouse, who performed the autopsy on newborn Angel Shuai, didn't consider other possible causes for the brain bleeding that caused her death, including a drug that Shuai received while she was in the hospital." *Bei Bei Shuai Pleads Guilty in Baby's*

Kevin Cole and Fred Zacharias have argued that defense attorney pretrial publicity – especially publicity vouching for a defendant's innocence – can influence a prosecutor to offer a better deal to avoid continued negative publicity.[156] Nevertheless, they express concern that if such pretrial publicity (even if true) is allowed to help one defendant, then other defendants would expect the attorney to engage in the same speech on their behalf. Thus clients who were guilty would be faced with the dilemma of telling their attorney all of the facts (and foreclose vouching), or lying to the lawyer so that they would vouch for their innocence.[157] Further, Cole and Zacharias argue that if vouching is allowed, then a failure to vouch will oust the defendant's guilt to the prosecution.[158]

Despite such concerns, the alternative – foreclosing such pretrial publicity – is unacceptable. It would contravene the role of the defense attorney, and their heightened duties to the accused, to forbid a defense attorney from publicly declaring the innocence of their client when accurate and when it is likely to operate to the client's benefit in obtaining a fair plea – or even getting charges dropped. As noted, plea bargaining is significantly skewed to favor the prosecution, which is able to exert considerable pressure on the defense to plead. The defense has close to zero ability to pressure the prosecution to advance an equitable plea deal or reduce or drop charges. Because it is the essential role of the defense attorney to protect the life and liberty of the criminal defendant in the face of the full weight of government power, the defense attorney cannot be denied from using one of the few tools available to exert pressure on a politically accountable prosecution: public opinion.

It is a known and established fact that innocent individuals plead guilty.[159] If a prosecutor brings unjustified charges, the defense attorney should be able to publicly call the prosecutor on it. Not only does this serve to protect that individual criminal defendant's interests, it also may serve to bring to light the fact that the prosecutor is not exercising their discretion appropriately. Such public scrutiny may in turn improve the integrity of prosecution. One major concern regarding the plea bargaining system is that it is done in the dark, and that prosecutors are able to "cover up faulty investigations that mistakenly target innocent suspects."[160] If prosecutors are aware that they are likely to receive negative publicity for unwarranted or substantially overcharged indictments, they may exercise greater care in ensuring that charges are warranted.

But the fears of Cole and Zacharias that every criminal defendant will want such publicity and will expect their attorneys to vouch for their innocence to the press are

---

Death, Huffington Post, Aug. 2, 2013 *available at* www.huffingtonpost.com/2013/08/02/bei-bei-shuai-guilty_n_3698383.html.

[156] Cole and Zacharias, *supra* Note 16, at 1648.

[157] *Id.* at 1665–66.

[158] *Id.* at 1665.

[159] *See supra* Notes 91–92 and accompanying text.

[160] Bibas, *supra* Note 73, at 2473.

unlikely to materialize. Under the access to justice theory, once the defense opens the door, the prosecution has a right to respond to the public and explain the decision to charge and the evidence that supports that charge. The right of the prosecution to respond to (but not to initiate) such publicity creates a disincentive for defendants to initiate publicity themselves. Only defendants who have little or no reason to fear publicity from the prosecution explaining the evidence against them would find defense attorney "vouching" useful to their case. But if the defendant is innocent or is grossly overcharged, then the chance of a successful prosecutor response is not as big a threat. In such a case, if the prosecutor responds by disclosing weak evidence, the defense can explain why the prosecution's response is unavailing. Ultimately, this may help both sides to properly determine the value of a case, resulting in a fairer plea bargain.[161]

Free Speech Right to Preserve Client Reputation and Liberty

In discussing the social value of pretrial publicity, Chemerinsky notes the importance for attorneys to protect their client's reputation, in turn quoting Uelmen, who states: "A client who is never prosecuted, or who is prosecuted and acquitted may have been ill-served by a lawyer who allowed public speculation about his guilt to go unchallenged."[162] The defense attorney has the ability to challenge, as a matter of law and fact, the legal appropriateness for pressing charges. Notably, Chemerinsky does not make this observation as part of his First Amendment analysis. Yet under the access to justice theory, defense attorneys' free speech rights include speech necessary to their role in protecting their clients' reputation in the face of criminal charges.

The existence of the common law tort of defamation shows the enduring societal recognition of the value of reputation and its time-honored status as a legally protected interest. Nevertheless, when criminal charges are brought against an individual, the prosecution is cloaked with immunity and the individual cannot sue the prosecutor for defamation to protect reputation. While it is necessary to protect the prosecutor in publishing charges in an indictment, such protection also means that accused individuals are left bereft of a traditional remedy to protect their reputation in the face of a publication that in any other scenario would be libelous per se.[163] Consequently, once indicted, criminal defendants and their constitutionally mandated counsel can only salvage reputation before family, friends, and associates in a timely manner by responding to the charges. Defendants should *not* be forced to wait until trial (months or years later) to protect their reputation.

---

[161] *Id.* at 2519.
[162] Chemerinsky, *supra* Note 14, at 869; Gerald F. Uelmen, *Leaks, Gags and Shields: Taking Responsibility*, 37 SANTA CLARA L. REV. 943, 951–52 (1997).
[163] Freedman and Starwood, *supra* Note 11, at 617.

To require otherwise would allow the government to deprive the accused of reputation during the pretrial period – with resultant personal and professional harms – without any remedy. Although criminal defendants and their counsel may decide that waiting until trial is the wisest course, they should have a right to protect the accused's reputational interests publicly and forcefully if they deem it necessary or desirable.

Thus it was perfectly consistent with his role as a defense attorney for Gentile to hold a press conference to protect his client's reputation and property interests once Sanders was indicted. Gentile recognized the severe reputational harm that his client, Sanders, had already suffered due to publicity regarding the crime. Although a jury, ultimately, would acquit Sanders, meanwhile Sanders' personal and professional life was on a ruinous trajectory. Defense attorneys are not required to await trial to publicly counter the disastrous array of personal and professional harms that come with indictment against their client.

Under the access to justice theory, because it is the central role of the defense attorney to protect the accused's life, liberty, and property interests – which liberty interests include reputation – the attorney has a free speech right to engage in pretrial publicity to protect the client's reputational interests pretrial. Although the Supreme Court has not recognized a constitutional remedy for reputation absent showing "stigma-plus,"[164] that does not undermine the importance of reputation as an essential component of a person's actual liberty interests as a member of society free to work, associate with others, and live, as Quintard-Morenas argues, "with the dignity and respect due to presumably innocent individuals."[165]

In an era where pretrial detention has become common,[166] pretrial publicity from the defense may not only protect the client's reputation; it may actually help bring about a plea or dismissal that would put an end to the accused's pretrial detention. Thus, the attorney would not only be protecting the accused's liberty interests in reputation but their liberty interests in being free from unlawful or unjustified incarceration. As noted, the framers considered freedom from unlawful restraint of special importance in our constitutional justice system.

Free Speech Right to Protect a Fair Trial

A criminal defendant's constitutional right to a fair trial by an impartial jury is not a formality but an essential populist check on the government's power to deprive people of life and liberty. Although few criminal cases proceed to trial, the right to a trial exists in every case up until there is a plea waiving that right. As noted earlier, empirical studies on pretrial publicity indicate that publicity generally works in favor

[164] *See supra* Notes 101–02 and accompanying text.
[165] Quintard-Morenas, *supra* Note 52, at 148.
[166] *See* Baradaran, *supra* Note 57, at 725.

of the prosecution and against the defense. Even emotional publicity of no inculpatory value has been shown to prejudice mock juries against the accused.[167]

Notably, one empirical study indicated that pro-defense publicity can lessen the effects of pro-prosecution pretrial publicity.[168] In the study, a control group was exposed to no publicity and all other participants were exposed to pro-prosecution publicity. Some of the exposed participants were additionally exposed to a brief article where the defense attorney questioned the motives of the press and the prosecution, indicating that the prior reports "knowingly ignore … facts which would point toward a defendant's innocence" and that the prosecution was trying to "sway public opinion."[169] Interestingly, a minority of subjects in the no-publicity group voted guilty (indicating the weakness of the mock prosecution's case), yet more than 75 percent of the subjects who were solely exposed to the pro-prosecution publicity voted guilty. Finally, those who were exposed to the pro-defense publicity "were *no more likely to convict* than were the participants in the nopublicity control condition."[170] Thus the pro-defense publicity (and its implication of innocence) did *not* prejudice the group in favor of the defendant, rather it leveled the playing field back to what it had been prior to the pro-prosecution publicity. Although this is only one study on the effect of pro-defense publicity, it illustrates that pro-defense publicity may be able to level the playing field for the defense, and restore the right to a fair trial by an impartial jury.

Because the role of defense attorneys includes protecting the accused's right to a fair trial, they should have a speech right to use publicity to lessen prejudice for a client publicly charged with wrongdoing. Even were we to imagine a situation where defense pretrial publicity resulted in a jury that was predisposed to find the defendant innocent,[171] that "presumption of innocence" would not run contrary to the proper functioning of the criminal justice system.

Model Rule 3.6 undermines the free speech rights of criminal defense attorneys to protect the fair trial rights of their clients. The rule forbids lawyers from commenting on the character, credibility, reputation, criminal record of the accused or a witness, expected testimony from parties or witnesses, or the results of forensic tests.[172] While the prosecution appropriately can be foreclosed from publicizing negative character evidence, the criminal record of the accused, and forensic test results, the "equality" of imposing these same prohibitions on the defense is problematic. If the defense has witnesses or forensic test results that undermine the prosecution's case and if the defense wants to use that information to publicly counter the weight of charges or level the playing field in public opinion they

---

[167] *See supra* Note 122 and accompanying text.
[168] Fein et al., *supra* Note 112, at 1218.
[169] *Id.* at 1220.
[170] *Id.*
[171] Freedman and Starwood, *supra* Note 11, at 607 (arguing that such a scenario could scarcely be imagined),
[172] MODEL RULE OF PROF'L CONDUCT R. 3.6 cmt. 5.

should be able to do so. Further, if the defense wants to present to the press positive evidence regarding the character, lack of criminal record, or reputation of the accused, the defense should be able to do so in order to preserve all of the interests noted herein: a fair trial, a fair plea, the presumption of innocence, and the accused's pretrial reputation and liberty.

If the defense commented on any of these items, as discussed later, the prosecution would be able to respond with information necessary to counter the publicity. Through this mechanism not only are the fair trial rights of the defense preserved but the other related constitutional rights of the defendant are properly put into the defendant's own hands. Commentators have argued that any effects of pretrial publicity can be fixed by other mechanisms, many of which require the defendant to give up a different constitutional right (speedy trial, venue, and jury trial) to regain a fair trial.[173] Under the access to justice theory, the prosecution constitutionally can be limited from initiating most publicity, and thus extensive attorney publicity should only be generated if the defense pursues it first. Consequently, if such publicity ultimately required one of the above fixes (and the concomitant forfeiture of one of the defendant's rights) it would often be because the defense pursued that option. Freedman and Starwood initially endorsed this approach, noting that if the defendant or her counsel's speech "should boomerang and result in so much prejudicial publicity that the defendant must waive one or more sixth amendment rights, so be it."[174] Defense counsel and the accused could weigh such potential consequences prior to initiating publicity.

GENTILE'S EQUALITY PRINCIPLE AND THE RIGHT TO RESPOND

Contrary to *Gentile* and Model Rule 3.6, the access to justice theory calls for differing rights for the prosecutor and the defense attorney. Prosecutors have extremely limited First Amendment rights to engage in pretrial publicity. They have a constitutional right to engage in publicity that is necessary to fulfill their purpose in the system of justice and have no constitutionally protected right to undermine the criminal justice system, including the rights of the accused, through pretrial publicity. Consequently, restrictions like those found in the Code of Federal Regulations are constitutional, and could be constitutionally imposed on state prosecutors. This does not mean that states are *required* to restrict prosecutors to the fullest extent that the Constitution allows. States are free to continue with lesser restrictions on prosecutorial speech, but the Constitution is not a barrier to state regulations foreclosing their prosecutors from engaging in pretrial publicity beyond what is necessary to conduct the investigation, prosecution, and trial.

Further, prosecutors do *not* have a constitutional right to divulge all information that is contained in some public record. Model Rule 3.6 contains a public record

[173] Freedman and Starwood, *supra* Note 11, at 617.
[174] *Id.*

exception, but the Code of Federal Regulations does not.[175] The Model Rule's public record exception has been interpreted in ways that generally swallow much of the force of the rule, even as to presumptively prejudicial materials.[176] For example, in *Attorney Grievance Commission of Maryland v. Gansler*,[177] the prosecutor avoided discipline under Rule 3.6 by invoking the public records exception when he published the prior criminal record of an accused based on the argument that criminal records are contained in public court records.[178] As noted earlier, the prior criminal record of an accused is one of the categories of pretrial publicity that has been found to prejudice jurors against criminal defendants and undermine their rights.[179] It is contrary to the role of the prosecutor to inject such information into the public view. It may be that media sources are able to dig up the information, but states can prohibit such information coming from the prosecutor, whose role includes protecting the accused's constitutional rights.

Defense attorneys have strong First Amendment rights to engage in pretrial publicity to protect their client's interests in a fair trial, a fair plea, reputation, and liberty. Consistent with their role in and the purposes of the criminal justice system, defense attorneys do have one significant limitation on their speech, which is reflected in Model Rules of Professional Conduct 4.1 and 8.4. In their speech to the press, defense attorneys lack a First Amendment right to knowingly make false statements of law or fact.[180] Model Rule 4.1, as proffered here as also representing the constitutional limitation, only prohibits the "knowing" false or misleading statement – requiring "actual knowledge," which can be inferred from circumstances.[181] This standard still leaves great leeway for criminal defense attorneys to engage in pretrial publicity, as long as they do not engage in blatant misrepresentations and falsehoods.[182] However, it is more restrictive than Chemerinsky's approach.[183]

---

[175] *Compare* MODEL RULE PROF'L CONDUCT R. 3.6(b) *with* 28 C.F.R. §50.2.
[176] *See, e.g., Muex v. State of Indiana*, 800 N.E.2d 249, 252 (2003) (no violation of Rule 3.6 by publicizing forensic results of inculpatory DNA tests because included in charging affidavit, a public record); *Attorney Grievance Comm'n of Maryland v. Gansler*, 377 Md. 656, 691 (2000).
[177] 377 Md. at 691.
[178] The Court noted that future attorneys "will have the burden of establishing that such information was contained in a bona fide public court record accessible to the general public," but that many criminal records could be found in "publicly accessible court records." *See id.*
[179] *See supra* Note 113 and accompanying text.
[180] MODEL RULES OF PROF'L CONDUCT R. 8.4 (including in the definition of misconduct, any "conduct involving dishonesty, fraud, deceit or misrepresentation").
[181] *See* MODEL RULES OF PROF'L CONDUCT R. 4.1 and 1.0(f).
[182] The overlap of Model Rules of Professional Conduct 4.1 and 8.4 with pretrial publicity already exists under the rules. For example, in *Iowa Supreme Court v. Visser*, 629 N.W.2d 376, 383 (2001), the court held that the attorney had not violated Model Rule 3.6 by his publicity, but that he had nevertheless engaged in dishonest conduct because he knew that part of what he said was untrue.
[183] *See* Chemerinsky, *supra* Note 14, at 885–86 (arguing that courts should employ the actual malice standard from *New York Times v. Sullivan* to pretrial publicity).

Even in this regime where prosecutors have limited free speech rights and defense attorneys have robust free speech rights, *Gentile's* equality principle does have play in one very important sense. Once the defendant opens the door by engaging in pretrial publicity, the prosecution should be constitutionally privileged to respond to such statements. The prosecutor represents a sovereign who is required to act impartially and whose goal in the criminal justice system is to convict the guilty in accordance with constitutional requirements and to spare the innocent.[184] To the extent that a defense attorney's statements indicate that the prosecutor – as the representative of the government – is abusing that power, the prosecutor has a right to respond. Further, prosecutors are political actors, using government resources, and exercising political discretion under public scrutiny. It is part of the prosecutor's role to protect the interests of the government, and it is not in the government's interests for the public solely to hear (and come to believe) that prosecutions lack justification when that is not the case.

A right to respond is already found in Model Rule 3.6(c), and, as with that provision, the prosecutor's constitutional right to respond is limited to disclosing information to mitigate the publicity from the defense.[185] The response right does not give the prosecution carte blanche to publicize all information and opinions about the case. Further, as with defense attorneys, the prosecution's response must comport with Model Rules 4.1 and 8.4. The prosecution has no free speech right to engage in false statements, misrepresentations, or dishonesty.

There is one area where the prosecution can respond but can be prohibited from responding "in kind": vouching for a client's innocence or guilt. While defense attorneys can vouch for their client's innocence if not a knowing misrepresentation, the prosecution cannot vouch for the guilt of the accused pretrial. To provide such a constitutional right to the prosecution pretrial is directly contrary to the presumption of innocence. The prosecutor can respond with information that mitigates defense vouching, and the very fact of continued prosecution of the accused will signal to the public the prosecution's continued belief in the defendant's guilt.

The criminal defense team that decides to use publicity to protect the accused's interests in reputation, the presumption of innocence, a fair plea, and a fair trial, must make that decision with proverbial fear and trembling. Once they open the publicity door, the prosecution will be privileged to respond. The defense must contemplate the reality that more publicity generally works to favor the prosecution, and thus publicity can backfire to harm the accused's interests. When Zimmerman's defense attorneys decided to create a webpage, Facebook page, and twitter account, commentators recognized the significant risks for the defense in fueling publicity, including

[184] *Berger v. United States*, 295 U.S. 78, 88 (1935).
[185] *See* MODEL RULE PROF'L CONDUCT R. 3.6(c).

social media. One attorney commentator aptly remarked: "You have to . . . understand that you're playing with a monster that will devour you if you screw up."[186]

Admittedly, publicity as to a particular crime or a particular defendant or victim may bring intense media scrutiny without initiation from either the prosecution or the defense. In such a case, the defense, of course, maintains the right to initiate publicity of its own; and if they do so, the prosecution has a right to respond in mitigation. Nevertheless, the prosecution has no right to respond to publicity not coming from the defense unless the media reports significantly undermine the prosecution's case. The prosecution lacks a free speech right to use media interest in a crime as an excuse to fuel the fire of publicity harmful to an accused.

The accused is thus given the choice to either close down nearly all publicity coming from the prosecution by refusing themselves to engage in publicity or, alternatively, to engage the press and allow the prosecution to respond. Putting this choice in the hands of the defense is appropriate in our criminal justice system in light of the constitutional mandates intended to safeguard the citizenry from abuse of criminal power, the constitutional undergirding of the presumption of innocence, and the reputational and liberty interests of the accused.

Rejection of differing free speech rights for the prosecution and defense – as argued by Freedman and Starwood in 1977 – has mostly arisen from *Gentile*'s equality principle. Moreover, from a First Amendment perspective, *Gentile*'s equality principle is founded on the First Amendment prohibition against viewpoint-based restrictions.[187] The primary objection to viewpoint-based restrictions is that they distort public debate and knowledge by allowing the public to hear only one side of an issue. Distortion of public debate is arguably more problematic whenever it involves government processes, such as the workings of the criminal justice system.

However, the alleged viewpoint discrimination problem is illusory. First, once the defense attorney opens the door to publicity, the prosecutor can respond. Thus, it is not accurate to say that this approach is viewpoint discriminatory. The public is *never given* only the defense version without the prosecution having a right to tell their side of the same story.

More importantly, even before the prosecution responds, allowing the defense to engage in pretrial publicity is not one-sided. The government has made the most devastating public statement possible about accused persons by officially declaring them wrongdoers and seeking forfeiture of their life or liberty through the indictment. That indictment, along with the charging affidavit, may contain the most damaging information that can be disclosed regarding the charged individual. Thus any publicity from the defense is already a "response" to the prosecution itself.

The defense has inherent incentives to limit pretrial publicity. Once the door is opened, the prosecutor can respond with information that may embarrass the

---

[186] Hochberg, *supra* Note 3 (quoting Scott Greenfield, a New York attorney and blogger).
[187] *See, e.g., R.A.V. v. City of St. Paul,* 505 U.S. 377, 384–88 (1992).

defendant, indicate guilt, or arouse public passion to the detriment of the accused. Many people charged with a crime will not want this kind of publicity, and if they can avoid it, they will. Thus knowledge of the prosecution's right to respond curbs the defense attorney's inclinations to ever open that door, rather than creating an advantage to be exploited. In contrast to the defense, the prosecution has no inherent incentives to limit pretrial publicity, and publicity will generally work in their favor both for their political goals and in influencing the jury venire.

Giving the prosecution First Amendment rights equal to those of the defense results in one of two undesirable regimes: either (1) the defense will have free speech rights appropriate to their role and the prosecution will have equal rights allowing the prosecution to undermine the defendant's rights to a fair trial, their reputation, and the presumption of innocence or (2) the prosecution will be limited in their rights to speech, and the defense will not be able to contest, except through trial, the full weight of government condemnation pretrial. Model Rule 3.6 can be seen as a compromise of these two undesirable alternatives forged in the desire to create an equal standard: The defense is deprived of much of its free speech rights and the prosecution is somewhat restricted in its speech, but is still allowed considerable leeway (particularly through the public records exception, which the prosecution can manipulate by including information they wish to publicize in the indictment or charging affidavit). Unfortunately, this regime results in the worst of both worlds. The prosecution can generally initiate publicity regarding a case and has no inherent or structural disincentive to do so, thereby undermining the rights of the accused. Yet the defense, unable to curb prosecutorial publicity, can only engage in limited pretrial publicity, which may be insufficient to protect the accused's interests. The result is completely backward: it inspires prosecutorial publicity without appropriately protecting the free speech rights of the defense.

The right to a jury trial, the presumption of innocence, and the social compact between the individual and the state are among the weighty interests in our criminal justice system that can be bolstered or undermined through attorney pretrial publicity. The procedural protections that exist in the Constitution for criminal justice are not technicalities or formalities. Rather, they are indicative of the inestimable value of life and liberty, and they act as a "bulwark between the State and the accused"[188] – protecting the personal liberties of the individual from state overreaching and forfeiture.

The traditional "compromise" of these interests is unnecessary to give the First Amendment rights of lawyers their proper scope. Unfortunately, the compromise of Model Rule 3.6 and *Gentile* has failed to produce the fair and equal regime it aimed at creating. Instead, the compromise violates the speech rights of defense lawyers to protect their client's rights to a presumption of innocence, a fair plea, and a fair trial. The compromise also improperly creates false constitutional walls that have kept

---

[188] *Southern Union Co. v. United States*, 567 U.S. 343, 348 (2012).

states from curbing their own representative, the prosecutor, from prejudicing the state's criminal processes. Both of these failings work to one end: undermining the rights and constitutional processes necessary to protect the guilty and the innocent in the face of state power to forfeit life or liberty.

THE RIGHTS OF THE CIVIL LITIGATOR TO ENGAGE IN PRETRIAL PUBLICITY

In the civil context, Chemerinsky's view that standard First Amendment doctrines should prevail is workable and does not undermine the civil justice system. An appropriate limitation is that neither party can make statements to the press that they know to be false, pursuant to the general obligations of attorneys to not make false or material misstatements of law or fact to third parties, as reflected in Model Rule 4.1. Further, it could frustrate the proper resolution of civil cases if one side was able to try to pressure settlement through publicity based on falsity. Notably, *Gentile's* equality principle should apply in the civil context. Both sides should generally have the same rights to engage in pretrial publicity.

Unlike the criminal context, in civil cases, the opposing sides are not inherently imbalanced with constitutional obligations that call for differing treatment and with differing incentives as to engaging in pretrial publicity. For example, in the criminal system, there is a presumption of innocence inhering in the defendant's constitutional rights that both the prosecution and defense counsel must maintain from the statement of charges until conviction has been obtained by a jury. But in the civil context there is no such thing as a "presumption of innocence" as to one side more than the other. Nor does resolution require one side to prove the other was guilty or liable beyond a reasonable doubt. The burden of proof is just a preponderance of evidence – what is more likely than not. In many, if not most, civil cases, there are claims made and counterclaims made in response – thus the parties are often both the plaintiff and the defendant in any given action.

Moreover, in civil litigation, there is no constitutional right to counsel for the defendant, and no obligation of counsel like that of criminal defense attorneys to defend their client even if the client lacks a colorable defense. Correspondingly, there is not an obligation on the plaintiff's side "to do justice," as there is for the prosecutor, which requires the voluntary dropping of charges if probable cause is lacking. Instead, both sides institutionally enter the system of justice equally suited with equal obligations.

Finally, the underlying civil controversy generally will involve the actions and activities of both parties. In the criminal system, the underlying crime involves the activities of the accused but not the activities of the prosecutor or their government client – and thus the prosecutor faces no inherent disincentive for engaging in pretrial publicity regarding the accused. Such publicity generally makes the prosecutor out to be the hero who is saving society, and the more negative information the prosecutor can dump regarding the accused, the more convincing that picture becomes. But in the civil context, the underlying controversy involves the acts of both parties. Thus, the decision of attorneys and their clients to divulge information to the press regarding the opposing party will often result in the opposition doing the same – as turnabout is fair play. Because the underlying controversy involves the activities of the clients of both attorneys, both sides often will appreciate and have a strong incentive to maintain confidentiality. Also, because each side represents an individual client (unlike our agent-principal prosecutor), information relating to the representation should only be divulged to the press if the client consents after consultation in compliance with the attorney's duty of confidentiality. Clients may be very hesitant to initiate a publicity stunt that will result in a mud-slinging battle to their own detriment and embarrassment. Even in more one-sided cases, both parties understand the settlement value of confidentiality, which weighs against running to the press.

Thus, in the civil context, attorneys should generally have free speech rights to engage in pretrial publicity with client consent for disclosure – unless the attorney knows the information is false or constitutes a material misstatement of fact or law. However, a major caveat to this First Amendment right to engage in pretrial publicity is the ability of the court in a given case to enter a protective order preventing dissemination of information obtained solely through court processes and not disseminated in open court. Recall from Chapter 9 that in *Seattle Times Co. v. Rhinehart*,[189] the Court held that litigants could be forbidden by a protective order from disseminating information obtained in discovery where the court had found "good cause" to prohibit dissemination.[190]

In *Rhinehart*, the defendant, the *Seattle Times*, sought membership records and information relating to the finances of the Aquarian Foundation through civil discovery. The Court ordered discovery – as the information sought related to the damages the Foundation had alleged in its lawsuit against the *Seattle Times*. But the trial court also entered a protective order that prohibited the defendants "from publishing, disseminating, or using the information in any way except where necessary to prepare for and try the case."[191] The *Seattle Times* argued that it had a First Amendment right to disseminate the information in that the protective order constituted a prior restraint on speech of public concern.

The Supreme Court upheld the constitutionality of the protective order, emphasizing that the order "prevents a party from disseminating *only* that information obtained *through use of the discovery process.*"[192] The Court explained that the defendants "gained the information they wish to disseminate *only* by virtue of the trial court's discovery process," and that the legislature and the courts had provided

---

[189] 467 U.S. 20 (1984).
[190] *Id.* at 36.
[191] *Id.* at 27.
[192] *Id.* at 34 (emphasis added).

liberal discovery "for *the sole purpose* of assisting *in the preparation and trial* or *the settlement* of litigated disputes."[193] The gist of *Rhinehart* is the Court's recognition that the government in creating a process like discovery that provides for state-compelled disclosure of information – a process essential for the just adjudication of civil cases – can limit the use of that information to the purpose for which it was provided. The courts can prevent "abuse of [their] processes" – specifically, abuse by disclosing to the press sensitive, private, proprietary, or embarrassing information obtained from the opposing party (or third parties) *solely* through the court's compulsory processes.[194] The Court explained that if courts could not protect sensitive information obtained in discovery from dissemination, "individuals may well forgo pursuit of their just claims," frustrating the right of court access.[195]

Importantly, the *Rhinehart* Court expressly recognized the *Seattle Times'* right to disclose "identical information" that was "gained through means independent of the court's processes." Further, the Court emphasized that the information at issue had *not* been admitted into court. It was instead "discovered by not yet admitted information," as pretrial discovery is generally done privately in places "not open to the public," and thus are "not public components of a civil trial."[196]

Again, while *Rhinehart* does not directly address the First Amendment rights of lawyers, it directly addresses the relationship between free speech and the disclosure of information obtained solely through compulsory court processes. Thus, and in the same vein, it directly speaks to the First Amendment rights of attorneys to disclose information obtained in civil cases as pretrial publicity. While, in general, civil litigators have First Amendment rights to engage in pretrial publicity, that right is limited and subject to the ability of a court to restrict the attorney's disclosure of information that the attorney obtained solely through use of court processes, in turn made possible by the attorney's license to practice law. As with *Rhinehart*, a court cannot prohibit dissemination of information obtained through other sources (even if also available through court processes). Such a restraint on disclosure of specific information regardless of its source would constitute an impermissible prior restraint – an exertion of judicial power to hide information – rather than the protection of the court's own processes from abuse.

Moreover, any such protective order or limitation on the attorney's publicity cannot prohibit disclosure of information that was disclosed in open court. The *Rhinehart* Court emphasized that the trial court could prohibit the dissemination of information about the Aquarian Foundation because that information was "discovered but not admitted." Once information is disclosed in open court, an opposing party or attorney is free to disclose it. Of course, in civil proceedings, if parties and attorneys want to contractually agree as part of a settlement not to

---

[193] *Id.* (emphasis added).
[194] *Id.* at 35.
[195] *Id.* at 36 n. 22.
[196] *Id.* at 33–34.

disclose anything regarding the case, they can contractually agree to do so, subject to breach-of-contract remedies. However, such an agreement does not bind non-parties, who should be free to discover and disseminate what occurred in open court.

Open courts are not a technicality – they are essential to the integrity of court processes and to judicial integrity. As the Supreme Court espoused in *Richmond Newspapers* v. *Virginia*, "the value in *open justice*" is not just "therapeutic" but is "the keystone" – for "[w]ithout publicity, *all other checks are insufficient*: all other checks are of small account."[197] In the criminal context, the Court expounded:

> *The open trial . . .* plays *as important a role in the administration of justice today* as it did for centuries before our separation from England. The *value of openness* lies in the fact *that people* not actually attending trials *can have confidence that standards of fairness are being observed*, the sure knowledge that *anyone* is free to attend gives assurance that established *procedures are being followed and that deviations will become known*. Openness thus enhances both the basic fairness of the criminal trial and the appearance of fairness so essential to public confidence in the system.[198]

In our justice system, open courts are *the check* on judicial power. For "[a] trial is a public event. *What transpires in the court room is public property*."[199] Thus, "[t]hose who see and hear what transpired can report it with impunity. There is *no special perquisite of the judiciary which enables it*, as distinguished from other institutions of democratic government *to suppress, edit, or censor events which transpire in proceedings before it.*"[200] Because open courts are *the* essential check on judicial power, it is important – as to proceedings that normally would be held in open court – that courts only close them in accordance with established procedures and pursuant to the Supreme Court's requirements for closure in light of the public's First Amendment and common law rights of access.[201] Moreover, it is essential that attorneys retain protectable free speech rights to raise – both inside and outside of court proceedings – unlawful closure, hiding, or sealing of cases by the judiciary. Otherwise, the judiciary can use an alleged power to limit attorney publicity of information obtained through court processes to cover up its own judicial mistakes or even unlawfulness.

Courts can protect from dissemination information obtained solely through court processes that is never admitted into open court (for whatever reason, including that it may be irrelevant to the ultimate disposition of the case or that the case settled). But the court cannot use that power to undermine *the* democratic check on its own power – the open court.

---

[197] 448 U.S. 555, 569 (1980) (emphasis added).
[198] *Press-Enterprise Co.* v. *Superior Court*, 464 U.S. 501, 508 (1984) (*Press-Enterprise I*) (emphasis added).
[199] *Craig* v. *Harney*, 331 U.S. 367, 374 (1947) (emphasis added).
[200] *Id.* (emphasis added).
[201] *See, e.g., Press-Enterprise Co.* v. *Superior Court*, 478 U.S. 1, 8 (1986) (*Press-Enterprise II*).

14

Attorney Civility, Harassment, and Discrimination

Two related movements have led to recent restrictions (and proposed restrictions) on attorney speech. One is the civility movement – a huge push by state regulators for lawyers to speak with civility and respect to each other, clients, witnesses, judges, court personnel, and any others involved in legal proceedings. For example, the Florida State Bar enacted a new civility regime in 2013, which prohibits members of the Florida bar from engaging in "substantial or repeated violations" of various professionalism standards, including the Florida Bar Creed of Professionalism (the "Creed").[1] The Creed proclaims, "I revere the law, the judicial system, and the legal profession and will *at all times* in my professional *and private lives uphold the dignity and esteem of each.*"[2] The Creed further states that the attorney "will abstain from all rude, disruptive, disrespectful, and abusive behavior and will *at all times* act with dignity, decency, and courtesy."[3] In 2015, the Florida Supreme Court suspended Robert Joseph Ratiner for three years for his incivility while conducting a document review, where Ratiner referred to female opposing counsel as a "dominatrix," stating, "you must enjoy dominating people."[4] Ratiner also attempted to take papers out of opposing counsel's hands – an index she was showing him, but did not give to him – until a security guard intervened.[5]

Similarly, the Utah State Bar adopted "Standards of Professionalism and Civility" in 2003, which, among other things, require attorneys to "treat all other counsel, parties, judges, witnesses, and other participants in all proceedings *in a courteous and dignified manner*" and "*avoid hostile, demeaning, or humiliating words in*

---

[1]   *In re Code for Resolving Professionalism Complaints*, 116 So. 3d 280, 282 (Fla. 2013).
[2]   FLA. STATE BAR, THE CREED OF PROFESSIONALISM (emphasis added), *available at* www .floridabar.org/wp-content/uploads/2017/04/creed-of-professionalism-ada.pdf.
[3]   *Id.* (emphasis added).
[4]   *See The Florida Bar* v. *Ratiner*, 2013 WL 12249742 (Supreme Court of Florida Nov. 13, 2013) approved and adopted by 117 So.3d 1274 (Fla. 2015).
[5]   *See id.*

written and oral communications with adversaries."[6] Unlike the Florida Creed, which purports to apply to the lawyer "at all times" in both "professional and private lives," the Utah civility standards appear to apply only to behavior in court proceedings and law practice, although providing very specific restrictions.[7]

Related to the civility movement, the ABA has recently urged states to enact a rule prohibiting lawyers from engaging in harassment and discrimination. Curbing harassment and discrimination is a very important goal. The #metoo movement has powerfully demonstrated the urgent need in our country to address and combat sexual harassment and assault, in particular. Nevertheless, the actual rule approved by the ABA's Board of Governors in August 2016 – Model Rule of Professional Conduct 8.4(g) – as a model for adoption by the States is fraught with First Amendment problems, reaching far beyond sexual harassment and beyond unlawful discrimination.

Model Rule 8.4(g) is exceptionally broad, and includes in its definition of prohibited "discrimination," any "harmful *verbal* or physical *conduct* that *manifests bias or prejudice*" as to "race, sex, religion, national origin, ethnicity, disability, age, sexual orientation, gender identity, marital status, or socioeconomic status."[8] The comments to the Rule define prohibited "harassment" to include not only "sexual harassment," but also any "*derogatory* or *demeaning verbal* or physical *conduct*" on any one of the aforementioned enumerated bases.[9] Additionally, the Rule's prohibition on speech that "manifests bias or prejudice" or is "derogatory or demeaning" applies not only in court proceedings and while representing a client, but also in any "*conduct related to* the practice of law."[10] The comments to the Rule confirm that conduct related to law practice is a broad concept that "includes representing clients; interacting with witnesses, coworkers, court personnel, lawyers, and others while engaged in the practice of law; operating or managing a law firm or law practice; and *participating in bar association, business or social activities* in connection with the practice of law."[11]

So far, the national response to ABA Model Rule 8.4(g) has been primarily negative. Of the states to consider it, only one – Vermont – has adopted it.[12]

---

[6]   UTAH STANDARDS OF PROFESSIONALISM & CIVILITY ¶¶ 1 and 3 (emphasis added).

[7]   For example, the Utah standards expressly instruct lawyers that "[n]either written submissions nor oral presentations should disparage the integrity, intelligence, morals, ethics, or personal behavior of an adversary unless such matters are directly relevant under controlling substantive law." *See id.* at ¶ 3.

[8]   MODEL RULES OF PROF'L CONDUCT R. 8.4(g) and cmt 3 (emphasis added).

[9]   *Id.* (emphasis added).

[10]   *See id.* R. 8.4(g) (emphasis added).

[11]   *Id.* R. 8.4 cmt. 4 (emphasis added).

[12]   Daniel Richardson, prior president of the Vermont Bar Association, surmised that the rule was adopted in Vermont without controversy in part because the bar "lack[s] any kind of vocal religious right and we just don't have diversity like so many other places" – noting that "Vermont is one of the least diverse states in the country." Essentially, and somewhat ironically, there was not a concern about the antidiscrimination rule because the bar is largely

Meanwhile, the Attorney Generals of Texas, South Carolina, Louisiana, and Tennessee have all written opinions that Rule 8.4(g) is unconstitutional as violating attorneys' rights to freedom of speech, association, and religion.[13] Illinois, Minnesota, Montana, Nevada, South Carolina, and Tennessee have all formally rejected the Rule.[14] The Montana legislature took the remarkable step of intervening and passing a resolution declaring that the Montana Supreme Court lacked the authority to enact such a rule regulating lawyers.[15] A number of other states are currently considering adoption of Rule 8.4(g) and have solicited, or are soliciting, public comments, including Colorado, Connecticut, the District of Columbia, Kansas, Maine, Michigan, New Hampshire, New York, North Dakota, Pennsylvania, and Utah.[16]

THE PURPORTED CONSTITUTIONALITY OF BROAD CIVILITY AND ANTI-DISCRIMINATION RULES

Of course, the pertinent question is *not* whether civility and antidiscrimination are laudable and even imperative goals in the abstract, but whether specific regulations to require lawyers to speak and behave in such ways are constitutional. And, of course, the answer is that it entirely depends on the specific rule – on what speech, association, or petitioning the rule suppresses and on the extent of the rule's reach. Nevertheless, courts, the ABA, and commentators assert the constitutionality of even very broad civility and antidiscrimination/harassment rules – but their arguments miss the mark.

---

homogenous. *See* Andrew Strickler, *Vermont's Anti-Bias Rule Vote an Outlier in Heated Debate*, LAW 360, Aug. 14, 2017, www.law360.com/articles/953530/vermont-s-anti-bias-rule-vote-an-outlier-in-heated-debate.

[13] *See* Op. Tenn. Att'y Gen'l No. 18-11 (Mar. 16, 2018), *available at* www.tba.org/sites/default/files/ag_18-11_corrected.pdf?fid=d96044608bcc5ac8ba3ab87f607fbff1ecdb5992; Op. La. Att'y Gen'l No. 17-0114 (Sep. 8, 2017), *available at* https://lalegalethics.org/wp-content/uploads/2017-09-08-LA-AG-Opinion-17-0114-re-Proposed-Rule-8.4f.pdf?x16384; Op. S.C. Att'y Gen. (May 1, 2017), *available at* http://2hsvzol74ah31vgcm16peuy12tz.wpengine.netdna-cdn.com/wp-content/uploads/2017/05/McCravy-J.-OS-10143-FINAL-Opinion-5-1-2017-01331464xD2C78-013 36400xD2C78.pdf; Op. Tex. Att'y Gen'l No. KP-0123 (Dec. 20, 2016), *available at* www.texasattorneygeneral.gov/opinions/opinions/51paxton/op/2016/kp0123.pdf.

[14] *See* AM. BAR ASS'N, *Jurisdictional Adoption of Rule 8.4(g) of the ABA Model Rules of Professional Conduct* (Mar. 20, 2018)), *available at* www.americanbar.org/content/dam/aba/administrative/professional_responsibility/chart_adopt_8_4_g.authcheckdam.pdf; Daniel A. Horwitz, *Tennessee Supreme Court Denies Proposed Rule Change Attempting to Police Discrimination and Harassment*, SUPREME COURT OF TENNESSEE BLOG (Apr. 23, 2018), https://scotblog.org/category/rules-of-professional-conduct/.

[15] *See* S. J. Res. 15 (Mont. 2017) *available at* http://leg.mt.gov/bills/2017/billhtml/SJ0015.htm; *see also* Lorelei Laird, *Montana Legislature Says ABA Model Rule on Discrimination and Harassment Violates First Amendment*, ABA J. Apr. 13, 2017, *available at* www.abajournal.com/news/article/montana_legislature_says_aba_model_rule_on_discrimination_and_harassment_vi.

[16] *See* AM. BAR ASS'N, *Jurisdictional Adoption of 8.4(g)*, *supra* Note 14.

Constitutional Conditions, Oaths, and Self-Regulation

Proponents of Model Rule 8.4(g) and broad-reaching civility codes rely on the same First Amendment theories and arguments that are reviewed in Chapters 1, 3, and 4. Thus, for example, proponents of 8.4(g) primarily rely on the constitutional conditions theory, starting with the Standing Committee that drafted and adopted the rule. Myles Lynk, the Chair of that committee, explained to the committee that "lawyers have always been subject to ethics rules that impinge on what *otherwise* would be their First Amendment rights."[17] Lynk then listed examples, such as rules protecting confidentiality and prohibiting pretrial publicity, and concluded that, consequently, the rule "does not violate a lawyer's First Amendment rights."[18]

Similarly, Stephen Gillers briefly addresses the Speech Clause problem in his defense of the rule by arguing that "we should recognize that even today the Model Rules contain provisions limiting speech." Gillers provides similar examples to those offered by Lynk, but additionally identifies, as a roughly analogous limitation on speech, the objective reasonableness interpretation of Model Rule 8.2 forbidding derogation of judges, which he notes has been upheld by courts (a rule discussed and excoriated in Chapter 11).[19] Finally, L. Ali Khan contends that Model Rule 8.4(g) does not "diminish" First Amendment rights of speech, religion, and association any more than other rules, explaining that "it is a well-established rule in American jurisprudence that lawyers surrender some (not all) of their First Amendment rights when they choose to practice law."[20]

Interestingly, earlier drafts of Model Rule 8.4(g) included a comment that expressly clarified that the Rule "does not apply to … conduct protected by the First Amendment."[21] That First Amendment proviso was dropped from the comment as ultimately adopted. Josh Blackman, in reviewing the legislative history of Rule 8.4(g), explains that at the February 2016 meeting, Laurel Bellows (a prior ABA president) urged the dropping of the proviso because "[w]e know the constitution governs."[22] Yet it borders on disingenuous for the Committee to remove the proviso on the theory that, of course, the rule is subject to the First Amendment but then also advance a constitutional conditions theory indicating that lawyers simply lack

[17] Andrew F. Halaby and Brianna L. Long, *New Model Rule of Professional Conduct 8.4(g): Legislative History, Enforceability Questions, and a Call for Scholarship*, 41 J. LEGAL PROF. 201, 250 (excerpting First Amendment analysis of the proposed rule presented by Myles Lynk to the committee).
[18] *Id.*
[19] Stephen Gillers, *A Rule to Forbid Bias and Harassment in Law Practice: A Guide for State Courts Considering Model Rule 8.4(g)*, 30 GEO. J. LEGAL ETHICS 195, 234–35 (2017).
[20] L. Ali Khan, *Disciplining Lawyers for Harassment and Discrimination: A Time for Change*, JURIST, July 11, 2017.
[21] Josh Blackman, *Reply: A Pause for State Courts Considering Model Rule 8.4(g)*, 30 GEO. J. LEGAL ETHICS 241, 248 (2016) (quoting Dec. 2015 draft of Model Rule 8.4(g)).
[22] *Id.* at 249 (quoting ABA House of Delegates, Tr. of Proceedings, Feb. 7, 2016).

First Amendment rights as to certain lawyer regulation (including this rule). Apparently, the rule is only subject to the First Amendment insofar as attorneys have any First Amendment rights against such regulation, which the Committee denies.

In a similar vein, Claudia Haupt relies on the concept of self-regulation by a "professional knowledge community" as justifying the constitutionality of Rule 8.4(g). According to Haupt, "conceptually the First Amendment is not a roadblock to regulation of *professionals' speech by the profession* via an antidiscrimination provision."[23] Haupt expresses concern about the constitutionality of forbidding lawyers from engaging in public discourse outside of the practice of law – but she defines public discourse very narrowly in such a way that lawyer Continuing Legal Education (CLE) programs or any bar-related debate or panel are excluded from her definition of public discourse. Haupt argues that it is constitutional for the profession to forbid its own professionals from contravening shared norms when acting as professionals. Haupt's concept is, at heart, a constitutional conditions argument as to alleged self-regulation. Importantly, Haupt fails to address the fact – discussed in Chapter 3 – that lawyers are not currently engaged in self-regulation but are subject to regulation imposed by a government entity (the state judiciary) and enforced through a state administrative agency (the state bar disciplinary authority).

Further, even if lawyers were truly self-regulated, that would not erase the First Amendment. As discussed in Chapter 3, our entire system of government is one of self-government, and yet everyone understands the need for a First Amendment even with self-regulation – particularly to protect minority viewpoints from majoritarian tyranny. Certainly tyranny of the majority can happen among professional communities.

Obviously, the primary problem with the constitutional conditions and self-regulation arguments – as noted in earlier chapters – is that they have no articulated limit or backstop. The state bar apparently has carte blanche to undermine lawyer First Amendment rights. Gillers and Lynk essentially say that it is fine for the bar to limit speech in Model Rule 8.4(g) because there are other rules that limit speech. Even Khan, who indicates there is some limit by saying that "not all" First Amendment rights are surrendered, does not explain what rights are surrendered and what rights are not – and how we can know which it is. Rather, he just concludes that because lawyers surrender some of their First Amendment rights when they become lawyers, Model Rule 8.4(g) is therefore constitutional and no more of a burden on First Amendment rights than other rules.

In the civility context, the same arguments persist. The South Carolina Supreme Court in *In re Anonymous Member of South Carolina Bar*, upheld the constitutionality of punishing a lawyer for writing an uncivil letter to opposing counsel based on constitutional conditions ideas and the oath of the lawyer. The *Anonymous* court

---

[23] Claudia E. Haupt, *Antidiscrimination in the Legal Profession and the First Amendment: A Partial Defense of Model Rule 8.4(g)*, 19 J. CONST. L. 1, 21 (2017) (emphasis added).

quoted the lawyer's oath to be civil and explained, "the United States Supreme Court has noted that lawyers are not entitled to the same First Amendment protections as laypeople."[24] Additionally, the Utah State Bar as part of its online annual registration in June 2017 required attorneys to "pledge to abide by the Utah Standards of Professionalism and Civility." As noted in Chapter 1, under Justice Rehnquist's view, such oaths constitute a waiver of any First Amendment defense to punishment for violation of rules sworn to.[25]

For both civility codes and antidiscrimination/harassment rules, the resort to constitutional conditions, oaths, and arguments of self-regulation are unavailing because they provide state regulators with carte blanche to suppress lawyer First Amendment rights to any degree they may wish. The invocation of these doctrines also reveals both the desire to avoid First Amendment constraints for perceived laudable ends and the lack of workable methodologies for analyzing the First Amendment rights of lawyers.

Speech or Conduct?

Another method to avoid or lessen First Amendment protection is to couch a restriction as being against "conduct" rather than "speech." The First Amendment protects expressive conduct, but the protection for conduct is not as robust as the Amendment's protection for speech.[26] For example, Lynk, in discussing the First Amendment with the Standing Committee, explained:

> [H]arassment and discrimination are illegal. No one, lawyer or non-lawyer, has a "right" to engage in such *conduct*. This is one reason why SCEPR [the ABA Standing Committee on Ethics and Professional Responsibility] moved away from "manifest bias or prejudice" as the conduct to be proscribed, and focused instead on the terms harassment and discrimination, because while *it could be argued that we each have a right to "manifest" (express) bias or prejudice against others*, we do not have a similar right to harass others or discriminate against others.[27]

Lynk's argument would have been well and good had the Committee decided to define the terms "harassment" and "discrimination" to mean unlawful harassment and discrimination as defined by substantive law, which laws typically require that verbal harassment be "severe or pervasive."[28] But instead, the Committee defined

---

[24] *In re Anonymous Member of South Carolina Bar*, 709 S.E.2d 633 (S.C. 2011).

[25] *See Gentile* v. *State Bar of Nevada*, 501 U.S. 1030, 1081 (1991) (Rehnquist, J.).

[26] *See, e.g.*, *O'Brien* v. *United States*, 391 U.S. 367, 381–82 (1968).

[27] Halaby and Long, *supra* Note 17, at 250 (excerpting First Amendment analysis of the proposed rule presented by Myles Lynk to the committee) (emphasis added).

[28] *See* Eugene Volokh and Keith Swisher, *Point-Counterpoint: A Speech Code for Lawyers?*, Judicature at 74 (statements of Eugene Volokh); Eugene Volokh, *The Volokh Conspiracy: A Speech Code for Lawyers, Banning Viewpoints that Express 'Bias,' Including in Law-Related Social Activities*, Wash. Post, Aug. 10, 2016; see also Blackman, *supra* Note 21, at 245.

harassment and discrimination specifically as "verbal conduct" – which is simply speech – that "manifests bias or prejudice" against others on certain bases.[29] That definition is precisely what Lynk stated would arguably be constitutionally protected speech; in his own words, "we each have *a right to 'manifest' (express) bias or prejudice* against others."[30]

The Committee and other proponents rally around the word "conduct" in order to avoid the Free Speech Clause implications of a prohibition on pure speech.[31] But at the end of the day, if a regulator defines harassment and discrimination as including "verbal conduct" that "manifests bias or prejudice" or is "demeaning or derogatory" – the use of a different term doesn't change the fact that it is a regulation on pure speech. "Verbal conduct" equals speech. As the *Button* Court emphasized, "a State cannot foreclose the exercise of constitutional rights by mere labels."[32] Virginia could not avoid the First Amendment in *Button* by using the term "solicitation" when enacting restrictions on speech and association, and states adopting 8.4(g) cannot avoid the Free Speech Clause by using the term "verbal conduct" instead of speech.

Pre-Existence of Anti-Discrimination Rules and Comments

Another major argument that Rule 8.4(g) is constitutionally sound rests in reliance on the fact that half of the states already have either an antidiscrimination rule proper or a comment to a rule forbidding discrimination on many of these same bases.[33] The major problem with this line of argument is that Rule 8.4(g) is far broader than the preexisting rules or comments. Even Gillers, a defender of Rule 8.4(g), recognizes and catalogs the significant difference between Model Rule 8.4(g) and the existing antidiscrimination rules found in various states. He summarizes as to the existing rules:

> Most contain the nexus 'in the course of representing a client' or its equivalent. Most tie the forbidden conduct to a lawyer's work in connection with the 'administration of justice,' or more specifically, to a matter before a tribunal. Six jurisdictions' rules require that forbidden conduct be done 'knowingly,' 'intentionally.' or 'willfully.' Four jurisdictions limit the scope of their rules to conduct that violates federal or state anti-discrimination laws … Only four jurisdictions use the word

---

[29] MODEL RULES OF PROF'L CONDUCT R. 8.4(g) and cmt. 3.
[30] Halaby and Long, *supra* Note 17, at 250 (emphasis added).
[31] *See id.* ("No one, lawyer or non-lawyer has a 'right' to engage in such conduct."); Gillers, *supra* Note 19, at 199–201 (arguing that Rule 8.4(g) is not a "sop to political correctness" but addresses "biased *conduct*," and the rule "tells the public that the legal profession will not tolerate this *conduct* in law practice" [emphasis added]).
[32] *NAACP v. Button*, 371 U.S. 415 429 (1963).
[33] *See, e.g.,* Khan, *supra* Note 20; Volokh and Swisher, *supra* Note 28, at 71 (statements of Keith Swisher).

'harass' or variations in their rules. [And] [i]n twelve states, anti-bias language appears in a comment only ... [34]

In short, the existing antidiscrimination rules are simply not analogous. The fact is that these rules narrowly proscribed bias by only limiting bias "in the course of representing a client" or in actual court proceedings, or by requiring that discrimination be willful, or tying violation to conduct that would violate federal or state antidiscrimination laws. The fact that there have not been constitutional objections to these narrowly proscribed anti-bias rules is thus entirely irrelevant to determining whether Model Rule 8.4(g) is constitutionally sound. Model Rule 8.4(g) has none of those limitations.

Khan argues that these rules are analogous because some states use the phrase "the practice of law," like Model Rule 8.4(g).[35] But the clincher for Model Rule 8.4(g) is that it extends not only to speech and conduct undertaken in "the practice of law," but also *"conduct related to* the practice of law," which expressly includes "operating or managing a law firm or law practice; and participating in bar association, business or social activities in connection with the practice of law."[36] The concerns of opponents that Rule 8.4(g) will extend to activities such as legislative lobbying or law school classes and functions are justified. In the ABA's own Report accompanying the adoption of Rule 8.4(g), the Committee noted that the prior comment regarding bias was insufficient because it "fail[ed] to cover bias or prejudice in other professional capacities" outside of law practice before a court, including, the Report notes, "attorneys as *advisors, counselors, and lobbyists* ... or other professional settings (such as *law schools*, corporate law departments, and employer-employee relationships within law firms)."[37]

The fact that courts have not declared existing anti-bias regulations on lawyers unconstitutional is simply not relevant to whether Rule 8.4(g) is unconstitutional because 8.4(g) is much more expansive than existing rules and comments. It is broader both in its expansive definition of harassment and discrimination (to include any speech that is "derogatory or demeaning") and it is far broader as it extends its scope to activities that are only "related to" the practice of law – including "social activities" and bar-related functions.[38]

The Mens Rea *Requirement*

Proponents of Model Rule 8.4(g) also point to the *mens rea* requirement – the required mental state for culpability – as providing a safeguard for protected speech.

---

[34] *See* Gillers, *supra* Note 19, at 208.
[35] *See* Khan, *supra* Note 20.
[36] MODEL RULES OF PROF'L CONDUCT R. 8.4(g) and cmt. 4.
[37] AM. BAR ASS'N, STANDING COMM. ON ETHICS AND PROFESSIONALISM, REPORT TO THE HOUSE OF DELEGATES (REVISED 109) 2 (Aug. 2016) [hereinafter ABA REPORT 109].
[38] MODEL RULES OF PROF'L CONDUCT R. 8.4(g) and cmts. 3, 4.

They indicate that lawyers will not be disciplined for accidental harassment or discrimination, but, as Model Rule 8.4(g) requires, only for speech and conduct "that the lawyer *knows or reasonably should know* is harassment or discrimination."[39] The ABA Report explains that the *mens rea* requirement "provide[s] a safeguard for lawyers against overaggressive prosecutions for conduct they could not have known was harassment or discrimination."[40] Similarly, Khan states that attorneys cannot "be disciplined under the Rule if the alleged harassment or discrimination is unintentional, accidental or even negligent."[41]

First of all, Khan is simply wrong that the rule doesn't punish negligence – reasonableness is the quintessential trait of negligence. If a person fails to act as a reasonable person, they have acted negligently. And Rule 8.4(g) ties culpability to what a reasonable lawyer would know is harassment – that is a negligence standard.

Be that as it may, the bigger problem with 8.4(g)'s *mens rea* requirement is the twofold assumption that (1) it will constitute a meaningful limitation and (2) that its inclusion somehow exempts speech from First Amendment protection. Neither is true.

Having read scores of cases from jurisdictions across the United States over the last decade that employ a reasonableness standard in cases dealing with punishing speech derogatory of the judiciary, I can affirm that a reasonableness standard for speech is all but meaningless. As noted in Chapter 11, despite the fact that the vast majority of states have adopted an objective reasonableness test for discipline under Rule 8.2 – asking whether a reasonable attorney would engage in the speech – I have yet to read a single case where a court actually analyzed whether or what a reasonable attorney would understand they could say. In the 8.2 context, the assumption of the cases is that reasonable attorneys know better than to make any statements critical or derogatory of the judiciary. Period. No analysis. No expert witnesses testifying about what reasonable attorneys would think or say. It's a foregone conclusion – courts proceed as though it just *is* inevitably unreasonable to engage in derogatory speech about the judiciary and that attorneys should know that. This is true even though the attorney's comments are patently political speech as to the qualifications and integrity of a public official and thus should enjoy impregnable First Amendment protection.

In states that adopt Model Rule 8.4(g), I predict a similar result – attorneys will be disciplined for making disparaging or derogatory comments and no real analysis of reasonableness will be undertaken. Instead, it will be assumed that *all* attorneys "reasonably should know" that they shouldn't make comments that are disparaging or derogatory on bases of race, ethnicity, religion, sex, sexual orientation, gender identity, marital status, socioeconomic status, etc. The bar can hardly do otherwise,

---

[39] *Id.* R. 8.4(g) (emphasis added).
[40] ABA REPORT 109, *supra* Note 37, at 8.
[41] Khan, *supra* Note 20.

because to hold that an attorney reasonably did *not* know that it is "out of line" to disparage people on such factors is to all but admit that the legal profession is backward or bigoted or somehow unaware of modern mores and sensitivities.

And indeed, the speakers often know – even those that *express* these views, who *believe* these views, are not unaware that many, if not most, in society think that such views are inappropriate, derogatory, or demeaning. Take for example, David French. David French is a prominent lawyer, war hero, and columnist for the *National Review*. He wrote a column in objection to Model Rule 8.4(g), explaining that he regularly expresses opinions that he is confident would fall within the ambit of the rule – and he does so at bar-related functions such as CLE programs and law school speeches and panels.[42] For example, French lists opinions that he has expressed in such contexts within the past year. These include opinions such as "that men cannot become women," that same-sex marriage is not protected by the Constitution and is "not truly a marriage," and that "violent jihad is deeply imprinted in the DNA of Islam."[43] He recounts that he is aware that "many of my legal colleagues" consider these opinions "biased" and "derogatory" – which means that French both knows and reasonably should know that they are. He, in fact, asserts that he has "a right to my biases" and "to be derogatory."[44] Does he?

Which brings us to the second assumption. Is speech in general – and lawyer speech in particular – divested of First Amendment protection because the speaker "reasonably should know" or even in fact *knows* that the speech "manifests bias or prejudice" or is "derogatory or demeaning" as to specific groups of people? Does the fact that David French apparently knows that the opinions he recounts "manifest bias or prejudice" and are "derogatory or demeaning" on bases of sexual orientation, religion, and ethnicity mean that the bar can punish him for expressing them at a CLE or bar-related debate or dinner? As discussed further in this chapter, the First Amendment answers this question for us – and it does and must protect French in expressing those views. That protection is not lost simply because the speaker knows or should know that the views are offensive to many. Whether you agree with French's statements or abhor them, they concern the great legal and social issues of our day – issues that fundamentally divide our citizenry, and about which we must have "uninhibited, robust, and wide open" debate.[45] As Eugene Volokh reminds: "This is America, where you're not supposed to lose your professional license because you dare to express certain views at a Continuing Legal Education debate or a bar association dinner."[46]

---

[42] David French, *A Speech Code for Lawyers*, Nat'l Rev., Aug. 11, 2016.
[43] *Id.*
[44] *Id.*
[45] *New York Times v. Sullivan*, 376 U.S. 254, 270 (1964).
[46] Volokh and Swisher, *supra* Note 28, at 72.

THE SCOPE OF ATTORNEY FIRST AMENDMENT RIGHTS AS TO CIVILITY, DISCRIMINATION, AND HARASSMENT

So what is the scope of attorney First Amendment rights as to civility, discrimination, and harassment? Are regulators powerless to protect their interests in legal processes that are fair, unbiased, and civil? It actually depends on the context involved. Regulators would do well to avoid broad prohibitions and instead specifically address and carefully define and shape regulation to the contexts where they can prohibit incivility and verbal expressions of bias or prejudice, as well as more traditional discriminatory and harassing conduct. As the Supreme Court cautioned in *Button*: "Broad prophylactic rules in the area of free expression are suspect. *Precision of regulation* must be the touchstone in an area so closely touching our most precious freedoms."[47]

Under the access to justice theory, the issue is whether speech is essential to the proper functioning of the justice system and to the attorney's role therein in invoking and avoiding government power in the protection of life, liberty, and property. Further, attorneys enjoy no protection for speech that frustrates the proper functioning of the justice system. Employing this analysis, we will examine the appropriate shaping of lawyers' First Amendment rights to speak in ways that are uncivil, derogatory, demeaning, and even biased.

Using Power Given through a License to Practice Law

An attorney is given power by the state that allows the attorney to exercise power over people and their property that a nonlawyer simply doesn't have. Thus attorneys – because of their state license – are empowered to use compulsory state processes to depose people, to examine witnesses, to compel production of documents, and overarchingly to harness the very power of the state by invoking law and judicial processes to protect client life, liberty, and property. The state has given the attorney this power for that end, and can limit abuse of that power by attorneys who are invoking and employing state processes.

Thus the state can limit abuse by the lawyer of people over whom the state has given him power – even if only temporarily. Lawyers are enabled by their license to depose people, and the state can forbid the lawyer from personally abusing the witness who is forced through state compulsory processes to attend and answer the lawyer's questioning. Thus, in the use of compulsory state processes, the state can prohibit lawyers from treating witnesses, parties, and even clients with incivility, bias, or prejudice. Even though controversial in many other contexts,[48] Model

---

[47] *NAACP v. Button*, 371 U.S. 415, 438 (1963) (emphasis added).
[48] *See, e.g.,* Eugene Volokh, *The Volokh Conspiracy: Banning Lawyers from Discriminating Based on "Socioeconomic Status" in Choosing Partners, Employees or Experts?* Wash. Post, May 5, 2016.

Rule 8.4(g)'s prohibition on discrimination and harassment on the basis of socio-economic status, for example, is largely justified in the context of deposing or examining a witness or party. The attorney can be prohibited from belittling or harassing a witness based on the witness's sex, socioeconomic status, gender identity, race, ethnicity, religion, or any of the other bases spelled out in Rule 8.4(g). As the Supreme Court recognized in *Rhinehart*, the government, in creating court processes essential for the just adjudication of cases, can prevent "abuse of [their] processes."[49]

Because the state provides attorneys with the ability to exert power over such people as part of the judicial process, the state can keep that process untainted and fair by requiring the attorney to treat participants with respect and civility. Further, the state can also require that the attorney not taint the proceeding with prejudice and bias. Similarly, the bar can preserve the integrity of fair trials, hearings, and proceedings, by prohibiting attorney incivility and prejudice in such proceedings.

Nevertheless, the State's power to punish attorney incivility even in the practice of law has limitations. A state cannot constitutionally use its power in such a way as to undermine the lawyer's First Amendment rights to protect client life, liberty, and property, and to petition on the client's behalf. Thus, as discussed in this chapter, lawyers retain their First Amendment rights to engage in protected advice and advocacy – and need appropriate "breathing space" surrounding devoted advocacy that they will not be punished unless their incivility constitutes an abuse of the power given by the state to practice law.

Protected Advice and Advocacy

Model Rule 8.4(g) specifically states that it "does not preclude legitimate advice or advocacy consistent with these Rules."[50] This provision begs the question – what constitutes "legitimate advice or advocacy"? Whatever the drafters of Model Rule 8.4(g) intended to mean by the adjective "legitimate," it cannot be interpreted in a manner that would infringe on the lawyer's core First Amendment rights of speech, association, and petition to invoke and avoid government power in the protection of life, liberty, and property – rights discussed in the foregoing chapters.

Lawyers thus must have a First Amendment right to advise their clients. As discussed in Chapter 9, the attorney must be able to fully and frankly explain the contours of the law, its purpose and function, and the potential for and extent of liability or criminal sanctions for violations thereof. As recognized in Model Rule of Professional Conduct 1.2(d), lawyers should "discuss the legal consequences of any proposed course of conduct with a client" and may "counsel or

---

[49] *Seattle Times Co. v. Rhinehart*, 467 U.S. 20, 34 (1984).
[50] MODEL RULES OF PROF'L CONDUCT R. 8.4(g).

assist a client to make a good faith effort to determine the validity, scope, meaning or application of the law."[51]

Further, client counseling can and should go beyond just legal technicalities where the client desires such advice. Model Rule 2.1 explains the lawyer's duty to render "independent professional judgment."[52] As an independent professional, the lawyer's advice should not be circumscribed by the bar. The lawyer is expressly allowed to discuss "other considerations such as moral, economic, social and political factors" with the client.[53]

Imagine a situation where a family lawyer represents a deeply religious client in a divorce. The client's (soon to be ex) husband has recently declared that he is homosexual. The client is horrified and does not want her children raised by someone who is openly homosexual, which she considers sinful. Can the lawyer discuss her religious concerns with her – concerns that shape her objectives for the representation and that she perceives as being essential to her life and liberty in raising her children consistent with her religious beliefs? Can the lawyer advocate for the wife in obtaining as full custody for the client as the law allows under the circumstances – even though the attorney knows that a primary reason that the wife doesn't want the husband to have custody is his sexual orientation?

Turning the tables, assume instead the attorney represents the husband. The husband wants as full custody as possible because he is upset about his wife's membership in a church that maintains that homosexual behavior is sinful. Can the lawyer and husband discuss his desire to undermine her custody of the children precisely because of her religion? Can the lawyer advocate for the husband in obtaining as full custody as the law allows under the circumstances – even though the attorney knows that a primary reason the husband objects to the wife having custody is her religion?

In both of these situations, full and frank discussion between the attorney and client – even of discriminatory intent and bias based on religion and on sexual orientation – is essential to the attorney's proper role in administration of justice, the client's lawful objectives (in both, the attorney is merely seeking custody to the fullest extent the law allows), and the client's own perception of his or her life and liberty interests.

The limitation on lawful advice between attorney and client is the same here as it is in the context of attorneys advising designated foreign terrorist organizations: The attorney lacks First Amendment protection for attorney advice intended to further or assist client crimes or fraud. Attorneys are delegates of state power – the state gives them a license that allows them to harness the force of law in protecting their clients'

---

[51] *See id.* R. 1.2(d). However, Rule 1.2(d) prohibits a lawyer from engaging or assisting a client in engaging "in conduct that the lawyer knows is criminal or fraudulent." *See id.*

[52] *Id.* R. 2.1.

[53] *Id.*

interests. It would frustrate the justice system if attorneys could use their knowledge of and access to the law to advise or assist clients to engage in unlawful activities. Thus, should this hypothetical play out in a state that forbids discrimination on the basis of sexual orientation or religion in determining child custody, the attorney and client should still discuss the matter frankly, including the client's concerns and objectives. The attorney should explain the contours of the law – that the client cannot obtain custody on the basis of the other's sexual orientation or religion if that is the law, and the validity, scope, and interpretation of any such law.[54] Additionally, the attorney is still able to advocate for as full custody as possible under the law – if that is the client's objective – but on different bases.

Moreover, the attorney must be able to discuss with any client and pursue "nonfrivolous argument[s] for extending, modifying, or reversing existing law or for establishing new law."[55] It is absolutely part of the lawyer's essential role in the system of justice to seek the extension, modification, reversal, or establishment of law. If lawyers could not pursue change in the law, then law would be entirely stagnant. Cases like *Brown* v. *Board of Education*[56] and *Obergefell* v. *Hodges*[57] could never have happened. Moreover, lawyers have to be able to discuss and pursue reversal of law in the context of an actual case for an actual client because the judiciary can only exercise its power as to cases and controversies.

In addition to being able to fully advise the client, the attorney must have the right to petition on behalf of the client. This includes the right to invoke court processes by filing cases on behalf of a client without punishment unless the claim is "objectively baseless."[58] Attorneys must also be free to make *all* material arguments regarding a case as set out in *Velazquez*. The *Velazquez* Court held that attorneys had First Amendment rights to "present *all* the *reasonable and well-grounded arguments* necessary for proper resolution of the case."[59] Thus, for example, in pursing arguments or even questioning a party or witness either through discovery or in court, the attorney should be protected from discipline for engaging in questioning that is relevant to a legal issue, even if that questioning seems to express bias or prejudice on one of the bases listed in Model Rule 8.4(g). Of course, if a court determines that a certain line of questioning is not relevant or is otherwise inappropriate, the opposing side may seek a protective order – which the court has a right to impose to protect its processes from abuse as set forth in *Rhinehart*.[60]

The *Velazquez* Court recognized that regulators cannot "prohibit the analysis of certain legal issues and to truncate presentation to the courts" because to do so

[54] *See id.* R. 1.2(d).
[55] See FED. R. CIV. P. 11; *see also* MODEL RULES OF PROF'L CONDUCT R. 3.1.
[56] 347 U.S. 483 (1954).
[57] 135 S. Ct. 2584 (June 26, 2015).
[58] *Professional Real Estate Investors, Inc.* v. *Columbia Pictures Indus., Inc.*, 508 U.S. 49, 60 (1993)
[59] *Legal Services Corp.* v. *Velazquez*, 531 U.S. 533, 545 (2001) (emphasis added).
[60] *Seattle Times Co.* v. *Rhinehart*, 467 U.S. 20, 37 (1984).

would "prohibit . . . speech and expression upon which the courts must depend for the proper exercise of the judicial power."[61] Ultimately, the *Velazquez* Court recognized that the First Amendment prohibited regulators from "[r]estricting LSC attorneys in *advising their clients* and in *presenting arguments and analyses* to the courts"; because to do so would "distort . . . the legal system by altering the traditional role of the attorneys."[62]

Pertinent to Rule 8.4(g), as discussed in Chapter 10, viewpoint-based restrictions are particularly problematic in the adversary system. The whole premise of the adversary system is that both sides of an issue will be heard by a court (or a jury) in search of a just result. If a rule like 8.4(g) is ever interpreted to forbid attorneys from raising relevant arguments in judicial processes where the opposing side is able to argue the contrary view, it would undermine a basic premise of the adversary system. Thus, as an essential component of the justice system, regulators should not impose viewpoint-based restrictions in limiting arguments made by parties. If one side is able to argue that a person can have more than one gender in a case dealing with bathroom or other policies, then opposing arguments – such as that it protects important privacy interests to require people to use the bathroom of their biological sex – should be afforded equal audience.

Attorneys have robust First Amendment rights to counsel with their clients and petition the judiciary under the First Amendment – even if such advice or advocacy could be considered to contain speech that could be viewed as prejudicial against others on one of the bases listed in Model Rule 8.4(g). Thus, for example, attorney and client can discuss going after a "deep pocket" defendant rather than a poor (but perhaps more culpable) defendant in order to maximize recovery – even though that conversation would involve bias on the basis of socioeconomic status. Further, if there is a colorable basis for the lawsuit against the less-culpable deep-pocket defendant, the attorney is protected by the First Amendment right to petition against punishment for filing that case.

Although the judiciary can prohibit lawyers from using the powers granted them through their license to abuse parties or clients, to fully represent their client's interests, lawyers often should "strike hard blows,"[63] or raise issues that are embarrassing to witnesses or parties, or even that may implicate stereotypes or seem biased toward one of the factors raised in Model Rule 8.4(g). If civility standards or anti-bias rules are interpreted strictly, attorneys may feel compelled to limit their advocacy on behalf of a client or "pull their punches." Thus, in order to fulfill their role in the system of justice as agents who protect their client's rights to life, liberty, and property, the scope of protected attorney advice and advocacy needs

---

[61] *Velazquez*, 531 U.S. at 545.
[62] *Id.* at 544 (emphasis added).
[63] *Berger v. United States*, 295 U.S. 78, 88 (1935).

"breathing space to survive" – as the *Button* Court recognized in the precise context of attorney advocacy and petitioning.[64]

Thus attorneys should not be punished every time an attorney makes too strenuous a statement or argument, invokes hyperbole to make a point, or makes an off-hand or ill-conceived comment that offends a case participant. Such stringent state control over lawyer advocacy will either cause cautious lawyers to retrench their advocacy to ensure never crossing that line or will result in punishment or even disbarment of devoted lawyers who were in fact working diligently to protect their clients' interests. Thus, in order to punish attorneys for incivility or expression of bias, the speech should rise to an "abuse" of the attorney's power and license to practice law – abuse that is incompatible with the proper functioning of the justice system and the use of the lawyer's license. A requirement that incivility or verbal expressions of bias be either "severe" or "pervasive" as required in the employment discrimination context would in large part alleviate punishment of devoted attorneys who are working to protect their client's interests.

Lawyers thus lack a First Amendment right to use their license to practice law in abusive ways, including abusing government processes. They also lack a First Amendment right to file cases or bring claims that are "objectively baseless," or to make frivolous arguments in court proceedings. In any of the above hypotheticals, if it would be frivolous – meaning lacking a basis in law or fact – to make a certain argument, then the attorney can be prohibited from making it. Attorneys also have no right to advise or assist a client to engage in crime or fraud. But these are very narrow exceptions. Outside of them and on the whole, attorneys are not circumscribed in either their advising of clients or their court advocacy. In pursuing the client's objectives, in securing client life, liberty, and property, and in enabling the exercise of the judicial power through bringing claims and making arguments the lawyer requires robust First Amendment rights.

Speech at Bar-Related Activities, CLEs, Debates, and Social Activities

Model Rule 8.4(g) did not stop at limiting speech made in court proceedings, or even in the practice of law – limitations that are properly contained in most of the existing anti-bias rules in American jurisdictions.[65] Instead, the rule expressly extended to *"conduct related to* the practice of law," which was expansively defined in the comments to include "participating in bar association, business or social activities in connection with the practice of law."[66] Moreover, the ABA's

---

[64] NAACP v. *Button*, 371 U.S. 415, 433 (1963) ("Because First Amendment freedoms need breathing space to survive, government may regulate in the area only with narrow specificity.")

[65] *See* Gillers, *supra* Note 19, at 208.

[66] MODEL RULES OF PROF'L CONDUCT R. 8.4(g) and cmt. 4 (emphasis added).

Report indicates the rule would additionally reach "lobbyists" and "settings . . . such as law schools."[67]

The ABA's Report and the legislative history indicates that this expansion was intended to capture sexual harassment at dinner events, CLEs, etc.[68] But if a jurisdiction wants to stop sexual harassment in such contexts, then the jurisdiction should narrowly define the prohibition as covering sexual harassment and *not* as prohibiting all speech that "manifests bias or prejudice" or is "derogatory or demeaning." It was this extension of the rule – to contexts outside the actual practice of law – that made way for the Montana legislature's primary argument that Rule 8.4(g) is unconstitutional. The Montana legislature explained that its Supreme Court is given the power to regulate the practice of law and to determine if lawyers are fit to practice, but does not have the power to impose general rules governing conduct outside of the practice of law. The legislature considered this rule as usurping legislative power to govern conduct outside of the practice of law because of its reach into "social activities," lobbying, law schools, etc.[69]

Keith Swisher, in advocating on behalf of Rule 8.4(g), argued that "it is hard to discern – and opponents do not identify – the value of such conduct."[70] Of course, when he said "conduct," that includes "verbal conduct" under the rule, which is speech. Importantly, when analyzing whether speech is protected by the First Amendment, one is not required to positively demonstrate ex ante "the value" of one's speech in order to engage in it. But here, where we are looking at the access to justice theory and considering whether attorneys have First Amendment rights, we consider the relation of the speech to the attorney's role in the system of justice, and from that perspective, the prohibited speech has significant value.

The speech that is clearly swept within the ambit of Rule 8.4(g) has implications for many of "the major public issues of our time"[71] – issues that decisively divide our country. These issues include marriage equality, gender identity issues including bathroom and locker-room usage, homosexual and single parent adoptions and surrogacies, birth control and abortion, terrorism, and immigration and refugee assistance – to name only a few. Importantly, Rule 8.4(g) tends to cut out expression on only one side of a given debate. For example, if an attorney says that he opposes bathroom usage in one's bathroom of choice rather than according to biological sex because it keeps out sexual predators, that argument may be considered demeaning or as manifesting bias on the basis of gender identity. But a person on the opposite

---

[67] ABA REPORT 109, *supra* Note 37, at 2.

[68] *Id.* at 11 (stating that "conduct related to the practice of law includes activities such as law firm dinners and other nominally social events at which lawyers are present," and explaining that the committee "was presented with substantial anecdotal information that sexual harassment takes place at such events"); *see also* Blackman, *supra* Note 21, at 244.

[69] *See* S. J. Res. 15 (Mont. 2017) *available at* http://leg.mt.gov/bills/2017/billhtml/SJ0015.htm.

[70] Volokh and Swisher, *supra* Note 28, at 72 (statements of Swisher).

[71] *New York Times* v. *Sullivan*, 376 U.S. 254, 271 (1964).

side of the issue is free to argue that everyone should be free to use their bathroom of choice, because that statement does not manifest bias. Similarly, to support and make arguments in favor of marriage equality is allowed, but to make arguments against it may be demeaning or expressing bias on the basis of sexual orientation. And so it continues, with exclusion heavily weighted against conservative views. Rule 8.4(g) stops such arguments before they are even made – it is a viewpoint-based prior restraint that disproportionately forecloses arguments and expressions of opinion on one side of issues of public concern.

These issues are of acute importance to millions of Americans – issues that drive people to vote for particular candidates or to belong to certain political parties. Ultimately, these issues will be resolved by laws, regulations, and policies, which will be determined and enforced through legislation, court cases, and executive action – all of which is entirely dependent on lawyers. Lawyers will write the legislation, will litigate the court cases, will draft policies, will evaluate constitutionality, and will execute the law. To cut lawyers on one side of these issues out of the conversation is wildly unconstitutional and completely undermines the role of the lawyer in the system of justice. Lawyers are the very people who have the knowledge, skills, and ability to articulate and implement legal policies, accommodations, and options – as well as to air and evaluate grievances and to propose legal remedies. Silencing lawyers from expressing their opinions on these issues – especially to other lawyers at law-related functions, CLEs, law school presentations, conferences, etc. – will forestall the wheels of political change; it will halt accommodation and conversation across the aisle of political divergence among lawyers. Such conversations and accommodations are desperately needed. Rule 8.4(g) constitutes viewpoint discrimination of political speech on the great issues of our times as to the very people who are necessary to consider and implement political change.

To say that no one has articulated the "value" of this speech is either to be oblivious to the implications of Model Rule 8.4(g) as to national issues or to declare that many conservative viewpoints have no value. Even if one whole-heartedly believes the second to be true and even if they are right (that the viewpoints have "no value" and are entirely wrongheaded), the First Amendment forbids government – including state courts and bars – from authoritative selection as to what is orthodox in national politics, society, and policy. If one disagrees with speech that indicates it is essential to protect privacy to require that people use bathrooms of their biological sex, that marriage should only be between a man and a woman as it has been for millennia before us, that a woman's primary role in society is as mother, that married heterosexual couples are the preferred choice for adoption of children, that a significant contingent of Muslims are radical Islamic terrorists, that the country would fare better with fewer immigrants and refugees (and for the record, I am not personally advocating *any* of these views here), then the First Amendment declares that the answer is *more speech* – one can and should explain why these views are wrong and are detrimental to individuals and to society.

"It is precisely this kind of choice" – between more speech and an enforced silence – "which the First Amendment makes for us."[72]

Yet Model Rule 8.4(g) is precisely that – an enforced silence. The First Amendment, as Justice Brandeis reminds us, "eschews silence coerced by law – the argument of force in its worst form."[73] And this is an argument of force rather than of deliberation and education. Lawyers are threatened with loss of their livelihood should they express such views. The First Amendment forbids such "authoritative selection."[74] The Supreme Court explained:

> If there is any *fixed star* in our constitutional constellation, it is that *no official*, high or petty, *can prescribe what shall be orthodox in politics, nationalism, religion, or other matters* of opinion or *force citizens to confess* by word or act their faith therein. If there are any circumstances which permit an exception, they do not now occur to us.[75]

State bars cannot declare what views are "orthodox" and thus allowed to be expressed at CLE programs, dinner parties, bar-sponsored discussions, and law school panels, presentations, and classes.

Additionally, to forbid or chill speech on one side of these issues in law schools, at CLEs, and at bar-sponsored discussions will undermine a healthy robust dialogue among lawyers as to how to represent and accommodate divergent viewpoints and interests. Again, it is lawyers who generally spearhead changes in law and policy, and they must collectively – precisely at CLEs, dinners, law school panels, and conferences – fully discuss these issues. As the *Sullivan* Court emphasized, debate on public issues must be "robust, uninhibited, and wide open." But by chilling speech on one side of these public issues, instead we would have "myopic, inhibited, and enclosed" debate. Political myopia – the inability to see, countenance, or even give a hearing to another party's viewpoints – seriously undermines the dialogue that is necessary to successful self-government. It was precisely in the context of punishment of lawyer speech that the Supreme Court asserted that "speech concerning public affairs is more than self-expression; it is the essence of self-government."[76]

And even for those who appear to be on the winning side of 8.4(g) – because only your opponent's speech is suppressed while you remain free to articulate your views – remember Justice Brandeis's warning: "repression breeds hate." It just does. And "hate menaces stable government."[77] That – maintaining a stable system of self-government where each citizen, including lawyers, retains the "freedom to think

---

[72] *Virginia State Bd. Pharmacy v. Virginia Citizens Consumer Council, Inc.*, 425 U.S. 748, 770 (1976).

[73] *Whitney v. California*, 274 U.S. 357, 375–76 (Brandeis, J., concurring).

[74] *New York Times v. Sullivan*, 376 U.S. 254, 270 (1964).

[75] *West Virginia State Bd. Educ. v. Barnette*, 319 U.S. 624, 642 (1943) (emphasis added).

[76] *Garrison v. Louisiana*, 379 U.S. 64, 74–75 (1964).

[77] *Whitney*, 274 U.S. at 375–76 (Brandeis, J., dissenting).

as you will and to speak as you think" as to public issues – is the value of allowing people who hold these views to express them.[78] It is the *only* path of safety – to allow people "the opportunity to discuss freely supposed grievances and proposed remedies" and accommodations.[79]

In the face of deep concerns that our country faced threats of violent overthrow, the Supreme Court recognized this same principle in its seminal association case, *De Jonge* v. *Oregon*.[80] The Court asserted that the *greater the threat* to our country – in that case violent overthrow, in this case a threat to equality as set out in Rule 8.4(g) – *the more important* it is to protect First Amendment rights, "to preserve inviolate the constitutional rights of free speech, free press and free assembly."[81] This protection of First Amendment rights is essential "to maintain the opportunity for free political discussion, to the end that government may be responsive to the will of the people and that changes, if desired, may be obtained by peaceful means. Therein lies *the security of the Republic*, the very foundation of constitutional government."[82]

Importantly, it is not enough to allow attorneys to represent people who hold these views but to forbid lawyers from personally advocating or expressing their own views in agreement therewith. Imagine if Thurgood Marshall and the NAACP were allowed by the *Button* Court to litigate cases, but prohibited from publicly advocating their point of view, or expressing or articulating their arguments in support of these causes at dinners, debates, law forums, and other venues. Imagine if they were prohibited from expressing or indicating their personal belief in the causes of their clients. Lawyers who understand and share viewpoints with their clients will often be vastly better at articulating those viewpoints and proposing solutions and accommodations than nonlawyers. It is insufficient to allow lawyers to represent clients with these views in court proceedings but then silence lawyers from discussing those issues outside of that representation, including expressions of their own views built in part upon representing such clients.

In September 1950, during the height of the second red scare, the ABA Assembly and House of Delegates adopted a resolution requesting that states enact a regulation to require each attorney to swear an anti-Communism loyalty oath and to file an affidavit periodically thereafter attesting as to whether the attorney was or ever had been a member of the Communist Party or other subversive organizations.[83] States were then to investigate and disbar any communist attorneys. As Zechariah Chafee recounted in THE BLESSINGS OF LIBERTY, written five years later, *not a single state*

Id.

Id.

[80] 299 U.S. 353, 365 (1937).

[81] *Id.* at 365 (emphasis added).

[82] *Id.* (emphasis added).

[83] *See* Mary Elizabeth Basile, *Loyalty Testing for Attorneys: When Is It Necessary and Who Should Decide?*, 30 CARDOZO L. REV. 1843, 1856–67 (2009).

adopted the ABA's proposed regulation.[84] Indeed, the New York City Bar Association in December 1950 adopted a resolution opposing the loyalty oath and affidavit requirement, and asserting that the *only* oath that should be required of lawyers is to uphold the US Constitution – the traditional oath of the American lawyer.[85]

The Association of American Law Schools (AALS) also opposed the ABA's loyalty oath. Noting that nearly all law professors are also members of a bar (even if inactive), the AALS asserted that the loyalty oath interfered with academic freedom.[86] In a similar vein, Model Rule 8.4(g) could negatively impact academic freedom of law professors and of presentations at law schools that include lawyer participants. The idea that Rule 8.4(g) could affect what can be said by lawyers and law professors at law schools is not far-fetched, because the ABA Report accompanying Rule 8.4(g) contends that the prior anti-bias comment to Rule 8.4 was insufficient in part because it did not reach into "other professional settings" outside of court proceedings, including, specifically, "law schools."[87]

It was in this context – in discussing regulations of the ilk of the ABA's 1950 loyalty oath – that Chaffee chastised regulators for undermining liberty "in the very process of purporting to defend" it.[88] In a similar vein there is significant irony that the ABA is attempting to promote diversity and eliminate bias through the means of silencing divergent and dissenting views. The ABA certainly can and should promote diversity – but it should do so by means that do not themselves undermine diversity (as well as Constitutional rights) by silencing a contingent of people with unpopular viewpoints. In retrospect it seems clear (and Chafee argued at the time) that rather than trying to improve loyalty among lawyers, "the true aim of the loyalty oaths was *to purge unpopular opinions or sympathies* among members of the bar."[89] The ABA wanted to sanitize the bar of any with communist ties, views, or sympathies. Eugene Volokh has come to a similar conclusion about Model Rule 8.4(g): "My inference is that the ABA wants to do exactly what the text calls for: limit lawyers' expression of viewpoints that it disapproves of."[90] As Chafee asserted, as a nation, "we are more especially called upon to maintain the principles of free discussion in cases of unpopular sentiments or persons, as in no other case will any effort to maintain them be needed."[91]

---

[84] Zecharaiah Chafee, The Blessings of Liberty 159 (1956).
[85] See *The Lawyer's Loyalty Oath*, ABA J. (Feb. 1951) 128–29.
[86] See Basile, *supra* Note 83, at 1861.
[87] ABA Report 109, *supra* Note 37, at 2.
[88] Chafee, *supra* Note 84, at 156. Chaffee eloquently explained:
> "The only way to preserve 'the existence of free American institutions' is *to make free institutions a living force*. To ignore them in the very process of purporting to defend them, as frightened men urge, will leave us little worth defending. We must choose between freedom and fear – we cannot have both."
> Id.
[89] Basile, *supra* Note 83, at 1850.
[90] Volokh and Swisher, *supra* Note 28, at 74 (statements of Volokh).
[91] Zechariah Chafee, Freedom of Speech 3 (1920).

Regardless of whether Volokh is correct about the purpose of the rule, the fact remains that the rule's language is so broad that it *will* have the effect of silencing certain lawyer speech. Even if jurisdictions that adopt it do not enforce it, lawyers will steer clear of expressing such viewpoints if there is any specter of discipline for so doing. Most lawyers do not go anywhere near the line of risking discipline – because being a lawyer is their livelihood, for which they have undertaken extensive schooling and cost. They will not risk it; they will acquiesce instead. As the *Button* Court explained in the context of prohibitions on attorney speech, association, and petitioning: "The threat of sanctions may deter their exercise almost as potently as the actual application of sanctions."[92]

Some may contend that silencing biased viewpoints or demeaning and derogatory speech is justifiable because such speech is not just "unpopular," but wrong. But that still doesn't solve the First Amendment problem because, again, if people, even the vast majority of people, think a viewpoint is wrong, the answer is more speech, not enforced silence.

Returning to the second red scare, Alexander Meiklejohn explains that speech regarding public issues cannot be suppressed "because it is on one side of the issue rather than another" even if a view is seen as being "false or dangerous," "unwise, unfair," or "un-American."[93] Certainly, equality is a central American tenet. Although never fully realized, it is proudly proclaimed as a self-evident truth in the Declaration of Independence: "all men are created equal."[94] The phrase "Equal Justice under Law" is inscribed above the entrance of the US Supreme Court. The idea of equality and of equality under law is an ideal that is central to the United States justice system and is absolutely worth every effort to achieve. Although views that express bias or are derogatory or demeaning are thus arguably contrary to this ideal and could even be considered "un-American," suppressing them is far more un-American.

As Justice Holmes explained, we must "be eternally vigilant against attempts to check the expression of opinions *that we loathe* and believe *to be fraught with death*."[95] In 2017, the Supreme Court in *Matal v. Tam*[96] emphasized this "bedrock First Amendment principle: Speech may not be banned *on the ground that it expresses ideas that offend*."[97] Further, the Court indicated that suppressing such speech has consequences for all of society:

A law that can be directed against speech *found offensive* to some portion of the public can be *turned against minority and dissenting views* to the *detriment of all.* The First Amendment does *not entrust that power to the government's benevolence.*

[92] *NAACP v. Button*, 371 U.S. 415, 433 (1963).
[93] Alexander Meiklejohn, Free Speech and Its Relation to Self-Government 26–27 (1948).
[94] The Declaration of Independence para. 2 (U.S. 1776).
[95] *Abrams v. United States*, 250 U.S. 616, 630 (1919) (Holmes, J., dissenting) (emphasis added).
[96] 137 S. Ct. 1744 (June 19, 2017).
[97] *Matal v. Tam*, 137 S. Ct. at 1751 (Alito, J.) (emphasis added).

Instead, our reliance must be on the substantial safeguards of free and open discussion in a democratic society.[98]

As recounted in Chapter 5, Meiklejohn posed the question of whether the government's right and duty to prevent evils allowed it to prevent "evil" and un-American speech. He asserted:

> In the judgment of the Constitution, *some preventions are more evil than are the evils from which they would save us.* And the First Amendment is a case in point. If that amendment means anything, it means that certain substantive evils which, in principle, [regulators have] a right to prevent, must be endured *if the only way of avoiding them is by the abridging of that freedom of speech upon which the entire structure of our free institutions rests.*[99]

The Supreme Court embraced this view in *New York Times* v. *Sullivan*, quoting James Madison and Thomas Jefferson in the Virginia Resolutions of 1798 that "the right of *freely examining public* characters and *measures*, and of *free communication among the people thereon* … has ever been justly deemed *the only effectual guardian of every other right.*"[100]

Speech Unrelated to Law Practice

Rule 8.4(g) did not purport to regulate speech completely unrelated to law practice, limiting its reach to conduct "related to the practice of law." Nevertheless, in defining that phrase, the comments extend regulation to include "social activities" related to a law function – which in some circumstances would in actuality be speech unrelated to the practice of law.[101] Moreover, some of the civility codes have purported to reach the lawyer's speech outside of law practice. For example, under the Florida Creed, lawyers affirm that they "will *at all times* in my professional *and private lives* uphold the dignity and esteem" of the judicial system and the legal profession and that attorneys "will *at all times* act with dignity, decency, and courtesy."[102] The Kansas Supreme Court, in a case dealing with speech regarding the judiciary, has likewise explained that "[l]awyers are subject to discipline for improper conduct in individual, personal, or business activities."[103]

Can regulation of lawyers go so far? For example, what if a lawyer tweets horrible things about other people, the judiciary, or protected classes – but all of the tweets

---

[98] *Id.* at 1769 (Kennedy, J.) (emphasis added).
[99] MEIKLEJOHN, *supra* Note 93, at 48 (emphasis added).
[100] *New York Times* v. *Sullivan*, 376 U.S. 254, 274 (1964) (internal citations omitted; emphasis added).
[101] MODEL RULES OF PROF'L CONDUCT R. 8.4(g) and cmt. 4.
[102] FLA. STATE BAR, THE CREED OF PROFESSIONALISM (emphasis added) *available at* www.floridabar.org/wp-content/uploads/2017/04/creed-of-professionalism-ada.pdf.
[103] *In re Arnold*, 274 Kan. 761, 762 (2002).

involve national issues and public figures rather than anything about the attorney's own law practice or clientele? Can the attorney be punished by the bar consistent with the First Amendment?

Todd Kincannon provides an example of speech that can and cannot be punished by the bar. During 2013 and again in 2015, Kincannon had a Twitter account on which he made horrifically outrageous statements about public figures, including racist comments about Trayvon Martin – the African American teenager who was killed by George Zimmerman, who in turn was acquitted on murder charges – and derided individuals who were transgender or homosexual. Kincannon claimed that the South Carolina bar threatened to discipline him for the racial and biased nature of his tweets.[104] But the tweets had absolutely nothing to do with the use of his law license. He was speaking as a citizen in a forum open to all citizens about high-profile controversies and issues completely unrelated to his own practice of law.

Similarly, in 2014, Law Professor Nancy Loeng filed a complaint with the relevant state bar against a public defender who made racist and sexual comments anonymously on her blog – although Loeng discovered his identity. The comments are horrible. However, they have nothing to do with his work or use of his law license. He posted comments on her blog the same way any other "cyber bully" – attorney or not – would. Loeng reported to the *ABA Journal* that the state bar ultimately decided not to pursue charges against the public defender for his blog comments.[105]

The First Amendment should protect such lawyer speech outside the practice of law to the same extent that it would protect similar objectionable speech by any other citizen. Again, the December 2015 version of proposed Model Rule 8.4(g) included a First Amendment proviso, explaining that the rule was subject to the First Amendment.[106] In the accompanying draft Report, the Committee included language that did not end up in the final rule or report – a very unfortunate exclusion because it accurately indicated the state's lack of power over attorneys in speech unrelated to their law practice. The draft Report clarified "that a lawyer does retain a 'private sphere' where personal opinion, freedom of association, religious expression, and political speech is protected by the First Amendment and not subject to the Rule."[107] Not only is such speech not subject to Rule 8.4(g) but it is also not subject to regulation by the judiciary or state bar.

As noted throughout this book, the categorical approach to attorney speech is erroneous in that it deprives lawyers of First Amendment protection whenever they

---

[104] *See, e.g.,* Andrew Branca, *South Carolina Licensing Officials Accused of Suppressing Lawyer's 1st Amendment Rights,* LEGAL INSURRECTION, July 16, 2014, *available at* https://legalinsurrection.com/2014/07/south-carolina-licensing-officials-accused-of-suppressing-lawyers-1st-amendment-rights/.

[105] Debra Cassens Weiss, *Blogging Law Professor Requests Ethics Probe of "dybbuk" Commenter,* ABA J., Jan. 7, 2014.

[106] Blackman, *supra* Note 21, at 248 (quoting Dec. 2015 draft of Model Rule 8.4(g)).

[107] *See id.* at 248–49 (quoting AM. BAR ASS'N, STANDING COMM. ON ETHICS AND PROF'L RESPONSIBILITY, NOTICE OF PUBLIC HEARING 6 (2015)).

are acting as a lawyer. As shown, such an approach undermines justice itself as lawyers must have First Amendment rights to fully protect their clients' interests and fulfill their role in the system of justice when acting as a lawyer. Nevertheless, the flipside of the categorical approach – that the lawyer has full First Amendment protection as would any other citizen in his activities outside of the practice of law – is an accurate principle, with only a few minor departures, discussed later in this chapter.

Thus, had Kincannon kept his abhorrent gibes to Twitter regarding national issues in which he had no involvement as a lawyer, it would have been a violation of his First Amendment rights for the South Carolina Bar to punish him for expressing his absolutely disgusting views. As it turned out, according to news reports, Kincannon decided to expand his aggressive antics to a court proceeding, where he sent "menacing" emails and faxes to case participants with photos of himself with a gun to his head after having a "meltdown" at a court appearance.[108] Now that speech – speech to case participants and in a court proceeding – is solidly within the power of the state bar to regulate. Kincannon was suspended from the practice of law that same week – apparently on mental health grounds, as he was put on "incapacity inactive status."[109]

The major objection to the view that lawyers have the same First Amendment rights as nonlawyers when acting outside their law practice or use of their law license is the fact that professional conduct rules have long since provided for discipline of attorneys for conduct (which may include speech) that demonstrates the lawyer is unfit to practice law. In particular, the ABA Committee pointed to Rule 8.4(c), which defines professional misconduct to include "engag[ing] in conduct involving dishonesty, fraud, deceit or misrepresentation."[110] Since dishonesty, fraud, deceit, and misrepresentation typically are performed through speech, the inclusion of this prohibition is used to demonstrate that state bars can and do regulate attorney speech that occurs outside the lawyer's practice of law.

Yet the basis for such discipline is the attorney's unfitness to practice law. And that factor – as Josh Blackman points out – is where the differential between dishonesty, deceit, and untrustworthiness, on the one hand, and engaging in speech that manifests bias or is otherwise demeaning or derogatory, on the other hand, becomes apparent.[111] Lawyers are fiduciaries. They simply cannot do their job – they cannot and should not be handling client funds or property – if they are not trustworthy. Evaluating a lawyer's dishonesty and untrustworthiness is not about whether the

---

[108] *See Supreme Court Drops Hammer on Todd Kincannon*, FITSNEWS, Aug. 29, 2015, *available at* www.fitsnews.com/2015/08/29/supreme-court-drops-hammer-on-todd-kincannon/.

[109] *In the Matter of J. Todd Kincannon*, Case No. 2015–001824, (S.C. Aug. 28, 2015), *available at* www.sccourts.org/courtOrders/displayOrder.cfm?orderNo=2015-08-28-01.

[110] *See* Blackman, *supra* Note 21, at 252; *see also* MODEL RULE OF PROF'L CONDUCT R. 8.4(c).

[111] *See* Blackman, *supra* Note 21, at 251–52 (quoting comments by Ben Strauss, a former President of the Delaware State Bar Association at the ABA's Feb. 2016 hearing on Rule 8.4(g)).

lawyer's viewpoints are on one side of the political spectrum or the other, or whether the attorney's ideas are un-American or contrary to certain ideals. It has nothing to do with examining the lawyer's views or opinions; instead, it is about examining the lawyer's character as to one essential aspect of lawyering: can the lawyer be trusted? Thus, evaluating lawyer dishonesty is about whether the attorney has a basic qualification to be a lawyer – to be a fiduciary of the client's money, life, livelihood, and legal interests. As I have written in a Professional Responsibility textbook: "If you cannot be trusted (whether due to malfeasance or negligence) to safeguard client money and property, then you cannot be an attorney."[112] The fact that one is untrustworthy categorically disqualifies an individual from the practice of law.

However, one's views on sexual orientation, on gender identity, or on marital status do not decidedly disqualify an attorney from being fit to practice law. The lawyer can still practice law. As long as the lawyer's biases are not used in the lawyer's law practice to prejudice the administration of justice, the bar has no business forcing the lawyer to either acquiesce in the ABA's view of those issues or lose their license. Although not stated in terms of First Amendment protection, the Montana legislature's rejection of Model Rule 8.4(g) is based in this basic dichotomy: The power of the judiciary and state bar to regulate lawyers is limited to the attorney's practice of law – the use of state power – and basic fitness to practice law.[113]

Notably, most of the existing state anti-bias rules contain a limitation that the bias must in some way prejudice the administration of justice. That qualifier is an essential First Amendment component to a rule that prohibits a lawyer's expression of bias. Because the bar has no business regulating a lawyer's private expression, that qualifier needs to be interpreted to mean that the bias is used in a court proceeding or in another law practice context. The phrase cannot be interpreted to mean that it is somehow prejudicial to justice for lawyers to express certain unpopular opinions publicly because such views reflect adversely on the profession as a whole.

Overarchingly, lawyers have full First Amendment rights to speech when acting outside of their law practice – including speech that manifests bias or prejudice, is demeaning or derogatory, is undignified, discourteous, rude, offensive, or even hateful. The fact that it embarrasses members of the bar that their colleagues have allegedly backward or bigoted opinions is not a sufficient justification to undermine lawyers' First Amendment rights outside of their law practice.

Compelled Representation

A particular thorny issue perhaps raised by Model Rule 8.4(g) is whether attorneys can be punished for *declining* to represent parties on one of the prohibited bases.

---

[112] SAHL, COOPER, CASSIDY, AND TARKINGTON, PROFESSIONAL RESPONSIBILITY IN FOCUS (2017).
[113] *See* S. J. Res. 15 (Mont. 2017) *available at* http://leg.mt.gov/bills/2017/billhtml/SJ0015.htm.

Model Rule 8.4(g) expressly states that it "does not limit the ability of a lawyer to accept, decline, or withdraw from representation in accordance with Rule 1.16."[114] While Rule 1.16 fully addresses when a lawyer is both required or permitted to withdraw, the rule only addresses situations where a lawyer is *required to* decline a case. Rule 1.16 simply does not address when a lawyer is *permitted to* decline a case. Nevertheless, once lawyers accept a representation, they can only withdraw as allowed by Rule 1.16 regarding permissive withdrawal. The reason for the omission in Rule 1.16 regarding when a lawyer is permitted to decline is clear. As Gillers recounts, lawyers have a right to decline to take on a representation for any reason or for no reason – it is not and has not been circumscribed by regulation.[115] Private lawyers are absolutely free to decline any representation they wish to reject. Does Model Rule 8.4(g) change that?

The best reading of Model Rule 8.4(g) is that it does not change the autonomy of private lawyers to decline cases, and should a jurisdiction adopt the rule, the lawyer retains complete autonomy to decline matters. The Rule says declining must be done "in accordance with Rule 1.16," but since Rule 1.16 says nothing that would restrict the lawyer's ability to decline a case, then attorneys retain their traditional autonomy to decline unless and until a jurisdiction amends Rule 1.16 to regulate when a lawyer is permitted to decline (or compelled to accept) particular matters. This reading is supported by the ABA's Report, which explains that Rule 8.4(g) "does *not* change the circumstances under which a lawyer may accept, decline, or withdraw from a representation."[116] If that's the case, then lawyers retain their complete autonomy to decline cases that they assuredly had before Rule 8.4(g).

However, after explaining that lawyers have autonomy to decline cases, Gillers oddly concludes that it would nevertheless be a violation of Rule 8.4(g) for a lawyer to decline to take cases based on gender, such as having a divorce practice that is limited to representing women.[117] He further concludes that it would be a violation of Rule 8.4(g) for family lawyers who prepare prenuptial agreements to decline to represent same-sex couples when their reason for declining is that marriage is only between a man and a woman.[118] How could it be a violation of the rule if the rule does not alter the traditional autonomy of private lawyers to decline cases?

The only way to read Rule 8.4(g) as Gillers does is through negative implication from Comment 5. Comment 5 to Rule 8.4(g) explains that "A lawyer *does not* violate paragraph (g) ... by *limiting the lawyer's practice* to members of underserved

---

[114] MODEL RULES OF PROFESSIONAL CONDUCT R. 8.4(g).
[115] Gillers, *supra* Note 19, at 225.
[116] ABA REPORT 109, *supra* Note 37, at 8.
[117] Gillers, *supra* Note 19, at 228.
[118] *Id.* at 232.

populations in accordance with these Rules and other law."[119] Gillers reads this comment to mean that lawyers *are* in violation of the Rule if they decline representations on one of the enumerated bases set out in Rule 8.4(g) – for example by declining to represent someone based on race, sex, ethnicity, gender identity, sexual orientation, religion, etc. – *unless* lawyers are limiting their practice to members of "underserved populations." Comment 5 thus indicates that lawyers can limit their practice, for example, to an underserved racial or ethnic group without violating the rule. But the comment is odd because the rule doesn't purport to change the private attorney's autonomy to decline cases. So lawyers should be able to limit their practice to *any* population – underserved or not – without running afoul of the rule.

But the Gillers reading is possible. By stating that limiting one's practice to "underserved populations" is *not* a violation of the rule, Comment 5 implies that limiting one's practice in other discriminatory ways *would be* a violation of the rule. This reading is not a preferable reading because, as the ABA's Report for 8.4(g) confirms (quoting the Model Rules Preamble), "Comments do not add obligations to the Rules."[120] Thus if Rule 8.4(g) does not forbid permissive declining of cases, then Comment 5 to that rule cannot add that obligation. The reading also is suspect because Comment 5 does not even expressly add that obligation; it just negatively implies that the obligation may exist.

Nevertheless, what are the First Amendment rights of lawyers in this regard? Assuming a jurisdiction adopts Rule 8.4(g) and interprets it to forbid declination of cases on the enumerated bases (race, sex, ethnicity, religion, gender identity, marital status, sexual orientation, etc.) do attorneys have a First Amendment right to decline cases that they do not wish to take? Gillers briefly argues that attorneys likely do *not* have any more right than a flower shop owner or cake decorator to decline cases that they object to on religious grounds. He also notes that Kim Davis was not allowed to discriminate against same-sex couples in issuing marriage licenses. Finally, he questions whether or not lawyers are somehow categorically different from other service providers because of the "intimate" nature of the attorney–client relationship.[121]

Notably, should enforcement be brought against a lawyer for declining a case under Model Rule 8.4(g), a lawyer should initially argue that the prohibition on declining cases is unconstitutionally vague – as it only exists through negative implication of a comment. The requirement is, in fact, contradicted by the accompanying Report, which expressly states that the rule does not change the preexisting rights of lawyers to decline cases.

---

[119] MODEL RULES OF PROF'L CONDUCT R. 8.4(g) and cmt. 5. In a similar vein, Comment 4 expressly allows lawyers to "engage in conduct undertaken to promote diversity and inclusion without violating this Rule." *Id.* R. 8.4 cmt. 4.

[120] ABA REPORT 109, *supra* Note 37, at 4 (quoting MODEL RULES OF PROF'L CONDUCT pmbl. and scope ¶ 14).

[121] *See* Gillers, *supra* Note 19, at 232–33 and n. 126.

Substantively, there is very little precedent on the question of whether a lawyer has a First Amendment right to decline a representation on the basis of a client's race, gender, religion, or sexual orientation (let alone on the nonconstitutionally suspect bases of socioeconomic status, disability, or marital status). Nevertheless, in 1997, the Massachusetts Commission against Discrimination fined Judith Nathanson for refusing to represent Joseph Stropnicky in a divorce.[122] Nathanson only represented women in divorces, and specialized in issues that often primarily affected women. Stropnicky had spent the early years of his marriage supporting his wife while she undertook a medical career and then was a stay-at-home father to their children for seven years. Stropnicky wanted Nathanson to review a separation agreement he was entering into because Nathanson had a reputation for advocating aggressively for women who had supported their husbands while foregoing their own careers. Nathanson declined the representation, explaining that she only represented women. The Massachusetts Commission against Discrimination fined her $5,000 for violating the Massachusetts public accommodation law by discriminating on the basis of gender.[123]

Nathanson explained her devotion to serving women in divorces – that she felt "a personal commitment" that was necessary to functioning "effectively as an advocate."[124] Further she "testified that her female divorce clients derive a specific benefit from her limited practice. They feel comfortable sharing their anxieties and concerns with an advocate whom they trust to be wholeheartedly as well as intellectually committed to their interests."[125] She also expressed her belief that she had "enhanced her credibility with judges" by arguing solely on behalf of women – judges recognized and credited her devotion to the cause of protecting women's rights.[126] Nathanson appealed the initial decision to the full Commission against Discrimination, which affirmed and specifically denied that Nathanson had a constitutional right to solely represent women.[127] The case was never adjudicated by a court.

The Massachusetts Commission against Discrimination erred in failing to recognize Nathanson's First Amendment rights to speech, association, and petitioning on behalf of women. Recall that in *Button* the Supreme Court recognized the political expression and association rights of the NAACP lawyers to specifically solicit and represent African American clientele.[128] The NAACP did not represent Caucasian clients – and, indeed, historically, the NAACP was devoted solely to advancing the

---

[122] *See generally, Stropnicky v. Nathanson*, 19 MDLR 39, 1997 Mass. Comm. Discrim. LEXIS 12 (Feb. 25, 1997).

[123] *Id.*

[124] *See id.* at *6.

[125] *Id.*

[126] *Id.*

[127] *Stropnicky v. Nathanson*, No. 91-BPA-0061, 1999 WL 33453078 (Mass. Comm. Discrim. July 26, 1999).

[128] *NAACP v. Button*, 371 U.S. 415, 428–31 (1963).

rights of African Americans.[129] The *Button* Court recognized that the First Amendment protected the NAACP's "vigorous advocacy" of "lawful ends" and that its association with African American clients "for litigation may be the most effective form of political association."[130] In speaking of regulation on lawyer speech and association, the Court maintained that our "government is built on the premise that every citizen shall have the right to engage in political expression and association" – including the NAACP lawyers in "seek[ing] through lawful means to achieve legitimate political ends."[131]

Attorney specialization and cause lawyering – such as that performed by the NAACP as to a specific race or Nathanson as to a specific gender – have played a major and beneficial role in the system of justice. It is not uncommon to have lawyers who specialize in women's rights, or LGBT rights, or fathers' rights, or immigrant rights, and so forth. While some of these bases would fall within the protective language of Comment 5 that the attorney's limited practice is focused on "underserved populations," others (like fathers' rights or women's issues) are not.

Lawyers have a freedom of association right (as well as speech and petitioning as required by the representation) to specialize their practice to protect or litigate on behalf of specific groups of people or legal rights – even if not directed at an "underserved population." If a battered woman decides to go to law school specifically to start a practice assisting and advocating for other battered women, she should have an association right to do so. If a divorced man feels like fathers have gotten a raw deal in custody battles, and wants to focus his practice on preserving father's rights, he should be able to do so. If a transgender individual wants to devote their practice to transgender rights – to the exclusion of assisting binary gender clients, they should be able to. Allowing this type of focused practice – where attorneys are personally committed to or identify a particular contingency of people or rights that they wish to focus on in protecting client life, liberty, and property – is and should continue to be fully protected by the attorney's First Amendment right to association.

The core idea underlying the historical right of association is that people should have a right to associate for political ends. Jason Mazzone explores the history of the First Amendment rights of assembly and petition as being essential to self-government and popular sovereignty. He explains that the "constitutional significance" of freedom of association is not so much the protection of speakers, but instead, "lie[s] in enabling people to influence government."[132] The lawyer's ability to associate with specific clients for the purpose of pursuing specific political ends and goals is and has been an important aspect of the lawyer's role in the system of

[129] *See Private Attorneys-General: Group Action in the Fight for Civil Liberties*, 58 YALE L. J. 574, 581–89 (1949).

[130] *Button*, 371 U.S. at 429, 431.

[131] *Id.* at 431, 430.

[132] Jason Mazzone, *Freedom's Associations*, 77 WASH. L. REV. 639, 743, 647, 711–12 (2002).

justice in the United States. It is precisely the type of associational right the *Button* Court recognized and upheld as to NAACP lawyers – namely, "association for litigation," which "may be the most effective form of political association."[133]

Crucially, the lawyer cannot engage in such advocacy without the client. No matter how strongly a lawyer wants to effect change through litigation, the lawyer cannot do it without associating with a client whose situation raises the precise issue for a court to adjudicate. The NAACP didn't want to take on just anyone's cause of injustice; they didn't want to take on the criminal cases of Caucasians who were innocent but criminally charged, despite taking on such cases for African Americans. They had a political mission. Nathanson's political mission to assist women in divorces was smaller, but it was still personally felt and she should have a First Amendment right to pursue it. Lawyers' ability to pursue their own personal and political goals is dependent upon their ability to carefully select their clientele in a manner that will promote and protect those interests.

Thus, association with a specific clientele or type of client is essential to the political advocacy of lawyers devoted to using their license to protect the rights of a particular class of persons or to secure specific social or political change. Further, the client cannot effectively invoke judicial power without the aid of the lawyer. Attorneys have First Amendment rights to associate with specific clients, to speak with them and on their behalf, and to petition on their behalf – and thus to pursue and achieve the political ends of both the attorney and client. Under the access to justice theory, such focused association is protected as an essential component of both the attorney's and the client's ability to invoke or avoid government power in a manner that will protect the rights of a specific group or cause.

Moreover, this right is not limited to representing "underserved populations." The *Button* Court emphasized that the fact that the NAACP "happens to be engaged in activities of expression and association on behalf of the rights of [African-American] children" was "constitutionally *irrelevant* to the ground of our decision."[134] The Court expressly held that *lawyers representing the opposite viewpoints* would be equally protected in their First Amendment rights of expression, association, and petitioning: "The course of our decisions in the First Amendment area makes plain that its protections would apply *as fully* to those who would arouse our society against the objectives" of the NAACP.[135] The court's recognition of this precept undermines Comment 5's carve-out solely for attorneys who limit and specialize their practice as to "underserved populations" but not to others. Lawyers have First Amendment rights of expression, association, and petitioning to focus and specialize their practice in protection of the rights of specific clients or causes – even if it results in declining representation of others who do not fall within that specified clientele.

---

[133] *Button*, 371 U.S. at 431.
[134] *Id.* at 444 (emphasis added).
[135] *Id.* (emphasis added).

Nathanson should have been protected in solely representing women, as she felt "personally committed" to advancing the rights of women – just as the NAACP lawyers were protected in their association and petitioning for African Americans. Both were using "lawful means to achieve legitimate political ends."[136]

In acting in their capacity as lawyers, members of the profession are engaged in political expression and association – as the *Button* Court recognized. They are invoking or avoiding government power on behalf of the client – and, by its very nature, that constitutes political activity. The lawyer who does not wish to further the exercise of government power in favor of heterosexuals – precisely because the lawyer believes and is personally committed to promoting the invocation of government power as to homosexual individuals whom the lawyer is devoted to assisting – should be protected. Such speech is political speech. It is political association. When an attorney invokes government power in favor of a client, the attorney has engaged in political expression and association, as *Button* held.

Yet what about Gillers' concern regarding lawyers – who really are *not* engaged in cause lawyering or advocating for a particular clientele or cause – who have a deep personal or religious objection to same-sex marriage or another substantive right such that they do not want to represent a particular person related to that right – typically dealing with homosexuality or gender identity? Gillers recommends that in such situations, "nothing in [Rule 8.4(g)] would prevent the lawyer from telling prospective clients that he has a religious objection" to the representation, for example, an objection to "adoption by same-sex, single, or unmarried couples."[137] But then the attorney must explain that they "will represent them if they wish because adoption is work he does and he is not allowed to discriminate against them."[138]

Despite Gillers' reassurance that explaining as much to a client would *not* be prohibited under Rule 8.4(g), a lawyer would have to be very careful in making such an explanation in a way that did not "manifest bias or prejudice" on the proscribed basis or was not "derogatory or demeaning."[139] If I were a lawyer advising another lawyer in a jurisdiction that had adopted Rule 8.4(g), I would advise the lawyer to absolutely not say anything at all indicating any bias or prejudice against those listed in the rule.[140] Any such statement could form a basis for a complaint. For example, in *Stropnicky*, the Commission specifically found that Nathanson lacked a First Amendment right *to tell* Stropnicky that she would not represent him because he

---

[136] *Id.* at 430.

[137] Gillers, *supra* Note 19, at 233.

[138] *Id.*

[139] MODEL RULE OF PROF'L CONDUCT R. 8.4(g) and cmt. 3.

[140] In confessing bias in a jurisdiction that adopted Rule 8.4(g), I would follow the advice noted by Justice White as to confessions in general: "'(A)ny lawyer worth his salt will tell the suspect in no uncertain terms to make no statement ... under any circumstances." *Miranda v. Arizona*, 384 U.S. 436, 516 n. 12 (White, J., dissenting) (internal citations omitted).

was a man.[141] She would have done so much better – and likely avoided the Commission and fine entirely – if she had come up with another reason (any reason other than gender) to decline the representation. Even something as simple as, "your case doesn't interest me," probably would have worked. Gillers solution of having attorneys explain their bias to the client could very well lead to a complaint under Model Rule 8.4(g) for engaging in "verbal conduct" that "manifests bias or prejudice" or is "derogatory or demeaning" on one of the enumerated bases.[142]

Allowing an individual lawyer to decline a case that is personally repugnant to the lawyer is not a novel issue in the practice of law. For example, the Model Rules generally recognize the lawyer's obligation to accept appointments – which are far less common in modern legal practice. Nevertheless, Rule 6.2 allows the lawyer to decline even an appointed representation for "good cause," which can be shown by the cause being "so repugnant to the lawyer as to be likely to impair the client-lawyer relationship or the lawyer's ability to represent the client."[143]

Lawyers understand the importance of access to justice and due process. They understand that the fact of representation does not mean that they agree with the objectives or actions of the client. Nevertheless, if a lawyer has a strong personal moral objection to the advocacy that the client is requesting, such that it would impair the lawyer–client relationship, there is no good reason to force the attorney to undertake the representation. In a private lawyering context, a lawyer's advocacy and litigation have political and societal results and the lawyer must work as the agent and the fiduciary of the client and of the client's interests. It would undermine the lawyer's role in the system of justice to act as a client's agent and fully protect that client's interests to require an attorney to represent a client when that representation *would actually be impaired* by the lawyer's deep moral objection to the client's objectives. In light of that reality, there is a decent argument that a private lawyer's personal and stringent objection to the action or objectives pursued by a prospective client combined with the lawyer's right to political association secures the lawyer's autonomy to decline a given case in such circumstances.

Publicly Employed Attorneys

A different scope of First Amendment rights to decline a representation is proper when considering a publicly employed attorney. The access to justice theory attunes the First Amendment rights of lawyers to their function, and it recognizes that some types of lawyers require differing rights.

---

[141] *Stropnicky* v. *Nathanson*, No. 91-BPA-0061, 1999 WL 33453078, at *3 (Mass. Comm. Discrim. July 26, 1999) (rejecting argument that Nathanson "had a right to tell Complainant she would not represent him because he is a man").
[142] *See* MODEL RULE OF PROF'L CONDUCT R. 8.4(g) and cmt. 3.
[143] *Id.* R. 6.2.

The publicly employed attorney does not have the same rights to decline cases as a private attorney. Private attorneys can engage in discriminatory declining of cases either because of their devotion to helping and focusing on assisting a particular cause or clientele or because a specific representation is so morally abhorrent to the attorney that it will impair the attorney–client relationship. Yet, publicly employed attorneys can absolutely be forbidden from discriminating on the bases stated in 8.4(g) in declining cases or in performing their services to the public. That is because the publicly employed attorney is not actually selecting an individual client – instead, the publicly employed attorney already has agreed to work for a client, and that client is the government. As noted in Chapter 12, that government sovereign's "obligation to govern impartially is as compelling as its obligation to govern at all."[144] Consequently, publicly employed lawyers must treat the public they serve with impartiality. They cannot discriminate in providing services to the public.

Gillers' concern that without Rule 8.4(g) same-sex couples will be denied marriage licenses by the likes of Kim Davis or Roy Moore are misplaced. Rules can and should be imposed requiring civil servant lawyers to fulfill their duties to their actual client – the government and its popular sovereign – by treating all people impartially. It is not necessary to impose a requirement of impartiality on all private lawyers in order to assure that the government acts impartially. It is not the role of the private lawyer to act impartially; but it is the role of the government.

Additionally, some have argued that Rule 8.4(g)'s constitutionality is demonstrated by existing rules for judges and recommendations for prosecutors that forbid them from acting with bias.[145] But this argument is unavailing. Public employees can be so constrained as necessary to fulfill their role in the system of justice and their duty to their sovereign client. But that in no way implies that such a rule is appropriate or constitutional to govern all private lawyers in practice.

Civility and Checking Judicial Power

Although, in general, lawyers in the practice of law constitutionally can be required to act with civility – as long as they are protected in their advice and advocacy with appropriate "breathing space" – there is a special problem surrounding civility codes and the checking of judicial power. Courts and disciplinary authorities have used civility codes or rules that require courtesy to punish attorneys for speech critical of the judiciary. After Utah had adopted its civility code, the buzz among members of

---

[144] *Berger v. United States*, 295 U.S. 78, 88 (1935).
[145] ABA REPORT 109, *supra* Note 37, at 6; *see also* Gillers, *supra* Note 19, at 210–11.

the Utah Bar was that the Utah Supreme Court or state bar would be looking for a case to "flex its arm" and discipline an attorney to send a message to the rest of the bar to be civil.[146] And, indeed, in 2007, the Utah Supreme Court did exactly that. In *Peters* v. *Pine Meadow Ranch Home* the court cited the civility code and struck the appellate brief of the party represented by an offending attorney, summarily affirming a lower court decision. Yet the Utah Supreme Court acknowledged that the lower court's opinion was both legally and factually erroneous.[147] Indeed, it was erroneous in precisely the manner argued by the offending attorney, but the attorney made the fatal mistake of being uncivil by attributing nefarious motives to the lower court.[148] In a subsequent decision, the Utah Supreme Court cited *Peters* and "remind[ed] attorneys of the pitfalls that may accompany" such an argument.[149] The court elaborated: "Any allegation that a trial judge became biased against a defendant should be supported by copious facts and record evidence" and "should be made in a reserved, respectful tone, shunning hyperbole and name-calling."[150] Similarly, in New York, attorneys who made arguments that certain judges in a case had acted unlawfully and unconstitutionally in a matter are being subjected to a disciplinary action for being "discourteous" to the court.[151]

As noted in Chapter 11, attorneys play a crucial role in checking judicial power – both inside court proceedings by raising arguments and petitioning on behalf of clients and by informing the public about their public servants, the judiciary. Attorneys are the only class of persons who can serve this function and check judicial power. It is problematic that courts have invoked civility provisions, not to protect witnesses or parties from abuse by attorneys, but to protect themselves from derogation. Courts do not need to protect themselves from attorneys. While attorneys can improperly use their license to practice law to harass and inflict harm on witnesses and parties (through discovery, etc.), they have no similar power against the judiciary. To the extent that an attorney's actions actually interfere with court order and processes, the Court can hold the attorney in contempt. But courts should not be able to end-run around the constitutional rights of lawyers to raise colorable arguments regarding judicial malfeasance or around the standard of *Sullivan* for speech critical of public officials by simply invoking their purported power to punish attorneys for being "uncivil" or "discourteous."

---

[146] I was a practicing member of the Utah State Bar at the time and heard many such conversations.

[147] 151 P.3d 962, ¶ 11 (Utah 2007).

[148] *See id.* at ¶¶ 5–6 (explaining the factual and legal arguments that were raised on appeal and gave rise to the attorney's accusations, and stating as to each that "[t]he court of appeals did err" as to the law and facts).

[149] *Utah v. Santana-Ruiz*, 167 P.3d 1038, 1044 (Utah 2007).

[150] *Id.*

[151] I am aware of this case as a consultant, but it is confidential and currently under court seal.

PROTECTING THE SYSTEM OF JUSTICE FROM
HARASSMENT AND INEQUALITY

Sexual harassment is a serious national problem in every industry, including the practice of law. The #metoo movement and the resignation of the iconic Alex Kozinski of the Ninth Circuit Court of Appeals have demonstrated that sexual harassment must be addressed and curbed.[152] In this climate, nobody wants to be the person who asserts that jurisdictions should *not* adopt a rule forbidding harassment and discrimination. But the fact that Model Rule 8.4(g) is unconstitutional does not mean that states are powerless to curb these problems – they must simply employ means that *are* constitutional to do so.

Josh Blackman recommends several "fixes" to Model Rule 8.4(g) that would render it largely unproblematic. These fixes include requiring harassment or discrimination to be "severe or pervasive," eliminating viewpoint discriminatory exceptions, and adding an express recognition of the lawyer's First Amendment rights outside of the practice of law to "personal opinion, freedom of association, religious expression, and political speech."[153]

Nevertheless, Blackman does not address the appropriate and necessary First Amendment protection of attorney advice and advocacy *within* the practice of law. Lawyers must be able to fully advise their clients and advocate on their behalf – including as to issues that may bear on one of the prohibited bases listed in Model Rule 8.4(g). This right includes the appropriate "breathing space" to allow for devoted protection of client life, liberty, and property.[154]

---

[152] *See, e.g.,* Editorial Board, *#MeToo Makes Its Way to the Judiciary,* WASH. POST, Dec. 23, 2017.

[153] Blackman, *supra* Note 21, at 263–64.

[154] *NAACP v. Button,* 371 U.S. 415, 433 (1963).

Epilogue

The purpose of this book is to begin the process of reclaiming – of defining and protecting – attorneys' First Amendment rights. And, appropriately, this book approaches that process by defining the core of protection. As shown, the First Amendment protects the full range of essential lawyer functions through its protection of attorney association, speech, and petitioning of the government for redress. It protects the ability of the lawyer to associate with others to form attorney–client relationships, and it safeguards attorney advice and counseling while allowing the state to protect client confidential information from disclosure. It protects the right of the attorney to invoke law and legal processes on behalf of the client to protect life, liberty, and property. It protects cause lawyering and the ability of lawyers to focus their practice on bringing about specific political and social change. This is so regardless of the popularity of the client or the cause. It safeguards the integrity and proper functioning of the judiciary by protecting attorneys in invoking judicial power and in exposing judicial incompetence, malfeasance, abuse, or corruption. It safeguards our constitutional criminal processes – including the right to effective assistance of counsel, the presumption of innocence, and the right to both an impartial jury and fair pretrial practices. In short, the First Amendment protects justice itself by protecting the means through which justice can be obtained.

But there is much beyond the core of protection, extending out into the periphery. While beyond the scope of this book, in considering other contexts implicating lawyers' First Amendment rights, the Amendment must be construed in such a way as to protect the core functions of attorneys to invoke and avoid government power in the protection of life, liberty, and property.

Further, this book does not specifically traverse into the related area of judicial First Amendment rights. The Supreme Court indicated that restrictions on judicial speech are subject to strict scrutiny in both *Republican Party of Minnesota* v. *White*[1]

---

[1] *Republican Party of Minn.* v. *White*, 536 U.S. 765 (2002).

and in *Williams-Yulee* v. *Florida Bar*.[2] Yet, the strict scrutiny applied in *Williams-Yulee* was arguably a watered-down variant, raising the legitimacy of Schauer's concern of dilution of First Amendment doctrines for regulations seen as particularly important.[3] As with attorneys, under the access to justice theory, restrictions on judicial First Amendment rights must be attuned to the judicial role. This does not mean that judges have no First Amendment rights, but that the core of those rights should be speech essential to fulfill their role in the system of justice. Further, if certain speech or other First Amendment activity frustrates the proper functioning of the judiciary, then it lacks First Amendment protection.

As noted in Chapter 4, a citizen who is admitted to practice law in a United States jurisdiction swears to uphold the Constitution of the United States and thereby becomes an "officer of the court." Rather than extinguishing their right to free speech, association, and petitioning, as traditionally understood, the oath and office of the attorney instead require attorneys to invoke their First Amendment rights and uphold the Constitution by protecting client life, liberty, and property, by checking government and institutional power, and by petitioning and enabling the judiciary to interpret and enforce the Constitution and other legal rights. Even assuming attorneys can waive their own personal First Amendment rights in exchange for a license to practice law, attorneys cannot waive their rights to speech, association, and petitioning essential to fulfilling their role in the justice system. And unlike an oath to an absolute sovereign, the attorney's oath to uphold the Constitution does not place the attorney in the arbitrary hands of carte blanche government regulation or repression of attorney rights. Instead, the Constitution reciprocally protects attorneys in undertaking those activities of speech, association, and petitioning necessary to fulfill their oath to uphold the Constitution and secure the proper functioning of our justice system.

---

[2]   135 S. Ct. 1656 (2015).
[3]   Frederick Schauer, *The Speech of Law and the Law of Speech*, 49 ARK. L. REV. 687, 693 (1997).

Index